Stepping-Stones to Happiness

BY

HARRIET PRESCOTT SPOFFORD

AUTHOR OF

"An Inheritance," "The Scarlet Poppy," "Hester Stanley at St. Mark's," "Hearth and House," Etc., Etc.

Psalm xxiii.1.2

Copyright © 2013 Read Books Ltd.
This book is copyright and may not be
reproduced or copied in any way without
the express permission of the publisher in writing

British Library Cataloguing-in-Publication Data
A catalogue record for this book is available from the
British Library

Harriet Elizabeth Prescott Spofford

Harriet Elizabeth Prescott Spofford was born on 3rd April 1835 in Calais, Maine, United States. She is now best known for her novels, poems and detective stories – a true pioneer of the American detective genre. When she was still a baby, Spofford's parents moved to Newburyport, Massachusetts, where she chose to stay for almost her entire life. Although she spent many of her winters in Boston and Washington D.C., Newburyport remained always close to Spofford's heart.

She attended the Putnam Free School in Newburyport and **Pinkerton Academy** in **Derry, New Hampshire** from 1853 to 1855. At Newburyport her prize essay on **Hamlet** drew the attention of **Thomas Wentworth Higginson** (a **Unitarian** minister, author, **abolitionist**, and soldier), who soon became her friend and gave Spofford much needed counsel and encouragement throughout her career. When Spofford was in her mid-twenties, her parents suffered from ill health, and of necessity she was set to work as a writer, sometimes labouring fifteen hours a day. She contributed to various Boston story papers for small fees, but her first major success came in 1859; this was Spofford's submission to *Atlantic Monthly* (a literary and cultural magasine) of a story about Parisian life, 'In a Cellar'. The magazine's editor, **James Russell Lowell**, first believed the story to be a translation and withheld it from publication. Reassured it was original, he eventually published it, and the narrative established her reputation. After this success, Spofford became a welcome contributor to the chief periodicals of the United States, both of prose and poetry.

Spofford's fiction had very little in common with what was regarded as representative of 'the New England mind.' Her **gothic romances** were set apart by luxuriant descriptions and an unconventional handling of female **stereotypes** of the day. Her writing was ideal and intense in feeling, revelling in sensuous delights and material splendour. Nowhere was this more evident than, in 'Circumstance', an allegorical short story which takes place in the woods of Maine. In this tale, the protagonist comes into contact with the Indian Devil, forcing her to come to terms with her own life, sexuality and fears. By the end of the story, her husband shoots the Devil with his shotgun in one hand and their baby in the other while the **'true Indian Devils'** destroy their home and town. When Wentworth Higginson asked Emily Dickinson whether she had read Spofford's work, Dickinson replied, 'I read Miss Prescott's '**Circumstance**,' but it followed me in the dark, so I avoided her.' Other notable works include *The Thief in the Night* (1872), *The Servant Girl Question* (1881), *A Scarlet Poppy and Other Stories* (1894), and *The Fairy Changeling* (1910).

In 1865, at the age of thirty, the authoress married Richard S. Spofford, a Boston lawyer, and the couple resided on Deer Island overlooking the **Merrimack River** at **Amesbury**, a suburb of Newburyport. They lived here for the rest of their lives. Harriet Prescott Spofford died on 14th August 1921, aged eighty-six.

Introductory.

IN all Ages, the Search for Happiness has been the ultimate aim and desire of human effort—Happiness here and hereafter. To those Searchers, in every station in life, this Book is dedicated, in the hope that it may be the means of guiding them, by pleasant paths, to the true Temple of Happiness, whence flow those delectable streams that refresh the hearts and rejoice the souls of all who enter the quest with a pure and resolute purpose.

Happiness is equally attainable to the poor and the rich, the youth and the veteran; and though multitudes have missed the Path, STEPPING STONES TO HAPPINESS will lead them back to the way, by which they may surely find it. May they, in turn, extend loving help to other struggling wayfarers on the same journey.

Go, Book of mine, go forth
  And give thy cheer,
Go where upon the hearth
  The fire burns clear;
Go where the evening lamp
  A rosy glow
Sheds while the storms without
  Their wild blasts blow.

Go under greenwood shade;
  Find open doors
Where babes like sunbeams play
  About the floors,
And say the hand that wrought
  Would only bless
And lend the simple art
  Of happiness.

Go then, the world is wide,
  And give thy cheer;
Perhaps some tender heart
  Will hold thee dear;
Perhaps some pleasant hand
  Thy pages turn;
Perhaps some gentle soul
  Thy message learn!

PREFACE.

WHEN one writes for publication, however great the surrounding solitude, there is always one companion present.

It is the personage known in literature as the Gentle Reader. This reader is kinder than one's self; has almost as much to do with the progress of the pages; cheers, encourages, and helps with both subtle and outright sympathy.

And when the manuscript has gone to do its work in the world, it is not of the great public that the writer thinks, but of this single debonair reader. It is for those of like manners and feelings that these chapters have been written. Gentle Reader, out in the unknown, be gentle still! Whoever and wherever you may be, when you open these leaves remember your old kindliness and forbear to criticise too harshly the pen that would help you on the way across the Stepping Stones to Happiness.

HARRIET PRESCOTT SPOFFORD.

Contents

PAGE.

CHAPTER I..17
    The Use of the Present—On a Texas Prairie—A Mirage—The Present Time—The Uses of This World—Advancing Years—Looking Backward—Disenchantment—Illusions—Idle Regrets.

CHAPTER II...38
    Going Over Dry Shod—Perpetual Hope—An Ideal World—A Child's Discovery—The Surprise—Mrs. Mulgrave's Story.

CHAPTER III..56
    A Pause By the Way—Self-Reliance and Self-Reverence—St. Augustine's Dream—The Spiritual Mind—Reticence—Real Troubles—The Armor of Patience—A Mutual Dependence—Man's Majesty—The Happy Warrior—Miss Moggaridge's Provider.

CHAPTER IV..88
    A Family Tree—Household Association—Plutarch's Advice—The Story of Xerxes and Ariamenes—Love of Ancestors—The Coat of Arms.

CONTENTS.

PAGE.

CHAPTER V..99

A Home in Town—Owning the House—The Sense of Permanence—Moving—Inside the House—The Vacation—Advantages of Town Life—City Children—Music at Home—The Piano-forte—Music Abroad—The Opera—Shopping—In the Street Car—The Cheery Town—The City Parlor—Old China—The Spinning Wheel in the Parlor—The Distaff—The Spinster—The Adventures of a Pound of Cotton—Society—The Gay Season—City Window Gardens—Louise Forester's Story.

CHAPTER VI...151

Under Green Boughs—Comparative Views of Town and Country—Great Ideas Start in City—In a Suburban Town—The Love of Nature—Michelet's Twilight Experience—Sunlight.

CHAPTER VII..167

Vine and Fig Tree—The Garden—The Almanac—The Apple-Tree—Woman in Agriculture—Among the Lake Dwellings—A Picturesque Sight—The Story of Mrs. Royal's Garden.

CHAPTER VIII...193

The House in the Country—Necessary Foresight—The Piazza—In the Furnishing—The Parlor—The Library—The Rosillon House.

CHAPTER IX...216

The Health of the Home—Old Water-courses in Town—Rock and Gravel—The Cellar—The Prevention That is Better than Cure—The Only Curse on the House—We or Providence to Blame—Children's Diseases—Disinfectants—The Scarlet Fever

CONTENTS.

—The Children of the Poor—The Lively Fly—At Autumn Time—The Birds When the Days Shorten—Light-Hearted October—By the Hearth.

CHAPTER X..243

The Light of the House—The Mother—The Ideal Mother—The Everyday Mother—The Story of Old Margaret and Her Boy.

CHAPTER XI...260

A Well-Spring of Joy—The Baby—The Care of the Baby—The Moral Growth of the Child—Help From the Great Educators—Froebel—The Kindergarten—The Gifts in Froebel's System—School Another World—On Visiting a Kindergarten—John Wesley's Mother—Slöjd—The Happy Result—The Story of the Hurricane Light.

CHAPTER XII..306

Other Children—Medicine Rather Than Punishment—Heredity—Sparing the Rod—Loving Children—They Who Really Love Children—Troublesome Children—Keeping Silence—Amusing the Small People—With Pencil and Paper—A New Game—Another Game—The Story of Laddy's Burglar.

CHAPTER XIII...343

Angels Unawares—What a Boy Thought of His Grandmother—Old Age—Growing Old Gracefully—The Satisfactions of Age—The Refinement of Old Age—The Town "Lady"—Ailments in the Family—The Right Sleep—The Grandmother's Charm—Delight in Poetry—The Story of a Perpetual Thanksgiving.

CONTENTS.

PAGE.

CHAPTER XIV. 376

About Pets—Poor Dog Tray—Famous L gs—The Dog in Literature—Harmless Necessary Cat—The Cat's Beauty—The Cat's Virtues—The Cat a Fireside Ornament—The Little Egyptian Cat—The Cat's Usefulness—The Norway Rat—The Bird in the Cage—Pretty Poll—The Children and the Parrot—Famous Parrots—A Kerry Cow—Advantages of the Cow—Pegasus—The Woman Who Used To Drive—The Woman Who Drives Now.

CHAPTER XV. 395

The Household Conduct—The Ideal Household—Managing and Ruling—Tyranny and its Result in Cunning—Working Together—Daily Cares—The Hired Housekeeper—The Strong-Box—A Vacation—Schools For Cooks—A Radical Procedure—Old Cookery Books—Ancient Feasts—The Peacock at Banquets—A Battle at Table—Some Economies—The English Woman's Economy—Saving On a Small Scale—Old Dishes—Different Kitchens—Undreamed Dishes—The Mushroom—The Story of Sylvia Dexte.

CHAPTER XVI. 429

Work—Mrs. Browning's Word—The Value of Work to Character—All Creation Works—Conscience in the Work—Work Here and Abroad—Love of Art Equaling Conscience—Those Who Are Down On Their Luck—Rest After Work—The Rest of Travel—The Mind in Travel—The Reader in Travel—Travel in Our Own Land.

CONTENTS.

CHAPTER XVII...449
    Love of Others—Associated Charities—Transmission of Initiated Organisms—Extremes of Wealth and Poverty—Giving at the Door—Lovely Examples—A Degrading Course—The Poor a Benison—What the Poor Have Done—The Story of Anstress.

CHAPTER XVIII..472
    The Genial Temper—An Unpleasant Idiosyncrasy—Love of Injury—Fancied Slights—Quid Pro Quo—The Undisciplined Temper—The Sinners Themselves—The Sulky Soul—A Remedy—The Perfecting of the World—Protoplasm and Dust—Right and Light—Transmuting Clay—Self-Forgetfulness—The Child's Troubles—Another World To Complete This—Changing Our Condition For Another's—Rejoicing in Another's Joy—The Golden Time For Love—On Tranquil Heights—Hand in Hand With Angels—The Riches of Angels—True Happiness At Last—Matthew Arnold's Wish.

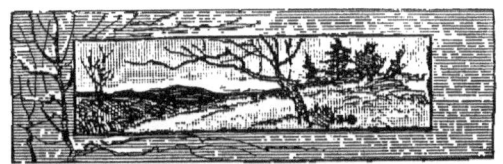

ILLUSTRATIONS

⚜ ⚜ ⚜

	PAGE
The Journey	18
Bells Ring Love's Story Song	19
As We Rolled on Through This Marvelous Landscape	20
Herd of Cattle Coming Down to Drink	22
Solitude	25
Truly We Are Not of Their Number	27
At Morning We Used to Feel It Was Going to Be Morning All Day	28
The Illusion that Surrounds the Dead with a Halo Is Certainly a Blessed One	30
The Home of Childhood	32
The Contemptuous Stare of Somebody in a Paris Hat	33
Dripping that Wears the Stone	34
Expectancy a much more Emphatic Thing than Hope	35
The Bright Drapery of Dreams and Pleasant Fancies	37
Never Birds Sang as I Heard Them	39
In the Wave-Washed Sand	41
The Ship that Is Coming into Harbor	42
If It had Been the Queen a-Coming In	44
You Couldn't Shut a Drawer	46
That Sea View Would Be Good as a Picture	47
I Was the Most Unhappy Woman	49
Dwelling upon the Spiritual	53
The Sweet Influence of a Loving Sympathy	57
A Happy Face Does a Service to Humanity	59
We Are Most of Us Inclined to Sympathize	61

ILLUSTRATIONS.

	PAGE.
The Good Are Lifting Up the Bad....	67
To Every Earnest, Striving Soul.....	69
A Letter Came to Miss Ann........	76
The Ship Went to Pieces.........	80
Bonds of Blood Relationship.......	87
The Same Mother's Knee.........	89
Reverence of the Young for the Old....	91
The Stiff, Prim Likeness of Some Grandam....	93
Tenderness for Those Dead and Gone.....	95
The Possession of a Home........	97
Industry..................	100
On the Wing...............	102
Sunshine of Pleasant Faces.........	104
Steamer Trips..............	107
Professors Find Their Support in Cities....	109
The Music-room Conservatory.......	111
Music's Largest Audiences in the Town....	113
Shopping................	115
Satchel-bearing Suburbans........	116
The Distaff...............	124
The Spinning-wheel...........	127
Rude as the Spinning-wheel Seems to Us Now....	129
Flock of Sheep.............	131
(From a Painting by Anton Mauve.)	
Always a Gay Season in Town.......	134
John Ruskin...............	137
(Bust by Sir Edgar Boehm, R. A.)	
Bowers of Loveliness...........	138
Flowers.................	139
Flowers the Only Comfort that I Had....	140
So Still and Dark and Solemn.......	143
A Box out of Every Window in the House....	144
I Came Home with Ladies' Tresses.....	145
The Corner of My Dear Wild Flowers....	146

ILLUSTRATIONS.

	PAGE.
This Place of Enchantment	150
You Must Have Known I Loved You	152
The Sweet Look that Nature Wears	154
The Loneliness of Rural Regions	157
A Sewing Circle	158
Some Lovely Landscape	161
Mountains Lifting Their Heads into Heaven	162
White and Innocent Fields	163
A Luxury of Life Is Theirs in the Spring	164
The Dark Shadow of the Branch-hung Stream	166
The Twilight Hour	168
Every Man Loves His Garden	171
The Modest Kitchen Garden	173
Title Page of Poor Richard's Almanack for 1733	177
Who Owns an Apple-tree and Does not Wish for Two?	180
The Harvest of the Grain Field	182
Making Grow Where Nothing Grew Before	185
A Picturesque Object in the Landscape	187
(Painted by Jules Breton.)	
Itself Draped with Vines	200
Such a Place Should be Made Attractive	212
Unable to Look a Man in the Face	217
Reeled and Fell Backward	220
Looking Down at Him	222
He Remembered the Place	224
Mother's Devotion	248
Sitting and Playing His Banjo	250
Practicing for a Long Migration	256
What a Singular Charm There Is about the First Fire of Wood	263
Rock Me to Sleep, Mother	268
She Spells out the Lesson with Her Child	274
Beauty and Glory of Motherhood	276
Helpless Morsel of Humanity	286

ILLUSTRATIONS.

	PAGE.
The Child Will Have a Love of Work	288
The Little Face Lies Near Her Own	290
The Hurricane Light-House	293
Love Lines of the Kindergarten Methods	308
Not to Fail in Exhaustless Gentleness	310
Little Merchants	312
The Young Expanding Intellect	315
Reprimanded	317
The Opening Soul of Childhood	319
Necessary that the Little Things Should Be Made Happy	321
Love of the Child for Drawing	323
Monument at New Plymouth to the Pilgrim Fathers	325
A Way of Making It a Charming Amusement	327
He Saw the Club Roll By	331
Laddy Slipped Out of Bed	335
The Sweet Serenity of Silver-haired Age	345
That Tenderness Felt for the Old	347
Gayeties of Her Grandchildren	349
Gentle and Well Bred, and that Is the Whole Lady	353
Drawing and Sculpture During the Palæolithic Epoch	364
Her Few Letters Were Spasmodic and Brief	366
That Turkey will be Looking Like a Big Heathen God	373
Not the Sole Constituents of the Family	377
Cats Are a Part of the Lares and Penates	382
The Ideal Household	399
Banquet of Vitellius	407
Look at the Jewels. Oh, What a Glitter!	422
From One Sick-bed to Another	425
Inundation of the Nile	439
Ascent of Mont Blanc	441
Dryburgh Abbey from the East	443
Kenilworth Castle	445
The Switzer Trail, Sierra Madre Mountains, California	447

ILLUSTRATIONS.

	PAGE.
More Agreeable if We could Sit down at Our Fancy Work	455
The Most We Can Do for the Poor is but a Debt We Owe	457
Love Is a Potent Shield against Many Troubles	479
It Is not Easy to Think It Is not as Fine as It Can Be	481
To Go to Bed Just as the Lamps are Lighted	488
Rolling by in Her Luxurious Coach	490

STEPPING STONES TO HAPPINESS.

CHAPTER FIRST.

One Stepping Stone—The Use of the Present.

HOW good is man's life, the mere living! how fit to employ
All the heart and the soul and the senses forever in joy!
—*Browning.*

Remember that man's life lies all within this present, as 'twere but a hair's breadth of time; as for the rest, the past is gone, the future yet unseen.
—*Marcus Aurelius.*

Now is the accepted time.
—*St. Paul.*

Nothing is there to come, and nothing past,
But an eternal now does always last.
—*Cowley.*

Catch, then, oh catch the transient hour.
—*Winter.*

Count them by sensation and not by calendars, and each moment is a day
—*Disraeli.*

O last regret, regret can die!
—*Tennyson.*

18 STEPPING STONES TO HAPPINESS.

THE JOURNEY.

On a Texas Prairie.

It was in one of the long journeys across Texas that the train stopping at a water-tank was boarded by a half-dozen children of the village that had grown up about the station, children to whom the train came like a herald and messenger from the great outside world. I sat at the end of the observation car, looking out over the wide prairie whose ineffable green under an immense arch of dazzling blue sky billowed away into the low horizon. The gentlemen had stepped down to look at some curiosity near by, and being mistress of the occasion I allowed the children the liberty of the car, which they enjoyed to the utmost. "I thought I would give you fifty dollars, if you would let me ride in this car," said one adventurous and

STEPPING STONES TO HAPPINESS.   19

BELLS RING LOVE'S STORY SONG.

bare-footed little damsel, who had never seen fifty cents in the world, although her father was rich in lands and herds.

"Why did you want to ride in this car?" I asked.

'Oh, I thought it would be such happiness!" she cried. "But I reckon I would like the burro best."

Her dream of happiness! To ride in the car. And mine so opposite—to be out of it. And then the porter came in his august plenitude of power and shooed the children off, and the gentlemen returned from their call upon the people who summered and wintered a dozen years in their tent, and we presently went our way again.

As we rolled on through the marvelous landscape, its great dells and dingles of live oak, its streams outlined by ribbons of white lilies, where the duck rose and skimmed away, its blazes of scarlet phlox, its coverts where the deer started at our coming, and its stretches where the wild horses galloped; there suddenly rose in the distance the vision of a river blue as blue crystal, mirroring trees hung with long wreaths of swaying moss, a herd of cattle coming down to drink there, and behind it the dim but gilded domes and spires of a city shone, the whole bathed in a soft atmosphere like that light which never was on sea or shore.

A Mirage.

It was a mirage that hung there before us for a little while, like reality, and then as we would have approached, it vanished.

"It is like happiness," I said to myself, "the little girl's, or mine, or another's. It is always before us; it disappears as we think we approach. No rapture is so sweet as its anticipation was. Happiness is a mirage." And an old verse came to mind: For here we have no abiding city.

Well, then, I thought, that mirage, at any rate, represents something to which we wish to attain. It is an image of that abiding city elsewhere; and every day of our lives there are stepping-stones for us to use in reaching it.

STEPPING STONES TO HAPPINESS.

AS WE ROLLED ON THROUGH THIS MARVELOUS LANDSCAPE.

If the mirage vanishes as we draw near, we have always in the present the measure of happiness that comes with brave endurance; in the future that comes with expectancy; and one day we reach the great goal. Let us be content then, day by day, with the stepping-stones.

The Present Time.

It is a singular thing that the present is something which most of us are always scouting. The past lies in an inwrapping mist that hides all pettiness, all daily annoyance, and leaves only the salient facts of pleasure or displeasure apparent, and has about it in our fancy some of the sacred character with which we surround the dead. The future, too, wears a halo rimmed with joyous expectancy, and is a Delectable Land gilded in a sunlight of possibility. But the present—the here and now—is our every-day life, is dull and commonplace, and worth little. What we might have done in the past we regard with a certain fondness; what we may do in the future, with eager anticipation; what we can do in the present, with doubt and disgust. Never do to-day what you can put off till to-morrow, is a reversal of the ancient maxim that goes to the heart of many of us. We are too apt to have that contempt for to-day which we have for all familiar things, and we disregard its opportunities, just as we think, in piping times of peace, that we could have done so much better if we had been born in a stirring era; or in war times, that we "should have come to something" if we had had the opportunities that peace affords; just as we think, if our surname is a common one, that it would have been very different with us if we had been born Montmorencys or Grosvenors; if we are poor, that with wealth we could have sprung upward as the vaulter flies with the upward impulsion of the spring-board; if we are rich, that perhaps poverty would have spurred us to a worthy exertion.

There are few of us that willingly take to-day as a stepping-stone, few of us who think of it as a stepping-stone at all. Yet if we so frequently fail to avail ourselves now of the opportunities of the moment, when to-morrow is to-day shall we regard it as any better worth, or do any more wisely with the new possession? And yet we all know that if we are going to do anything with to-morrow we must be making ready to-day. When to-morrow comes rising over us it may be as full of opportunities as the cloud is of lightnings, but if we have not our kite ready to fly, we shall draw none of those lightnings down.

But while, on the one hand, this disregard and waste of the present is loss to ourselves, on the other hand, it involves a peculiar selfishness, a sort of psychological anomaly, that is seldom guessed or considered. We delay the disagreeable duty, put off the laborious effort, till to-morrow, for what reason? Because to-morrow is another country, another climate, an unknown region, and because the person of to-morrow is quite another person from the person of to-day—so very much another that the person of to-day saves himself all the difficulty and trouble possible by pushing it over to the person of to-morrow. It is only another form of that selfishness which we exhibit when we indulge ourselves in any license, in any pleasure of the present, for which we know to-morrow will bring in a heavy price and penalty to be paid. The person of to-day is to have the license and the pleasure, the person of to-morrow must pay the penalty. It is indeed only another form of that terrible selfishness which allows the parent to practice a self-indulgence which shall some day ruin the child, who does not inherit any share of the pleasure of that self-indulgence, but only the ruin of its penalty.

But the selfishness of this evasion of the present rises into more metaphysical regions. The folly of it is something that even the simplest thinker can hardly fail to see. For the present is all that we certainly have, and to let it slip by unimproved is to make ourselves so much the poorer, since the mo-

HERD OF CATTLE COMING DOWN TO DRINK.

ment that we improve is ours forever, but the moment that we do not seize, do not improve, escapes us, has nothing to do with us, never enriches us, never was, indeed, so far as we are concerned, and our life is by that much more a blank. The present is as safe as time; to-morrow is as vague as eternity. Eternity may have its own uses; we know nothing about them; it is among infinite things, and we are among finite. The uses of time we know well, and that one of them is to make ourselves round and complete as a star for our course through that infinity.

"Ages past the soul existed;
Here an age tis resting merely,
And hence fleets again for ages."

The Uses of This World.

The poet Browning, in some of his verses, speaks of this world and this life as something that sets the scene, as one might say, of this particular portion of the drama of our soul's existence; and that act incompletely rendered, the whole drama fails of perfection. Suppose, for instance, it were the stage set merely for the love scene of the drama; were that lost, then the whole thing would want point and meaning, and the soul be by that much the more barren.

> "Else it loses what it lived for,
> And eternally must lose it;
> Better ends may be in prospect,
> Deeper blisses, if you choose it,
> But this life's end and this love bliss
> Have been lost here."

It would be but a poor and material supposition, though, to conjecture that the world were only the resting-place for spirits on the wing, pausing but long enough for that one experience, however great, however beautiful, it may be. To the young it might possibly seem a charming fancy; they do not give the world for love, but have an idea, indeed, that the world was given them for love, and in that view they certainly cannot be accused of not improving the present, which is the world. But love, the love of man and woman, is merely one wondrous phase of our soul's existence, like the ray that sparkles in the brilliant jet of some special color as the crystal takes the light. Love of another kind, the love of fellow-men, the love of man and God, is the very medium, indeed, that surrounds us and gives us communication, atom by atom, with the universe, that will accompany us forever, it is to be hoped. And there are far other purposes apparent in life than the wedding of twin souls. For, since this love is the to-day of youth and the yesterday of age, it can not be the present of any other era, and one era deserves as much of fate as the other. But whatever the present be, whether the time to love or the time to hate, the time to weep or the time for rejoicing, it is only those that live in it that can do anything with it. And they who forget all its claims, and live only in the future, live only to and for the future Even those who make a religious point of it, as if the future were a thing any dearer to the Creator than the present, are quite as unwise as they who risk everything on the sea of the passing moment. "This world is all a fleeting show," says the one side. "Let us eat, drink, and be merry, for to-morrow we die," says the other. And the one side forgets that God lives in His world, and that it is not theirs to contemn it or to deride a portion of His work, and the other side forgets that this mortal shall put on immortality.

Of a truth it befits us to make the most of the present; for there comes at last to most of us a season when all at once we wake to the fact that we are no longer young, and something angry with fate, with ourselves, with the laws of the universe, and with those that observe them in relation to us, we experience surprise and indignation, as if we were the only ones who ever grew old.

Advancing Years.

Any trifle will scratch the match, but it kindles a great fire, in which the dreams and hopes of youth begin to dissipate in smoke and vapor. Some one incidentally speaks of us as "middle-aged," whereas our mothers hardly seem to us to have passed that meridian, the boundary line of a different 'and from youth; but after a fair debate with facts and the looking-glass, we have had to yield the point.

The daughter of our old schoolmate, married on or about her graduation-day, who has now grown up and come before us to replace her mother in some mysterious way, receives our embrace as a "good motherly kiss," and arouses us to the circumstance that whatever we have been thinking of her as our contemporary, she has been thinking of us as her mother's contemporary.

We have never given the subject a thought before; it has been one of the things taken for granted with us that of course we are young, just as the sky is blue or the earth round, because we always have been young—that, in truth, all people are young till they feel old. But what are the facts? For the first time we consider them. As far as years go to make up the count, we must admit that we have crossed the median line, perhaps: our years are no longer the years of romance and poetry. As far as looks go—well, it is true there are silver threads among the gold; we had regarded them as accidents, but they were not accidents—they were necessities; there are wrinkles round the eyes, more or less, which have no longer the firm young muscle to hold them full; some teeth are missing, or the dazzle of the enamel is gone; there is the suspicion of a horrid hollow on the cheek; under the best conditions, and however attractive the face may remain, the rosy roundness there is gone. So far as feelings go—well, it has seemed to us till now only as if life deepened and enriched itself each year. Then we begin to look about us, peradventure to see how the thing strikes the rest of the world. We have spent years in listening, in learning, in making ourselves companionable and possibly entertaining; we see the veriest chit, with her luscious flesh and color, ignorant of life and of everything else but her own senses, preferred before us. Ah! then other people found out long ago what has just been revealed to us: we are old, and have been making fools of ourselves in masquerading as young. We declare to our self-investigation, then, that we do not care for the successes of the pretty girl; it may be that we had as much in our day; we do not find it in our heart to envy her: perhaps we pity her that the beam in which she sports so soon must fade. Then suddenly we see that we are pitying the young; truly we are not of their number! And if we had no sensation of the sort before, henceforth we acknowledge that we have one foot in the grave. Then, by slow access of meditation, we are aware that much of the freshness of feeling is gone, much of that which once gave us rapture, our power of joyous appreciation, our fullness of enthusiasm; we are not again rapt by the spell of any great painting into fairy-land, as the case has been with us, when all the lovely hues and aerial distances seemed to be portions of the region to which we traveled, that region into which the coming years were sure to bring us; no single dash of color in the sky fills us with unspeakable delight and longing after the unknown; we do not lean out into the star-lit nights with conscious companionship of the spirits of the stars and the deeps and the dark—we are a little afraid of the damps and draughts and rheumatism; we remember all these things; we do not feel them afresh. Nor do the same books please us,

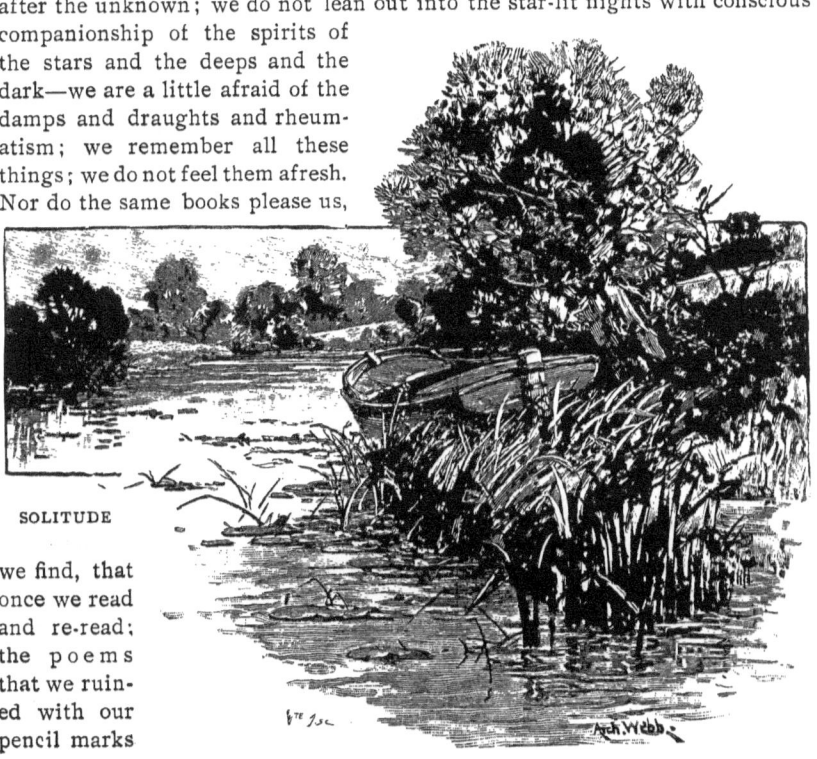

SOLITUDE

we find, that once we read and re-read; the poems that we ruined with our pencil marks and underscoring have ceased to charm, and the volumes that in the days of those pencil-marks we would have scorned, now attract us at first sight; the bread-and-butter novel moves us to derision; we feel sufficient acquaintance with life and its passions and subtle motives and secret springs to read the books of darker dealings. Dancing does not seem to us, either, the pleasantest way in the world in which to spend time. We do not think a youth of twenty-one or twenty-two the ideal being for whom the heavens and earth were created. Possibly we prefer lamp-light and people to all the moonlight and solitude in the world. What then? It seems that middle age has its pleasures, which it would not exchange for those of youth; why will we persist in looking back so regretfully on those of youth, which we would no longer enjoy if we had them?

Looking Backward.

If we do not wish to dance, why do we envy those who do? If a dried date does not taste to us now rich with all spicy flavors of unknown lands, but like a commonplace sweetmeat, compensation comes in the fact that we have no craving for the date. And yet it seems to be insufficient compensation: we wish we had that craving, remembering the pleasure of its satisfaction. We are not like the old proverb's dog in the manger, that neither wants a thing himself nor is willing that another should have it; on the contrary, we are much more like the little boy who eats his cake and wants it, too. Nothing would induce us to forego the various happinesses of the period to which we have arrived, the calmness and repose, the clear-headed comprehension of vexed problems, the wealth of memory, the power of looking out on the world and not only seeing as in youth, but of summarizing and philosophizing on what we see. Yet, for all that, we remember how round was the cheek of youth, how delicious was life at the dawning; and here is the shadow of the unknown future beginning to fall over us, and full soon shall we feel the breath of the dark river; and we see fresh meaning in the words of the old preacher: "Truly the light is sweet, and a pleasant thing it is for the eyes to behold the sun, but if a man live many years and rejoice in them all, yet let him remember the days of darkness, for they shall be many." As the monarch considers a demand for the surrender of his sceptre, so do we hate to lay down our sovereignty, to retreat as the new generation becomes regnant, to become not only the mere commoners and superannuaries of the present, but the pensioners of the past, to feel, perhaps, a passing remembered and reflected thrill of the keen, quick joy at the fragrance of a wind, at bell notes on the evening air, at

TRULY WE ARE NOT OF THEIR NUMBER.

AT MORNING WE USED TO FEEL IT WAS GOING TO BE MORNING ALL DAY.

so many other delightful things that once we felt in full, to feel, when that wind blows, and that bell rings, and that love story is sung, and that evening air grows purple, that our thrill is only the memory of the thrills of years and years ago, to know that a multitude of choicest pleasures now are no more the objects of actual experience, but are only an impalpable procession of bloodless ghosts.

But for all that, the past was not so perfect when it was the present that we need to compare it too strenuously with to-day. While that itself was the present there was much amiss with it. It is true that when we were very young every object in creation seemed gilded with the glory of our own dawn. At morning we used to feel that it was going to be morning all day, with blue sky and sparkling dew and flower scents and freshness; but at noon we hardly remembered another joy than those under the meridian; and our only shadow of vexation was that night must needs come to put an end to it all. But when we ceased to be very young how sorry we sometimes were to open our eyes and find it morning! How glad we were fain to be when night came and brought another day to its close! Fortunate they who, in middle life and in still more advanced years, carry the morning always with them, and love the hour, whatever it may be, and the fortune it brings with it.

Yet, sooth to say, there are very few of us who bring our ideals up to the end with us all unbroken. The mists of early day magnify the objects we see through them. This fruit is sweeter to the virgin palate than it ever will be to the taste accustomed to all impressions; that flower scent never can be found again; that music on the water never sounds to us, now that even-song has sung, as it did when blown on the winds of morning. When Henry Esmond met Father Holt, after he had grown to be a man, he "smiled to think that this was his oracle of early days, only now no longer infallible or divine."

Disenchantment.

How many a young person there must be who, dominated over by a maturer mind and personality, with attractions and conjurations of its own, shakes off the spell in after-times, and sees with amazement that the god, if not made of putty, yet is only common flesh and blood! How many a woman has waked, after years of marriage with the one idolized at the outset, to find that the idol had feet of clay! How many a man has married a doll, and by the slow process of disenchanting years has felt no surprise when at last he saw the sawdust! Yet they who find the demi-god of youth still a demi-god, when middle life has rubbed the cobwebs out of their eyes, when the high noon has dissipated those magnifying mists of morning, they who preserve their idols and find them and their informing spirits golden still, they who have no occasion to be reminded that there is such a thing as sawdust in the

THE ILLUSION THAT SURROUNDS THE DEAD WITH A HALO IS CERTAINLY A BLESSED ONE.

world—how blest are they, blest with the good fortune that is theirs, blest even if it is illusion and they themselves are not wise enough to be aware of it!

Illusions.

For surely there is a pleasure in our illusions, so long as we do not know them to be illusions. So long, indeed, as we are ignorant of that, they are not illusions, but as blessed verities as any of the fixed truths of the universe. To believe a person great and good is to endow him with all the great and good qualities we revere, and if by the added exaltation which we might derive from him if he really exerted those qualities upon us, it does not actually matter, for, on the contrary, by insisting upon it that he shall have the noble characteristics, they have to be created somewhere, and if only in our imagination, then at least that far we have been exalted by being their creators ourselves. It is our own natures that have been the matrices of the statue we have reared to him, and he is none the worse and we are somewhat the better.

The illusion, too, that surrounds the dead with a halo is certainly a blessed one, all that was ignoble or unlovely in them sinking out of sight and memory and only the beautiful remaining, till, if they are not angels in the unseen sphere they visit, so much of them as remains in our memory is altogether angelic. And if we may have blessed illusions concerning those that are gone away from us, how equally blessed are those concerning the affairs that might have come to us but never do! The songs we never sang are far the sweetest; the wife who was never wed, the hero for whom the maiden waits, the little children never born and never to be born—what perfectness enwrap them all! Elia's Dream Children were lovelier and sweeter, and dearer, too, than any children that Charles Lamb ever met. It is a thing to be thankful for when any experience of our earlier years is left to us untouched by the tarnishing fingers of time; that we can still visit the house that used to seem to us in our childhood the House Beautiful, and find there the fair chamber looking to the east; that the young girl who hardly needed wings for her translation seems as ethereal still; that the child who went early and never grew up to mundane coarseness is still to us a cherub out of heaven, who folded his wings awhile ere he fled back to heaven again.

And perhaps it is another thing to be quite as thankful for, the illusions we all have more or less about ourselves. As we never fairly see ourselves in the mirror, the right side there becoming the left, so that we get none but a false and distorted vision of ourselves, what virtues, what triumphs of truth, kindness and generosity do we not seem in that inner vision to possess! For

THE HOME OF CHILDHOOD.

would we not make such and such great gifts, and perform such and such magnanimous acts, if things were only a little different with us? If we had the bank account of that billionaire, would we not be paying off the national debt? As it is, we have hardly enough for ourselves. And what Ithuriels we are, too, in that inner vision—we who scorn all untruth except that which may be absolutely necessary to save ourselves from other people's ill opinion! and what angels of mercy are we in that picture we delight to look at—we who roll the last scandal under our tongue for a choice morsel, and are glad when what we have is better than what our neighbor has! Well, if we are to sit in sackcloth and ashes for our sins, our bad traits, hereditary or otherwise, our good traits uncultivated, we shall have a sad time of it; and so blessed be these, with all the other of our illusions that hinder us ever from seeing a grain of sawdust in any doll we have. For if a sorrow's crown of sorrow is remembering happier things, how often the reverse is true, and how we find ourselves forced to smile at the very affairs that seemed unbearable in the bearing, but which have proved to be, if not angels in disguise, yet things that took a glory on their flying wings. Last year how bitter and detestable was that experience! This year the conditions are changed; the situation is otherwise; it seems to have been a very trifle about which to make such a fuss; we laugh at ourselves and at that trouble of the past.

The fact is that a person must be of a very sympathetic cast in order to feel intensely the troubles of others; it is not quite possible to realize them; every one has not sufficient self-forgetfulness to be able to displace himself, or sufficient imagination to plant himself on another centre as regards the

THE CONTEMPTUOUS STARE OF SOMEBODY IN A PARIS HAT.

DRIPPING THAT WEARS THE STONE.

universe, and occupy the position of another party. But that is what must be done if one would feel very keenly the pains of the past, for to-day you are yourself, but yesterday, as it has been said, you were quite another person; the kaleidoscope has taken another turn, and the relation of atoms is a new one.

Idle Regrets.

Last year's toothache does not hurt us; it seems as though it hurt some one else; in truth it seems as if that tooth might have been saved. Last year's affront makes us smile to think we should have been such fools as to mind it; the misery we endured a twelve-month since, in our old bonnet, from the contumelious stare of somebody in a Paris hat, is now, in the distance, too infinitesimal for us to condescend to remember. But then it is quite possible that we have a new hat ourselves this year, that nobody is affronting us, that our teeth are in fine order; we should not dream of allowing ourselves to be unbalanced by such trifles anyway now—what are they to be compared to the sore hangnail of the present moment, to the sudden cracking and unexpected shininess of our best silk, to the bill with no money to pay it! Yesterday's troubles vanish in the perspective of two narrowing lines, to-day's hover just before the sight, and shut out everything else. We cannot, to be sure, forget the facts of the past troubles, but all their sting and anguish is over and gone.

Of course we are not speaking of the real and significant griefs, the vital sorrows of the past, the unavailing regrets, the losses never to be made good —events whose meaning has entered into our being, and incorporated itself with our soul. Those things die only when we do, and will not, it may be, die even then, for their discipline may have been the thing we needed most, and nothing that is really valuable and necessary for us can ever be lost out of our posssesion.

In "My Summer with Dr. Singletary," Whittier says: "The present will live hereafter, memory will bridge over the gulf between the two worlds, for only in the condition of their intimate union can we preserve our identity and

EXPECTANCY A MUCH MORE EMPHATIC THING THAN HOPE. (35)

personal consciousness. Blot out the memory of this world, and what would heaven or hell be to us? Nothing whatever. Death would be simple annihilation of our actual selves and the substitution therefor of a new creation in which we should have no more interest than in an inhabitant of Jupiter or the fixed stars." Still, although memory may thus be the vital current of our identity, we doubt if we shall carry with us into any life whatever, memory of the little teasing details of our annoyances, although their effect may be felt forever in countless touches on our natures, like the fret of that ceaseless dripping which wears a stone. It is, indeed, only the exceptional nature, and often the morbid one, that is able to recall pain, that is saddened by its recollection, but we can all of us thrill again with the recollection of old joys; and the optimist might well argue, from experience of the truth, that pain is perishable, but joy is immortal.

Perhaps if we recognized this more forcibly, the petty provocations, the little teasing troubles, that are so "tolerable and not to be endured" while we are laboring through them, would cease to make the present uncomfortable, would wear less detestable aspects as they came, would no longer excite, in the rebellion against them, our ill temper, malice, hatred, and all uncharitableness, and would make less final impressions upon our nature than even now they do; we might refuse to be provoked or teased by them, and remembering the evanescence of pain and vexation, and the permanency of joy, we might yet learn a lesson from the trees of the forest that heal their wounds with precious gums; from the oysters that mend their shells with pearls.

> Led by a kindlier hand than ours,
>   We journey through this earthly scene,
> And should not, in our weary hours,
>   Turn to regret what might have been.
>
> And yet these hearts, when torn by pain,
>   Or wrung by disappointment keen
> Will seek relief from present cares
>   In thought of joys that might have been.
>
> But let us still these wishes vain;
>   We know not that of which we dream;
> Our lives might have been sadder yet;
>   God only knows what might have been.
>
> Forgive us, Lord, our little faith,
>   And help us all, from morn till e'en,
> Still to believe that lot the best
>   Which is—not that which might have been.
>
>   —*G. Z. Gray.*

THE BRIGHT DRAPERY OF DREAMS AND PLEASANT FANCIES. (37)

CHAPTER SECOND.

Dry Shod.

'Tis expectation makes a blessing dear,
Heaven were not heaven if we knew what it were.
—*Sir John Suckling.*

If a flower
Were thrown you out of heaven at intervals
You'd soon attain to a trick of looking up.
—*Elizabeth Barrett Browning.*

In all the splendor farther on
We missed the morning's maiden blush,
The soft expectancy was gone,—
The brooding haze, the trembling flush.
—*Margaret E. Sangster.*

I place faith in three friends—and they are powerful and invincible ones—namely, God, and your head, and mine.—*Wolfgang Amadeus Mozart.*

For every minute is expectancy
Of more arrivance.
—*Shakespeare.*

Hope to joy is little less in joy than hope enjoyed.
—*Shakespeare.*

But although the art of living chiefly in the present, and of letting the dead past bury its dead, gives us two of the stepping-stones to happiness, still, would we go over dry-shod, the next one must not be overlooked. It is the joy of perpetual hope.

Perpetual Hope.

For there are few joys of life comparable with that of expectancy, especially the expectancy of people of imagination. This is a singular fact, and speaks largely for the spiritual side of our nature; for few of the joys of realization and possession ever quite reach the heights of hope and imagination. Expectancy is, however, a much more emphatic thing than hope, since it signifies certainty, where the other is uncertain—signifies assurance and right,

NEVER BIRDS SANG AS I HEARD THEM.

signifies hope with the seal of authority upon it. We hope for many things without a shadow of ground for our hoping; we only expect that which we feel is sure to come. And what a pleasure is there in the expectancy, calling upon senses that know no sating! As the world within the looking-glass is an ideal world; as the scene in the Claude Lorraine glass is transfigured; as any commonplace thing, when reflected out of the actual and tangible, takes on an aura of grace and refinement—so expectancy gives us sensations just beyond reality, refines the real and idealizes facts.

An Ideal World.

One living in a state of expectancy, however temporary, lives really in an ideal world while it lasts. Every thing that comes within it is taken out of bald facts, and clothed in the bright drapery of dreams and pleasant fancies. Exactly what is expected never comes, to be sure, and unconsciously in these seasons of expectancy all of us are more or less poets. The maiden who wonders if her lover's steed "keeps pace with her expectancy and flies," is looking for a lover many degrees finer and tenderer than the lover who at last arrives, and divides the enjoyment of his love-making with the enjoyment of his cigar. The wife who awaits her husband, her heart beating at every sound, "listening less to her own music than for footsteps on the walk," pictures to herself, although perhaps without an articulate thought about it, a sort of model King Arthur, a noble pattern of all the excellencies, and in her love of this superior being of her conjuration forgets all about the real man, who, when he comes, will complain if his slippers have not been warmed, if his supper is not to his mind, who wants his wife well dressed on nothing a year, wants his table well set, but grumbles over the bills, and in general plays the part of that Pharaoh who would have bricks made without straw. And in turn, the husband whose wife has been absent, and who has missed her ordering, her bustling, her fault-finding, her presence in the house, so long that he has had time to forget the disagreeable part of her and remember only the cheerful and sweet, strangely recalls, now that he awaits her return, the wife of his youth, the girl he fell in love with, and who seemed to him at that time far "too good for human nature's daily food," and is somehow so fondly expecting that seraphic being, that he experiences an actual shock of surprise over the arrival of the woman who does come at last, only to dispute the hackman's charge, to reproach the servants, to complain of the misdoings during her interregnum, to set things straight with fury, and to tease for money. The merest trifle, in short, when we expect it and it has not yet arrived,

IN THE WAVE-WASHED SAND.

THE SHIP THAT IS COMING INTO HARBOR.

seems something better than the truth. Even the bonnet on its way from the milliner's is changed in our waiting from a tolerably pretty affair into a bewitching and delicate confusion of straw and lace and ribbons and flowers, that with some throws a glamor of itself over the commoner bonnet when that arrives, and with others utterly annihilates the poor bonnet that falls under none of its provisions. And so of every other mote in the world—it is gold while it swims in the sun; it is dust when it falls on our arm.

The pleasures of this expectancy are something that you may see little children begin to indulge in early. Half of their plays are made of it, and this, that, and the other joy and glory are to be theirs when they are big boys and girls; when they grow up; when they take off petticoats, forswear knickerbockers, wear long dresses, have a tall hat; when they are ladies; when they are soldiers; when they go to college; when they have children of their own; when the great future arrives, with all that they expect in it. Who of us, even in middle life, is not expecting his ship to come in? And who of us cannot recall the magnificent expectancy concerning that vague realm of unknown labors and rewards which we used to call the great world, and to think of as a delightful region into which we should presently be launched, which lay always just below the horizon? And what would life be worth if that other world were cut off from it—that world lying just beyond the horizon of life, which somehow casts its glory back over this actual world of to-day, and serves in our expectancy as perpetual compensation for all the ills and wrongs existing here?

Everybody remembers that child experience of Mrs. Browning, when in her sylvan rambles she came across a spot that never seemed the same again, if again she ever found it:

> I affirm that since I lost it,
> Never bower has seemed so fair;
> Never garden creeper crossed it
> With so deft and brave an air;
> Never bird sang in the summer
> As I saw and heard them there.

A Child's Discovery.

We recollect, ourselves, a child of our acquaintance who, playing on the beach at Newcastle, discovered a deposit of garnets there in the wave-washed sand, and ran hallooing up the shore for spades and bags to carry off the treasure, and whose dismay was only surpassed by that of the fox whose buried goose had been unearthed and stolen by another fox, when, on her

IF IT HAD BEEN THE QUEEN A-COMING IN.

returning full of expectancy, with a quickly assembled party, there was not a garnet to be found; and she would have been deemed guilty of falsehood or of fancy if her little apron full of rough gems had not been witness to her veracity, and Hugh Miller had not afterward come to her support with relation of similar facts. So far from quenching the spirit of expectancy within her, the circumstance seemed to stimulate it during all the rest of her life, as if time and fate must needs atone for the loss by giving everything else she looked for a value beyond itself.

Many of our mental processes are as yet quite inscrutable and past finding out, and thus it would be of little use to endeavor to say why expectancy so doubles the value of consummation.

Surprise.

There is a sudden joy and ecstatic heart-beat in the very welcome surprise that sometimes overtakes us, but who would exchange it for the long-drawn-out sweetness of that expectation in which we count the days, the hours, the moments, picture to ourselves the truth, gloat over every item of the coming joy, live it and re-live it, and extract the last drop of its deliciousness before it is actually here? The surprise is precious, doubtless; it lasts a moment. The expectation is equally precious; it lasts for hours. Our heart goes out and flies before the ship that is coming into harbor, goes out to greet the guest, goes out to receive the blessing, and is doubly dowered with every reasonable day's delay. To expect sorrow, and supreme sorrow, surely to expect it, is as wearing and wearying and unendurable as the suffering is when the blow falls; to expect joy, and surely to expect it, is to enjoy it by so much the longer and by so much the more exquisitely as it may happen with us that the ideal in our being exceeds the real. Thus it may be seen that happy expectation, almost another name for content, is an important factor in our happiness. I suppose it was a lesson of content in the present and of joy in the future, of the delight of vague expectancy and constant hope, that Mrs. Mulgrave had when looking at her new house in process of construction, she saw what she described as "Two Sides to a Bureau."

Mrs. Mulgrave's Story.

It is Mrs. Jim, however, who speaks first. This is one side of it: You must know, she said, that when I turned round and she was coming in the door, I'm sure I thought I was dreaming. If it had been the Queen a-coming in, I shouldn't have been more surprised; and the three children with their three faces like little pigs! "Here, you," whispered I to Benjamin Franklin, "you just go 'long and stick your face in some water, quick metre! And give Johnny's a scrubbing, too." And I wet the corner of my apron between my lips in a hurry, and rubbed Sue's mouth; and then I made believe I hadn't seen her before and dusted the other chair for her; and she sat down, and I sat down, and we looked at one another. Lord! she was that fine! Her flounces were silk, and they were scalloped like so many roses, and lace showing under the edges of them; and she had such boots, setting like gloves—just enough to make your eyes water. But the flowers in her hat—you should have seen them—I declare you could have smelled them! Well, she seemed to fill up the little room, and if ever I was glad of anything, I was glad that I'd scrubbed the floor that very day, so that it was clean enough to eat off of—glad, too, that I'd taken Jim's old hat out of the broken window and put in the smooth bottom of a box with a good respectable-looking tack. Jim might have mended that window, for he's a perfect Jack-at-all trades; but he'd rather play the fiddle than eat, and he was a-playing it out in the tie-up that moment, with all the wind there was blowing. However, I couldn't complain, for he'd just mended the chair, so that it was almost as good as new, and had put me up as tidy a shelf as you please over the stove for the brush and comb and the hair-oil bottle. If I'd been a little slicked up myself, with my new print and my pink apron, or if I'd only had my bang on, I wouldn't a-minded.

But when Benjamin Franklin came back with just the top dirt rinsed off, and the rest all smears, I did feel so vexed that I gave him as good a shaking as a nut-tree gets in harvest.

"Bless my heart!" says she, "what are you doing that for?"

"Because he's so aggravating," says I. "There, you go 'long;' and I gave him a shove.

"Why," says she, "don't you remember how it used to feel to be shaken yourself?"

"I don't know as I do," says I.

"As if you were flying to atoms? And your body was as powerless as if it had been in the hands of a giant, and your heart as full of hate?"

"Why, look a-here," says I. 'Be you a missionary?"

YOU COULDN'T SHUT A DRAWER.

THAT SEA VIEW WOULD BE GOOD AS A PICTURE

"A missionary?" says she, laughing ; No. I m Mr. Mulgrave's wife. And I came up to see how the new house was getting on; but the house is so full of plaster dust inside and the whirlwind is blowing the things off the roof so outside, that I thought I would venture in here till the cloud passed."

"Oh," says I.

"I knocked, but you didn't hear me."

"I'm real glad to see you," says I. "It's a dreadful lonesome place, and hardly anybody ever comes. Only I'm sorry everything's so at sixes and sevens. You see, where there's a family of children, and the wind blowing so," says I, with a lucky thought—it's always good to have the wind or the weather to lay things to, because nobody's responsible for the elements— "things will get to looking like ride-out."

"Children do make confusion," says she; "but confusion is pleasanter with them than pimlico order without them."

"Well, that's so," I answered; "for I remember when Johnny had the measles last year I thought if he only got well I'd let him whittle the door all to pieces if ever he wanted to again. Here, Benny," says I, for I began to feel bad to think I'd treated him so—if he'd mortified me, 'twas no reason why I should mortify him, and right before folks so—"take that to little sister," and I gave them something to keep them quiet. "I suppose you wouldn't care for any water?" says I to her then. "Not if I put some molasses in it? I didn't know but the wind would have made you dry. Yes, children do make trouble. One of Jim's songs says,

> 'Marriage does bring trouble;
> A single life is best;
> They should never double
> Who would be at rest.'

But there! I wouldn't be without them for all the fine clothes I used to have when I was single and worked in the shop I worked down at Burrage's— I suppose you never buy shoes there any?"

"What makes you suppose so?" says she, smiling.

"Well, because your boots don't look like our work; they look like—like Cinderella's slippers. Yes, I worked at Burrage's, off and on, a good many years—on most of the time. I had six dollars a week. Folks used to wonder how I got so many clothes with it, after I'd paid my board. But I always had that six dollars laid out long before pay-day—in my mind, you know—so that I spent it to the best advantage. There's a great deal of pleasure in that."

"A great deal," says she.

"That's what I say to Jim; and then he says his is all spent before pay-day, too—but with a difference, you know. I suppose you've got a real good, steady husband?"

"Oh, yes, indeed," says she, laughing some more.

"You must, to have such a nice house as that is going to be. But there! I shouldn't know what to do with it, and I don't envy you a bit."

'Oh, you needn't," says she, a-twitching her shoulder; "I expect to have trouble enough with it."

I WAS THE MOST UNHAPPY WOMAN.

"Not," says I—"I don't mean that Jim isn't steady. He's as steady as a clock—at that old fiddle of his. But sometimes I do wish he loved his regular trade as well, or else that that was his trade. But I suppose if fiddling was his trade, he'd want to be wood carving all the time."

"Why don't you speak to him," says she, "seriously?"

"Well, you can't," says I. "He's so sweet and good-natured and pleasant that when I've got my mind all made up to give him a sound talking to, he makes me like him so and sets me to laughing and plays such a twirling, twittering tune, that I can't do it to save my life."

You see, I'd got to talking rather free with her, because she listened so, and seemed interested, and kept looking at me in a wondering way, and at last took Sue up on her lap and gave her her rings to play with. Such rings! My gracious! one of them flashed with stones all round, just like the Milky Way. I should think it would have shone through her glove.

"But," says she, "you should tell him that his children will be growing up presently, and"——

"Oh, I do that," says I. "And he says, well, he'll do for the bad example they're to take warning by; and, at any rate, it's no use worrying before the time comes, and when they do grow up they can take care of themselves just the way we do."

"And are you contented to leave it so?" says she.

"Well, I'm contented enough. That is, in general. But I do wish sometimes that Jim would go down to his work regular every day, with his tin pail in his hand, like other men, and come back at night, and have a good round sum of money in hand at once, instead of just working long enough to get some flour and fish and pork and potatoes and sugar, and then not so much as lifting his finger again till that all gives out; it's such a hand-to-mouth way of living," says I. "And of course we can't get things together, such as a rocking-chair, and a sofa, and a good-sized looking-glass, and an eight-day clock. Not that I care much; only when a lady like you happens in I'd like to give her a seat that's softer. And there's a bureau. Now you wouldn't believe it, but I've never owned a bureau."

"Indeed," says she.

"Yes. I don't think it's good manners to be always apologizing about the looks of a place; and so I don't say anything about all the boxes and bundles I have to keep my things in, that do give a littery look; but I am always meaning to have a bureau to put them in, if I can compass it ever. You see, it's hard getting so much money in a pile; and if I do happen to, why then there's something I must have, like Jim's boots, or flannel and yarn and cloth, or a little bed—because you can't sleep with more than two children in one bed. And so, somehow, I never get the bureau. But then I don't give it up. Oh, I suppose you think my notions are dreadful extravagant," says I, for she was looking at me perfectly amazed; really, just as if I was a little monster, and she'd never seen the like. "And perhaps they are. But people must have something to ambition them, and it seems to me as though, if I ever could get a bureau, I should 'most feel as if I'd got a house!"

"Well, I declare!" says she, drawing of a long breath.

STEPPING STONES TO HAPPINESS. 51

"I did come precious near it last fall," says I—for I wanted her to see that it wasn't altogether an impossibility, and I wasn't wasting my time in vapors—"when Jim was at work up here, helping lay out the garden. He was paid by the day, you know; Mr. Mulgrave paid him; and he was paid here, and I had the handling of the money; and I said to myself, 'Now or never for that bureau!' But, dear me, I had to turn that money over so many times to get the things I couldn't do without any way at all, that before I got round to the bureau it was every cent gone!"

Yes," she says, "it's apt to be so. I know if I don't get the expensive thing when I have the money in my purse, the money is frittered away and I've nothing to show for it."

"That's just the way it is with me," says I. "But somehow I can't seem to do without the shoes and flannel, and all that. Oh, here's your husband! That's a powerful horse of his. But I should be afraid he'd break my neck if I was behind him."

"Not when my husband's driving," says she. And she bids me good-day, and kisses Sue, and springs into the wagon, and is off like a bird, with her veil and her feathers and her ribbons and streamers all flying.

Well, so far so good. Thinks I to myself: "She'll be a very pleasant neighbor. If she's ever so fine, she don't put on airs. And it does you good once in a while to have somebody listen when you want to run on about yourself. And maybe she'll have odd chores that I can turn my hand to—plain sewing, or clear-starching, or an extra help when company comes in. I shouldn't wonder if we were quite a mutual advantage." And so I told Jim, and he said he shouldn't wonder, too.

Well, that evening, just at sunset—now I'm telling you the real truth and if you don't believe me, there it is to speak for itself—Jim was a-playing "Roslin Castle," and I was a-putting Sue to sleep, when I happened to look out the window, and there was a job wagon coming straight up the hill, with something in it that had a great canvas hanging over it. "It's a queer time o' day," says I to myself, "to be bringing furniture into Mr. Mulgrave's house, and it not half done, either. But it s none of my business. Maybe it's a refrigerator to be set in the cellar." And I went on patting Sue, when all at once Jim's fiddle stopped short, as if it broke, and I heard a gruff voice saying, "Where'll you have it? Here, you, sir, lend a hand." And I dropped Sue on the bed and ran to the door, and they were a-bringing it in—there, look at it, as pretty a bureau as you'll find in a day's walk. It's pine, to be sure, but it's seasoned, and every drawer shuts smooth and easy; and it's painted and grained, like black-walnut, and there's four deep drawers, and a shallow one at the bottom, and two little drawers at the top; and in the upper drawer of the deep ones there's a place for this all parted off, and a place for that, and a place for the other; and, to crown the whole, a great swinging glass that you can see yourself in from head to belt. Just look! Oh, I tell you it's a great thing. "With Mrs. Mulgrave's compliments," says the man, and went off and shut the door.

I never waited for anything. Sue was screaming on the bed; I let her scream. I never minded Benny's rassling nor Jim's laughing. I got down every bandbox and basket and bundle I had on the shelves, got out every bag there was under the bed and behind the doors, and in ten minutes that bureau was so full you couldn't shut a drawer. Then I took them all out and fixed them all over again. "It's ours, Jim!" says I; and then I just sat down and cried.

The Other Side of the Bureau.

"Well, Lawrence, I'm so glad you've come! I thought you never would. And I've had such a lesson read me!"

"Lesson? Who's been reading my wife a lesson, I should like to know?"

"Who do you think? Nobody but that little absurd woman there—that Mrs. Jim. But I never had such a lesson. Drive slow, please, and let me tell you all about it—this horse does throw the gravel in your face so! I'm expecting every moment to see the spokes fly out of the wheels There, now, that's reasonable. This horse is a perfect griffin—has legs and wings, too."

"Well—steady, Frolic, steady!—now let's have your lesson. If there's any one can read you a lesson, Mrs. Fanny Mulgrave, I should like to hear it."

"Now, Lawrence! However, you know I came up to look at the house, for I've been having my misgivings about that big room. And when I went in, it did look so big and bare! I was dismayed. I paced it off this way and paced it off that way, and thought about what I could put in the corners; and how that window with the sea view would be as good as a picture: and how the whole mantel-piece from dado to cornice, with its white marble carvings and gildings and mirror, was a perfect illumination; and how I must confront it in that great square alcove with a mass of shadow; and we haven't a single thing to go there; and how magnificent an ebony and gold cabinet like that Mrs. Watrous and I saw at the Exhibition—the one I went into ecstasies over, you know, that goes from floor to ceiling—would fill the place. And the more I thought of it, the more indispensable such a great ebony and gilt cabinet seemed to be. And I knew it was perfectly impossible"——

"How did you know it, may I inquire?"

DWELLING UPON THE SPIRITUAL. (53)

"Oh, they cost—oh, hundreds of dollars. And, of course the house itself takes all you can spare. But I felt that it would be utterly out of my power to make that room look anything like what I wanted without it. And I kept seeing how beautiful it would be with those gold colored satin curtains of your aunt Sophy's falling back from the windows on each side of it. And I sat down and stared at the spot, and felt as if I didn't want the house at all if I couldn't have that cabinet. And I thought you might go without your cigars and your claret and your horses a couple of years, and we could easily have it."

"Kind of you, and cheerful for me."

"Oh, I didn't think anything about that part of it. Just fancy! I thought you were the most selfish man in the world, and I was the most unhappy woman; and all men were selfish, and all women were slaves; and—and that ebony and gold cabinet was obscuring my whole outlook on life. I felt so angry with you, and with fate, and with everything, that hot, scalding-hot tears would have shaken down if you had happened to come just then. I'm so glad you didn't, Lawrence, dear; I couldn't have spoken to save my life, and I should have run directly out of the room for fear, if I did speak, I should say something horrid.'

"Should you, indeed? And do you imagine I shouldn't have followed?"

"Oh, I should have been running."

"And whose legs are longest, puss?"

"Well, that's nothing to do with it. Just then the whirlwind came up, and the window-places being open, all the dust of the building, all the shavings and splinters and lime and sand about, seemed to make a sudden lurch into the room, and I couldn't see across it. And there I was in my new hat! And I made for the door as fast as my feet could fly."

"Silliest thing you could do."

"I suppose so; for when I was out-doors, the boards on the scaffoldings were pitching through the air at such a rate that I could neither stay there nor go back; and I saw that little shanty just round the corner, and ran in."

"That was sensible."

"Thanks. And there she was, pots and pails about the door, and a hen just blowing in before me, and a parcel of dirty-faced, barefooted children tumbling round. And such a place! It fairly made me low-spirited to look at it. I was in mortal fear of getting a grease spot on my dress. But I was in before I knew it, and there was no help for it, and the wind was blowing so I had to stay."

"And the lady of that house read you a lesson?"

"Such a lesson! You'd have thought, to begin with, that it was a palace. She did the honors like a little duchess. It didn't occur to her, apparently, that things were squalid. And that made it so much easier than if she apologized, and you were forced to tell polite fibs and make believe it was all right, you know. She was a trifle vexed because the face of one of the children wasn't clean, and afterward she repentingly gave him the molasses jug to keep him quiet; but another of the children was such a little darling! Well, presently her tongue was loose."

"Humph!"

"Humph? Didn't you want to hear about it? Oh, I know the whole story of my tongue, but I find you like to listen to it."

"So I do, my dear; so I do. And then?"

"Well, as I was saying, presently her tongue was loose, and I had the benefit of her experience. And I know she has a good-for-naught of a husband, whom she loves a great deal better than I love you—oh yes she does, for she seems never to have thought one hard thing concerning him, and I was thinking so many of you, you know! And there she is, and has been, with her cooking stove and table, her two chairs, a bed, and a crib, with a contented spirit and a patient soul, and her highest ambition and her wildest daydream just to have"——

"An ebony and gold cabinet?"

"Oh, no, no! Do drive faster, Lawrence. How this horse does crawl! I want to get it up to her to-night. A bureau. To think of it, only a bureau! You needn't laugh at me. I've an awful cold in my head. And I mean she shall have it, if it takes every cent you gave me for my new jacket. I'll wear the old one. I think I can get what she'll consider a beauty, though, for twelve dollars, or thereabouts. Drive to Veneer's, please, dear. I do feel in such a hurry, when it takes such a little bit to make a woman happy."

"An ebony and gold cabinet, for instance."

"Oh, nonsense! How you do love to tease, Lawrence! I never want to hear of such a thing again. I wouldn't have it now."

"Stop, stop, goodwife! You'll say too much. You silly little woman, didn't you know that ebony and gold cabinet which you and Mrs. Watrous saw was made for the place between your windows?"

CHAPTER THIRD.

A Pause By the Way.

Who know to live and know to die,
Their souls are safe, their triumph nigh.
—Anon.

Who sweeps a room as to God's law
Makes that and the action fine.
—Herbert

Never content yourself with doing your second best.
—Gen. Phil. Sheridan.

Has made me King! Now in my new estate
What duties must I do, what honors bear?
More than all men the King must feel the weight
Of constant self-restraint, of watchful care;
Beneath his firm control his passions bring,
And rule himself if he would be a King.
—S. M. Day.

But Pallas where she stood
Somewhat apart, her clear and bared limbs
O'er thwarted with the brazen-headed spear
Upon the pearly shoulder leaning cold,
The while, alone, her full and earnest eye
Over her snow-cold breast and angry cheek
Kept watch, waiting decision, made reply.
"Self-reverence, self-knowledge, self-control,
These three alone lead life to sovereign power.
Yet not for power (power of herself
Would come uncalled for), but to live by law,
Acting the law we live by without fear;
And, because right is right, to follow right,
Were wisdom in the scorn of consequence."
—Tennyson.

Self-Reliance and Self-Reverence.

We should do poorly with our content with life as it is, if we did not find one of the strongest and firmest of our stepping-stones as we cross the stream to our shining goal of happiness, in the habit of self-reliance and self-rever-

STEPPING STONES TO HAPPINESS.

THE SWEET INFLUENCE OF A LOVING SYMPATHY.

ence. The eloquent preacher Whitefield is reported to have asked Tennant: " Do you not rejoice that your time is so near at hand, when you will be called home and freed from all the difficulties of this checkered scene? '

"No," was the reply. "My business is to live as long as I can, as well as I can, and to serve my Lord and Master as faithfully as I can, until He shall think proper to call me home."

The aged saint knew that to every one is appointed his place and duty, and that he is to fill it and to fulfil it till relieved, and that thus his character is developed and strengthened. "The greater the power of thought in any individual," some one has said, "the greater is his spontaneous action; and the greater the spontaneous action the more completely will he live and be. A thousand influences lie in wait to ensnare mortal man. The whole world is an influence. The strongest of all is individual character. Character makes the man. Man can boast of nothing as his own, except the energy which he displays. If unable to arouse this energy let him assume it, let him place himself by a sudden effort in circumstances where he must will." Character then is developed by doing and not by dreaming.

St. Augustine's Dream.

When St. Augustine determined to give three days and nights to prayer and meditation concerning the deep mystery of the Trinity, on the third night he was very naturally overcome with sleep. In his sleep he dreamed that he was walking by the sea, where a child had made a hole in the sand with his tiny heel and then pouring water into it from a shell he held in his little hand. "What dost thou?" said St. Augustine. "I am pouring the sea into this hole," said the boy. "That cannot be done, my child," said the saint, with a pitying smile. Then all at once a gleam of heaven shone in the child's eyes—it was no longer a child. "I can do that, Augustine," he said, with a mighty voice, "as readily as thou canst understand the nature of thy thoughts and of the Trinity."

The Spiritual Mind.

But this does not imply that one should not dwell upon spiritual thoughts at the proper time, should not, in effect, be more spiritually minded than anything else, for to be spiritually minded is to have a sense, a conviction, an assured knowledge of the reality, solidity and security of spiritual things. "To find in the unseen region of a heavenly existence a source of motive power, a vast auxiliary, an inexhaustible reservoir of strength, coming in aid of natural conscience, which alone is insufficient to direct or reclaim us, but which we enforce from the divine works, irresistibly triumphs with our first moral

A HAPPY FACE DOES A SERVICE TO HUMANITY.

(59)

victory. A supreme uncreated excellence and glory must haunt, elevate, sanctify, and draw us to another citizenship than that which we hold amid these clay-built abodes, before the spiritual mind, which is life and peace, can be unfolded within us." Apropos of this, it is Bishop Huntingdon who says "that spiritual serenity is spiritual strength; it comes in by no softness of sentiment, but by thorough work. It comes by a faith that emboldens and energizes the whole soul." Spiritual or not, every one has his own life to live, and to live alone, alone as he came into being, alone as he will go out into the next stage of being. "There is something awful in this terrible solitude if we look at it. . . . One may indeed strive to break in upon the stillness of our solitary being, by crowding others around us, by the fever of excitement, or the sweet influence of a loving sympathy, but in all the pauses of outward things the solemn voice comes back and the vision of our single, proper, solitary being overshadows the spirits. We have each one this burden of a separate soul, and we must bear it. How do all deep-thinking persons, even in the daily routine, live apart from others, and more or less feel that they do so. Even ordinary life hears voices which add their witness to the truth if we will listen to them." It is in this inner solitude in which we all live that our habit of self-respect, of something more, of self-reverence, takes rise.

Reticence.

We cultivate it at first, very like, by a fit and proper reticence. We remember that the world is not very much interested in our especial suffering or joy, and that our haps and mishaps have not the interest of romances to other people. There are, indeed, let us say by the way, many sorrows and troubles of which the old proverb, "least said soonest mended," holds true. There are some things best hidden in secret receptacles with the lid shut down, rather than aired in the sight of all. Whoever wears a happy face does a service to humanity; for it is infinitely better that the world should seem full of sunshine than of gloom, that the general heart should be lifted in gratitude rather than abased with rankling injury; and happiness meanwhile, or its semblance, begets happiness, like a dollar at usury, and enriches the moral world as sunshine does the earth. Those who go about baring their private woes might learn, if they were able to lose the thread of their discourse for one moment, that most of the rest of the race are busy with the thread of their own discourses, and that although they turn to listen to a plaint and even to give a share of sympathy and pity, it is quite as a matter aside. an affair as much of self-respect as of respect for us, and they are presently hurrying on with their own

WE ARE MOST OF US INCLINED TO SYMPATHIZE.

interest again almost as indifferently as Nature herself seems to hurry. But even allowing that the sympathy is very great, given for a long time, without stint, and actively felt, there comes an end to all things, and perpetual draughts must only reach the lees of that. If one is going to demand sympathy forever, one should be very careful as to the manner in which it is demanded, as it is no impossible thing to wear out the patience even of those who love us most.

Real Troubles.

Real troubles can never fail to receive the tribute of warm and enduring compassion; but real troubles do not last forever, nor are they the ones concerning which the most rout is made, for deep sorrow is apt to seek to wrap itself in silence, and of the literally cureless diseases of the body, these the sufferer conceals to the last possible moment, and those, by the very fever they excite in the blood, kindle cheerfulness. We are so constituted, both physically and spiritually, that, under too heavy a burden for us to bear, we sink and fail; and real trouble of any amount wears us out, be it of body or of soul, before any great lapse of time, and puts an end to any need of sympathy—wears us out before we have a chance to wear patience out. It is, except for very rare and phenomenal cases, the unreal troubles, the actually slight ones, those to be in some measure avoided, mitigated, or overlooked, that are spread before other people with loudest iteration and demand for sympathy.

This is especially to be noticed in cases of partial illness, where much discomfort is experienced, some pain, great weariness, perhaps, yet not positive danger; but you will observe that where there is an invalid suffering such illness, no guest enters the door who is not hospitably entreated with a detailed account of that invalid's least symptoms—and, unless the guest be nurse or physician, to what result? It is even then ten to one if the complainer be well listened to, the first words having recalled some similar instance in the guest's experience, impatience to recount which, according to the very same tendency, dulls the ear to all the rest of the sickly recital. It is perhaps exceedingly sad and dreary to be obliged to suffer as this invalid does; we pity greatly; but when the invalid still lives on, growing no worse, we sometimes feel obliged to husband our resources, and to question if good taste would not try to wear the bright face instead of saddening the world with the darkest side. In reality, we are most of us inclined to sympathize generously with sorrow, with injustice, with pain; but the instinct of self-preservation prevents our being able, if we are willing, to endure a too prolonged strain, and it may be pronounced as an axiom that the individual receives the best and surest sympathy who makes the least outcry, and bears the sad lot with fortitude.

It is a little singular, withal, tnat the possessors of these numerous private woes—private? one should rather say public!—so frequently forget common self-respect. What would the same individuals say of the beggar who goes about showing his sores? And are they doing any differently? Are they not exhibiting a corresponding sort of uncleanness, the same want of modesty and shame, making themselves, as far as in them lies, and with the mere difference—and not always that—that exists between the ills of body and mind, as loathsome in all comparative degree?

The chief thing to be done in this regard by those who consider themselves the victims of any remarkable affliction is always to remember that, in spite of all kindness shown, nobody is so interesting to another as he is to himself, and that dignity requires one to keep one's sorrows, as well as one's joys, rather sacred than otherwise. As a rule, in the ecstasies of our great happiness or our great grief, we prefer to be alone. Why in our small happinesses and small griefs do we need so much more companionship? It seems as if one must, after all, be the possessor of a very reassuring amount of vanity to suppose that one should receive more consideration or consolation from one's acquaintances than Job did from his friends.

If keeping our woes to ourselves is one help to self-respect, another is the habit of taking life as it comes, sure that it is the best for us that comes, that we are not inferior wretches in the divine eyes, but that we are here to perform an appointed part. We will not then spend time in waiting for a path to open for us: "We will go ahead and open it." "By doing my own work," says Ruskin, "poor as it may seem to some, I shall better fulfil God's end in making me what I am, and more truly glorify His name than if I were either going out of my own sphere to do the work of another, or calling another into my sphere to do my proper work for me."

The Armor of Patience.

There are people to be sure, who may not open the path, to whom it is appointed to wait. "They also serve who only stand and wait," said the blind poet. And we shall find those who really seem to have little else to do than to wait: perhaps they lost their places early in this great procession of travelers from one darkness to another, and so nothing comes to them at the appointed time; they wait for love, for home, for happiness, for work, for wealth, for fame; usually they wait in vain, and at last they have only to wait for death. Whether it is owing to some of the cross purposes of fate that these people are so unfortunate, or whether it is the fault of their own organism that they have failed to profit by occasion, there is always something very pathetic about the thought of their unsatisfied lot. Others of us know something of the annoyances of waiting, are acquainted with the impatience, the nervousness, the disappointment, if not anger, the vexation of vainly expecting some trifle that in reality is unimportant; some of us know the misery of waiting for those who do not return;

every one has listened for desired footsteps, heard them coming from afar, heard them go by; and if such waiting be misery, we can paint to ourselves what a lifetime of waiting is. Of course, with the patient sufferers there is not the poignancy of acute disappointment in a matter of pressing present interest, such as that where hangs the life or welfare of a beloved one, or the pivot of our personal fortunes; but with them it is one dull expectancy, one long ache; other waitings come to an end, but this knows neither the piercing pang of certain sorrow and denial, nor ever any sudden lifting of gratification and content. The outlook, the hopes, the experience, narrows as chance never arrives, and fruition never happens, and they who look at the enduring patience of one thus waiting are sure that, if for no other reason, there must needs be an immortality in order to do justice to those thus wronged of what their soul most craves, although they have everything else in the world. For it is of no consequence to any what else they have in the world if they have not the one precise thing wanted. He who wants the hymns of Homer can not be put off with the *Mécanique Céleste*, or, to go from great to less, it makes no odds to the woman who has no gloves that she has two dozen handkerchiefs; under no conditions will she who longs for a home of her own be quite satisfied with the home of other people, and he who wishes for recognition of genius does not care to be pointed out for his fine eyes. He waits for recognition; she waits for love and home; another waits for a chance of self-education; another for freedom from a hated bond; and whether they wait all their lives, or get the desire at last, while they are waiting it is pitiful. It seems as if there were not happiness enough in this world to go round. "There's chairs enough," said the suddenly inundated country host, "but there's too much company;" and in this case there is no help for it but that some must go to the wall and wait.

Possibly there are some of these waiting ones who are waiting for something more serious than any of the small affairs of the daily paths, who await an answer to the great riddle of life, for the first glimpse of the things beyond, and have girded themselves with the armor of patience, till sight and knowledge shall be vouchsafed; and others there are who, undisturbed by such emotion, wait only for the leading of the power that rules the universe to do the will of that power, and help onward its work; and yet others who, all hope of further helping over, fold their hands and wait only for the word that gives them the freedom of the eternal city. But all such are waiting in good company—they wait with the hosts who stand with folded wings about heaven's throne.

If there is something lofty in this sainted waiting, not for the blisses of this life, but for the communion of saints beyond, all the other waiting depends for its merit upon the spirit in which it is taken. If it is quarrelsome, petulant, impatient, we fail to be touched by it; if it is idle and shiftless it renders us indignant, and disapproval almost destroys pity; if it is, on the whole, merely a waiting for opportunity to come, as the boy waited for the river to flow by that he might cross, unaware that opportunity is almost always in the passing moment if we have the knack of seizing it, it receives only a pity that is too near contempt to be pleasant.

Yet it behooves us, be the waiting of what sort it may, to keep some sparks of a better pity undestroyed, as we hope for it ourselves, for in one shape or another we are all of us waiting for something that in all our three-score years and ten we fail to find.

A Mutual Dependence.

Although we must stand alone in the spiritual life, we can not stand alone in the material one, for life is like a great interwoven fabric where one thread holds another. Think of the way in which all the relations of our social life are complicated, so that no one lives in the civilized world who is not doing something for some one else, either physically or intellectually or spiritually, paying rent, it might be said, for the lease of life. The bad are pulling down the good, the good are lifting up the bad, the poor are working for the rich, the rich are spending for the poor, and even the baby of the pauper is creating a demand that some one must supply.

The wealthy woman stepping from her stone mansion to her carriage is an illustration, in her mere material affairs, of the way in which all humanity works together, and works for each member of itself. To say nothing of those influences that have shaped her heart and soul, how many workers have contributed to send her abroad in the guise in which she appears? to how many workers has she contributed a fractional support? The quarry-man has wrought the stone for the mansion; the kiln-man has burned the brick; the woodman has felled the lumber; the miner has sent the iron and lead; carpenter and turner, mason and blacksmith and marble-worker and plumber, and all the kindred trades, have been at her service. The watchman has patrolled the street at night for her soft slumbers in that mansion; the laborer has made that street, and has cleaned it; the lamp-lighter has lighted the gas before it; powerful officials, learned doctors of the boards of health, committees of the city government, have seen that all this was properly done, and she has paid her stipend to assessors, recorders, and receivers of taxes for having it done. Slaughterers, leather-dressers, carriage-makers, again, have afforded her the coach into which she steps; some one of the old countries, or rather the influences working there, have probably sent her coachman and footman; the farmer, who supplies much on her table, has raised her horses. And for that same table has the vaquero driven the herd of steers that came sweeping up from bayou and prairie of the far New Mexican and Texan regions; have flocks of fowl been brought from the Northwest; have fruits been pulled in the tropics, and sweetmeats been sent from the East; has the fisher in the Columbia taken salmon, and the Hindoo on the bank of the Ganges sent hot sauces; has the peasant of the Rhine tended his grapes, and pressed the must. Look then at her array: the negro has bent under the sun picking the cotton that enters into some portion of it; the flax-raiser has been in her employ; the barefooted Irish girl at home has turned the woven linen for her in sun and dew; the maidens of France have tended the silkworms for her, and reeled the cocoons; the shuttles have tossed to and fro for her in the looms of Lyons; swarthy Orientals have squatted at their rude frames embellishing the rich stuffs she folds about her; while slaves in the diamond mines have dug and delved for her at one side of the globe, and fishermen have stripped the seal at the other. For her, too, have the keels of ships been laid, to bring her these silks and cashmeres and furs and jewels; for her have sailors braved the mid-ocean storms, have pilots gone out to bring the ships to port through curling breakers; for her the watcher in his solitary sea-washed tower kindles the light-house lamp each evening on the edge of dark. For her, too, have the shining lines of railway steel been laid, and the trains led thundering over them by engineer and fireman, bringing her fineries and dainties; for her has the daily paper been struck off, with editor, reporter, and printer on her payroll; for her delectation did the morning news run at midnight over the telegraph wires; for her safety has the sentinel paced all night on the lonely seawall in the harbor defense, and have bodies of troops been moved up and down on the frontier haunted by the tomahawk. For her pleasure has the inspiration of the musician come, has painter painted, and statuary carved; has the performer spent weary hours of practice with his instrument; has the actor plodded through his lines, the dancer through her steps, before the curtain rises on the scene where all joy and suffering are fused in swift sparkle and beauty. For her the judge sits on his bench to administer justice; for her even the chief of the nation holds the reins of power, and one might say that for her all the nations of the earth exist, and kings and queens and emperors sit upon their thrones. And to each and all of these, from peasant to prince, who thus work for her she pays tribute, and is, in turn, their feudatory. She can not do without them, as they can not do without her; her life is their life, her wishes give them their wishes. And what is true of the rich

THE GOOD ARE LIFTING UP THE BAD.

(67)

woman is true of the poor woman as well. For although she have not a dollar but what she earns with her hard and pitiful laundry-work, she does not spend it without receiving service and paying tribute also to all the crafts and trades that supply her needs, and the radius in which she is felt is just as the circle of her wants is wide or narrow; and the rich woman is her "bound woman" again, for one furnishes the other with the clean linen that she wants, and one furnishes the other with the money that she wants! With the unequal fortune of the two there is also a mutual dependence.

And if the dependence is so intimate in purely material things, how close is it in things of the spiritual domain, in the mental and moral world. What surmise and suspicion of evil does not swing from one to another in scandal, till it mows down its swath before it? What theft, in the simple injury of the loss of the loser, does not entail trouble passing again from one to another, and in the injury of the crime to the taker does not entail other trouble on all with whom his degradation comes in contact, not only in his diminished power to do good, but in his increased aptitude to do evil? What wicked thought can prompt the speaking of a wicked word that its vibration shall not cause the air to thrill, and make some other voice its echo? For we can neither do nor think wrong without injuring, in degree—as the cuttle-fish darkens the water about him—all those within the limit of our influence. Let us be ever so much accountable to fate and to our consciences as separate individuals, we are yet more certainly congregated and bound together in one great circulation and interchange than the atoms of some vast polyp building its coral reef in the South Pacific, and every one's self-respect and reverence must have its effect upon the individuality of every other soul.

Man's Majesty.

There are, however, those who call themselves philosophers to whom self-reverence, in any high degree, seems as futile as any of their early hopes and dreams, since they consider the human race and its concerns to be only among the smaller affairs of the universe. These people declare that there is something a little mortifying to their vanity in the sense of the insignificance of the human race which almost invariably overcomes them when they see it in a mass. Not, be it understood, when they see it in the roaring, turbulent mass of an infuriated mob; then it assumes, indeed, some of the greatness of elemental forces, and swells and surges like the sea, with one wave fortifying another; but in the common stream of population going to and fro upon a thousand pitiful small errands along some thoroughfare. Watching this stream for any length of time, it irresistibly occurs to them that just so the ants go and come with their little burdens, their wealth of grains of wheat and barley bigger than themselves, just so their soldiers march to battle, just so their slaves toil on at home; and they half wonder if to any superior eyes that chance to rest on us we can be of more consequence than these ants are in our own. At the same time they confess that it is odd that recurrence and multitude should make small and common that which in the single and isolated instance is often found to be grand and uncommon— in the great senator, mighty soldier, singing poet, lovely woman. Yet we have only to take the separate features of any of

TO EVERY EARNEST, STRIVING SOUL.

these isolated instances of humanity—say, the malcontents—to find the same sensation recurring, and to feel assured that if man be made in the image of any thing divine, it is his inner and spiritual body, and not all the varying eyes and ears and noses. For if it were one of these, even so much as one ear, for example, which one, of all that we meet? This little curled, pink-rimmed, and shell-like ear of the maiden, with its jeweled tip, this pair that stand out on either side of the head like vase handles, these that remind one of the answer of the worthy who, on being asked if the story he was about to relate was fit for the auditor's ears, replied that they were long enough, or those where old age, as it too often does, has smoothed out all the charming whorls and creases, and left only a large flat surface of cartilage, those that hold themselves pricked up, alert companions, as if they meant no whisper should escape them, those pinned back so flatly that what goes in on one side may easily come out at the other, those that wag as the scalp moves, those that have the pointed segment of the faun's ear, those that are lobeless, or those that project themselves into space like a trumpet? Yet when one can find so much in the mere outward guise of so small a portion of the frame, so tiny a member as the ear, and is aware that its inner construction is so complicated and delicate with vibrant membrane and labyrinthine passage, it is not easy to recur to such a fancy as that of the insignificance of the owner of such an instrument. No! Man who has dared, and who has been given the power to dare, to search almighty secrets, to weigh the sun, to catch the colors of the elements from which stars are made, is a being of importance in the creative eyes, and he owes a debt of self-respect to the Power that made him. "Your body," says Rutherford, "is the dwelling-place of the spirit, and therefore for the love you carry to the sweet Guest give a due regard to His house of clay, for the house is not your own." We read in the "Records of a Quiet Life" that it is one of the hardest things in the world to be true to one's self in one's intercourse with others. "There is scarcely anything that requires more real courage. How little is there of true freedom from all put-on conversation and manner! The more truly Christian is our spirit, the more truly shall we rise out of this bondage, which is of the earth earthly, to preserve our truth and uprightness of character, to be in all places and at all times and with all people one and the same, not equally open or equally communicative, but equally free from what is artificial and constrained, and steadfast in keeping fast hold of those principles and feelings which are known to be according to God's will and law." The great poem of the "Happy Warrior" does not apply to the soldier merely, but to every earnest, striving soul on earth.

> "Who is the Happy Warrior? Who is he
> That every man in arms should wish to be?
> It is the generous spirit, who, when brought
> Among the tasks of real life, hath wrought
> Upon the plan that pleased his boyish thought;
> Whose high endeavors are an inward light
> That makes the path before him always bright;
> Who, with a natural instinct to discern
> What knowledge can perform, is diligent to learn,
> Abides by this resolve, and stops not there,
> But makes his moral being his prime care.
> * * * * * * * *

> But who, if he be called upon to face
> Some awful moment to which heaven has joine-
> Great issues, good or bad for human kind,
> Is happy as a Lover, and attired
> With sudden brightness like a man inspired;
> And through the heat of conflict keeps the law
> In calmness made, and sees what he foresaw;
> Or if an unexpected call succeed,
> Come when it will, is equal to the need."

I have thought that the story of Miss Moggaridge's Provider was an illustration of that sweet self-reverence which implies absolute belief and truth in Providence, and of the truth of the saying of Thomas À Kempis that, "From a pure heart proceedeth the fruit of a good life."

Miss Moggaridge's Provider.

The way in which people interested themselves in Miss Moggaridge's affairs would have been a curiosity in itself anywhere but in the seacoast town where Miss Moggaridge lived. But there it had become so much a matter of course for one neighbor to discuss the various bearings of all the incidents in another neighbor's life, and—if unexplained facts still remained to supply the gap from fancy—in addition to the customary duty of keeping the other neighbor's conscience, that it never struck a soul among all the worthy tribes there that they were doing anything at all out of the way in gossiping, wondering, conjecturing, and declaring this, that, and the other about Miss Moggaridge's business after a fashion that would have made any one but herself perfectly wild.

But Miss Moggaridge was a placid soul, and as the fact of her neighbor's gossip implied a censure which perhaps she felt to be not altogether undeserved, while, on the other hand, their wonder was not entirely uncomplimentary, she found herself able to disregard them altogether, and in answer to query, complaint, or expostulation concerning her wicked waste, which was to make woful want, always met her interlocutor with the sweet and gentle words, "The Lord will provide."

Poor Miss Moggaridge's father had been that extraordinary phenomenon, a clergyman possessed not only of treasure in Heaven, but of the rustier and more corruptible treasure of this world's goods—an inherited treasure, by the way, which he did not have time to scatter to the four winds in person, as it was left to him by an admirer (to whom his great sermon on the Seventh

Seal had brought spiritual peace), but a few years before his death, which happened suddenly; and the property was consequently divided according to his last will and testament between two of his three children, giving them each a modest competency, but leaving the third to shift for himself, as he always had done. The first thing which Miss Moggaridge did with her freedom and her money was to imitate the example of the "fearless son of Ginger Blue," and try a little travel, to the great scandal of souls in her native borough, who found no reason why Miss Moggaridge should want to see any more of the world than that borough presented to her, and never shared her weak and wicked desire to see what sort of region it was that lay on the other side of the bay and the breakers.

"The idea, Ann!" said Miss Keturah Meteyard, a well-to-do spinster whose farm and stock, and consequently whose opinion, were the pride of the place—"the idea of your beginning at your time of life to kite round like a young girl. The eyes of the fool are in the ends of the earth," quoted Miss Keturah, with a long sigh. "For my part, the village is good enough for me!"

"And for me too, Kitty," said Miss Moggaridge. "I am not going any great distance; I—I am going to see Jack."

Now Jack was the scapegrace Moggaridge, who had run away to sea and therewith to the bad; and the stern clergyman, his father, having satisfied his mind on the point that there was no earthly reclamation possible for Jack, had with true, old-style rigor commenced and carried on the difficult work of tearing the boy out of his heart, that since Heaven had elected Jack to damnation there might be no carnal opposition on his own part through the weak bonds of the flesh; and Jack's name had not been spoken in that house from which he fled for many a year before the old man was gathered to his fathers. For all that, every now and then a letter came to Miss Ann and another went from her in reply, and her father, with an inconsistency very mortifying but highly human, saw them come and saw them go, convinced that he should hear from Ann whatever news need might be for him to hear; and so it came to pass that Miss Ann knew of Jack's whereabouts, and that Miss Keturah, hearing her intent of seeking them—Miss Keturah with one eye on the community and one on her old pastor—held up her hands a brief instant in holy horror before memory twitched them down again.

'Ann!" said she, solemnly—"Ann, do you know what you are doing?"

"Doing?" said Miss Moggaridge. "In going to see Jack, do you mean? Certainly I do. A Christian duty."

"And what," said Miss Keturah—"what constitutes you a better judge of Christian duty than your sainted father, a Christian minister for fifty years breaking the bread of life in this parish?"

"Very well," said Miss Moggaridge, unable to answer such an argument as that—for Miss Keturah fought like those armies that put their prisoners in the front, so that a shot from Miss Moggaridge must necessarily have demolished her father the clergyman—"very well," said his faithful daughter, "perhaps not a Christian duty, we will say not; but, at any rate, a natural duty."

"And you dare to set a natural duty, a duty of our unregenerate condition, above the duties of such as are set apart from the world?"

"My dear Kitty," said Miss Moggaridge, "I am not sure that we ever are or ever should be set apart from the world; that we are not placed here to work in it and with it till our faith and our example leaven it."

"Ann Moggaridge!" said the other, springing to her feet, with a lively scarlet in her yellow face, a color less Christian perhaps than that of her remarks, "this is rank heresy, and I won't stay to hear it!"

"O pooh, Kitty," said Miss Moggaridge, listening to the denunciation of her opinions with great good-humor, "we've gone all through that a hundred times. Sit down again—we'll leave argument to the elders—I want to talk about something else."

"Something else?" with a change as easy as Harlequin's.

"Yes, I want to talk to you about that corner meadow. It just takes a jog out of your land, and I've an idea you'd like to buy it. Now say so, freely, if you would."

"Humph! what has put that into your head, I'd like to know? You've refused a good price for it, you and your father, every spring for ten years, to my knowledge. You want," said Miss Keturah, facing about with uplifted forefinger like an accusing angel—in curl-papers and brown gingham—"you want the ready money to go and see Jack with!"

"Well, yes. I don't need the meadow and I do need the money; for when you have everything tied up in stocks, you can't always get at it, you know."

"That's very shiftless of you, Ann Moggaridge," said Miss Keturah. "When the money's gone, it's gone, but there the meadow'll always be."

'Bless your heart, for the matter of that, I've made up my mind to get rid of all the farm."

"Get rid of the farm!'

"Yes. I'm not well enough nor strong enough to carry it on by myself, now father's gone, and his means are divided. Your place would make me blush like a fever beside it. No, I couldn't keep it to advantage; so I think

I shall let you take the corner meadow, if you want it, and Squire Purcell will take the rest."

"And what will you do with yourself when you come back from—from Jack, if you really mean to go?"

"O, board with the Squire or anywhere; the Lord will provide a place; perhaps with you," added Miss Moggaridge, archly.

"No, indeed," said Miss Keturah, "not with me! We never should have any peace of our lives. There isn't a point in all the Westminster Catechism that we don't differ about, and we should quarrel as to means of grace at every meal we sat down to. Besides which, you would fret me to death with your obstinacy when you are notoriously wrong—as in this visit to Jack, for instance."

"Jack needs me, Kitty. I must go to him."

"It is your spiritual pride that must go and play the good Samaritan!"

"Jack and I used to be the dearest things in the world to each other when we were children, you know," said Miss Ann, gently. "We had both our pleasures and our punishments together. The severity of our home drove him off—I don't know what it drove him to. I waited, because father claimed my first duty; now, I must do what can be done to help Jack into the narrow path again.'

"The severity of your home!" said Miss Keturah, who had heard nothing since that; "of such a home as yours, such a Christian home, with—with"——

"The benefit of clergy," laughed Miss Moggaridge.

"Ann, you're impious!" exclaimed Miss Keturah, bringing down her umbrella hard enough to blunt its ferule. "Much such a spirit as that will do to bring Jack back! It isn't your place to bring him back, either. You've had no call to be a missionary, and it's presumption in you to interfere with the plain will of Providence. You will go your own gait, of course, but you sha'n't go without knowing that I and every friend you have disapprove of the proceeding. And it's another step to total beggary, for the upshot of it all will be that Jack coaxes and wheedles your money."

"My money?" said Miss Ann. "There will be no need of any coaxing and wheedling; it's as much his as mine."

"His!"

"I know father expected me to do justice, and so he didn't trouble himself. I should feel I was wronging him in his grave if I refused."

"And what is Luke going to do, may I ask?" inquired Miss Keturah, with grim stolidity

"Because Luke won't give up any of his, is no reason why I shouldn't."

"Luke won't? That's like him. Sensible. Sensible! He won't give the Lord's substance to the ungodly."

"So he says. But I m afraid not to the godly, either. I'm afraid he wouldn't even to me if I stood in want, though perhaps I oughtn't to say so."

'Not if you'd wasted all you have on Jack, certainly."

"I shall divide my property with Jack as a measure of simple justice, Kitty," said Miss Moggaridge, firmly. "It is as much his as mine, as I said."

"And when it s all gone," continued Miss Keturah, "what is to become of you then?"

"When it's all gone? O, there's no danger of that."

'There's danger of anything between your butter-fingers, Ann. So if it should happen, what then?"

"The Lord will provide," said Miss Ann, sweetly.

"The Lord helps them that help themselves," said Miss Keturah. "Well, I'm gone. I'd wrestle longer with you if it was any use—you're as set as Lot's wife. I suppose," she said, turning round after she had reached the door, "you ll come and see me before you go. I've—I've something you might take Jack; you know I ve been knitting socks all the year and we've no men-folks," and then she was gone.

Poor Miss Keturah—a good soul after her own fashion, which was not Miss Moggaridge s fashion—once she had expected the wicked Jack to come home from sea and marry her; and the expectation and the disappointment together had knit a bond between her and his sister that endured a great deal of stretching and striving. The neighbors said that she had pious spells; but if that were so, certainly these spells were sometimes so protracted as almost to become chronic, and in fact frequently to assume the complexion of a complaint; but they never hindered her from driving a bargain home to the head, from putting royal exactions on the produce of her dairy, from sending her small eggs to market, and from disputing every bill, from the tax-man's to the tithes, that ever was presented at her door. But somewhere down under that crust of hers there was a drop of honey to reward the adventurous seeker, and Miss Ann always declared that she knew where to find it.

So Miss Moggaridge went away from the seacoast for some seasons, and the tides ebbed and flowed, and the moons waxed and waned, and the years slipped off after each other, and the villagers found other matter for their gossip; and the most of them had rather forgotten her, when some half dozen years later she returned, quite old and worn and sad, having buried the wretched Jack, and a goodly portion of her modest fortune with him, and bringing back nothing but his dog as a souvenir of his existence—a poor little shivering hound that in no wise met the public approbation.

A LETTER CAME TO MISS ANN.

But Miss Moggaridge did not long allow her old acquaintances to remain unaware of her return among them. The very day after her arrival a disastrous fire in the village had left a family destitute and shelterless; and, heading a subscription list with a moderate sum, she went round with it in person, as she had been wont to do in the old times, till the sight of her approaching shadow had caused the stingy man to flee. And now, with every rebuff she met, every complaint of hard times, bad bargains, poor crops, she altered the figures against her own name for those of a larger amount, till by night-fall the forlorn family had the means of being comfortable again, through the goodness of the village and Miss Moggaridge; for had not the village given the cipher, whatever might be the other figures which Miss Moggaridge had of herself prefixed thereto? True to her instincts, Miss Keturah Meteyard waylaid her old friend next day. "I've heard all about it, Ann, so you needn't pretend ignorance," she began. "And you may think it very fine, but I call it totally unprincipled. Are you Crœsus, or Rothschild, or the Queen of Sheba come again, to be running to the relief of all the lazy and shiftless folks in the country? Everybody is talking about it; everybody's wondering at you, Ann!"

"Everybody may reimburse me, Kitty, just as soon as they please."

'Perhaps they will, when they're angels. The idea of your''——

'But, Kitty, I couldn't see those poor Morrises without a roof over them; and if you want the truth," said Miss Moggaridge, turning like the trodden worm, "I can't imagine how you could. Why, where on earth could they go?"

"There was no need of seeing them without a roof. The neighbors'd have taken them in till they rebuilt the place. Perhaps that would have spurred Morris up enough to make an exertion, which he never did in his life. If he'd been one atom forehanded, he'd have had something laid by in bank to fall back on at such a time. I declare, I've no patience!" cried Miss Keturah, with nobody to dispute her. And any one would be glad of those two girls as help," she continued. "Great lazy, hulking, fine ladies they are! And the first thing they'll do with your money will be to buy an ingrain carpet and a looking-glass and a couple of silk gowns, whether there's enough left for a broom and a dish-cloth or not. Go?" cried Miss Keturah, now quite at tne climax of her virtuous indignation. "They could go to the poorhouse, where you'll go if some of your friends don't take you in hand and have a guardian appointed over you!"

But Miss Moggaridge only laughed and kissed her censor good by, and made up her mind to save the sum of her prodigality out of her own expenses in some way; by giving up her nice boarding-place, perhaps, and boarding herself in two or three rooms of a house she still owned, where she could go without groceries and goodies, for instance, in such things as fruit and sugar and butter and eggs and all the dainties to be concocted therewith; for bread and meat and milk would keep body and soul together healthily, she reasoned, and acted on her reasoning. But instead of making good, by this economy, the sum she had extracted from her hoard, she presently found that the saving thus accomplished had been used upon the outfit of a poor young minister going to preach to the Queen of Madagascar. Miss Keturah was not so loud in her disapproval of this as of some of Miss Moggaridge's other less eccentric charities; but as giving away in any shape was not agreeable to her, she could not help remarking that, if she were Miss Moggaridge, she should feel as if she had lent a hand to help cast him into a fiery furnace, for that would undoubtedly be the final disposition of the unfortunate young minister by the wicked savages of the island whither he was bound. She herself only bestowed upon him some of her knitted socks to walk the furnace in. What she did cavil at much more was the discovery that Miss Moggaridge was living alone. "Without help, Ann Moggaridge!" she said, laying her hands along her knees in an attitude of fine Egyptian despair. "And pinching yourself to the last extremity, I'll be bound, for these Morrises and young ministers and what not! What would your father say to see it? And if you should be sick in the middle of the night and no one near to hear you call"——

"The Lord'll provide for me, Kitty," said Miss Moggaridge, for the thousandth time.

"He won't provide a full-grown servant-girl, springing up out of nothing."

"But there's no need of worry, dear, with such health as mine."

"It's tempting Providence!"

"Tempting Providence to what?"

"Ann!" said Miss Keturah, severely, "I don't understand how any one as good as you—for you are good in spite of your faults"——

"There is none good but One," Miss Moggaridge gently admonished her.

"As good as you," continued Miss Keturah, obliviously, "and enjoying all your lifelong privileges, can indulge in levity and so often go so near the edge of blasphemy, without a shudder."

"Dear Kitty," said Miss Ann, laughing, "we shall never agree, though we love each other so much; so where is the use? For my part, I think it blasphemy to suppose Providence could be tempted."

"Ann! Ann!" said Miss Keturah, solemnly. "Don't indulge such thoughts. They will lead you presently into doubting the existence of a personal Devil! And now," continued she, reverting to the original topic, "I sha'n't go away till you promise me to take in help, so that you needn't die alone in the night, and be found stiff in the morning by a stranger!" And poor Miss Moggaridge had to promise, at last, though it upset all her little scheme of saving in groceries and firewood and wages, and went to her heart sorely.

It was not very long after this expostulation of Miss Keturah's that—a stout-armed serving-woman having been added to Miss Moggaridge's family—another more singular addition made itself on the night when a ship was nipped among the breakers behind which the town had intrenched itself, and went to pieces just outside the cove of stiller water, at whose head stood the house in which were Miss Moggaridge's rooms. Of all the freighting lives on board that doomed craft, one thing alone ever came to shore—a bird, that, as Miss Moggaridge peered from the door which Bridget held open for her, fluttered through the tumultuous twilight air and into her arms. Miss Moggaridge left Bridget to set her back to the door and push it inch by inch, till one triumphant slam proclaimed victory over the elements, while hastening in herself to bare her foundling before the fire. It was a parrot, drenched with the wave and the weather in spite of his preening oils, shivering in her hands, and almost ready to yield to firelight and warmth the remnant of life that survived his battling flight. Miss Moggaridge bestowed him in a basket of wool in a corner of the heated hearth, placed milk and crumbs at hand, and no more resumed her knitting and soft-voiced psalm-singing, but fidgeted about the darkened windows and wondered concerning the poor souls who, since they never could make shore again themselves, had given the bird the liberty of his wings. She was attracted again to the fireside by a long whistle of unspeakable relief, and, turning, saw the bird stepping from the basket, treading daintily down the tiles, and waddling to and fro before the blessed blaze, while he chuckled to himself unintelligibly, but quite as if he had practiced the cunningest trick over storm and shipwreck that could have been devised. Bridget would have frowned the intruder down, and did eventually give warning "along of the divil's imp," as she called him; but Miss Moggaridge was as pleased as a child; it was the only thing of the sort in the village, and what a means to attract the little people, whom she loved, and at the same time to administer to them diluted doses of the moral law! Had she chosen, to be sure, it would have been one of the great gray African things she had read of, that spread a scarlet tail and seemed the phœnix of some white-washed brand in which the smouldering fire yet sparkles. But this was a little fellow with scarlet on his shoulders and his wings, a golden cap on his head, and it would have been hard to say whether the glistening mantle over his back were emerald crusted with gold or gold enameled with emerald, so much did every single feather shine like a blade of green grass full of flint. While she looked, and admired, and wished, nevertheless, that it were gray, another door was pushed gently open and Folly entered—Jack's slim white hound, as much a miracle of beauty in his own way—made at the bird with native instinct, then paused with equally native cowardice, and looked at Miss Moggaridge and wagged his tail, as who should say, "Praise my forbearance."

THE SHIP WENT TO PIECES.

But the parrot, having surveyed Master Folly on this side and on that from a pair of eyes like limpid jewels, opened his mouth and barked. Nothing else was needed; the phantom of the gray parrot disappeared whence he came; more intelligence no child could have shown. Miss Moggaridge caught him up, received a vicious bite for her pains, but, notwithstanding, suffered him to cling upon her fingers, tightly grasping which, he looked down upon the hound, flapped his gorgeous wings and crowed; then he went through an astonishing series of barn-yard accomplishments, finally ending in a burst and clatter of the most uproarious and side-splitting laughter. Having done this, he had exhausted his repertory, and never for all the time during which he delighted the heart of Miss Moggaridge and forced Miss Keturah to regard him as a piece of supernatural sin created by the Evil One in mockery of the creation of man, so that had she but been a good Catholic she would have crossed herself before him, and, without being an ancient Persian, did frequently propitiate him after the fashion of the Ahrimanian worship—never during all that time did he catch a new sound or utter an articulate syllable to denote from what nationality—Spanish, Portuguese, or Dutch—he had received his earliest lessons. But he had done enough. Folly, never particularly brilliant in his wits, and not more strongly developed in his affections, was given hearth-room on sufferance for his lissome limbs, and on general grounds of compassion for himself and Jack together; but the parrot, luring one on with perpetual hopes of new attainment, and born of the tropical sun that made a perpetual mirage in her imagination, became cherished society, and had not only a shining perch, but a nest in Miss Moggaridge's affections as well—a nest that cost her dearly some years afterward.

But before the town had much more than done wondering at Miss Moggaridge's parrot, and telling all the gossipry of his deeds and misdeeds—of the way he picked the lock of his cage, walked up the walls, tearing off the papering as he went, bit big splinters from the window-blinds, drove away every shadow of a cat, and made general havoc—Miss Moggaridge gave such occasion for a fresh onslaught of tongues, that the bird was half forgotten.

It was when her name was found to have been indorsed upon her brother Luke's paper—Luke being the resident of another place—and in his failure the larger portion of her earthly goods was swept out of her hands. One would have supposed that Miss Moggaridge had been guilty of a forgery, and that not her own property, but the church funds, had been made away with by means of the wretched signature; and a particular aggravation of the calamity, in the eyes of her towns-people, seemed to be its clandestine character; if they had been consulted or had even been made aware that such a thing might possibly be expected, much might have been condoned. As it was, they were glad, they were sure, that she felt able to afford such fine doings, but they had heard of such a thing as being just before you were generous, and they only hoped she wouldn't come upon the town in her old age in consequence, that was all; for much that close-fisted Luke would do for her, even if he got upon his feet again—Luke who had been heard to remark that the loss of a cent spoiled the face of a dollar!

But Luke never got upon his feet again, and during the rest of his life he struggled along from hand to mouth, with one child binding shoes and another in the mills, a scanty board, a thread-bare back; and though Miss Moggaridge was left now with nothing but a mere pittance of bank stock over and above the possession of the house in which she reserved her rooms, yet out of the income thus remaining she still found it possible now and then to send a gold-piece to Luke—a gold-piece which in his eyes looked large enough to eclipse the sun, while she patched and turned and furbished many a worn old garment of her own, in order that she might send a new one to her sister-in-law, of whom Miss Keturah once declared that she put her more in mind of an old shoe-knife worn down to the handle than of anything else in the world.

"As if it would make the least difference in her appearance," said Miss Keturah, who had a faculty of mousing out all these innocent crimes against society on Miss Moggaridge's part, "whether she wore calico or homespun? Dress up a split rail! And you rigging yourself out of the rag-bag so as to send her an alpaca. Why can't she work? *I* work."

"Bless you, Kitty, doesn't she work like a slave now for the mere privilege of drawing her breath? What more can she do?"

"That's no business of mine, or yours either. Your duty," said Miss Keturah, "your bounden duty's to take care of yourself. And here you are wearing flannels thin as vanity, because you've no money left to buy thick ones; and you'll get a cold and a cough through these Luke Moggaridges that'll carry you out of the world; and then," exclaimed she, with an unusual quaver in her piercing tone—"then I should like to know what is to become of"——

"The Lord will provide for me, Kitty."

"So I've heard you say!" she snapped. "But I was talking about myself —He won't provide me with another Ann Moggaridge"—— And there Miss Keturah whisked herself out of sight, possibly to prevent any such catastrophe as her friend's seeing a tear in those sharp eyes of hers unused to such weak visitants.

Yet as a law of ethics is the impossibility of standing still in face of the necessity of motion, either progressive or retrograde, so Miss Moggaridge went on verifying the worst prognostications of her neighbors; and it was surmised that the way in which she had raised the money to pay for having the cataract removed from old Master Sullivan's eyes—eyes worn out in the service of two generations of the town's children—which she was one day found to have done, was by scrimping her store of wood and coal (Bridget's departure having long left her free to do so), to that mere apology for a fire the winter long to which she owed a rheumatism that now began to afflict her hands and feet in such a manner as to make her nearly useless in any physical effort. It was no wonder the townsfolk were incensed against her, for her conduct implied a reproof of theirs that was vexatious; why in the world couldn't she have let Master Sullivan's eyes alone? He had looked out upon the world and had seen it to his satisfaction or dissatisfaction for three-score years and over; one would have imagined he had seen enough of a place whose sins he was always bewailing!

But a worse enormity than almost any preceding ones remained yet to be perpetrated by Miss Moggaridge. It was an encroachment upon her capital, her small remaining capital, for the education of one of the Luke Moggaridges, a bright boy whom his aunt thought to be possessed of too much ability to rust away in a hand-to-hand struggle with life. Longing, perhaps, to hear him preach some searching sermon in his grandfather's pulpit, and to surrender into safe and appreciative keeping those barrels full of sacred manuscripts which she still treasured, she had resolved to have him fitted and sent to college. Very likely the town in which the boy lived thought it a worthy action of the aunt's, but the town in which he didn't live regarded it as a piece of Quixotism on a par with all her previous proceedings, since the boy would have been as well off at a trade, Miss Moggaridge much better off, and the town plus certain tax money now lost to it forever. It was, however, reserved for Miss Keturah to learn the whole extent of her offence before the town had done so—to learn that she had not been spending merely all her income, dismissing Bridget, freezing herself, starving herself, but she had been drawing on her little principal till there was barely enough to buy her a yearly gown and shoes, and in order to live at all she must spend the whole remainder now, instead of waiting for any interest.

"Exactly, exactly, exactly what I prophesied!" cried Miss Keturah. "And who but you could contrive, let alone could have done, such a piece of work? You show ingenuity enough in bringing yourself to beggary to have made your fortune at a patent. You have a talent for ruin!"

"I am not afraid of beggary, Kitty," said Miss Moggaridge. "How often shall I quote the Psalmist to you? 'I have been young and now am old; yet have I not seen the righteous forsaken, nor his seed begging bread.'"

"I know that, Ann. I say it over often. It's the only thing that leaves me any hope for you." And Miss Keturah kept a silent meditation for a few moments. "As if it wasn't just as well," she broke forth at length, "for that Luke Moggaridge boy to dig potatoes or make shoes, as to preach bad sermons, or kill off patients, or make confusion worse confounded in a lawsuit!"

Whether Miss Moggaridge thought it a dreadful world where every one spoke the truth to his neighbor, or not, she answered, pleasantly, "Kitty, dear, I should have consulted you as to that"——

"As to what? Shoes or sermons? He might have made good shoes."

"Only," continued Miss Moggaridge, meekly but determinedly—"only you make such a breeze if you think differently, that I felt it best to get him through college first"——

"Why couldn't he get himself through?"

"Well, he's sickly."

"O dear Lord, as if there weren't enough of that kind! Serve Heaven because he can't serve the flesh! Taking dyspepsia and blue devils for faith and works!"

"You mustn't now, Kitty, you mustn't. I meant for us all to advise together concerning the choice of a profession after his graduation. For he has real talent, he'll do us credit."

"Well," said Miss Keturah, a little mollified, "it might have been wise. It might have saved you a pretty penny. *I* might have lent the young man the money he needed, and it would have done him no harm to feel that he was to refund it when he was able."

"That is exactly what I have done, Kitty. And I never thought of letting any one else, even you—though I'd rather it should be you than any one —while I was able. And I'm sure I can pinch along any way till he can pay me; and if he never can pay me, he can take care of me, for he is a noble boy, a noble boy."

"And what if he shouldn't live to do anything of the sort?"

"O, I can't think of such a thing."

"He mightn't, though. There's many a hole in the skimmer."

"I don t know—I don't know what I should do. But there, no matter. I shall be taken care of some way, come what will. I always have been. The Lord will provide."

"Well now, Ann, I'm going to demand one thing by my right as your next friend, and one caring a great deal more about you than all the Lukes in the world. You won t lend that boy, noble or otherwise, another penny, but you'll let him keep school and work his way through his profession himself."

"No indeed, Kitty! That would make it six or seven years before he got his profession. There are only a few hundreds left, so they may as well go with the others."

"Light come, light go," sniffed Miss Keturah. "If you'd had to work for that money—— What. I repeat, what in the mean time is to become of you?"

"Don't fear for me; the Lord will provide."

"The poorhouse will, you mean! Why in the name of wonder can't he work his way up, as well as his betters?"

'Well, the truth is, Kitty, he's—he's engaged. And of course he wants to be married And"——

But Miss Keturah had risen from her chair and stalked out, and slammed the door behind her, without another syllable.

Poor Miss Moggaridge. It was but little more than a twelvemonth after this conversation that her noble boy was drowned while bathing; and half broken-hearted—for she had grown very fond of him through his constant letters and occasional visits—she never called to mind how her money, principal and interest and education, had gone down with him and left her absolutely penniless, save for the rent of the residue of the house where she kept her two or three rooms. But Miss Keturah did.

Miss Moggaridge was now, moreover, quite unable to do a thing to help herself. Far too lame in her feet to walk and in her hands to knit, she was obliged to sit all day in her chair doing nothing, and have her meals brought to her by the family, and her rooms kept in order, in payment of the rent, while her time was enlivened only by the children who dropped in to see the parrot—an entertainment ever new; by a weekly afternoon of Mrs. Morris', who came and did up all the little odd jobs of mending on which she could lay her willing hands; by the calls of Master Sullivan, glowering at the world out of a pair of immense spectacles, through which he read daily chapters of the Psalms to her; and by the half-loving, half-quarreling visits of Miss Keturah. She used to congratulate herself in those days over the possession of the parrot. "I should forget my tongue if I hadn't him and the hound to talk with," she used to say, in answer to Miss Keturah's complaints of the screeching with which the bird always greeted her. "He is a capital companion. When I see him so gay and good-natured, imprisoned in his cage with none of his kind near, I wonder at myself for repining over my confinement in so large and airy a room as this, where I can look out on the sea all day long." And she bent her head down for the bird to caress, and loved him none the less on the next day—when Miss Keturah would have been glad to wring his neck—for the crowning disaster of her life, which he brought about that very evening.

For the mischievous fellow, working open the door of his cage, as he had done a thousand times before, while Miss Moggaridge sat nodding in her chair, had clambered with bill and claw here and there about the room, calling in the aid of his splendid wings when need was, till, reaching a match-safe and securing a card of matches in his bill with which he made off, pausing only on the top of a pile of religious newspapers, on a table beneath the chintz window-curtains, to pull them into a multitude of splinters; and the consequence was that presently his frightened screams woke the helpless Miss Moggaridge to a dim, half-suffocated sense that the world was full of smoke, and to find the place in flames, and the neighbors rushing in and carrying her, and the parrot clinging to her, to a place of safety, upon which Miss Keturah swooped down directly and had her removed to her own house and installed in the bedroom adjoining the best-room, without asking her so much as whether she would or no.

"Well, Ann," said Miss Keturah, rising from her knees after their evening prayers, "it's the most wonderful deliverance I ever heard anything about."

'It is indeed," sobbed the poor lady, still quivering with her excitement. "And, under Heaven, I may thank Poll for it," she said, looking kindly at the crestfallen bird on the chair's arm, whose screams had alarmed the neighbors.

"Indeed you may!" the old Adam coming uppermost again—strange they never called it the old Eve—"indeed you may—thank him for any mischief—picking out a baby's eyes or setting a house afire, it's all one to him. But there's no great loss without some small gain; and there's one thing in it I'm truly grateful for, you can't waste any more money, Ann Moggaridge, for you haven't got any more to waste!"

"Why, Kitty, there's the land the house stood on, that will bring something"—profoundly of the conviction that her possession was the widow's cruse, and with no idea of ever taking offence at anything that Miss Keturah said.

"Yes, something. But you'll never have it," said Miss Keturah, grimly. "For I'm going to buy that land myself, and never pay you a cent for it; so you can't give that away! And now you're here, I'm going to keep you, Ann; for you're no more fit to be trusted with yourself than a baby. And I shall see that you have respectable gowns and thick flannels and warm stockings and the doctor. You'll have this room, and I the one on the other side that I've always had; and we'll have your chair wheeled out in the daytimes; and I think we shall get along very well together for the rest of our lives, if you're not as obstinate and unreasonable"——

"O Kitty," said Miss Moggaridge, looking up with streaming eyes that showed how great, although unspoken, her anxiety had become, and how great the relief from that dread of public alms which we all share alike—"O Kitty! I had just as lief have everything from you as not. I had rather owe"——

"There's no owing in the case!" said Miss Keturah, tossing her head, to the infinite danger of the kerosene from the whirlwind made by her ribbons.

"O, there is! there is!" sobbed Miss Moggaridge. "Debts, too, I never can pay! You've always stood my next best friend to Heaven, dear; and didn't I say," she cried, with a smile breaking like sunshine through her tears—"didn't I say the Lord would provide?"

BONDS OF BLOOD RELATIONSHIP. (87)

CHAPTER FOURTH.

A Family Tree.

And hie him home at evening's close
To sweet repast and calm repose.
—*Gray*.

He that hath a house to put's head in has a good head-piece.
—*Shakespeare*.

She is my home,
My household stuff, my field, my barn.
—*Shakespeare*.

From our own selves our joys must flow
And that dear hut our home.
—*Nathaniel Cotton*.

Who hath a family
Stands not alone,
Buttressed by clansmen,
Holpen by bannermen,
Battle all merrily
Many as one.
—*Old Song*.

Such is the patriot's boast, where'er we roam,
His first best country ever is at home.
—*Goldsmith*.

When one has made up one's mind to live in the present and to find a great joy in expectancy, that is to foster a sunny disposition and cease regretting the past, and when one is entrenched in a firm self-respect, one turns first for happiness to the family relation. God setteth the solitary in families is a text that we all receive with grateful hearts, and the more so the older we grow. The homely saying that blood is thicker than water is one of the truths that it is usually held there is no gainsaying, and it is believed that it contains, as many another law does, the concentrated wisdom of years. Yet we have always doubted if, after all, it were natural feeling that predominated among us so much as family feeling, if one can discriminate between the two; for natural feeling is shared with brutes and savages, but the other belongs

THE SAME MOTHER'S KNEE.

truly to those that are bound in the bonds of blood-relationship. The brute shows none of it, except in relation to the mate, and not always then, and for a very brief season to the offspring.

The love of brothers and sisters, of grandparents and cousins, does not distinguish savages, many of whom are known to leave their old and sick to lonely and speedy death. But the moment that civilization advances at all, families and clans become established, the blood that flows in kindred veins begins to be recognized and felt. Some of this sentiment might possibly be traced to the sense of possession, for although we do not reason it out in corresponding words, we are aware of it—perhaps through those dark senses that are to the others what the dark rays of the spectrum are to the seven colors—these people are ours, are in some degree a part of ourselves, certainly of our lives; their conduct is an honor or a dishonor to us; we are forced to think of them, and it flatters our self-love to think well of them; what they are it is possible that we, of the same descent, may be also, and this little thread of pride feels a pull at the third generation

Household Associations

But cannot much more of the sentiment be traced to association? There must be ties, equal to those of blood, in life from the earliest remembrance about the same hearth and at the same mother's knee—that mother who remains sacred, we will not say either because of instinct or because of the result of long teaching, but because she bore us. And while we are a portion of the flesh and blood of our parents, and love is thus compelled, they would be strange beings if we might not also love them for themselves. But whether or not, we see that there is no time, in all that season when emotions are fresh and character is forming, in which the others of the family are not integral and inherent portions, and again through our very love of self they are dear to us.

But whether this family feeling is, in its essentials, a God-given instinct or a matter of growth and education, it is at the foundation of all our civil polity, and the family is at the base of the town, as the town is at the base of the State; and so long as the family relation is kept pure and undefiled among any people, so long as children honor their parents, as parents bear in mind their responsibility concerning those whom they have brought into the world, as the hearts of brothers and sisters beat as one, so long will that people possess shields and safeguards against enemies in having homes and altar-fires worth fighting for.

There are few things more beautiful to see than this family affection, the solicitude of the old for the young, the reverence of the young for the old, the gentle ties of affiliation between sister and sister, the noble loyalty of brother for brother, the attention to trifles that makes happiness for one another, the deadening of strife and destruction of envy, the mutual aiding and uplifting.

REVERENCE OF THE YOUNG FOR THE OLD. (91)

Plutarch's Advice.

Something of this was known to Plutarch, who advises his readers to imitate one who, "when he knows himself far superior to his brother, calls for his help and advice, whether it be the business of a rhetorician, a magistrate, or a friend; in a word, he that neglects or leaves him out in no honorable employment or concern, but joins him with himself in all his noble and worthy actions, employs him when present, waits for him when absent, and makes the world take notice that he is as fit for business as himself, but of a more modest and yielding disposition, and all this while he has done himself no wrong, and has bravely advanced his brother." This same old heathen author, indeed, who speaks so commendably of brotherly honor and help, has a great deal more to say in the same vein, which makes one see that fine family feeling, if not universal with the ancients, was yet by no means confined to our later day; and one can not but be struck at the advice he gives a young man in relation to a married brother, adjuring him to "have the highest esteem and honor for his brother's wife, respecting and honoring her as the most sacred of all his brother's sacred treasures, and thus to do honor to him; condoling with her when she is neglected, and appeasing her when she is angered; if she have a little offended, to intercede and sue for her peace; if there have been any private difference between himself and his brother, to make his complaint before her in order to reconcilement. . . . . When he has children, let him express his affection and respect to both parents with the greater ardency. Let him love the children equally with his own, but be more favorable and indulgent to them, that, if it chance that they commit some of their youthful faults, they may not run away and hide themselves among naughty acquaintances through fear of their parents' anger, but may have in their uncle a recourse and refuge where they will be admonished lovingly, and will find an intercessor to make their excuse and get their pardon."

If all this were in accordance with advice and custom among the best in heathen times, how much further should fraternal feeling go now, led along in the gentle paths of Christianity! Yet although great things are sometimes more easily done than small ones, we doubt if there are, in our own virtuous days, any better instances of brotherly love than that between two Eastern brothers whose dust has for thousands of years been a portion of the common earth, "in a question," to quote our good old Plutarch again, "not concerning a little patch of land, nor a few servants or cattle, but no less than the kingdom of Persia. When Darius was dead, some were for Ariamenes' succeeding to the crown, as being eldest son; others were for Xerxes, who was born to Darius of Atossa, the daughter of Cyrus, in the time of his reign

THE STIFF, PRIM LIKENESS OF SOME GRANDAM.

over Persia. Ariamenes, therefore, came from Media, in no hostile posture, but very peaceably, to hear the matter determined. Xerxes, being there, used the majesty and power of a king. But when his brother was come he laid down his crown and other royal ornaments, went and, meeting, greeted him. And sending him presents, he gave a charge to his servants to deliver them with these words: 'With these presents your brother Xerxes expresses the honor he has for you; and if by the judgment and suffrages of the Persians I be declared king, I place you next to myself.' Ariamenes replied: 'I accept your gifts, but presume the kingdom of Persia to be my right. Yet for all my younger brethren I shall have an honor, but for Xerxes in the first place.' The day of determining who should reign being come, the Persians made Artabanus, brother to Darius, judge. Xerxes excepting against him, confiding most in the multitude, his mother, Atossa, reproved him, saying: 'Why, son, are you so shy of Artabanus, your uncle, and one of the best men among the Persians? And why should you dread the trial where the worst you can fear is to be next the throne, and to be called the King of Persia's brother?' Xerxes, at length submitting, after some debate Artabanus adjudged the kingdom to Xerxes. Ariamenes presently started up and went and showed obeisance to his brother, and taking him by the hand, placed him in the throne. And from that time, being placed himself by Xerxes next in the kingdom, he continued the same affection to him, insomuch that, for his brother's honor engaging himself in the naval fight at Salamis, he was killed there."

It is not every crowned Christian that in the years since Salamis has rivaled the behavior of these brothers. It is not every one in private life that rivals them to-day. For, however the blood may run in our veins, neither natural affection nor family feeling is always quite sufficient to carry us through all the temptations and trials and small annoyances of daily life without constant use of the Golden Rule, without hourly remembrance of that Divine love which shadows forth all family love.

It is true that the jest concerning the man who, in settling the estate left him by his brother, had so much trouble with it that he "almost wished he hadn't a' died," is still for some households more a literal interpretation of the prevailing spirit there than anything hyperbolic and absurd. But we thank Heaven that we are able to believe such households are not many; that, so far as domestic happiness and union go, most of our homes are as full of peace as the House Beautiful; that our land is one long succession of such homes; and that few of us need to learn a lesson in these high morals from such a people as the Persians, or from such a man as Xerxes.

But although doing their whole duty to the living, there are many people

TENDERNESS FOR THOSE DEAD AND GONE.

who are unable to feel an interest in those of their race who have passed from earth, beyond at furthest the last two generations. Perhaps they have half a sensation that these people are strangers, they are so remote they would not care for them, so why should they do more?

Love of Ancestors.

Yet, if they think of it, in every link of the chain of relationship the tenderest closeness of affection has probably subsisted; they themselves were kissed by lips that in turn received the kisses of those behind, and they again received the love and caresses of those yet behind, kisses and caresses forming the long chain between people dear to one another, and not strangers, though the last known be many generations gone. As they look at the stiff, prim likeness of some grandame five or six times removed, they would not regard her so critically if they bethought themselves how that face had lighted up with smiles, and those lips had gathered sweets from the babies that grew up to hand down the line that ends in themselves; they would feel as if they, too, had come in for some share of the warmth of her nature, and recognize the kinship of race; they would possibly find themselves even loving this woman whom they have never seen, and of whom they know nothing but that she lived and loved. It is not easy always to throw ourselves into the personality of those who belonged to a life so long past and so different from our own; but we are sure to know that, whatever their lives were, their hearts were the hearts of mothers and fathers, and into those imagined natures, then, there is not a heart of their posterity which beats that cannot pulse some of its own warm life-blood, and make them for the nonce alive.

There can hardly be too much closeness in family ties between the members of an existing generation; there is none too much love broadcast in the world, and if it is not our duty to value and cherish those of our own blood, it would be hard to say whose duty it is. The more this obligation is recognized, the better for the world in general, and surely for the world in particular, for there is nothing that smooths the way through life like love, and love that is also a duty has an added force, and is twice love

Family Traditions.

Few things stimulate this family love more than the treasuring in common of family love and tradition, the looking for the repetition of family traits in mind and body, and a certain jealous respect for the honor of those who are not here to maintain their own honor, no matter should it even go so far as to make sure that the descendants of these ancestors shall themselves be decent and honorable people. A certain tenderness for these dead and gone persons is a worthy feeling that, far from doing harm, is deepening and enlarging to the nature; a certain determination to feel this tenderness puts one already into the attitude of reverence that, if it does no other good, inclines one to consider more warmly the good of their other descendants and bind more nearly the family tie. One need not, in order to do fit reverence to the old root of a family tree, follow the example of the Chinese, and make

STEPPING STONES TO HAPPINESS.

THE POSSESSION OF A HOME

a solemn business of worshipping one's ancestors with prayer and sacrifice and genuflection; nor even the example of those among ourselves who, judged by their conversation with its boasts of past splendor, would seem to be trying to make other people worship their ancestors in order to throw glorification on themselves. For, after all, the most fit act of reverence that we can possibly show this old family tree of ours is to prove to the world that the best part of it is not that which is under the sod.

To be sure there is a certain pride in armorial bearings and titled descent, with which a republican people have and should have little or nothing to do, and which to those who believe ardently in our institutions seem but agencies of harm, even if looked at more as matters of curiosity and art than in any other way.

The Coat of Arms.

Yet it is pleasant to know, albeit in a country where coats of arms are out of order, what the coat of arms was that fell to one's ancestors in the great strifes for existence and booty in previous centuries, as historically illustrative of the character and attainment of a man whose ever-so-many-times-diluted blood may run in our veins, and of the standard which he was obliged to live up to, as we now try to live up to our blue china. And one also naturally takes pride in the motto that indicates, if it chances so to do, a lofty character in the man from whom we have some part of our character as well as of our blood. Many a coat of arms, indeed, as well by its bearings, its crest, as its motto, indicates the whole character and nature of a family—a nature impressed so powerfully that all the other sides of the house have failed to make themselves felt in material modification, and if the family were to be characterized by heraldry to-day, it might be in the same manner. Thus one may actually have an interest in the arms of the family that is perfectly legitimate, and not a subject of pompous parade or improper pride—an interest in the expression of heroism, or force, or whatever it may be that they commemorate, shut up in that little space as if it were crystallized there; and one feels a right to hope that something of such worthy ancestry may at some time re-appear in one's self or in one's children.

For other use than this, which may be called a virtual and virtuous use, citizens of a republic have no need of a coat of arms, which is recognized neither by the laws nor the customs of a republic; and it is to be expected that it will be looked on with suspicion, when blazoned abroad in all its bravery, by those who are jealous of the preservation of so costly a boon as liberty, wrenched as that was from the hands of those who still display their armorial bearings in countries that do not present so fair a view of human nature in the masses as this one, in which the common people mount heights of thought and education and comfort hand in hand with the liberty that their fathers gained.

CHAPTER FIFTH.

A Home in Town.

> He that holds fast the golden mean,
> And lives contentedly between
>   The little and the great,
> Feels not the wants that pinch the poor,
> Nor plagues that haunt the rich man's door.
> —*Cowper's Translation of Horace.*

> Dear God! the very houses seem asleep,
> And all that mighty heart is lying still.
> —*Wordsworth.*

> As many ways meet in one town
> As many fresh streams meet in one salt sea.
> —*Shakespeare.*

> I must live among my neighbors.
> —*Shakespeare.*

> I will go lose myself
> And wander up and down to see the city.
> —*Shakespeare.*

> Good talkers are found only in Paris.
> —*François Villon.*

> The axis of the earth sticks out visibly through the centre of every town or city.
> —*Dr. Holmes.*

> Then rose Elaine and glided through the fields
> And past beneath the weirdly sculptured gates
> Far up the dim rich city to her kin.
> —*Tennyson.*

Having our personal condition satisfactory, in the determination to make the most of the present, and to surround ourselves with the atmosphere of hope and of self-respect, we find our next stepping-stone to happiness in the possession of a home. There are many of us who, on account of our work, our business, or our family relations, or from a long habit of generations of our people, must have our home in the city, and so prefer it.

Owning the House.

It is not always easy to own a house there; not only because large holders of property there are unwilling to part with it, but because the first expense is too much for the light purse. If it is the want of funds that oblige one to forego the happiness of owning the house, it is not impossible to practice a strict economy till enough money is laid by for a first payment, if the house is purchasable; and then a mortgage is easily to be negotiated at any savings bank or with any money-lender, and the house is practically ours. We find then that there is something to live up to in laying by money each year that otherwise we should have wasted in uncourted and unthinking ways; and it gives us presently a great pleasure to do this, and almost before we know it the mortgage is wiped out. But if that may not be, it is our best interest to obtain a long lease of the house, not only that the rent may not rise upon us, but that we may not lose it at a landlord's caprice or at the wish of another tenant, and also and more important than either, that we may secure permanence and establish the idea of home. For when our children have to note the years of their lives "when we lived in the Blank Street house," and "when we were living in the Naught Square house" and the rest, it is impossible that they should have the idea of home that a permanent stay in any one spot gives. The house is a residence then and not a home. As it is, moving from house to house has become a sort of habit with us, and one of the first signs of advancing spring among us is a certain restlessness beginning to be apparent in every house-holder, together with an anxious inspection of those placards that are then blossoming out in the windows, and in the advertising columns of the daily news, with more unerring instinct as to season than the dandelions have in the parks. As the days grow longer, and the robins are seeking us out again, and the swallows are flitting round the eaves, these other migratory beings are also on the wing running from house to house in search of a proper place for their nests; that is to say, judging whether or not their furniture will look better in this house than it does in that, and if all other things are equal, not to say a trifle superior. It is a singular commentary upon the insufficiency of our builders that this is so

Moving.

People do not move for the sake of moving, for the pleasure to be found in ripping up and putting down carpets, packing books and trunks, having mirrors smashed and paintings gashed and china destroyed and tables scarred, for the sake of going through all the trouble of hanging curtains, driving nails, directing labor, repairing damages, living in a world of dust, and taking the risks of soaking rains on all their household gods. There are pleasanter ways of spending one's time: smoking at the club, visiting one's friends, lying on a sofa and reading novels, counting one's money—are all of them more cheerful and agreeable occupations; and when they are put by for all the excitations of moving, it is only because there is reason, and people are flying from the ills they have to those they know not of. To those they know not of, we say, because they will no sooner be established in their new quarters, where all looked as if it might be made so comfortable, than they will find the world is hollow even there; and if the drains are not out of order, then the water-pipes are, or the heaters are, or the next neighbors are, or the attic is haunted, and there is a pea-hen somewhere.

Of course those people would be very foolish who endured a wrong that they saw any way of righting, but they should be very sure it is going to be righted before they bring upon themselves all the calamities of moving, reduced to a science now though moving be.

But besides the breakage and ruin and irritation and fatigue, too frequent moving brings a worse effect to pass, for it has a tendency to uproot character, and make one like floating weed; there is no sense of stability, nor much of that recognition of social responsibility which it is desirable to have in order to be saved from the Bohemian, and which a more permanent resting-place of the Lares and Penates gives. There is a certain moral support in the walls that have surrounded us for any length of time, and that are

ON THE WING.

known to have done so; we share their permanence and acquire their respectability; they fit us now, and the new ones are to be broken in.

In the annual march of which we are speaking there is too often the mere desire for change, and restless dissatisfaction with circumstances that will hardly be improved by such means. The surrounding walls are different, but the discontent has removed, too, and remains the same. To these cases we would recommend the old story of the farmer who, troubled by the persistent attentions of a ghost, packed his goods for another place, and on the way encountered an inquiring neighbor:

"What! you're flitting?"

"Yes, we're flitting," says the ghost (for they had packed the spectre among their beds).

"Oh, well," says the farmer, "you flitting with us, too?—Jack, turn the horses' heads, and home again!"

Better than the moving, when the family has increased, and when the circumstances are sufficiently improved to warrant a house of twice the size, would be the total disregard of unfashionable neighborhood, and the purchase or hire of the next house, turning both into one. No matter whether the street be the most desirable or not, it is the spot where home is, the spot to which we wish the children's thoughts to return when absent, and it is better to enlarge, enrich and beautify that than to move into other houses so frequently that it is impossible for them to call any place home.

Inside the House.

Nevertheless in the city it is not so much the location or anything of the exterior that has to do with happiness so much as it is the inside of the house. Outer sunshine is important there, of course; but the sunshine of gentle manners and pleasant faces is more important still, and the social enjoyment of friends that is to be had in the city is something that is impossible anywhere else for a length of time. The large rooms, the airy sleeping rooms, the hot and cold water and gas, the bath at any hour of day or night, the physician at telephone call, comfortable conveniences for getting about, cheap means of reaching some of the most superb gardens of the world, such as Druid, Fairmount, Prospect, and Central and Franklin parks; all these things add a great deal to the enjoyment of life

The Vacation.

If one wants more there is the summer vacation for many, in which the clerk, the student, the tired house-keeper, the business man, the journalist, the

SUNSHINE OF PLEASANT FACES.

professional man, can go out and lie in the sun on the grass, and feel the pulse of the old planet, or sit on the sand, watching the rise and fall of the sea like the placid heaving of a mighty breast, hide in the shadow of the woods, till they feel like the wildwood creatures themselves, launch their boat in the breakers, and know the exhilaration of conquering the unconquerable, or slip it through lily-pads, and watch their doubles in the depths below, receive the freedom of the fields, as heroes are given the freedom of cities, and take hold of the real business of life when they return to town with renewed youth; each enjoying the enjoyment of friend or neighbor, as it is narrated to him, as if it were his own again.

Social Pleasure.

And even when there is no vacation, the city gives a social pleasure of companionship when sitting on steps and stoops in the warm evenings, in the strolls after ices, in the visits to the roof gardens, the steamer trips, the trolley rides, that have a pleasure all their own. It is certain that there is a great human happiness in the congregation and aggregation of life in towns, of which the widely separated rural populace can know but little, while the free interchange is stimulating to mental growth and the reception of new ideas.

Advantages of Town Life.

The opportunities for growth and improvement are innumerable. Is there a painter whose canvases bring the beauty of the world into the compass of a few feet—the sight and the inspiration are at our command; is there a speaker of world-wide repute, a singer to whom kings and emperors are glad to listen, a preacher that moves men's souls, it is ours to listen, too; is there a play that thrills, a spectacle that delights, a song that charms, it is all within our reach in the city. We gather the news of the world there on a larger scale than that on which it is given to rustic communities, and we have absorbed and assimilated the last new thing before it has reached what is sometimes called the Provinces, and have gone on to something newer yet.

City Children.

The children of the city, too, have, in the mass, the advantages of schools that are the most enlightening, and of teachers in art whose talent and rank make it impossible to have them outside of the wealthy city. Take music alone; the best professors of that art must needs find their support in cities, and the child who has their instruction from the start has the best chance of success.

Music at Home.

We frequently hear derision cast upon the prevailing habit of instructing young ladies indiscriminately in the art of music, and especially of piano-playing, when they have shown no very peculiar talent for it. But we think this derision a great mistake. These young people would be doing nothing better if they were not practicing their finger exercises. They give themselves, undeniably, a great pleasure, and they make themselves able to produce a great deal for others throughout their little circle. The mistake is to be found in the supposition that it is necessary they should play like Aus der Ohe, as if nobody might be allowed to read who could not roll his periods like Edmund Kean. It seems reasonable that children should be taught the alphabet of all arts, and go farther if nature prompts the desire. As for the piano-forte, perhaps both maker and inventor would feel repaid for their centuries of thought and work if they could see, as we have done, those tired fathers that, hearing their young daughters thrum their tunes on the instruments they have toiled so hard to buy, close their eyes and listen delightedly to the poor little music and feel as if they enjoyed indeed a foretaste of heaven.

It is nearly a hundred and twenty-five years ago since an announcement of a concert was made in a London newspaper, and it was promised that a certain singer would sing, accompanied by Mr. Dibdin "on a new instrument called the piano-forte."

The Piano-Forte.

A hundred years ago—and to what a growth has that new instrument attained! Then it was comparatively of rude manufacture, a slender case, standing on slight supports, and with keys tinkling like a music-box, and scarcely so much like the modern piano-forte as the little tea-kettle engine with which the inventors first ran over the road is like the ponderous locomotive of the present day that bites the rail as it thunders on with a planetary tread.

There had been one or two pianos, though, nearly seventy years before that era, but so very imperfect that it took a multitude of new ideas, improvements and patents to bring even the perfection of the one of 1776. Still some of the great composers had written wonderful music for the instrument even in that crude state, whether satisfied with it or foreseeing its advance. And from what it had advanced! The timbrel, the dulcimer, the clavichord, the spinet, the harpsichord, the harp itself, each contributed its separate idea to the composition of the wonderful mechanism on which Mr. Dibdin played that day, and which has advanced so much farther now that it seems to be as perfect as an instrument that does not meet the pure euharmonic scale can hope to be, and that stands, when its lid is closed, as some one has described it, like the sarcophagus of unrisen music, and whose manufacture, moreover, has reached in London alone an average of more than a hundred thousand instruments a year, produced by some two hundred makers, and giving employment and livelihood, of course, to an immense train of workmen and their families.

It is interesting to note how many various countries enter the lists in ca-

STEAMER TRIPS.

tering for our daily music and in finishing the case and works. Take, for instance, a fine Erard. Switzerland has sent the fir, Norway the deal, England the pear and sycamore and holly wood and the iron, Riga the oak, the tropical forests of Honduras the mahogany, and of South America the cedar; from Ceylon comes the ebony, from Rio the rosewood, from India the satinwood, from Africa the ivory, from Russia the leather, from America the pine, and copper and silver and cloth from almost every meridian. And all this is brought together; for this great minds have wrestled, great minds have written, and all to delight the heart of the little miss who longs to rattle off her notes as she sees her elders do it, and breaks her little back for hours every day in the effort.

And why not? Why should not great minds write and wrestle for such results? Is there any better result than that of bringing the pleasure into the household that this instrument does? As you sit and hear it and look about on the group of pleased listeners, you think it equal to a hearth any day in its power to gather and to cheer; and it has seemed to me in certain family circles where the members clustered round the piano-forte as a center that it was a sort of household altar at whose shrine the family assembled, and where the father looks on his little daughter, who can evoke this magic, as on something too precious and perfect to be his, and that the moral health and refinement of the whole household are assisted by the music, no matter how imperfect it may be when measured by great standards; and I have thought that every child ought to feel repaid for all her toil in the happiness she affords the fond father and mother in these hours of their satisfaction.

Music Abroad.

Music, on a broader scale, moreover, has its best cultivation and its largest audiences in the town, where opera has asserted a sort of sovereignty and immense throngs never think of grudging immense sums of money, glad to get music at its best on any terms. For the opera is the idealization and apotheosis of the drama; it is the drama set to music, and where the subtile inflections and far-reaching influences of tune and harmony shall do more than words can do—shall make the prosaic impassioned, and the impassioned divine.

The Opera.

Beside the opera, to those that understand its spirit and love its exaltations, the spoken drama is something infinitely petty; the mask and the co-

PROFESSORS FIND THEIR SUPPORT IN CITIES.

thurn seem then to belong only to the region into which song lifts them. For the opera is, after all, little else than the old Greek play perfected in the matter of its representation, and with the eloquence of language translated more thoroughly into music. There is the chorus and there are the instruments, both of them far transcending the old simple idea; all the appliances of modern illumination and machinery take the place of the ancients' open roof of the blue in those theatres that were

> "clean scooped
> Out of a hill-side, with the sky above,
> And sea before our seats in marble row;"

and after all that, all passion and suffering and joy being crowded into the action now as then, tone and tune lift it on their mighty wings, and love and sorrow are heightened and deepened into the universal sympathy by the magic of modulated numbers, the ineffable power of music.

But in old times all Greece attended the representations of the drama. The merits of the new play were discussed by the populace as freely as the price of provisions. Balaustion and her listeners were not the only ordinary Greeks who knew Euripides and Sophocles by heart; their verses belonged to the people, and they had their roots in the common soil.

But with us, on the contrary, the opera is as costly as all other exotics are; it is designed only for the rich—the boys who sang the women's part to the Greeks did not dream of being able to melt pearls in their drink in the way our prime-donne can do if they will—and by force of circumstances the poor have little part in it. Nevertheless, among those who do frequent it here there are several perfectly distinct classes of patrons: there are those who go because it is the fashion, as they would stay away if it were the fashion, who go because opera hats and cloaks are becoming, who go because they are invited, because all their friends are there, because they want to say they went, want to be seen, want to be excited; then there are those who go as a matter of curiosity, because it is a novelty to them, because they want to educate themselves in all those things that touch the finer senses; and lastly, there are those who go to intoxicate soul and sense in a luxury of sound, to revel in the beauty of motion and light and color, the eagerness of dramatic interpretation, the satisfaction of song—who go because to them the opera is a real thing, a thing they love, and that repays them with an affluence of pleasure.

Shopping.

And there is still another pleasure and advantage of life in the city that affords a singular exhilaration and satisfaction—the pleasure of going shop-

THE MUSIC ROOM CONSERVATORY.

ping. There is an excitement about this shopping that must be forever unknown and unfelt by the masculine shopper, we fancy.

In point of fact, though, there is no masculine shopper. A man goes and orders what he wants, and there an end, but a woman flutters from shop to shop and from street to street, day after day and week after week, like a bee humming over sweets, and only retires from the work at last when not only she herself, but all her friends as well, have no money left.

And what a throng it is of which these shoppers make a part—the haughty urbans stepping from their satin-lined carriages; the satchel-bearing suburbans; the young country school-mistress who thinks the firm would possibly become embarrassed if she did not buy her new black silk there, and, the article once bought, feels a happy consciousness of benefits conferred, and a proud sense of having enlarged the trade of the place in all the markets of the world; then there is the penniless companion of the shopper, who has no purse to open, and before whose indifferent eyes all these things—the people, the noise, the bustle, the confusion—pass like disordered phantasms; there is the woman who never lets her purchase out of her sight after the money has passed, and laughs to scorn the parcel delivery, and the woman who wears a circular cloak and is afraid to go near the counters for fear she shall be accused of stealing, and the woman who wears a circular and takes precious good care to keep near the counters and watch her chance for stealing; there is the professional shopper who buys for others on commission, and who knows what there is in the place better than the clerks themselves know; the young bride who never thinks of blushing as she adds treasure after treasure to her trousseau; the young mother who is nothing but a blush as she chooses her nainsooks and long lawns and edgings and insertings; there is the wretched gentleman who accompanies some shoppers as purse-bearer, and in all the crowd of women never felt so exquisitely uncomfortable in his life; and there are the shoppers who have no idea of buying at all, but who have come only to see what it is that the rest of the world is buying.

And what beautiful things they are that the world is buying! One would say ingenuity in design and beauty of fabric and prodigality of undreamed-of colors never reached before the point they touch to-day; for although stuffs have been made more barbarously rich, we doubt if they have ever been more artistically beautiful. The shopper whose check-book is not unlimited needs to pause bewildered among all the brocades and damasks, to beg for patterns, and then to go home and ponder and balance and decide in peace, where her fancy will not be disturbed by rival claims, where the jostling of the crowd will not have made her nervous and cross and difficult to please, and where the elation of the recently given largess for her shopping will not have so turned her head that she is pleased too easily and buys too soon.

And, after all, the whole business is much like a lottery. One starts out in the morning quite ignorant whether one is to draw prize or blank; whether the bargain will prove a bargain or otherwise; whether what looked precisely right in the shop will not look precisely wrong at home, away from its acces-

MUSIC'S LARGEST AUDIENCES IN THE TOWN.

sories, and face to face with the necessities of its future companion pieces of dress; whether the silk will not wear shiny, the basket cloth wear satiny, the damasse rub up fluffy. One's ideas, too, are apt to build such charming pictures of unattainable shapes and colors that the result may be heart-breaking. One marvels that out of all that wilderness of beauty and lustre in the shops,

STEPPING STONES TO HAPPINESS.

to which the four quarters of the globe have contributed—muslins from Farther India, shawls from Cathay, gold-wrought wefts from Egypt, silks from France, furs from the North Pole—one has contrived to reach only such a beggarly and unbecoming end. And then to the disappointed young shopper, who has not been broken in by a long series of disappointments, there seems to be little more to live for, until some rival shopper, when all is over, says how perfectly that plume falls along the brim! what a lovely contrast that color is with the skin! with what grace that stuff takes folds and falls! groans for such a knack of making herself picturesque, and begs for her company when next she rides abroad, and knows well that neither theatre, nor dance, nor drive, nor sail has any such swift and sweet excitement as shopping has for the skillful shopper.

In the Street Car.

But in all the delight of shopping there is still a drawback, and that is the street-car and its discomforts and the discussion of her conduct there. She knows that it is said of her that it is she who swings her parasol at the car-driver, from the greatest allowable distance, and walks with more or less deliberation toward the car while it waits, where a man would have run with good speed; that she holds the car, the door open, while she gives her friend the last message or the superfluous kiss and takes her parcels, and drops them, and has to pick them up on the steps; that it is she who refuses to budge an inch to make room for the new arrival; that it is she who slips into the vacated seat without a word of thanks.

All these things, it cannot be denied, are offenses; yet, if we look into them, we may find some little excuse for their existence. "It must needs be that offenses come; but woe to that man by whom the offense cometh." On our first glance, for instance, at the woman who swings her parasol a square off, and walks deliberately to the car, we see no apology; but she sees one perfectly in the fact that every man in the car will make her a subject of merriment and of unpleasant remark if she runs, that her clothes make it very difficult for her to run, and that the laws of deportment, which have had to receive the stamp of masculine approbation in all ages before they could pass current, make it one of the high misdemeanors for a woman to be seen running. For another count in the indictment there is really nothing to be said. The woman who keeps the car waiting for her kisses and good-bys and mutinous parcels is a child who should be taken by the shoulders and pushed in. Nor can much defense be made for the woman who refuses to budge, since that is an unkindness, a churlishness, in which she is untrue to her sex; yet

SHOPPING.

the truth is that, having paid for her seat, she has a right to enjoy it without relinquishing a third of it on either side only to have her apparel ruined by

SATCHEL-BEARING SUBURBANS.

the heavy weight crushed upon it, and frequently not merely a heavy weight, but a soiled and contaminating one. For the last accusation, and the one more dwelt upon than any, it is, without doubt, occasionally true that women take a proffered seat and neglect to express their obligation. Yet here again it may be said in their behalf, in the first place, that they would almost invariably rather stand than force another person to do so, and generally take the seat only to avoid a scene and the appearance of anything conspicuously ungracious. In the next place, the confusion and embarrassment incident probably divert the mind from the conventionality—for a conventionality it is, when the giver in his own mind knows that, of course, the taker can not help but thank him, whether she says so or not. Again, it is not easy to thank a person who perhaps vacates his seat without a word or a nod, and whose back is too quickly turned for him to receive them if there are thanks to give; and one is in as unpleasant a position when sending thanks at a man's back as in not rendering them at all. And finally, to say nothing of the fact that a woman's fare is as good as a man's fare, and entitles her to a seat, or of the circumstance that it is an affair of *noblesse oblige* with the stronger party to care for the weaker, and the man thus does it as something due to himself, and not at all in order to please the individual woman, and therefore does not make her his debtor, yet so long as men refuse to women their obvious equality in human rights, she does not so much wrong, after all, as we implied in the beginning, in claiming privilege; and since all that she might be and do and rise to is taken from her in exchange for protection, a seat is her privilege, for which she owes no more thanks than a convict does for fetters. Nevertheless, we think no woman of any self-respect ever fails in giving thanks when the opportunity is allowed her.

In the mean time the men who stare the women out of countenance; who put their arms unnecessarily about the women in helping them along their way; who soil the floor, according to their unclean custom, where the women must tread and drag their dresses, even if they do not exercise their skill in targetry on those dresses themselves—such men (and there are, to say the least, as many of them as of the thankless women) should have very little to say about courtesy in the cars.

The Cheery Town.

With all these pleasures and distractions, even with their drawbacks, the city-dweller will tell you there is no place one-half so good, so bright, so cheery as the town. He will tell you that throughout sacred Scripture itself Heaven is described as a city, the celestial city, and the most splendid vision of the Apocalypse is of a city descending from the sky. He will tell you that all great movements have their origin in the lively thought and action of the town.

The City Parlor.

And he will tell you that in lesser matters the city, always in advance, has reached elegance and an inhabited appearance much earlier than the country at large, and drawing-rooms were darkened there the first and crowded with plenishing, and there were paintings and statuary in them before these objects traveled farther, and there were portieres and screens and placques and brass-work and bronze and old silver and china and beveled glass and needle painting, dark walls and multiplied mantels shelf over shelf, short curtains and long curtains, huge vases and little panels and the rest. And all this while the rural parlor was ornamented only with the framed sampler, and the family-tree, and the lady with the big handkerchief at the tomb under weeping willows, with at best four prints in gilt frames or possibly a couple of crude portraits or black silhouettes, always excepting, of course, those colonial mansions that rejoiced in "Smyberts" and "Copleys." Surely the city parlor had the right of it. The moral forces are not necessarily strengthened by contact with bare and uninviting walls; the nature, instead of being developed to better things, will be constantly returned upon itself, in the absence of objects stimulating the fancy and leading the thought outward. And certainly the intellectual forces in almost every such instance are starved, and where one is of such build that he chances to be improved by the concentration of thought that such ascetic dwellings might foster, others are only dwarfed and withered.

The age that has become famous for its unhealthy self-introspection could hardly do a better thing than make the surrounding material walls of its daily life diverting and interesting, while all that hangs upon them or lies between them leads the thought out to larger life and experience, to the past history of art, to its future hopes, and to its effect upon humanity; and if the harmony of all, the lovely and luxurious combination, excite the pleasure-loving senses, the controlling brain also is excited in memory, imagination, invention, and appreciation. One realizes the falsehood of that old, strict idea that one could not be good and be comfortable, understands that enjoyment of fine colors and fine contours does not belong exclusively to the Scarlet Lady, and that beauty and brimstone are really not inseparable.

Old China.

If the city parlor, in its best estate, of course, had nothing else but its old china on which to rely, it would have sufficient excuse for its being.

The fabric itself is so exquisite, in the translucent material, in the enamel, in the tints, in the shapes, that one would search in vain outside the kingdom of jewels and flowers for anything so alluring to the eye as that bit of china in which, when held before the light, the spirit of lambent flame seems to float as it does in an opal, and whose designs, even when not intrinsically charming, are always interesting through history and through suggestion, and the love of which among our own people dates back more than two hundred years.

There is more quaint and curious tradition clustering round the story of pottery and porcelain than of any other of the arts, from the tale of the man who, in despair, after ceaseless efforts to produce the quality at which he aimed, leaped into his furnace, and produced the desired flux in the consuming of his own body, and has been worshiped ever since among the less enlightened practicers of the ceramic art, to the touching story of Palissy the Potter, and the noble work of Wedgwood.

As far back in Roman record as the time when Numa Pompilius reigned a king, we find a school or college of pottery founded, from which we can judge that the subject was held in high esteem even at that day. The Greeks already had potteries at Samos and at Corinth and elsewhere—and we all know the absolute charm which the Etrurians had reached in such productions—while the most exquisite enamel has been found in the tombs of the Egyptians. At perhaps still remoter periods, in the gloom of what we call the early twilight of civilization, the Orient had reached perfection in pottery, and rivaled the best the world has done in porcelain, the tower of Nankin, whose tiles are of the rarest faience, being the one concerning which the above legend of the sacrifice of a life is related.

It is not merely for their beauty, though, that these things acquire their interest. The historian has made them subserve many a matter of profound research. When he finds the remnants of a race—some bones scattered in a cave or under a bank of earth, weapons round about, and even traces of food —he knows instantly at what point of civilization that race perished, not by its stone or copper knives and axes, but by its jars and pipkins or the absence of them; for their presence signifies that a race has reached, as we may say, the boiling-point; shows that man then was no longer in the condition of the mere animal, devouring raw meat with teeth and talons. And the antiquarian, meanwhile, in his search among the ruins of the buried Asian cities, is enabled by the style of the pottery he finds to say what power ruled, and what people obeyed the rule.

Of course the manufacture of china is something far beyond that of pottery in importance, but the one is the crude alphabet of which the other is the poem; and pottery itself has now and then risen to a height where even china falters, as in those instances of majolica that it has not been disdained to adorn with the work of Raphael and Julio Romano and Titian. If one could but own such marvelous specimens to delectate the eyes, one's ears could endure all the sarcasms of those in ignorance of such beauty with exceeding equanimity. Addison, to be sure, was among the ignorant in this respect, or pretended that he was. "There is no inclination in women that more surprises me than this passion for china," he somewhere takes occasion to say. "When a woman is visited with it, it generally takes possession of her for life. China vessels are playthings for women of all ages. An old lady of forescore shall be as busy in cleaning an Indian mandarin as her great-granddaughter is in dressing her baby." But when we remember that Horace Walpole was of precisely the opposite persuasion, that Kingsley was an amateur and Gladstone a collector, we can afford merely to pity one who did not know how to enjoy the bits of delicate color and light with which we are fond of adorning our cabinets.

What is there, in sooth, that can be lovelier than a cup of that delicious sea-green called the Celadon, a concretion of sea-foam out of which the nereids themselves might sup, and one of which Robert Cecil gave Queen Elizabeth, as being a fit gift for royalty, unless it is that egg-shell cup through which the light falls rosy as through a baby's upheld fingers, while the odd designs upon them both tell strange tales of life and worship and floral fancies among the curious people who make them. And yet one would pause a moment before giving them the palm over this claret-colored Chelsea cup, with its gold anchor mark; over that delicious Dresden candelabrum where the hand of Summer seems to have scattered the flowers; or this vase in Capo di Monte china, where the high relief of the figures dancing round about it throws a shadow on the tints beyond; or these miracles of Sèvres, exhibited every Christmas in the Louvre along with the latest work of the Gobelin looms, the cups and vases painted after Watteau, now in *bleu du roi*, now in *rose du Barry*, now in *vert pré*, looking as if the wings of birds and the petals of blossoms had simply been cast under a spell beneath the gloss of enamel, and now made more precious yet with jewels.

Where all are so lovely it is hard to choose; and a collector is tolerably sure that if she selects a vase of Henri Deux, with its yellow glory, she will long for a basket of Palissy's ware in violet relief; if she has Dresden, she will want Berlin, that she will never think her china closet complete without a bit of old Bow with its bee beneath the handle; and that, in fact, having once begun, she will never be happy again so long as the snow-white shapes encircle the blue of the Portland vase itself and are not hers.

And meanwhile the lover of the quaint and the suggestive has united town and country in another article of ornamentation—only the good country housewife would never have it in her parlor, as the city wife is eager to do. Perhaps its adoption yields a little too much to the rococo, but, it is interesting inasmuch as it makes the necessary article of earlier centuries the plaything of the later. It can, indeed, hardly be anything but a plaything, for what machinery already does so perfectly is unlikely to be rivaled by the amateur fine lady's fingers; and the thing is now only saved from absurdity by its history, which is something inquisitorial in the bondage it imposed, by its associations, which are sacred, and by its outlines, which are those of clear beauty

The Spinning-Wheel.

The spinning-wheel is certainly a pretty sight, whether we should see it in a drawing-room or in the moty sunbeam slanting through some old garret; and the little linen-wheel which our great-grandmothers used to stand at their knees is a real object for an artist.

Who can see its slant lines, its lovely curves, see its swift revolving circles, and the fine thread trembling to a mist as it draws out its length, and hear the pleasant hum it makes, without thoughts of sunny mornings, and bees in flowers, and all sweet rural sights and sounds? Few of us in looking at it think of the imprisonment of the spinner, still wetting her broadening thumb as the sunshine fell without, and she longed to be there, too—the spinner like her of Mendelssohn's "Song Without Words," who sings her tune to the whirr of the wheel while the birds carol and the bees hum outside.

Rude as the spinning-wheel seems to us now, it was as wonderful an advance in its day from the hand-distaff as the jenny and mule and power-loom have been in their turn from the spinning-wheel. The distaff, indeed, made few improvements in itself in all its long career, the only notable changes being that from the time when very primitive people, who had little or no use of metal, loaded its spindle with a perforated stone, and others carried the load at the top instead of at the bottom of the spindle; but save for these simple changes, and the fact that the distaff which princes' daughters used was overlaid with gold, the distaff with which Clotho spun was the same as that which Burns' Jean took to her "rocking on Fasten's Eve"—"rock" being the old term for the distaff and spindle. It was the simplest sort of pretty apparatus, not much more inelegant to carry than the modern tatting. No dame or damsel went abroad without it. The good spinner loaded her distaff with the tow at its upper end, and carried it protruding from under her left arm, and as she pulled the thread out between thumb and finger, the weight of the hanging and loaded spindle twisted it round and round still closer, and she wound it measure by measure about the body of the spindle as she twisted.

The Distaff.

The first day after the twelve winter holidays used to be known as St. Distaff's Day, for then the women renewed the work that play had so long interrupted. It was still, in real fact, only another holiday, for the men made a point of leaving their own work to set fire to the flax the women were bringing out, and the women, in turn, provided themselves with buckets of cold water to dash over the depredators, and all was good humor.

> 'If the maids a-spinning go,
> Burn the flax and fire the tow;
> Bring in pails of water then,
> Let the maids bewash the men,'

sang Herrick; by which we may judge the custom to have been tolerably prevalent.

It is observable that the occupation of the distaff and the spinning-wheel has associated itself with women even to the point of contempt, our first pictured memorials of the race on Egyptian and Hindostanee monuments showing women with the useful toy in hand—the toy despised by all men but Achilles and Hercules. "On the side of the spear" was an old legal phraseology to signify a descent in the male line, "on the side of the distaff" to indicate female descent. In the early times, when rapine and all violence were the distinguishing masculine traits or, we may say, employments, honor was held to come only from such work as bloodshed, conquest and plunder; there was none given for the quiet performance of the duties at home; and as women stayed at home pursuing their quiet duties, preparing food and clothes and nursing the wounded, the distaff became disdainfully associated with them. "The Crown of France never falls to the distaff," said the contemptuous French proverb; but it is more than a French proverb that woman's wit cannot overreach, and the distaff has in reality frequently and secretly been the sceptre there, the power behind the throne, making and unmaking the fortunes of the nation.

It was not till the fourteenth century that the distaff was superseded by the spinning wheel, and not till about a hundred years later that the wheel appeared at which the spinner could sit instead of stand; and almost immediately afterward the term spinster in our language was modified so as to be descriptive only of an unmarried woman below the rank of a viscount's daughter, and not of all unmarried women—though why unmarried at all is a question we leave for Rosa Dartle; for although the farm-wives of good condition were wont to hire their spinning done by any spinner in need of the work, there was never a farm-wife who did not know how to do it herself.

The Spinster.

The distinctive nature of the term spinster, as applicable to none above a viscount's daughter in rank, is a slight curiosity in history: it is probably due to the fact that the increase of wealth and the introduction of printed literature enabled ladies of rank to find amusement and employment otherwheres than at the wheel, which was abandoned to the use of those unable to command the luxury of their own time—women presumably below the rank of a viscount's daughter. Wonderful things used to be done with the wheel, though in those times before machinery made nothing of wonders. One girl was known to spin a pound of wool into eighty-four thousand yards of thread, almost equal to forty-eight miles; and another at a later period spun the same quantity into a thread something more than one hundred and fifteen miles in length—but she was a famous spinner.

The Adventures of a Pound of Cotton.

Since steam, that great afrite, has put the hand to shame, these wonders have probably been eclipsed, and the adventures of a single pound of cotton, borne on its wings, and for sale in the London market, are like a tale of the *Arabian Nights*—journeying from the Indies to London docks, thence to Lancashire to be spun, thence to Paisley to be woven, to Ayrshire to be tamboured, to Dumbarton to be hand-sewed, back to Paisley, on to Glasgow for a finish, and once more in London, having traveled five thousand miles by sea and one thousand by land, supporting by the labor spent on it one hundred and fifty people, and increasing its own value some two thousand per cent.

The spinning-wheel, certainly as much as anything, has been a badge of woman's servitude. For while all her time was needed to make the clothing for her family, there was none for her to spend in illuminating her mind. And so it is not unpleasant to-day to see this old badge made the sport of circumstance, and what was once a slavery now affording pastime in the drawing-room. Broken and disused, and in dishonor, and shorn of its locks, as it is, it was once a mighty tyrant; and we should think the lovely ladies, free to pursue pleasure, art, learning, to mount the ladder to the stars with men, and who have adorned their drawing-rooms with the mimicry and mockery of its old estate, might in some twilight be haunted by a strange dream of it, pulling down the temple of their freedom and happiness about them. And as they play with it now, in all their liberty and possibilities and comparative

THE DISTAFF

enlightenment, they may do well to be mindful of the bondage in which it held their "forebys," and in which its rude forerunner, the distaff, still holds certain of their sisters. "The art of spinning," says an elegant writer, "in one of its simplest and most primitive forms, is yet pursued in Italy, where the country-women of Caia still turn the spindle unrestrained by that ancient rural law which forbade its use without doors. The distaff has outlived the consular fasces, and survived the conquests of the Goth and the Hun But rustic hands alone now sway the sceptre of Tanaquil, and all but the peasant disdain a practice which once beguiled the leisure of high-born dames."

Society.

Such rooms as those of which the old china and rich draperies and costly bric-a-brac make part are necessary in a place where what is known as Society takes on its most splendid guise, and where there is such a positive thing as the gay season. For it makes no difference how much want and suffering may be abroad in the town or in the land, there is always a gay season in town, and probably there always will be one. For as one generation tires, another is springing upon the scene, and all the fardels belonging to the glitter and frolic that these are dropping from their hold those are ready to catch as they dance on. The new belles and the new beaux will always have a mutual attraction; the old belles drop off, to be sure, but the old beaux linger to see these fresh young beauties who are just taking up the business of life with such a sparkle in their wondering eyes, such a vitality in their veins, and when any of these old beaux drops off, some one of the young belles usually drops off with him.

The Gay Season.

Yes, there probably will always be a gay season so long as society holds together by its present structure, and even those who have and desire to have nothing to do with it must witness more or less of it and be aware of it, however unwillingly. Artistically considered, it has a certain value, if only as showing the possibilities of beauty attainable under the present conditions of favorable life. We need not go to the ancients in these times for the ideal of loveliness in the outward forms of social mingling. Some daylight sacrificial festival by the blue waters of the Ægean, with torches turning pale in the sunshine, with the flower-decked and filleted victim, the dancing youths and maidens under the festoons of their floral ropes and wreaths, may have been more remotely poetical; a Roman supper may have been more voluptuous; a Pompeiian revel may have been more wild and wanton; but a mask of the gods could hardly be more beautiful than are some of the nightly entertainments of the gay season of the present. Winter changed to summer, night into softly glowing day, bare walls to bowers of bloom out of which gleam statues like the gods just alit, and pictures like dreams of a yet lovelier life—all this constitutes an enchanted background for the throngs that troop across it, the dark shadows of one class of the participants in the pleasure throwing out all the brilliance of the other portion with its rosy flesh and glistening hair and starry eyes and curving outlines, the brilliance, moreover, of the material in which this beauty robes itself, to whose lustrous wealth neither the dreams of poets nor the facts of antiquity ever approached; for laces and silks and velvets, at any rate, are of the modern world, and the substance in which poets clothe their dreams of beauty is filmy and vaporous stuff as thin as moonshine. And meanwhile, if the gay season is an artistic success, wherever it kindles the wit in any degree and puts a sparkle into conversation, it is intellectual success as well. Those who admire and excuse this series of festive pageants declare that there is another view of it worthy of a pause, and that is a consideration of its beneficent nature in our social economy, in the part of the good Samaritan which it so undoubtedly plays. Does this seem an impossible or Quixotic view? Give, then, but a glance to the army of workers—glad and thankful to be workers—whom this gay season calls to the front; not merely housemaid and cook, coachman and groom, milliner and seamstress, but the multitude of those who produce and prepare the raw material which these ultimately handle, the multitude of underlings who assist them all, till the work ramifies through a thousand far-extended avenues, so that some single ball not only calls into requisition the forces of market-men, the finest fancies of florists and designers, the running of the steamships that import its novelties, but saves from starvation and beggary the denizen of many an attic.

The gay season may in itself—as those who roll to swell its triumph, with plume and jewel, with epaulet or train, forget the existence of any others less fortunate than themselves—be called as heartless as any other great machine; but, like most great machines, it does unconsciously a tremendous work, and, with the industries it necessitates, tides over the dark and cruel winter months, when there is little hope and less joy to those who otherwise might have no season at all. May there always be a gay season, then, its upholders exclaim—not too gay a season, not a mad revel, but a brief and brilliant tournament of youth and beauty! May the early years enjoy it, and the advancing years look on well pleased with the pageant! May it charm for the passing moment, but not captivate one instant beyond its proper power; and, while its light burns ever so brightly, may it not put out the sun! For, after all, there are those of good reason who totally disapprove of the extravagance and the waste of time. The philosophers and the political economists deny that there is any advantage in the expenditure of wealth after this fashion, assuring us that only injury is wrought thereby.

Mr. Ruskin says that as long as there is cold and nakedness in the land, splendor of dress is a crime. "As long as there are any," he says, "who have no blankets for their beds, and no rags for their bodies, so long it is blanket-making and tailoring we must set people to work at—not lace."

Society is of course a charming thing: the reunion of kindred souls in scenes made as lovely as artifice can make them; people always at their best, and conscious of it; with every enjoyment to pass the time—pleasure, excitement, admiration, the dance, the opera, the theatre, the drive. But it is life in too concentrated a form, like the nourishment where nothing goes to waste,

THE SPINNING WHEEL.

and which, while it enriches the blood, causes the atrophy of certain of the organs. The experiment having been tried of feeding guinea-pigs with sugar alone, it was found that the little creatures lived a short space of time, and then those that did not die became blind. Too long and too undiluted a diet of gay life would be no better for the soul than the undiluted saccharine matter was for the unfortunate animal; and it is a merciful arrangement that, after the faculties have received sufficient stimulus and the senses sufficient enjoyment, puts an end to it all with the total and arbitrary change of habit that the Lenten season brings. Then the swift rout is succeeded by the quiet life, the nightly revel by the morning walk, the call of charity, the household duty, the neglected book, and the performance of all those little acts postponed when the days only waited on the nights to bring the next one round. Then one has time to recall the fact that there are those less favored by fate than one's self; then one has time to put one's self in one's enemies' place and see what their justification may be; time to look over one's own life, and learn what has been amiss, to make new resolutions, and indulge them a little while before beginning to break them; then there is time to enter on the search for those less favored ones, if they are not at the door, and to do what may be done toward striking the balance in this life that death will strike at last when the earth is cast upon one.

City Window Gardens

But there is another gay season for the city lover than that of the winter and its routs; it is when spring opens, and before people begin to leave town, and the flower-boxes in varied windows are called into bloom. To be sure, all winter long the florists' windows are bowers of loveliness, and so are many of the windows of the wealthy, under which the children of the poor often stop in admiring groups. But let the chill once forsake earth and air and even in the poorer quarters of the town the little boxes at the windows begin to show that nature will everywhere repay love and care. How to make these flower-boxes answer a purpose, and how to make the miserable little backyards beautiful and useful, Miss Louise Forester may tell us in a way that shall perhaps help another young gardener in her work.

A City Window Garden.

I never was the pretty one, said Louise Forester, or the bright one; and I had no accomplishments and no lovers. And I suppose that is what made it all surprise me so at the end. Perhaps I was well-looking enough,

RUDE AS THE SPINNING WHEEL SEEMS TO US NOW.

being healthy; although nobody would give me a second glance; and I had common sense, of course; and sometimes I used to wish the other girls hadn't such a turn for accomplishments, and would help me a little more about the house. But then Clara was like somebody made of roses and lilies, so tall, so slight, so fair; and Emily could read the most difficult music, and could talk about high art in a way that sounded to me like Japanese; and you ought to have heard Annabel recite, and have seen her go through the thirty-five gestures, alarm, fascination, listening, delight, and all the rest. I used to think it was Siddons come again, and twice as great, and needing only her opportunity—and she was always so obliging, and would give you the gestures every time you asked. We all knew that if Annabel went on the stage she would make the family fortunes and her own everlasting fame.

For you see the family fortunes needed making or mending or some other very particular attention. We owned our house and yard in the narrow street of the crowded city, and took care of ourselves with the money we made by taking in lodgers; and sometimes we had enough to scrimp along on, and sometimes we didn't, and that was oftenest; and then we got on as we could, pinching in our clothes, and pinching in our food, and never going anywhere. At least *I* didn't go anywhere; the girls used to go to the theatre, or down to the sea, with the particular lover in favor at the time—for most of our lodgers were young gentlemen who came to us with letters of introduction, or came to me, rather; since, although I was the youngest, I was the one that the girls put forward and made transact the business. They were awfully shrinking and sensitive, Clara, and Annabel, and Emily; and somehow they always used to feel, and so did I, when we had an unsuccessful season, that it was all owing to my inefficiency.

"I'm sure we might do better if you made more exertion, Louise," Clara would say. "If instead of wasting every spare moment, the way you do, over your absurd flower beds and boxes, you ever made a business of talking with the lodgers and getting them interested in us, they might stay on. We can't go and talk about ourselves; but you, being the ostensible manager, could often meet them, or make them little calls when you carry up the monthly bills, instead of leaving those bills under the door the ridiculous way you do, and so gradually get into conversation, and speak of our circumstances, and praise Emily's music, and Annabel's elocution, and wish she could have an engagement at the theatre—not to say anything that might be said about me. But there! what do you care about your sisters, so long as you can attend to your flowers? I never saw such selfishness. Sometimes I feel so enraged with the things I could go and trample them down!" and her blue eyes flashed like great angry sapphires.

FLOCK OF SHEEP.
(From a Painting by Anton Mauve.)

Of course this was very unjust; as if I were not doing all I could for them every day. And I really could have cried if I hadn't also felt some indignation at the talk about my flowers—my flowers, the only pleasure or comfort that I had. The other girls had their talents, and their flatteries, their people to take them to the park or to the concert, their own consciousness, too, of what they were and what they could do, which was truly a pleasure; and I had nothing at all but my flowers. But then the thought of Clara in one of her rages trampling down my flowers, and of what it was that *might* be said about her and her tempers, if I chose, made me laugh. And so I went out of the room quite gayly; and I heard her say to Annabel before I closed the door: "Any heart was left out of her composition. She hasn't the least atom of one." And Annabel said nothing, but Emily replied, "No, she doesn't care for anything in the world but her ridiculous flowers." And Clara was pinning in her belt a big bunch of red roses that I had just given her off my bush, and Emily was putting on her hat, which was the third hat she had had that year out of my share of the four divisions of the income after the household expenses had been paid. But nobody ever thought of such things as that; there was no reason why I should have new bonnets when I looked as well in the old one; and why in the world should I not give Clara my flowers when they set off her white beauty so through the open window as young Mr. Annersley let himself in?

But I had a heart; and Allen Annersley knew it. For I had talked with him about the girls, and had canvassed with him the ways and means of having scholars found for Emily, or an opportunity for Annabel to show some theatrical manager what she could do; and he kept a book and music store over on the Avenue, where the theatrical people went. It was a long time before the girls knew that he kept a book and music store; they insisted that he was the son of the rich Mr. Annersley, on the Heights, who had been a member of Congress; and that he probably had a whim of having separate lodgings of his own because it was English. And after the blow fell, and they knew he kept a shop, they could not get out of their heads what they had so firmly implanted there, the idea of his belonging to something or somebody on a different scale of grandeur. 'He is, maybe, an Anarchist," said Annabel, "or a Nihilist, or a Socialist of some sort. And he has left his father's splendid surroundings and is seeing for himself what life means among those that have to earn their living."

"He visits a great deal next door, and the people there are very well off," said Clara.

"There are no people there but the housekeeper and old gentleman, and he does writing there," said I.

"You always so contrive to dampen every enthusiasm, Louise," said Clara.

"I'm sure," said Emily, "if I didn't think he was something superior to most of our lodgers I should never give him a second thought. He is insignificant enough to be the very pink of gentility.'

"How can you talk so?" said Clara. "As if the aristocracy hadn't every opportunity for physical perfection."

"Maybe they have," said I. "But they don't improve their opportunities. The fathers and mothers keep marrying for money and for lands, and not for love, or good looks or intellect, and they are the result; that's what the old housekeeper says next door"——

"How in the world did you know her?"

"Oh, we made acquaintance over the garden wall, and she told me that Mr. Annersley keeps books for her master, and he's not only poor, but in debt for his stock in trade, and never had any rich or grand relations "

"The idea of your talking like that with our neighbors' servants! You always did like low company, Louise!" said Emily.

"But I must say! How perfectly abominable!" cried Clara. "What is he here for, with his false pretences! It's a regular imposition—going about with his air of seclusion, and keeping a coat of arms in his room"——

"Did you think that was a coat of arms?" asked I. "Why, it's the diploma of a commercial school."

"I don't spend so much time as you do, Louise, in the lodgers' rooms, studying up their belongings. As if I cared what it was—a low-bred person!"

"It's very unkind of you to talk so, Clara, when he's trying to do so much to help us. He is going to take Annabel himself to the manager of the Avenue theatre to-morrow morning. And I'm to bring Emily to his store this afternoon, when the Director of the Symphonies is to hear her play, and give her pupils if he is satisfied."

"Satisfied! I rather think there's no danger that any one Mr. Annersley's likely to know will be anything else but satisfied with Emily's playing!"

I thought so myself. And I must say I was thunderstruck, after Emily had played two of her very best pieces that afternoon, to hear Mr. Deboisson, the director, who, at first sitting in dead silence, presently fidgetted enough to drive one wild, cry out: "It is utterly useless. It is utterly hopeless! Of what can the young lady be thinking? Has she a mind to think with at all? It is necessary to be plain. How can she give lessons without talent, without technique—with absolutely no qualification! Her hand was spoiled in the beginning. She has no idea of the master's meaning. She cannot even read the music. It is childish play, Mr. Annersley!" and he stalked out of the shop as if he had been insulted.

ALWAYS A GAY SEASON IN TOWN.

But Emily, for whose sake I felt so badly, was not in the least disturbed. "What a crusty old simpleton!" she exclaimed. "As if nobody knew anything but himself! And who knows whether he does or not?" And she rattled off one of her show pieces in great disdain of him, and went home with me scolding about Allen Annersley all the way. For if he had taken the least pains to prejudice Mr. Deboisson in her favor, it would all have been different, she said.

I must confess that, when Annabel came home crying, the next noon, and told us that the manager had pronounced her efforts idle, weakly amateurish, and out of the question for business, I felt as if Fate was against us, and there was some gigantic mistake somewhere. And I hated the manager even while I wondered at his blunder, and I cried a good deal myself over my flowers, as I trimmed and watered them. But my crying only made Emily indignant. "I should think you thought our enemies were in the right," she cried. "*I* don't cry. What such a person as that Mr. Deboisson says makes no odds to me. There are people who say he's no sort of a director! I shall go on with my playing just the same, and so will Annabel with her elocution. And you can attend to your precious flowers and not worry yourself about us!" But Annabel kissed me that night before she went to sleep.

So I went back to my flowers; and they were the greatest comfort to me. I had a box out of every window in the house, and when they were full of blossoms it did make the house mightily attractive; and I used to think that was one reason why the lodgers came. But when I said so, the girls greeted me with shouts of laughter and with reproaches for my self-conceit; and Clara said she shouldn't wonder if beautiful young women in a house were quite as attractive as flower-boxes at the windows. But all around the edges of the yard, at first, I had my beds, and at last I covered every bit of space in the yard with them. I had a world of trouble, though, because the soil was so hard and clayey there; and I did question if I were not too selfish to live when I had a cart-load of fresh loam and some fertilizers hauled on the yard once, at a time when the girls had all gone out. But I went without butter and sugar for two whole months, so as to be sure that I had not wronged them in doing it. And I was sorry then that sugar was so cheap; if it had only been a dollar a pound, I need not have gone without anything like as long.

Everybody must have some pleasure, I fancy, and the pleasure I had with those flowers of mine was past reckoning; and sometimes Mr. Annersley came home when the girls were out, and went about from window to window with me, admiring them as much as I did. He knew a good deal about flowers, and once in a while he brought home some rare little thing that he had got in a greenhouse, and I felt richer than if it had been a pearl; and sometimes I found something that I could root, in an old chance bouquet thrown from her carriage by some beauty going home from a ball, maybe. One day the friendly next-door housekeeper asked me, over the fence, if I would not like to take a drive into the woods with her old master; and as all the rooms were in order, and lunch just over, I was delighted. For the old gentleman and I were very good friends in a small way, and after we were off the pavement he began to talk about my flowers; he was something of a botanist, he said, and he had enjoyed looking over in my little yard and seeing me make something out of nothing; and he thought if I were so fond of flowers as all that, I might like a drive in the woods (where I had hardly ever been), to see some of them in their own homes, although it was still only the last of May.

How lovely it was in the woods! So still and dark and solemn, with long vistas away into golden green sunshine, and, when you were wonted there, the murmuring whisper of the treetops, swelling and falling like the echo of a wave upon a distant shore. We left the carriage, and went wandering into the mossy glades, I often in advance, for my old friend was too feeble to go very far, and I came back to him with this and that treasure of the wild growth that I found—white violets, anemones, straw-bells. "Ah!" said he, as I came back once with a strange and charming pink-purple flower, as much of the wet black earth about it as I had been able to take from the ground, "now you have a real treasure! That is the Showy Orchis. Yes, I am glad you have found that; and doubtless there are others here. It belongs to the most interesting and curious of all the flowers—flowers that mimic animal life. Do you know, there is a damp shady corner in your little yard, under the pear tree, that you can make rich enough to grow this and several others of its kind. We will come again with a big bag and fill it with this peaty soil." And so we did, several times, the girls marveling why I liked driving out in the country with that old creature, and not at all admiring the weeds that I brought back. And in those times I found many wonders, and among them one that he told me was the Arethusa, the loveliest purple thing alive, and a Calypso, too; and he was just as pleased as I was.

Sometimes, once or twice, after he heard about it, Allen took me in the street cars as far as they ran, and we walked the rest of the way, although somehow I never liked to tell the girls; and it is certainly odd how your senses are trained and warned all unconsciously, to find what you are looking for; but I had no sooner seen the old gentleman's pleasure over my Arethusa, than what should I spy, one sweet June day, but the small white moccasin flower, and then the big yellow one, and presently the little yellow one. fragrant as a tropical jungle might be. And I carried them home to the old gentleman, with Allen, and he said it was an unexampled find, all in one day. "Three different specimens of Cypripedium," said he, "all in one day! But flowers know their lovers. They know to whom to reveal themselves. Come July, we will go through the woods again, and I dare venture you'll come

JOHN RUSKIN.
(Bust by Sir Edgar Boehm, R. A.)

BOWERS OF LOVELINESS.

home with the big pink ladies' slipper, a perfect balloon, and the crane-fly, to boot!" And of course I really did —it would have been impolite to seem to contradict him by not doing so, you know. And I came home, moreover, with the greenish-white ladies' tresses, and the adder's mouth with its tiny green blossom, too; and one day I found myself half crying for joy over the sudden beauty of the white fringed orchis; and in August—there never was such luck!—I found the yellow fringed orchis, and the ineffably sweet purple fringed one; and by that time the little rich wet corner of my yard was a perfect chamber of jewels to me, with more than the treasure-house of any Oriental king, with here a quaint rose-purple flower whose white lip was spotted purple, and here a sweet-scented, blushing begonia. For the other flowers in the yard had grown as all common flowers do; but these things that I had brought home from the dark, wild wet woods and swamps seemed to belong to some other planet, and to tell of some other life —some strange, fantastic, foreign principle of life. They told of another life for human beings, too, different from this crowded brick and mortar one. "A life," I said to Mr. Annersley once, "that I suppose I never shall have—but a life on a farm in the country with one corner of a garden running down into wet woods." He stopped and looked at me, quite gravely, a moment. "Perhaps you will have it," said he. "I think it depends on yourself whether you will or not."

Well, well, those things were not all my wealth by any means. What pinks I had, such great globy crimson carnations and white ones, too; one box, outside the parlor floor lodger's window, was all nothing else, and another box was full of snowy sweet alyssum and forget-me-nots and mignonette, and another box was all yellow oxalis and blue lobelia, and just as soon as they could blow out doors I had all sorts and colors of double columbines shaking in the wind, white, golden, blue, purple and scarlet, in the box out of Mr. Annersley's window, and over the sides another box brimming with yellow escholtzias and marigolds; I had crimson cypress vines, and sulphur tinted canary bird flowers, and nasturtiums of all deep, rich impossible blood-colors streaming; and then I had purple cinerarias and yellow coreopsis and Star of Bethlehem, all an odd prickly velvet, over its midnight blue, and bachelors' buttons and balsams and four o'clocks; and there were pots full of violets, full of geraniums, of purple and carmine colored gloxinias; and an oleander-tree that when it bloomed was like a rosy sunrise in the room; and in the yard was the corner of my dear wild flowers, and my June peonies, and my larkspurs, bluer than blue, and my little rows of sweet peas, and morning glory and scarlet runners covering all the sides of the fence, and a vast orange trumpet flower and a purple clematis and a wistaria running up the back of the house, and hollyhocks, stately as old-fashioned lovely ladies, and a dahlia and a prince's feather, each in their season, and last of all my white chrysanthemums and scarlet salvias—a perfect little wild garden, every inch used, and not a half an inch wasted. I used to look out over the yard in the morning and wonder at myself, and I used to look up at the house when I came home from market, and think it looked as if it ought to be Paradise inside. But it wasn't.

FLOWERS.

I really don't know where they all came from, these darlings of mine. This person gave me one, and that person gave me another, and some I

(140) FLOWERS THE ONLY PLEASURE AND COMFORT THAT I HAD.

begged, and some I bought, and one, yes, one I stole. You'll never believe how wicked I was. I stole it walking in the Park. And I tried so hard to look innocent, passing the policeman, that I know he knew I was guilty, and I hope I made up for it afterwards a little, by scattering a whole handful of its very own seed in the same spot in the spring; and I do believe that the great patch you see there like live brown and gold velvet in the sun, came from those identical seeds.

Those seeds, and the seeds of the others, too, gave me no end of trouble, by the way; for people all up and down the street, and people who passed that way, strangers, too, and all our acquaintances of course, used to come and beg me for some of the seed of this, that, or the other. And it grew to be a real nuisance, it took so much of my time, and I was afraid, too, I would have none left for myself. I was doing some up to give away one day, when Mr. Annersley came in. "It isn't generosity at all," I said. "I don't like to do it. I wouldn't mind so much, though, if I thought they really wanted them. But it's only a freak, because our flowers look so pretty. I don't believe they'll ever come to anything. They're just wasted."

"Sell them, then. Don't give them away. It will amount to something in the year."

"Oh dear, no—I should be ashamed. "Ashamed of turning an honest penny? I'm not." "But they're not worth a penny." "Oh yes, they are. Why, you know there are some establishments for nothing else than the sale of flower seeds. Do them up in neat packages, and I'll take them to the store. Those that want them will want them enough to pay for them. And they won't be wasted, either." I should never have done it, you see, but for him; he was always looking out for my interest that way. And what did I see the next week but a great black and white placard in the shop window: "Flower seeds from Miss Forester." The girls were so outraged! But he didn't take the placard down for all that; and I kept putting up and sending round to him my flower seeds as fast as they ripened, and in the late spring he handed me more money than I would believe could come from their sale.

One way and another, all the time, the house gradually became an actual bower. Once some men came staggering in, not looking at all like men, but more like Birnam Wood, and they carried between them an immense azalia bush, a mound of snow and sweetness, with the compliments of the old gentleman next door. The girls said of course it couldn't be for me; but as they couldn't make up their minds for which one of them it was, it didn't matter; and I returned thanks, and did it so carefully not to mention any names, that Mr. Annersley, who was writing in there, looked up at me with a laugh in his brown eyes, and the old gentleman said, "You're a little girl as sweet as those flowers themselves, and I know somebody else that thinks so." And then I ran away.

A few days after that Mr. Annersley bought me a tiny Southern orchid, just the least flower of one, an air-plant that had no root, and which there couldn't be any doubt he gave to me. "There's a fortune in those things," he said, "although I fail to understand why. And if you would like, Miss Louise, there's an exhibition of orchids to-morrow, and we might see them together, if you will."

If I would! Of course I would. And I hurried along with him next day, my pleasure and ardor not at all abated by the wonder and disbelief and contempt of the girls, whom he didn't ask, although I should have been delighted if he had.

But I thought no more of the girls when I was once in the hall of the exhibition. The anteroom, full of startled cyclamens, plats of primroses, dishes of pansies, and great jacqueminots with half-yard long stems, was nothing beside this place of enchantment where, tier over tier, rose the weird, wondrous creatures with their threads and filaments sailing on the air, with all their beauty and diablerie, like flowers and serpents speaking together, each uncertain if it were not the other. "They resemble, more than anything else, the floral ornament of the cinque-cento painting and carving," said Allen. "You think it is a fish, with all its scales and contours and colors, and suddenly it is a flower. Nature had done with work when she made them and was in a mood of wanton freak and frolic."

"See that upper one over there," I said. "It is a flower—but how it is trying to be a bird!"

"Perhaps it is a bird," he answered, "that has just succeeded in becoming a flower "

"And there are others in disguise, trying not to seem the flowers they are, but other flowers. If they were not so cool, so calm, so refined, wouldn't you say they were full of the wildest fun, playing surprises and making jests?"

"There is a sort of dignity through it all, though, as if they were of a separate order of creation, and were only obedient to the elfin law of their being. Perhaps the dignity takes root in their prices," he added gayly.

"Are they dear?"

"Immensely so. This collection is worth thousands and thousands of dollars. They outweigh gold in preciousness."

"Oh!" and the falling accent in my voice, I suppose, told him the story of my little secret hope of wearing my old gown and boots another while, and getting some bulb or shoot or seed among them all. "Oh, that caps the whole!" I exclaimed. "That just shows they are the very spirits of flowers,

SO STILL AND DARK AND SOLEMN.

to be capable of such work as outweighing gold. Perhaps they are ghosts of the dead and gone gnomes and trolls who handle the gold and gems in the heart of the hills in the fairy stories. I suppose that gnomes could have ghosts. See that scarlet fellow with the white spathe—they are the witches and warlocks of flowers. How I should like to look in here when the moon

A BOX OUT OF EVERY WINDOW IN THE HOUSE.

shines to-night through the great windows, and see them at their wild play all alone! If one only had ears fine enough to hear their language!"

"Do you know," said he, suddenly stopping and turning toward me, for we were in a corner by ourselves, "that you have something in common with these orchids? Yesterday a little unnoticeable body, suddenly something has clothed you to-day with a beauty lovelier than Clara's. What freak was Nature playing when she gave you this color, this smile, this sparkle, to hide yesterday and come to-morrow?"

"Oh, hush, hush!" I said. "You musn't speak to me so. Nobody ever speaks to me so. They talk so to the other girls. They don't talk so to me."

"I can think it just the same, can't I?" he said, smiling. "There you go again. The enthusiasm has died down, the flame is wrapped in gray smoke, the cloud has come over the sun, the great shining orchid that you were, with your illumined eyes and changing blush a moment ago, has turned back and become the little forget-me-not. But I have seen it before, many a time, as I looked at you out of the windows next door, when you found one of your new plants in bloom."

"I—I am sorry you said so," I murmured. "For now—perhaps I shall never feel quite free again when—when I'm there."

"Then I must never look at you out there again, and that would be a good deal more than I would like to deprive myself of," he said. "So you think I am jesting?" he said, all his old barriers suddenly seeming to give way. "Look up at me, look up at me a moment. Why do you keep those blue eyes veiled so? Lift those white lids just for one swift, shy glance, one sweet shy glance, and see if I am not in earnest." And I tried to, and my lip quivered; but determined not to yield I did raise my eyes, and out spurted the tears. "Louise!" he exclaimed, but under his breath, and standing between me and the crowd beyond. "My darling, I didn't dream I was hurting you! Do you suppose I would hurt the thing I love best in the world?"

I CAME HOME WITH LADIES' TRESSES, ETC.

146   STEPPING STONES TO HAPPINESS.

THE CORNER OF MY DEAR WILD FLOWERS.

"You love best in the world!" I repeated, in amazement, looking up at him through all my tears and in spite of them.

"Yes," he said. "Does that surprise you? It ought not. I have always wanted to tell you when I felt I might. Does it surprise you? Why, who is it that you love best in the world?" he asked, quickly.

"You!" I said, before I thought a word. And then, when in a moment I could have cried out at myself, and would have turned and tried perhaps to run away, "That is all right then," he said, coolly. And he took my hand and tucked it under his arm in a perfectly matter-of-fact way, and walked off with me. "You must have known I loved you," he said. "I never doubted that you loved me. After my stock is paid for and the day for our marriage is fixed, I shall tell you all I have thought about you for this long time as I have seen you going and coming. I shall tell you I was always afraid you would put out wings like any other angel, and fly away and leave me desolate."

"I—I think you musn't—say any more to me—just now," I murmured. "I am afraid I—I shall do something—silly."

"Whatever you do," answered he, "will be the best and wisest thing a woman could do. But come! I've a greater surprise than this in store for you. For I believe you knew this all the time"——

"I—I—never dreamed of it!" I answered, catching my breath, for fear it would turn into a sob of joy. And just then we stopped before some shelves clothed in moss, and there, in several trays, in pots and baskets, were some wild flowers which I couldn't see, and a large card which I couldn't read, for the unshed tears and doubles of everything, dancing like sparks before my eyes. "I will read it for you then, my darling," he said. "'Prize for the best collection of native specimens of Orchidaceæ, Miss Louise Forester, fifty dollars.' The old housekeeper and I took them up the moment you went in after watering them."

"I—I think I must go home," I half sobbed "It is all too much for me. I don't know what the girls will say."

"I know what the president and manager of the Horticultural Society will say," he exclaimed. "They will say: 'Buy your flower seeds of Miss Louise Forester, at Mr. Annersley's book and music store.' And people will flock to buy at once, you see if they don't! so many of them that it will crowd out all the books and music. And our fortunes will be made in the twinkling of a snap-dragon seed!" And so he ran on, to direct the current of my too intense feeling. And while he was talking, there they were all about me, the president, and managers, and the board of ladies, saying all sorts of pleasant things about my pretty orchises, not all of which, of course, were in bloom, asking me questions, and waiting for my replies. And before I was conscious of it, I was talking with them just as easily as with the friendly housekeeper, and telling them all the little I knew. "And I was proud of you," said Allen, when on the way home. "There wasn't one among

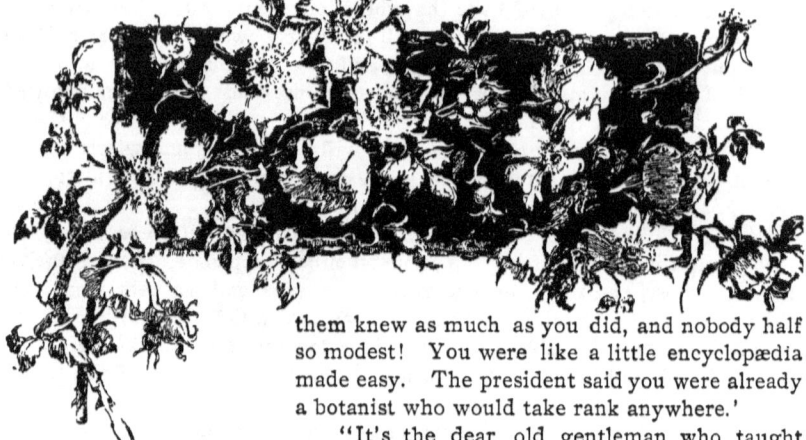

them knew as much as you did, and nobody half so modest! You were like a little encyclopædia made easy. The president said you were already a botanist who would take rank anywhere.'

"It's the dear old gentleman who taught me," I said. And then the house was near; and it seemed to lift itself so strangely and look so like another place, that at first I couldn't make out what was the matter. "Oh, the whole world has been changed, Allen!" I said. And he drew me inside the door, and in the dark hall he folded me close in his dear arms and gave me one long deep kiss—the first lover's kiss I had ever had, the first kiss, except for Annabel's, that had ever touched my lips since my dear mother died.

It seemed to me the next day as if everything were happening at once. I had hardly told the amazed girls about my prize, and I was going round the house in my light-hearted, happy maze, singing with a whole heart in my songs, when the dear old gentleman next door sent for me to come in. Allen was there, and we stayed for an hour or two, and a lawyer came, and we signed our names to papers, and I don't know what and all.

When I came back Annabel was waiting for me. "I've been making you a bonnet," said she. "It made me ashamed to see you yesterday, and we flaunting about in all the finery we could catch."

"I am so glad that you did it, Annabel, before you knew," I said.

"Knew what?"

"That I am going to be married—and to live in the country, ten miles from here, on a little farm that the old gentleman is to let us have till we can pay for it. A flower farm it is to be, and the Horticultural Society will sell my seeds for me. And as soon as we get it well under way Allen will give up his other business, and we shall do nothing else than raise and sell flower seeds. And we expect to pay for the place, and create a great business, and make our fortune and make, besides, oh, such great and beautiful flowers by giving our whole souls to it and having all out-doors to do it in!"

'Oh, Louise!" she cried. "What a life you are going to live! Who would have thought of it from just the beginning of those window-boxes and tiny beds in the yard? Oh, it isn't because of the flowers only—it's because you were in earnest and never thought of yourself! And now you are going to be so happy"——

"Would you like to come with me?" I said. "Clara and Emily can take care of the house and themselves here, and you can help me enough to have a salary, presently, if all goes right. Allen said something about it, his very self." And then Annabel flung her arms about me and we both cried together —for all at once I felt that I had found a sister as well as a lover. And I can tell you I took care never to lose her.

But you ought to see my garden now—no little back yard at all, but acres of blossom. There is one half-acre of tuberoses alone that drives the wind

THIS PLACE OF ENCHANTMENT.

before it heavy with deliciousness. And there, at another season, are the roses, such roses! they climb over walls and poles and trellises, and they fill whole garden plots, drift-white, and maiden-blush, and cream, and crimson red, and purple red to blackness. And sometimes, in late spring, when Allen and I go out and stand in the middle of a bed of violets, and the satiating sweeting rises round us in heavenly clouds, we feel, not as if we were in a little flower seed farm that had paid for itself and was making a large income, but as if we were in the very heart and center itself of the Garden of Eden!

CHAPTER SIXTH.

Under Green Boughs.

> No tears
> Dim the sweet look that Nature wears.
> —*Longfellow.*

> And not from Nature up to Nature's God,
> But down from Nature's God look Nature through.
> —*R. Montgomery.*

> I have heard the mavis singing
> Its love-song to the morn,
> I've seen the dew-drop clinging
> To the rose just newly born.
> —*Charles Jeffreys.*

> The meanest floweret of the vale,
> The simplest note that swells the gale,
> The common sun, the air, the skies,
> To him were opening Paradise.
> —*Gray.*

> The breeze of Nature stirring in his soul.
> —*Wordsworth.*

> O Love! what hours were thine and mine,
> In lands of palm and Southern pine;
> In lands of palm, of orange blossom,
> Of olive, aloe, and maize and vine!
> —*Tennyson.*

They who best cherish this family tradition, and this family feeling, are they who most value the home and its influences and are eager to make it all that is good for its various members. For a home is the best of all the stepping stones to happiness. Where the home may be is a matter of comparatively little importance beside the character of the home itself. Wherever it is, in city or in country, its occupants will probably congratulate themselves that their lives are better spent than if it were in the other place. There is so much less to distract the attention and so much more to help toward the concentration of thought in the loveliness of rural regions that people there are

THE THEATER FOYER.

wont to think the absence of frivolity among them is a question past dispute, although perhaps a circumstance on which they have no right to pride themselves, since they can hardly claim a voluntary agency in this affair of the favor of Providence, but which, if not to be set down to their credit, certainly is to their advantage. In the city, they reason, are the unceasing entertainments of all sorts, complicated and simple, lectures, concerts, theatres, operas, crowds on Sundays at the churches where this choice singer or that draws a large salary, picture stores, galleries, libraries, exhibitions of things from the four corners of the earth, morning calls, strolls down thoroughfares as good as foreign lands, dinner parties, afternoon teas, one perpetual round of change and excitement, not the least part of which is the mere observation of the throngs that line the streets, with the equipages and the way-farers—streets which to the rustic are a theatrical entertainment in themselves, of which one is not immediately wearied; and in the mean time when life in the country has subsided to quiet sleep, it is under full headway in the town for hours afterward.

Comparative Views of Town and Country.

In the country, on the other hand, the reasoner continues, how few are the changes and how necessarily less frittered are time and attention by the need and habit of giving a thought to this and a thought to the other. All public entertainments, with the exception of a possible weekly lyceum course, are things unknown, and church-going and evening meeting and preparatory lecture are the only general assemblages. Social calls are but half-yearly ordinations, although neighbors may go across lots of a winter evening to be regaled with new cider and apples, or loiter a half-hour or so about each other's gates in the summer dark before the nine-o'clock bell rings everybody into bed with its remembrance of the ancient curfew. The missionary meeting and sewing-circle exist; but what are gatherings taking place once a fortnight or once a month, where every one is expected to be busy, where a good book is read, or where there is time for solid conversation, compared to the kettledrums and high teas of every day in the city life, where to get into a serious talk would be bad taste? For what time there is left to the country resident after these mild pleasures—and they occupy but a small fraction— there is an unremitting industry requisite for those who, living away from the emporiums in which every desire may be gratified for money, have to do everything for themselves, and have not the money for such gratification anyway, if the rest were equal. A new book there is not to be thrown aside and succeeded by a newer after a light skimming; if it is anything to read at all, it is something to exhaust, to repeat, to talk about for a goodly season; and news is so rare that when anything takes place, not only the history of

STEPPING STONES TO HAPPINESS.

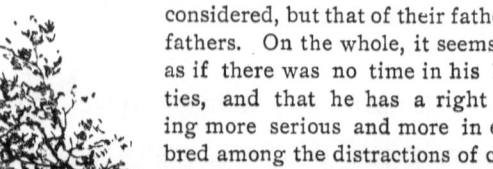

the actors is   considered, but that of their fathers and
their grand-   fathers. On the whole, it seems to the
countryman   as if there was no time in his life for
the frivoli-   ties, and that he has a right to the
claim of be-   ing more serious and more in earnest
than those   bred among the distractions of cities.

Yet again, the dwellers in cities will have something to say for themselves, and be heard to set up the same claim. In the first place they will urge on their side, possibly, the preposter-

THE SWEET LOOK THAT NATURE WEARS.

ousness of there being any distraction for them in the throng of the city streets; they were born among them; they have been familiar with them since the day they could walk alone; every alteration in them has come gradually, and stamped itself on their consciousness without any intellectual effort on their part, or any consequent waste of thought; the unending processions in those streets occupy no more of their attention than the pebbles of the country road do that of the rustics. If, to go on, the day begins later and prolongs itself later in the city, the amount of time compassed is equal, and the possibilities of time greater. As for the strolls and rides and the shopping, they have their rural equivalents, or ought to have, as they merely belong to the concerns of health or of necessary life. For other things, such as the routs and balls and visits, it is but a limited class that have them to enjoy, and with those that do have them they are a sort of routine, after all, which from continued custom requires certainly little expenditure of brain tissue, if they do require expenditure of time. As the conjurer Houdin, from long practice, could tell every article in a show-window at a single glance, and without conscious endeavor at all, so the persons frequenting these entertainments do it as a stale custom; they give so much time and so much thought, and no more, and the rest is left free for earnest work; while it is not to be denied that many of the entertainments are but a stimulus to earnest work, are creators of thought, kindlers of ambition, rest and refreshment after effort, and far from feeders of frivolity to those who use them as a means and not an end.

Certainly great things are done in the cities, as it has already been said in these pages; great ideas are started there, great works go forward there, great charities have their origin and bring about their wonderful results there, and it takes people with but little of the frivolous about them to attend to them all. And when we come to individual life we shall find that there is hardly any girl in the city who has finished her direct attendance at school who is not still pursuing some special study, and that far from superficially, but in

earnest, either because her interest is deep, or because some rivalry has spurred it, or because it is the custom in her set; or who is not engaged in personal charities that require her careful oversight, and use half her day in deeds that are neither vain nor frivolous, nor unnecessary to the health of the world.

The measure of human nature is probably the same wherever it is found, and the men and women of the country are not very different from those of the town. Condemnation of either by the other is the most frivolous affair that either encourages, while it will surely do neither of them any harm if a serious rivalry should exist between them as to who shall make the most of life, and leave the world better behind him. For our own part, were we called to decide the dispute, since the farm is needed for the city and the city for the farm, we would let them balance the matter between them and would decide for the golden mean—that is—home near a large suburban town, not too remote from a great city on occasions, but sufficiently remote to let one enjoy rural life and indulge the love of nature.

The Love of Nature.

Indeed, is not this love of nature itself a stepping stone to happiness? Few things so soften the asperities of life. Let other things go awry, let the roof leak, the dinner burn, the goodman grumble, and after a glance from the window at some lovely landscape that chances to lie below—a good long gaze in which the beauty works its spell upon the soul—all the troubles seem light and easily to be borne: that is, if one really loves nature, and does not merely pretend to do so. They with whom the love of nature is a passion find her rising to meet them in all their joys, to quiet them in all their vexations, to solace them in all their sorrows. "What I wanted when my father died," said a musician, "was to hear a certain piece of music. If I could have heard that, it would have seemed like a precious friend comforting me. But I could not, and so I was desolate, and my heart fed on itself." And it is just so with the love of nature in any similar stress. The soft meadow scene of a champaign country, where the purple vapors veil the distant edges, and the sunbeams slant across them with that straight-cutting line in which light penetrates a jewel; the infinite joy of the wide sea scene, with the everlasting play of its frolicking waves by day, its infinite melancholy, tenderness, and mystery by night; the magnificent inclosure of the mountains, lifting their heads into heaven to catch the light and translate it for the beholder, companions of the stars and yet companions of ourselves—all these speak to heir

THE LONELINESS OF RURAL REGIONS.

A SEWING CIRCLE.

lover as some delightful friend might speak, as some great all-wise friend, indeed, sometimes the very voice of God Himself. They comfort insensibly, when comfort is needed, too, not by the mere pleasure of the eye, but, as beauty always must, by composing and resting, by silent influence, and by the inevitable consciousness that the existence of such a thing shows an ever-living and ever-loving care; and beholding the scene so perfect, it would seem as if we were, almost unaware to ourselves, called upon by all these viewless forces to do our best toward perfection, too. We have known a person, very sensitive to all these forces, who in a season of religious despair was made whole merely by a winter's walk in the country, looking toward sunset, where the snow-white and innocent fields grew faintly rosy and smiling, and a ruddy orange lay low in the west, like a vast hearth-fire, and in its suggestion of warmth and home and shelter, made the sufferer in some way feel that the universe was under care, and every atom of it was regarded as precious and not to be spared by its Maker. And are we not, all of us, atoms in it?

And if the lovers of nature can be satisfied in such wise in the time when her pictorial and delightsome effects are less easy to be felt, what joy can they experience in the other seasons, when she is an utter spendthrift of beauty, like a player at whist who plays trumps because he has nothing else at all in his hand! What a luxury of life is theirs in the spring, when the callow willows make a sort of green sunshine near and far, and scatter their delicate fragrance through the land; in the summer, when the boat slips along the dark shadow of the branch-hung bank, the shadow full of deep olive tints, with now a yellow star-glint beneath, and a heaven of stars bright as the brede of some immortal scarf hung overhead; or in the fall, when the sun shines through the gilded and reddened leaves and transfigures them to flame, and earth seems a vast garden of brilliant bloom, whose vividness is only softened by the tender hazes everywhere dropping and folding about it! If all the ineffable charm of such scenes will not, indeed, pluck out a rooted sorrow, it will, at all events, if once really felt, go far towards alleviating the sorrow, acting perhaps as chloroform is said to do in spasmodic diseases, obtaining possession of the brain first, and rendering it in some way less acute to the touch of the other.

Micnelet's Twilight Experience.

To those who sincerely and understandingly cherish these influences of nature, with whom the love is no intellectual pretense, she assumes a real personality—a personality so strange that sometimes when night or twilight is superadded, this thing that is so dear to us puts on a mystery that becomes weird and uncanny, as if we were visited by the ghost of one we loved. "La petite chaîne, par exemple, qu'on appelle le Rocher d'Avon, nous avait saluée le matin, dans la senteur des bruyères, de la plus gaie lumière de l'aube, d'une ravissante aurore qui rosait le grès; tout semblait sourire et s'harmoniser aux études innocentes d'une âme poétique et pieuse. Le soire, nous y retournous, mais la fée fantasque a changé. Ces pins qui nous accueillirent sous leur ombrelle légère, devenus tout à coup sauvages, ils roulent des bruits étranges, des lamentations de mauvais augure. Ces arbustes, qui le matin invitaient gracieusement la robe blanche à s'arrêter, à cueillir des baies ou des fleurs, ils ont l'air de recéler maintenant dans leurs fourrés je ne sais quoi de sinistre—des voleurs? ou des sorcières? Mais le changement le plus fort est celui des rochers qui nous reçurent et nous firent asseoir. Est-ce le soir? Est-ce l'orage imminent qui les a changée? Je l'ignore; mais les voilà devenus de sombres sphinx, des éléphants couchés à terre, des mammouths et autres monstres des mondes anciens qui ne sont plus. Ils sont assis, il est vrai; mais s'ils allaient se lever? Quoi qu'il en soit, l'heure avance, marchons . . . L'on se presse à mon bras."

This singular personality which Michelet here gives the rocks and stones, others have been known to give to members of the vegetable kingdom. All growing things are alive to them, and full of purpose and intelligence; a flower is not to be plucked with inadvertence; a river rolls because it is called by the sea, as youth is called by love; and even the trees assume the same intelligence that elder mythology gave them in peopling the green or hollow stems with dryads. A botanist once declared to us that he had seen a tree manifest all the intelligence of a human being. This tree grew in the chink of a rock on the brink of a slight precipice, with a mere handful of soil to nourish it, and it was nourished so poorly that it spindled and had few leaves, and seemed altogether worthless. One day the person claiming the "animula, vagula, blandula" for the little sapling saw a thread that had been put forth from among the roots—a mere slender white thread—creeping over the brink of the precipice and dangling there, blown about by the wind, and growing longer every day. At the foot of the precipice was a spring of water and some deep, rich soil; on the hither side the soil was boggy, on the farther it was rich and suitable. The little thread did not merely drop into the nearest place and take root in the boggy hither side; it wavered and wavered and pushed out till it landed at last on the other side of the spring, where the ground was firm and good; and before long the fine thread was a coarse one, the coarse one was a yarn, the yarn was a cord, a rope, a great stem, and in time it looked as if it were the tree itself and not a mere rootlet that it thrust down where it felt the water. Very soon after it struck root, the sapling, re-

SOME LOVELY LANDSCAPE.

MOUNTAINS LIFTING THEIR HEADS INTO HEAVEN.

ceiving the rich food and drink of the spring, sent out a fresh head of leaves, presently fresh branches, and began to flourish with a vigor that had never been dreamed of for it—with such a vigor that the winds caught in the full-leaved head of the top-heavy little thing, and it was in danger of being uprooted. What now did intelligence do? It put forth a rootlet on the other side, curled it round and round the main stem in the crevice, till finally, as the root grew large and thick, it looked as though it had been poured fluid into the mould of that crevice to anchor that tree, which it did securely, and probably for generations.

If we may not accord intelligence, rather than the mere accident of situation, to the work of this sapling, yet do we all of us on occasion personify some noble oak or pine, as Olive's lover did the oak that stood knee deep in fern and brake; we all of us personify a mountain eternally couchant, and we all of us find the love of nature a free-masonry that even when circumstances, station, and education are all at odds, make us the children of one mother.

WHITE AND INNOCENT FIELDS.

Sunlight.

If we have decided that that home is happier which is in a measure in the country, we must further resolve that the home shall be full of sunshine, both of the soul and of the heavens. There is more than idle fancy in the old sun worship of the Persian and of the Mexican, the inhabitants of two regions with the diameter of the globe between them, but where kindred climate gave birth to kindred instincts. There, with the sun powerful and beneficent above them, at the touch of whose rays earth seemed to blush with bloom, like attendants upon which the winds came laden with perfume and delicious warmth, with whose reign life resolved itself into a mere pleasure of existence, under such circumstances, and with no revelation of another form of religion, it was not wonderful that to these people the sun seemed to be the splendid shroud of a divine power dwelling within it.

They saw the sun the center of the universe, and all things seeming to revolve around him. They saw the seed lying, for eons it might be, in the bosom of the mother earth, but never springing into life till touched by the fructifying power of the sun. They saw those portions of the earth remotest from his influence wrapped in ice and frigor, desolation and darkness, while between such parallels as lay perpetually beneath him a prodigious vegetation and life and beauty reveled; and they felt that behind this creative power the Creator Himself must be ensphered—the Creator, the Friend, the Benefactor, the Father of all, Who when He came brought hope and joy with Him, and when He went left darkness and doubt and fear to creep in behind Him.

A LUXURY OF LIFE IS THEIRS IN THE SPRING.

STEPPING STONES TO HAPPINESS.

After all, it was at once the simplest and the most beautiful of the ancient and heathen religions. It had none of the complexity of the Grecian paganism that, a natural offshoot under Ægean winds and skies and the artistic fancy indigenous there, became an utterly artificial manufacture when transplanted into the Roman atmosphere. It had in its early form none of the mysticism of the Hindostanee, none of the barbarity of the Polynesian and its related religions. It was the idea that must have suggested itself at once to the reason and the imagination of primitive man in a happy and comfortable condition. It cumbered itself with no personalities, and it perplexed itself with no dogmas. Before the revelation of the truth, of a religion of self-sacrifice and endeavor, nothing could have been purer or more joyous than this worship of the sun.

We have learned better now than to worship the instrument as the originator. But for all that, the most of us remember our home in the East, that great breeding-place of the race; some traditions of it cling to us yet, and among them we have a veneration for the sunshine, the ancient and unalterable sunshine. Whatever melancholy there may be in our composition asserts itself at the twilight hour when the sun is withdrawing from us. All our gladness and gayety break forth in the morning hour when his smile kindles the heavens. The dark days when cloud hides him throw their veil over our own spirits also, and it seems in that thick weather as though nothing would go amiss if only the sun were out. Nor is it anywise strange that it should be so; for apart from the physical pleasure it affords, this sweet, soft, penetrating sunshine is the emblem of all tenderness and strength, of all benevolence and impartiality; like the rain, it falls on the just and on the unjust, and wherever it falls a blessing springs up to meet it. For when the sun shines, we can all of us cry out with the joy of the old Earth in the "Prometheus:"

> "It interpenetrates my granite mass;
> Through tangled roots and trodden clay doth pass
> Into the utmost leaves and delicatest flowers;
> Upon the winds, among the clouds, 'tis spread;
> It wakes a life in the forgotten dead—
> They breathe a spirit up from their obscurest bowers!"

(166)   THE DARK SHADOW OF THE BRANCH-HUNG STREAM.

CHAPTER SEVENTH.

Vine and Fig Tree.

> Throw hither all your quaint enameled eyes
> That on the green turf suck the honied showers,
> And purple all the ground with vernal flowers.
> Bring the rathe primrose that forsaken dies,
> The tufted crow-toe and pale jessamine,
> The white pink, and the pansy freakt with jet,
> The glowing violet,
> The musk-rose and the well attired woodbine,
> With cowslips wan that hang the pensive head,
> And every flower that sad embroidery wears.
> —*Milton.*

> God Almighty first planted a garden.
> —*Bacon.*

> There is no ancient gentleman but gardeners.
> —*Shakespeare.*

> And add to these retired Leisure
> That in trim gardens takes his pleasure.
> —*Milton.*

> When tillage begins other arts follow.
> —*Daniel Webster.*

> No daintier flowre or herbe that growes on grownd,
> No arborett with painted blossoms drest,
> And smelling sweete, but there it might be fouwnd,
> To bud out faire and throwe her sweete smels al arownd.
> —*Spenser.*

But if the house is in what is called the country or on the country's edge, we shall find another stepping stone to happiness in the possession and cultivation of a garden, and if we live in town, still we love a garden. Every man loves his own garden. It is the delight and the desire of the farmer's wife and the dream of the old sailor coming off the sea. The turning up of the earth is in obedience to one of the natural instincts, perhaps almost the only inheritance we carried with us out of the Garden of Eden. Gardening

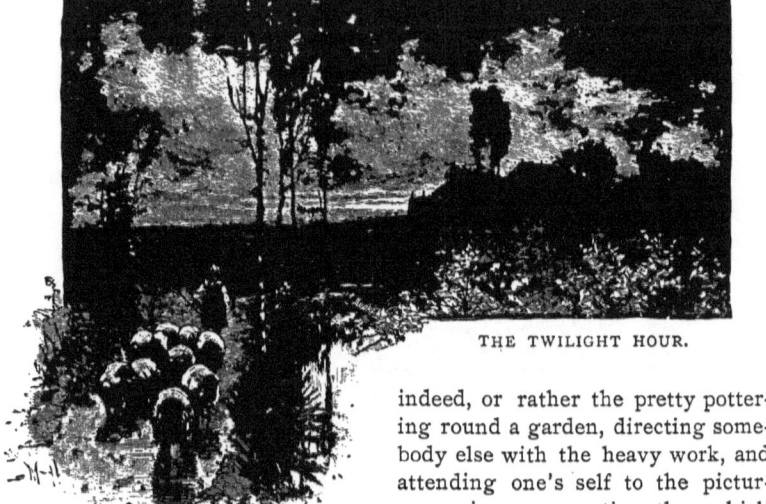

THE TWILIGHT HOUR.

indeed, or rather the pretty pottering round a garden, directing somebody else with the heavy work, and attending one's self to the picturesque, is an occupation than which there is none pleasanter, as all those know who are blessed with a bit of ground. The first pulling over of last year's flower bed is like coming back from long absence and enjoying the society of a mother; and as strength and vigor come to us while we meddle with the soft brown soil of the healing and purifying earth, we easily understand that Antæus as well as Adam was a gardener.

The Garden.

Nor is there anything more soothing than this same occupation for a mind vexed and worried by many cares. The breaking up of the ball of loam, the raking together of scattered waste, the sowing of seeds, the cutting of weeds, the removal of worms, the trimming of branches—all that distract the thoughts from trouble, together with the slight fatigue of bodily labor—calm the nerves and reduce things to harmony.

And while the occupation is both pleasing and soothing, it is the one work of all which has most promise and most accomplishment in it; we know that little is done there in vain, the reward is constantly before us, and the fulfillment of the first part comes while we are working on the last. We see the thing grow under our hands—the seed sprouts, the bud sets, the flower blooms, the fruit ripens, and all so that we can count ourselves, if not like the Oriental conjurers under whose hands the seed springs from shoot to fruit in twenty minutes' time, yet, at any rate, as if we had had a small hand in helping on the seasons and the fruits of the earth, each after its kind.

An Old-Fashioned Garden.

And what in the world is there lovelier than an old-fashioned garden—one not so carefully kept as to be a nuisance rather than an enjoyment? Over the old walls clamber the grape-vines and the scrambling blackberries, beneath them are the currant bushes, and here and there is a rare plum or pear tree, or honeysuckles, trained on tall trellises, to keep a sentinel's watch on the rest. Here stand the queenly hollyhocks in all their splendid hues, here the sweet stocks; here beds of carnation spice the air all day long; and pansies, violets, roses, southern-wood, evening primroses, and lilies—all in their turn, and sometimes altogether—make the mere breath a luxury; while in some neglected corner a forgotten sunflower absorbs all the warmth and wealth of its region, and suddenly spires up and spreads its broad disk like a fiery illumination. We do not care for scientific work in our old-fashioned garden, nor do we perplex ourselves with massing and separating the colors much: the sight of them all, as nature happened to throw them together, is pleasure enough; while in the distance the modest kitchen-garden throws in a sturdy background of greenery, with its fluttering bean and pea blossoms, with the great green roses of its cabbages, with the reddening beet-tops, the feathery carrots, and the waving plumes of corn.

When the chief care and labor are over—not great at any time, certainly —to sit on summer days with book or work in a garden chair on the reserved grass-plot of such a place, is a satisfaction that few who are not bound by the city have need to deny themselves. And when we add to the satisfaction of the senses the fuller satisfaction of looking on a scene that would not have been but for our own hands, of feeling that we have added by our personal exertion to the beauty and to the wealth of the world, that summer is more summer for our flowers, and mankind is richer for our potatoes and tomatoes, we wonder everybody does not hasten to the study of the almanac and the task of laying out a garden!

The Almanac.

For in the habit of studying the almanac lies a part of the pleasure of having a garden. When we open the Old Farmer's or the first pages of our handy volume diary, we hunt up our birthdays, consider on what days the festivals of the next year may be found, look to see if any eclipses will happen in our part of the world, and take more or less unconscious pleasure in the cabalistic pages, some of which still, in spite of all that has been done for us, we understand no better than the peasant, who, bewildered with his first one, cried, "Well, well, it maffles and talks; but all I could make out is that Collop-Monday falls on a Tuesday next year."

The almanac as we have it was not enjoyed by our grandmothers. If they wanted such a thing at all, they had to be content—and doubtless were—with one full of fortune-telling and astrology, to which the days and tides and moons were quite subsidiary—lucky if they could read it any way. For in its present state the almanac is almost a modern invention, since, although the Greeks of Alexandria had one as early as the first century, it would hardly be taken for a poor relation of ours. In Rome, in the primitive times, an officer proclaimed the day and the weather in the streets, and a placard of the fact was put up in public places. But the first almanac worth attention at all must have been that of Solomon Jarchus, issued in the middle of the twelfth century. Even the origin of the thing's name is a subject of as much mystery as any other of its facts, these holding that it belongs to the Arab *almanah*—a record—and those, that it is from the Saxon *al-mon-aght*—the heed of the moon—all the changes of our satellite having long been carved on a stick thus named; indeed, a stick or "clog" having been brought in from Denmark so artistically carved with symbols of time as to be a subject of a good deal of scholastic interest.

In a library at Oxford is an almanac computed by Peter of Darcia in 1300, and in this that mythical, allegorical, and, to most, inexplicable figure called the "man of the signs" makes his début. Oxford, indeed, after this, gave its authority to all the English calendars of the Middle Ages, and one made there in the last years of the fourteenth century had the calendar of the rainy days to be expected, and the precise statement of what season it is good to build or marry in, and all the science of the day, the "Houses of the Planets, events from the birth of Cain, short notes on medicine, movable feasts, and blood-letting," which, after all, was not so unlike some still among us. However, the second, if not really the first, one printed on the European continent came from Buda, in Hungary, and was calculated for three years, containing little but the eclipses and the places of the planets. But we may well take heart of grace in this age of free distribution when we remember that this sold for ten crowns in gold.

The *Sheapard's Kalendar*, translated from the French, is thought to be the first one *printed* in England, which did not have printed ones till fifty

STEPPING STONES TO HAPPINESS.   171

EVERY ONE LOVES A GARDEN.

years after France. In 1558 comes one that carrieson its title-page the words, "Wherein is expressed the Change and Full of the Moone, with their quarters. The varietie of the Ayres and also of the Windes throughout the whole yere, with Vnfortunate Times to Bie and Sell."

Nevertheless, in Leonard Digges' time, a half-dozen years earlier than this last brochure, there had already arisen numerous doubters and sneerers at the astrological portion of the almanacs, whom this worthy stoutly combated. Having declared that the rising of Orion, Arcturus, and Corona provoked tempestuous weather, and the Hyades rain, "Who is ignorant," he exclaims, "though poorly skilled in astronomy, that Jupiter with Mercury, or with the sun, enforces rage of winds? What is he that perceives not the fearful thunders, lightnings, and rains at the meeting of Mars and Venus, or Jupiter and Mars? Desist, for shame, to oppugn these judgments so strongly authorized!"

In France, the astrological character of the work had allowed the taking of great liberties, and it was found necessary to forbid the prophesying against affairs of state or of people—the fulfilled prophecy of the downfall of the Du Barri having given great encouragement to true believers. But in England full latitude was never interfered with by the state, except that a monopoly of the publication was given the Company of Stationers and the two universities, the latter, however, soon selling out to the former. This done, there came to be two strong parties in the matter of almanac-making, the philomaths and the astrologers, and hot was the warfare between them. But in the time of the civil wars superstition was still rampant, and those with the most gloriously impossible predictions were the most eagerly bought.

Poor Robin's Almanac did, perhaps, as much as anything else in the extermination of this kind; it was published in 1664, and although often low and coarse, had much good-humored raillery at the ignorant sort. "We may expect," it ran, "some showers of rain this month, or the next, or the next after that, or we shall have a very dry spring." Robert Herrick had a hand in this, as Decker had in a slightly earlier one of a similar nature. John Evelyn, of "Diary" fame, had already published one of an entirely serious and suitable nature for the sole use of gardeners. At last, in 1708, Dean Swift tried his hand at this literature, and issued one in which he satirically declared that a certain Partridge, an importer in the line of astrological almanacs, should die on a fixed day, at eleven at night of a fever. Partridge, after that fixed day, certified to the fact that he was still alive. In Swift's amusing epitaph on the man are the lines:

> "And you that did your fortunes seek,
> Step to his grave but once a week,
> This earth, which bears his body's print,
> You'll find has so much virtue in't,
> That I durst pawn my ears 'twill tell
> Whate'er concerns you full as well,
> In physic, stolen goods, or love,
> As he himself could when above."

Half a century after all this, Andrews was doing work on the regular almanac so as to increase its circulation to five hundred thousand, although himself never receiving more than twenty-five pounds a year. Yet the first really decent one of all appears to have been our own *Poor Richard's Almanac* by Benjamin Franklin; and it was not until the first quarter of the present cen-

STEPPING STONES TO HAPPINESS.

tury that the astrological parts disappeared from the usual British almanac, while we all still tolerate the promise of snow or rain "at about this time." We may, then, thank the stars, that are no longer consulted in the making of almanacs, that we may open our diaries, or our little *Lady's Almanac*, and no longer be tormented with predictions of the destruction of the world, being glad that almanac-makers, at any rate, have relegated that work to the astronomical savants, who may tell us that the earth is drying up to-day, and dropping into the sun to-morrow, without troubling us a whit if we do not have to read the fact every day of our lives in finding the day of the month.

But for all this we have known the almanac do strange things in its way. Indeed, we knew a family where it was not only a cloud-compelling Zeus, ordaining the weather, making the days of the month walk up to the mark, and bringing about eclipses and convulsions of nature at its will, but where it really wrought nothing less than magic. It always hung by the side of the huge chimney-piece, along with other mystical paraphernalia of that hearth; and when an offence had been committed whose perpetrator was undiscoverable by common earthly means, the family of chil-

THE MODEST KITCHEN GARDEN.

dren were summoned, and were ranged in a solemn row before the head of the house, who took down the almanac, read aloud those terrible things about Aries and Libra and Scorpio and Gemini, and made the awful signs of the Zodiac with the tongs in the ashes, and turned the leaves and consulted the quarters of the moon and flow of the tides, all interspersed with swift-scrutinizing glances at the waiting row, till suddenly the pale and trembling culprit of the ordeal was singled out by name; and great was the birch rod, and the almanac was its prophet there

But it hardly needs the almanac to tell us that when snow is gone, the sun is shining and the birds are building; then it is time to begin to turn up the earth, and let the air of heaven in to nitrogenize the under side of the clods.

The Apple Tree.

It is often a pathetic sight as one drives along the rural roads to see the effort that the wife of the laborer, or the small farmer, has made to get her little garden with its patch of color. But if it be in the spring-time that one drives, the pathos is some time lost in the beauty of the apple orchard that rises behind the garden and throws it into foreground. For who, living in the country or the large country town, in the parallels of its habitat, pretends to own a home without an apple tree?

And who owns an apple tree and does not wish for two? And who would own a farm without an orchard? And who that has one does not feel a kind of family affection for the old gnarled and moss-grown stem which has so rooted itself in the soil, and has so long been a part of the family life, as to seem little less than an ancestor?

There are harvests the world over, each having a peculiar charm and beauty of its own. In one place it is the harvest of the vineyard on the castled slopes of the Rhine, on the hills of France, or the volcanic sides of Vesuvius, in the fields of Greece—harvests around whose bald facts are woven images of beauty in form and hue that painters and sculptors and singers have been swift to seize. Then there is the harvest of the grain field, with its reapers, its sheaves, its wains, its sweet old stories, such as that of Ruth in the corn; its pictures, such as that famous one of the "Blessing of the Wheat"; its vast Western existence on this continent of boundless horizons, and wonder-working machines tossing sheaves to right and left like giants at play. If less universal than these, yet hardly less beautiful, is the hop harvest, with its lovely blooming bunches in a sort of simulation of the grape, and the scenes of its merry pickers down their long green lanes. But quite as full of attraction as any other is the apple harvest of New England and those regions where the apple-tree is as much an institution as the house itself.

From the first flake of the pink snow that drifts across their boughs in May with clouds of fragrance and songs of nestlings and lights of glancing wings, to the heavy drooping of their branches dropping thick shade in the deeps of summer, to the time when they are starred with their ruddy wealth, the apple-tree is a pleasure to the eye and to the senses—perfect in its spring-time beauty, and with an air of homely heartiness and health the rest of the year; a matronly, motherly thing, happy, it would almost seem, in giving happiness, as if it knew how grateful was its summer shade, its autumn juices; as if it knew the good times it furnished to the gay guests of the "paring bee"; to lovers sitting by the fire and watching their greenings sputter as they roast before the coals and tell the tale of which loves the best; to the roysterers of All-halloween ducking their heads in water tubs for the red retreating sphere; to friends and neighbors on a winter night who, having trudged across the snowy fields, are regaled with mellow fruit and mellower cider; to all the light-limbed gatherers on autumn days who climb among the boughs or roll the bright heaps together in the orchard corners.

There are few scenes pleasanter to the eye of those that from childhood have known the apple-tree in garden and field and about the back door than those of the apple gathering. The branches, that all the summer have hung a little more heavily day by day, have long been hiding under their dropping weight the far-stretching orchard aisles whose arched roofs and turfed floors have seemed fit for fairy dancing-halls; now men and boys have climbed among them with baskets and ladders, or are emptying their loads by the piles of barrels, this load yellow as the apples of the Hesperides, that red as rubies are, and all as fragrant as the first apple that ever tempted Eve. The girls and the women of the family are usually as busy as the men are, too; and even the horses of the waiting teams arch their necks and turn their wistful eyes, appreciative of the sweet morsels that they love so well. In all the time of the harvest no other work is to be done, no men can be hired to lay stone or haul gravel or cart wood; the "appling," before the frost can work its mischief, or the high winds toss and hurt the fruit, has tasked the energies of a whole neighborhood.

How picturesque, then, are the cider mills with their enormous heaps of fruit about them! how far and how deliciously on every hand you can scent the air they load with their aroma as you ride along, as if the virtue of golden pippin, and of the gillyflowers, the richness of whose deep red skin stains the snowiness of the black-seeded white flesh with a crimson tinge of snow-apple, and of nonesuch, had all melted into the atmosphere, and become a part of it! And although the sky be full of the promise of winter, and although the heap of fruit be chill to the touch, one feels, in receiving the rich odor, in looking at the rich colors of the glittering heaps on the ground, something of the warmth and cheer of which they will presently be a part; of red-embered fires, and beaming faces round them that they will help illuminate—fires no more red and shining than the apples that toast before them; of "turn-overs," and of "pan-dowdies," and of "apple-jack"; and one feels that the apple harvest is valued none too much, and that, from the blossoms of May to the "dried-apple sauce" of March, the apple tree is the special blessing of its owners and growers, all that the date is to the Arab, a rough-coated, warm-hearted friend, a vegetable guardian angel of hearth and home and happiness.

Woman in Agriculture.

But whether she has an orchard or not, every woman who has ten feet of earth about her door thinks herself an object of blame if she has not at least a rose-bush, a cluster of coleus, and a honey-suckle in it; and she may be seen in spring and fall and in the heats of summer watering and pruning and digging as she would think herself abominably used if it were expected of her now-a-days in relation to any matter pertaining to the economies, such as hoeing the corn or digging the potatoes, or doing anything of the sort, let it be lighter or heavier work, whose end is not purely æsthetic. She has no idea of returning to the tasks of her savage ancestress; she has sublimated and idealized those tasks. But unconsciously though she makes the offering, yet nevertheless every blossom that blows under her hands is a tribute to that ancestress, an offering on her altar, a memorial service to her who first discovered and turned to her advantage the warmth and fertility and creative power of the mother earth.

Among the Lake Dwellings.

"The ruins of so-called lake dwellings," says a graphic address of Mr. Lyman before an agricultural society, "covered for long ages with water, have revealed the beginnings of such culture in Europe. Among the charred piles which once supported wooden cabins built in a lake have been found bones of oxen, dogs, and goats, and beside them heaps of wheat and barley. No writing, monument, or tradition remains to tell us who were these primitive tillers of the soil who thus sought safety from enemies amid the waters. By their implements, fished up in quantities from the bottom, we know that some of them still maintained the good old fashion of stone tools, while others, more

Poor Richard, 1733.

AN
Almanack

For the Year of Christ

1733,

Being the First after LEAP YEAR:

And makes since the Creation   Years
By the Account of the Eastern Greeks   7241
By the Latin Church, when ☉ ent. ♈   6932
By the Computation of W. W.   5742
By the Roman Chronology   5682
By the Jewish Rabbies   5494

Wherein is contained

The Lunations, Eclipses, Judgment of the Weather, Spring Tides, Planets Motions & mutual Aspects, Sun and Moon's Rising and Setting, Length of Days, Time of High Water, Fairs, Courts, and observable Days

Fitted to the Latitude of Forty Degrees and a Meridian of Five Hours West from *London*, but may without sensible Error serve all the adjacent Places, even from *Newfoundland* to *South-Carolina*.

By RICHARD SAUNDERS, Philom.

PHILADELPHIA:
Printed and sold by *B. FRANKLIN*, at the New Printing-Office near the Market.

ambitious, were able to cast implements of bronze—another lesson from mother earth, who yielded her copper and tin for the melting-pot. They were barbarians, with the manners of barbarians; and it is safe to infer that women did all the field-work, and held undisputed possession of what the French call 'the sacred right to labor.' The man goes into the Swiss forest intent, with flint-headed arrow, to slay a red deer; the woman must till the field, and be back in good season with a bundle of firewood to boil the venison, which her lord may eat while she dresses the hide with a stone scraper. To her the duty of gathering, quartering, and drying the wild apples for winter use; their fragments have been found—prototypes of apple-sauce. She must bring the grain in from the small clearings, and store it safely in the lake-dwelling, under the eye of its master, who sits lazily chipping a pebble, whereof he will fashion, by some weeks of labor, a spear-head. That woman wrought better than she knew. While, perchance, her thoughts were only on her finery—her bronze bracelets and hair-pins—she was founding an ever-glorious reputation as the Discoverer of Agriculture. It passes my comprehension that writers on woman's rights and woman's superiority have not earlier hit on this capital fact—woman was the discoverer of agriculture. The classic nations recognized it. Ceres of the Romans, Demeter of the Greeks, was not a god, but a goddess, who taught the uses of corn. On the eve of her festival the women drove out of the temple men and dogs, shut the doors, and had a good time by themselves. Alas, genius lives on unconscious of itself! Women planted and garnered all through the last of the stone period and the beginning of that of bronze unconscious that her praises would be sung ages afterward by the Norfolk County Agricultural Society. When she quartered and dried those sour wild apples, did she dream of pomological clubs? Did she suppose it would ever be possible to propagate three hundred varieties of pears? There is encouragement to be drawn from such late recognition of genius."

Perhaps it was "genius" in this early woman, perhaps it was the instinctive turning to the creative earth, perhaps it had nothing to do with the circumstance that the savage lord and master found the wild exhilaration of the hunt something vastly more pleasant than bending with the rude implements of the time over the furrow, and fighting the wild boar infinitely gayer work than fighting weeds. Whatever may have been the power that impelled her to the work, it is interesting to remember that gardening was woman's work ever since Eve plucked the roses of Eden, and that her descendants, over their little trellises and rockeries, their vases, and window boxes, are only following out what hundreds of generations may have now trained into a purely feminine instinct.

A Picturesque Sight.

Nor could there be a pleasanter illustration of feminine instinct than the delight of making something grow where nothing grew before, the delight of creation, and of producing and increasing beauty to gladden the eyes of the world. It is, perhaps, to be doubted, if flower-gardening were a plebeian occupation, whether feminine instinct would turn to it quite so willingly, although we fancy that even in that case there would be surreptitious little boxes of mignonette and violets hidden away in corners for private, if vulgar, enjoyment. But since even duchesses handle now and then a garden rake and play the pastoral, no woman of lesser degree, or of any republican degree, feels that her dignity suffers any derogation from the use of her little hoe and sprinkler. She knows that she not only adds beauty to the world, but is a picturesque object in the landscape while doing it, not only in the tender spring and summer, but at a time when the out-door world is cheerless, and needs such an enlivening object as her bright colors and busy movements make her. Moreover, if she herself is not conscious of it, others are conscious that the work is a refining one, that rude movements are impossible where such delicate objects are concerned, and that ungracious thoughts cannot have wide range in the mind of her who watches the slow, sweet progress of the bud becoming a flower, and takes heed to feed and nurture it something as a mother cares for a child, while she sees loveliness growing under her hand as it grows under the hand of painter or carver. Meanwhile the bountiful old earth remembers well those who take pleasure in occupying themselves with her; and for all the toil in the damps of spring, the heats of summer, or the chills of autumn, she gives a robustness and rosiness that make the beauty of the flowers not the only beauty evoked from her processes. She repays the effort expended on her by a fine familiarity with her ways, which makes the fair gardener seem to be more a thing of nature than of art herself; and every once in a while she causes one to think that, but for women, those flowers which are merely objects of beauty and not utility might perish out of the world. In his charming "Out-door Papers", Colonel Higginson describes a piece of statuary, a fountain in a garden, whose fine fall wrapped three marble maidens in a veil of spray, and in winter sheathed them about with glittering, many-rainbowed ice. Such a sculpture in a garden is but a monument to those women who were possibly, it seems, the first gardeners ages ago, and who are the tutelary genii of all flower gardeners now.

Perhaps Mrs. Royal's garden was a trifle disappointing, but such as it was, would you like to hear about it?

(180) WHO OWNS AN APPLE TREE AND DOES NOT WISH FOR TWO?

Mrs. Royal's Garden.

There are few greater luxuries in life than the possession of a garden, a fine old kitchen-garden, where from long care the soil has a tropical richness; where there are corners for balm and "yarbs" and spicy shrubs; where rows of currant bushes shut you off from rows of tomatoes; where there are long arbors of case-knife beans; where melons surprise you among thickets of corn, and pumpkins and squashes climb over the stone wall and hang their yellow wealth on the other side; where the carrot shreds her lovely tresses, the red-veined beet leaves make a patch of color, the cabbages are like apotheosized green roses; where shady grass-plots are left about apple-trees and nut trees, about some one pear-tree famous the country round, some rosy peach or bearer of translucent plums; where industry and idleness, shadow and sunshine, pleasure and thrift, are blended in one charming composition; a place sacred to long sunny mornings, to the working off of megrims; where one works and pretends to play, where one plays and pretends to work; where one dreams of the subtile chemistry by which the seed he buries, with the atoms of earth and ordure, dew and sunshine, around it, is metamorphosed till ashes become gold, eking out a narrow income, and wakes to find that, on the other hand, it was gold he buried and only ashes that remain, leaving him profoundly convinced that gold is not one of the original metals, since he himself has reduced it to its constituent elements and gases—a place, in fact, which one discovers, after infinite loss and disappointment, is the sole common ground of two great classes of society, and can belong only to the millionaire or to the day-laborer.

We were neither millionaires nor day-laborers, but when we moved to Craigie we were resolved to have a garden—"a real old-fashioned kitchen-garden, Royal," said I.

"It takes years to make a real old-fashioned garden," was the reply.

"No; only money. There are half a dozen apple-trees for a nucleus already, and we only need to set out the largest raspberry bushes and quinces that can bear transplanting. No, it will only take money."

"But we haven't a great deal of money."

"We don't need a great deal—just enough to buy our top-dressing, and have the earth spaded and planted, and then the things will come up of themselves, you know—we can't effect that. Major Bayley will be delighted to give us some dwarf pears, and we can buy a few standard roses"——

"Roses in a kitchen-garden?"

"Oh, yes; it is charming to come upon some great flower when you are hunting for a last pod of peas—like unexpected wealth, you know. And we

THE HARVEST OF THE GRAIN FIELD.

shall get a mine of happiness out of it, and save the cost of all our vegetables, and have some to give away, and perhaps—yes, very probably—add a surplus to our income. Oh, I wouldn't be without a kitchen-garden on any account. I'd rather be without a drawing-room. There was no use in moving down to Craigie if we were not to have a kitchen-garden."

All which meant that Mr. Royal was opposing me enough to make me think I was having my own way, when in reality he was having his, and intended a kitchen-garden from the start.

"Well," he said, "if you really will have the garden—I warn you it will be a great deal of trouble"——

"Oh, no matter about the trouble," said I.

"Well, then, the first thing to do is to have that spot ploughed—should have been done last fall, and the sod turned up to rot."

We had decided upon the precise place at last—on the south side of the apple-trees, having quarreled over every inch of ground, sowed it with salt and watered it with tears, so to say, in our endeavor to locate the garden with reference to sunshine, security, privacy, and pleasure, till it became as memorable to us as the landmarks where every spring the old Germans used to take their children and box their ears solemnly all round that they might never forget the locality.

"The first thing to do," repeated Royal, "is to have the ground ploughed. It's virgin soil. I don't believe the share has ever turned a sod of it since the days of the primeval forest."

Which conjecture was a sound one, as we discovered next day when Neighbor Weldon's broken ploughshare assured us that our garden-plot was founded on a rock. "Well," I overheard Royal saying to the men, "my wife has set her heart on a garden, and she shall not be disappointed. We'll have to blast." And so for a day or two the click of drills and hammers resounded, and then came a shock as if heaven and earth were coming together, and they had blasted indeed—a premature explosion had broken every window on that end of the house, and cracked the parlor mirror from side to side.

Of course at the breaking of the mirror grandma cried out in horror, and felt that she had lost or was about to lose every friend in the world, and I think it weighed more heavily on her mind than Royal's broken arm or the hired man's burned face. But his arm being set again, Royal's blood was up; fate itself now was not going to balk him of that garden; if he couldn't see to it, I must; and we went on blasting, having a great ox-team to haul out the broken rock, till we had taken out ninety tons of granite, and it wasn't a ledge either, going into central earth, but just some drift and huge boulders. "We had better have turned it into a quarry," growled Royal. "We might have made our fortune at that."

"You can't quarry drift and boulders; they give out presently. And if you could, it would have been a fine thing, a quarry, with hammering and yelling and oxen and derricks under our eyes forever. Mr. Weldon will buy the rock of you, though; he wants it for his new cellars."

"He can't have a pebble of it!" cried Royal. "I shall want it for cellars of my own, hen-houses and rockeries and things."

"Ninety tons of rocks! Nonsense! He will pay you twenty dollars for it."

"What's twenty dollars, if I have to buy stone myself?"

"But there's plenty where that came from."

"No, there isn't. I've taken out the last splinter; there were only some enormous fragments, left by the glacier, perhaps, that scratched those cliffs out there—no permanent wealth of stone."

"But"——

"Now don't let us discuss that, Prim. He can't have it."

My Christian name of Primrose had become a sort of measurer of moods, for when Royal was vexed he always said "Prim," and when he was pleased he always called me "Rose."

But the holes left by that ninety tons of rock were something appalling. "It's the greatest undertaking that ever I undertook," said Royal. "We've not only to make the garden, but really to make the earth first."

"But when it's done it is done," said I. "The first cost is all."

"That's so," he answered me. "The first cost is all."

So we hauled the earth from a distant pasture, where it was black as a prairie with richness. They gave us the earth and a welcome, but it cost a dollar a load to haul it, and we had two hundred loads.

"Well, now, Rose," said Royal, as we walked down the paths that had been staked out about the beds, "we have really begun the garden."

"And how lovely it will be to sit on this stone wall and look out across the sea under the shadow of this gnarled old russet tree, hidden from sight by the corn, and all that, growing by day and by night, and bringing us in money for hardly turning our hands over!"

"Yes," said Royal, "I must say I anticipate a great deal of enjoyment in seeing these things come forward."

'Let alone all that about benefactors in making two blades of grass grow where one grew before. Oh, Royal, here's a bean come up!"

"By George! so it is." And we stood over that absurd little cotyledon with our hands clasped, in an ecstasy, as if it were the first thing that had ever come out of the earth since creation.

"Oh, I always was so fond of beans!" I cried. "Don't you remember Alphonse Karr's chapter about the delights he could trace to the fact that the beans were in blossom? Oh, I am so glad! The armies of the Crimea got roast beef and ice-cream and marmalade from their beans by skillful manipulation. Nobody needs to starve that has beans; and you know Pythagoras deified the bean, Royal, and"——

"Yes, I know, Rose," said Royal, laughing at me. "But it's a pity there isn't a pea, too. I suppose the birds ate up the radish seeds, but I thought perhaps we should have some early cucumbers. Don't you suppose that the potatoes mean to come up at all?"

Perhaps the spell of wet weather had spoiled the planting; perhaps the corn and peas hadn't been soaked long enough; perhaps—— But there, what use is it? They didn't come up, and we planted them over again. Then when the corn did sprout we couldn't quite make out whether it was grass or corn, and had to let weeds and all grow together for a while before we dared to hoe; and the peas were so late that when they came straggling along, the hot weather shriveled them to nothing. But the beans—the beans were simply splendid. The cabbage plants, too, were quite thriving, and the tomatoes were a wilderness of green leaves and strong odors; the squash vines were perfectly rampant, and the potatoes really began to hill up. I was sorry about the peas; there was a white mould all over them like a bloom—and they never had any other bloom to speak of—while Royal, who had dreams of a vineyard, was entirely disgusted with the fifty dollars' worth of grape-vines and pear-trees he had set out, the leaves on the latter curling up in a curious

MAKING GROW WHERE NOTHING GREW BEFORE.

fashion, but on the former disappearing altogether. "By George! Prim," he exclaimed at last, "it's those confounded hens of yours!"

Now contumelious mention of the hens, I must confess it, touched a sore spot. They were the prettiest creatures that ever stepped as if the earth were not fit to tread on: black just dusted with white, and with the loveliest great cropple-crown of feathers hanging all over their eyes. To be sure, I had had them now six months, and they had never laid an egg, nor shown any disposition to hatch a chicken, and had eaten whole bags of grain; but they were of grand family, and everybody knows that Black Polands seldom lay, and never set; it's enough to be allowed to look at them. These in particular seemed the very fairest of fowl; and the rooster, with his long plumes that sometimes tipped him backward, his dainty ways, and delicate outlines, never reminded me of anything but Oberon. I admit that I should have liked to see some little Poland chickens, but perhaps I shouldn't have thought half as much of those hens if they had condescended to any such commonplace thing as eggs. "Oh!" I cried, "oh, my hens!"

"Yes," said he, "your hens. If those hens were worth a rap," cried Royal, severely, "do you suppose they'd leave these things on the vines?" and he held up a branch of the potatoes thick with great brown slimy creatures.

"I suppose that's what's destroying the pear-trees, too," I exclaimed, breaking off a twig.

"It's just inattention," he cried. "If there'd been any oversight of things at all, this would have been nipped in the bud."

"In the bug, you mean. But whose inattention is this?" and I tossed him the twig of the pear-tree, covered with just as nasty a brown slug. "I don't suppose I'm to climb trees."

"You mean to infer it is mine?" he exclaimed. "I, who have to be in town all day long in order to get enough to keep up this intolerable expense and luxury, coming home tired out with my day's work, must hurry out here, and toil like a swinking laborer!"

"Well, if you think I've nothing to do but to spend my life picking bugs off plants, you— How—how utterly outrageous! Oh, I never imagined you'd expect anything of the sort. When you married me, you said the winds of heaven—— I never thought—I wouldn't have believed"—— and I burst into tears, and flounced out of the garden and into the house, and hid myself in my sewing-room, and didn't speak to Royal all night, and he went off to town in the morning without his breakfast.

Of course the first thing I did after that was to send for a quantity of paris green, and go to the district school and beg a half-holiday for all the small boys, that they might be turned into my garden, armed with tin pans, for a crusade on the beetles. They trod down every other row of the potatoes, to be sure, but they didn't leave a beetle on the place, nor a penny in my purse. Yet, for fear of accident, I sifted the paris green over the vines thoroughly, and then procured ashes from the house and paid my respects to the pear-tree slugs. A strong wind was blowing at the time; and although I destroyed the slugs, I destroyed my gown as well, the ashes clinging ineradicably to the fibre. And as the stupid servant had brought them from the range, a hot cinder blew into my eye and fastened itself, and when Royal came home at last he found the house in confusion, with the doctor just coming, and the people running this way and that, and my eyes, already inflamed with a night's crying, in a condition with that cinder before which the eyes of Leah would have had to pale ineffectual fires. Of course it was all his fault, and he acknowledged it like a man, and we had a reconciliation that made it seem as if we had just become engaged, and had never been married at all.

A PICTURESQUE OBJECT IN THE LANDSCAPE.
(Painted by Jules Breton.)

"Well, Rose," said Royal, "if a reconciliation is like marriage, a quarrel is like divorce, and the fewer we have the better."

"Then you mustn't call me names," said I.

"I never called you names, Prim," said he.

"Oh, how can you say so?" I cried. And I suppose we should straightway have plunged into another skirmish but for the little servant, who ran in and begged me to go out to the garden.

"Garden be"—— began Royal. But I tied a handkerchief over my aching eye, and we went; and there lay my six hens and their lovely little lord and master, on their backs, with their drooping claws in the air. *They* had eaten the paris green, and had been exterminated.

I must say that I shed tears over their little corpses, but not very bitter ones, as they dried themselves on the discovery that the golden pippins were ripe—a cream-colored apple with black seeds and delicious flesh and flavor. What lovely desserts were here! what crates to send away to relatives with watering mouths, what baskets to friends in town! What was there so choice as a smooth yellow apple, warm with sunshine? Who blamed Eve? Why couldn't we have an apple-bee, and invite everybody to the picking? We would. The next morning we found that the bee had been held over night without invitations. Those dreadful little boys of the district school had not been in the garden for nothing; they, too, had learned that the pippins were ripe, and there was not an apple left on the tree.

"We will have to get a dog," said Royal.

We got a dog. When that dog had scratched up the celery trenches for the purpose of burying his bones there, had rolled in the asparagus beds, and the carrots, and over the late-coming cucumber vines till they were worthless; had chased the calf into the corn just as it was ripening, till not one ear was left standing on another; had pulled down a dozen sheep, and brought home as many dead young turkeys from the neighbors', for all of which we had to pay; had sensibly added to the butcher's bill; had bayed the moon till sleep forsook the place; had frightened the baby into fits, and had given the rest of us a hydrophobic horror—we began to think him as doubtful an experiment as the garden. He was fastened upon us, but celery, asparagus, carrots, and corn had fled. However, that corn, as we began to look forward to it, had developed a hideous fungus, so that nearly every ear was as big as ten, and that was to be subtracted from Bruno's debtor account. "Well," I said, "at any rate there are going to be millions of tomatoes; they are just reddening, and we shall have a salad of them by day after to-morrow. And there will be quantities for chowchow besides; and then, with ginger and lemon, you know, they make the most luscious Oriental sweetmeat. And you really can't tell a preserved melon from citron; so Bruno and the calf did some good in trampling down the corn, for it has let the sun in on the melons.'

"What melons?" said Royal.

"Why, the water-melons, and nutmegs, and"——

"Do you see any there?" he asked.

Upon my word, not one. The district school had levied on that melon patch, and we might have perished with thirst, for all the imps had cared.

"I don't care!" I exclaimed, after the first of the dismay. "I hate melons, anyway; they always taste like a raw squash, and they are full of cholera morbus; while a tomato"——

Alas! what was that clucking under the tomato plants? I bent to see the cause, and beheld the whole harem of Neighbor Weldon's black Cochin fowl comfortably disposed there, and not a tomato of them all that those bills of theirs had not broken and emptied. It was no use to shoo those hens out of the garden and beyond the farthest bounds of Craigie; they seemed to descend out of the air or come up out of the ground; and when you assured yourself that they were utterly routed, there they were again pecking away at the tomatoes, and there they stayed as long as a single love-apple did, enjoying the first-fruits of the garden, and leaving neither sweetmeats nor chow-chow to us for second-fruits.

I pledge you my word that by this time Mr. Royal had hedged, pretending that the garden was none of his, but a little indulgence allowed me, and that he took a magnanimous sort of interest in it for my sake, and gave himself some mild merriment over it at my expense. Of course at that I was put to my trumps, and determined to have something from that garden. We had the beans, to be sure; we had them every day, and out of the necessity of my enthusiasms I was compelled nearly to live upon them. They certainly were the nicest beans I ever tasted. But the only other thing left me now on which there was any possibility to make or keep a reputation for my garden was a certain squash that had early manifested an intention of distinguishing itself. There was to be a county fair and agricultural display, and if I could but take the prize for my squash, would Royal, would any one, dare laugh at my garden? Now it is not universally known that near the stem of every squash is a little proboscis which it puts down and roots round within the earth, and through which it sucks up further nourishment than that given by the roots. "Further nourishment it shall have," said I. And I secretly brought a great flat pan of milk every day, and set it down beneath the vine, lifting the stem carefully, and plunging that little proboscis into the contents, and you would have laughed to see it suck up the whole of that milk, like a live creature, and fairly grow beneath your eyes. How it did grow! How it

stretched its great yellow sides as it lay warm in the sun, like a child waking from sleep! I began to get fond of it, and to experience a certain gratitude toward it as the redeemer of the garden's good name. What a monster it was becoming! I trembled for a time lest it might be stolen over night, but at length the danger was past—it was too heavy for mortal thief. Forty pounds, fifty pounds, sixty pounds: it grew as those huge balls grow that boys roll before them in the snow till they are higher than their own heads. I don't dare to say it was a hundred pounds, or two hundred pounds, or a ton—it never was weighed. I used to make Royal come out and walk round it admiringly with me. "By George!" he used to say, "there's something uncanny about it. I'm afraid of it. We'll have to rig a derrick to get it to the fair!" The derrick was a couple of Irishmen; and as the great thing rose in their arms, big as the moon in August through the mist, a clumsy foot contrived to slip, and over went Irishmen, squash, and all, in an indistinguishable mass of slush and pulp, and I sat down and cried.

It was the end of the garden. The beans had all been stacked and dried and threshed; a dozen squashes, misshapen and warty, as if one needed practice in growing them, and the thimbleful of potatoes, had been put into the cellar. Everything was dry and sere and rustling; presently there came a black frost as if a fire had run along the ground. I went out and pottered about the forsaken beds now and then; but it was generally thought in the family that the subject of the garden was one best to avoid in conversation with me; and at last the snow came and covered all that battle-ground with a robe of peace, and we forgot about the thing.

One day a robin twittered under the window; a bit of sunshine lay so warm there that I saw a snow-drop piercing the moist ground with his shining little helmet; I thought I saw a blue-bird's wing; certainly the buds were swelling; it was time to think of the garden. There had been a great snowfall, and it had suddenly melted under a few strong suns, in pools and streams of water, and now there came a week's steady down-pour of rain, enough to soak through to the nadir. "I'm sure it's lucky they have tanka boats in China, Royal," said I, waking up one morning and hearing the steady downpour still. "The whole population will take refuge in them if this lasts much longer. It will have flooded Symmes' Hole by this time and washed it out, so that we may expect to see great things floating down from the pole this summer. There can't be any drought this year with the ground so soaked. What do you say about the garden, Royal?"

"What do *you* say?" said Royal. "I don't know. It hardly seems worth while."

"Worth while?"

"Well, let us cast it up."

"Cast up the garden?"

"I mean the cost of it, of course. What are you so irritable about? Let me see—debit: a broken ploughshare, drilling, blasting powder, hire of men, teams, and oxen, the doctor's bill for my broken arm, the glazier's bill for the windows, a new mirror, the price of two hundred loads of muck, wages of a man for ninety days, seeds, paris green, district school boys, price of potatoes destroyed, of your dress ruined by ashes, apples stolen, melons stolen, of the dog, of all the mischief that he did, of six hens and the cock poisoned, of"——

"Oh, my goodness! As if there were no credit to the garden side!"

"Yes; I was coming to that eventually: one bushel of potatoes, a dozen small squashes, one mess of tomatoes, ninety messes of beans."

"And a world of pleasure!" I cried.

"Well, you may call it so, Prim. I can find more pleasure for the same money in some other way. Every one of those beans cost more than if it had been raised in a hothouse."

"Well, I declare!"

"Do you call it pleasure to have the sharp edge of a hundred-weight of stone snap your bones like a cleaver, as my arm"——

"You have plenty to say about your arm, but I don't hear a word about my eye."

"Oh"——

"I know exactly what you were going to say, Royal. You were going to say, 'Hang my eye!'" But just then a hand was clapped over my mouth.

"Not another word," said Royal, "or we shall quarrel again, and we haven't quarrelled since that wretched garden has been covered up; and I wouldn't quarrel with you to-day for the Garden of Eden! Don't you know what day it is, Rose?"

And in consideration of its being the anniversary of something—we had so many anniversaries, from the day when we first made mouths at each other as children to the day when we first made love to each other as grown people!—I was about to express my forgiveness, when there came the strangest shock and shatter and crash you ever knew, so that the bed rocked, and the brackets pitched, and my very eyes shook in their sockets. And as at the same instant there rose a terrible yelping from Bruno, I sprang to the window. "Oh, Royal! Royal!" I cried, "what has happened to the garden?"

He sprang to my side, and looked over to the cliff. There wasn't any garden there. A tremendous land-slide, whether caused by the rains or by an earthquake shock, had scooped it out as neatly as one cuts with a knife, and the great sheet of earth and boulders, with the young plum-trees and the dwarf pears and the old apples, was sweeping down, and taking Bruno with it, and burying itself in the sea with a gigantic plunge and hiss and roar, leaving only an unfathomable bed of dry sand in the hollow behind it. "So that settles it," said I. "Nature takes your side. The stars in their courses fight against Sisera. What a pity," I cried, in a sudden fury, "that there wasn't a land-slide in the Garden of Eden that would have carried Eve and her apple over the edge, and left the world alone to Adam and you men!"

"There was," said Royal; "and the apple of discord has taken root here. Yes, that settles it," said Royal, complacently. "And now we'll have to buy our vegetables."

CHAPTER EIGHTH.

The House in the Country.

> Not a mouse
> Shall disturb this hallowed house.
> —*Shakespeare.*

> I can tell you why a snail has a house. Why? Why, to put's head in.
> —*Shakespeare.*

> Sir, he made a chimney in my father's house, and the bricks are alive at this day to testify it.—*Shakespeare.*

> The stately homes of England
> How beautiful they stand,
> Amid their tall ancestral trees,
> O'er all the pleasant land!
> —*Felicia D. Hemans.*

> And hie him home at evening's close
> To sweet repast and calm repose.
> —*Thomas Gray.*

> In Xanadu did Kubla Khan
> A stately pleasure-dome decree.
> —*Coleridge.*

> I knew by the smoke that so gracefully curled
> Above the green elms that a cottage was near,
> And I said, "If there's peace to be found in the world
> The heart that was humble might hope for it here."
> —*Moore.*

> This castle hath a pleasant seat; the air
> Nimbly and sweetly recommends itself.
> —*Shakespeare.*

> The house of every one is to him as his castle and fortress, as well for his defence against injury and violence as for his repose.—*Sir Edward Coke.*

Necessary Foresights.

One approaches the house through the garden, and having made sure of a pleasaunce there, it is tolerably certain that the house is going to be a sort of a pleasaunce, too. In the first place it has been oriented in the right way, squared to the southeast, so that the sun comes into every room in it at least once a day, and in some rooms lies all day long Besides being supplied with this wealth of sun, it has been remembered that another requisite of health, and so of happiness, is pure water; and care has been taken that the well, if there is no high-spring to pipe into the house, is more than a hundred feet from any drain, and so a multitude of poisonous microbes has been kept at a distance. And when everything else to give comfort in the house has been foreseen, one thing more will be thought of, and almost before the house is built its owners shall make sure of a piazza.

The Piazza.

For both country and seaside life in America during the summer season, and even for a part of the winter, has become largely an affair of the piazza, or, as it is more prettily styled throughout the South and Southwest, of the gallery—has become a sort of out-door existence, in which there is all heaven to breathe and all heaven's light to see by.

It is no longer the little skimped piazza of old times with which people now content themselves, where one could scarcely stretch a sea-chair without dangling one's feet over the edge of the place, that hardly served to shade a seat anywhere at noonday and was as barren as the plank sidewalk of a muddy town; nor is it the imposing Grecian imitation of an ancient portico whose pillars soar above the ceiling of the second-story rooms, and whose use nobody can conjecture, since nobody ever sat upon it. So long as architectural appendages of the nature of these were the sole piazzas known to the country or the country town, people lived inside their dwellings, hot and stuffy as they might be; nor could they ever cool off these dwellings as might be done with open doors and windows, as they can now when the burning outer air gets its first cooling in the lovely out-door room which the modern piazza makes; and they consequently lived in a far less wholesome atmosphere than that which it is possible to enjoy to-day.

Not but that homes are healthy without piazzas, which are not an absolute necessity of existence, but that generous piazzas are one of the many alleviations with which this generation surrounds itself, and the benefit of which will be shown in the superior health and vigor and bloom of the generations to follow.

Any piazza, no matter if it is the merest open porch, of no size, comparatively speaking, dresses a house out more or less agreeably, especially if it be itself dressed with vines, and not to drape it with vines is not to curtain one's windows or ornament one's house in any respect. The vine in its infancy costs but a few cents if bought; costs only a thank-you if begged from a friend;

costs only a walk if brought home from the woods, as the sweet-brier and the Virginia creeper can be brought any day; and this vine, if set out at night-fall and well watered for one season will take care of itself forever after, and no costly art of the florist can equal the superb effect of the long-continuing scarlet bunches of blossom on the luxuriant trumpet flower, or the huge waving purple feather of the wistaria that twists and climbs from the piazza to the top of the house, and looks back to shake its resplendent plumes in the wind and sun.

The architects of most of our late houses, so far as those houses have architects, are prone to remember all this, and in the place of the three-foot-wide shelf of olden time, they make something that is almost an integral part of the house, and only fails to be a room through the want of walls, at once a part of the house and a part of all out-doors. These modern piazzas are as large as the usual rooms of the house, and seem larger yet through the want of inclosure; they are raised from the ground and kept cool with under-currents of air; they are very lofty, but are intended to be shaded with vines or cheerful awnings. Pots of semi-tropical plants adorn them, great rosy oleanders and mysterious cacti, that country people always seem to know how to grow, slip propagating slip from one neighbor to the other, and in statelier houses, besides these, there will be the more expensive palms and other frailer exotics appearing. Here and there a curtain flaps in the breeze across these airy piazzas; doors open on them, and windows level with the floor; there are canvas and rattan lounges; there are sea-chairs, telling of foreign travel by members of the family; there are those willow woven articles of superlative comfort that are carried about the land swung on the sides of huge wagons; there are wicker stands and baskets, and desks and tables, too, that rain and sun are not going to ruin, gay ribbons wrought in which, even when the ribbons are only bright tapes and calicoes, make the whole effect still more charming. The ease, and one might almost say the *abandon*, of this pleasant spot are equaled not even by the famous "mother's room" of the inside house.

Here is the cradle brought, that the child may sleep with all the sweet air in the world about it, lulled by the birds' song, the bees' hum—for the birds will sing in the poorest sidewalk tree, and the bees will hum wherever a leaf opens, in the hope that it may have a flower behind it—and here that child, well protected, will gather strength twicefold over that given by sleep in comparatively closer quarters. Here, also, is the caller received, the *négligé* in the nature of the place making stately dress a thing to be dispensed with, and allowing the sewing, the writing, the restful lounging, to go on as if all that were proper to the hour and spot. Here, moreover, in this out-door room—if the country custom of the hearty noon meal is followed with tea and a lighter repast at sunset—is the tea-table often laid, perhaps at first with a little more trouble to the maids, perhaps, in the long run, with not so much, in so far as floors are easier to sweep than carpets, and such absence of formality as the habit of the place allows making also an absence of steps and work. It is always an elastic tea-table, too, in that tea-room where there are so often apt to be other guests than breezes and bird songs and flower scents, for one may take one's cup to any cozy corner of the place, or one may be waited on without leaving one's hammock or settee, and there is always the same sort of space for another.

In fact, the piazza of to-day is a living-room, with all out-doors as a friend; one sleeps, works, reads, plays, eats there, and one even dances there, if dance one must when the thermometer is up among the high figures. In this lofty and deep piazza, where it is only the ever welcome and level beams of sunset and sunrise which can fall straight across it, there are always spots of cool shadow where one may lie with a book, undisturbed by flickering sun and shadow falling elsewhere in the inclosure; and what a charm is added to the book by this atmosphere in which one reads it, an atmosphere that seems a very part of the blue of the sky or the green of that forest sending its *avant-courier* in the shadow of the maple or the linden at the corner! And then in pure idleness, that necessary food for nerves and soul and body, how great is the charm of lying there and doing nothing, any more than the leaf that shakes outside, and how familiar we become with certain aspects of nature without the physical exertion of leaving our own vine and fig-tree, while here again at night at last we learn the secrets of the stars themselves! Take it for all in all, it seems to us that the large and lofty vine-shaded summer piazza is a blessing added to life that has a right to put in rival claims with the telephone, the bicycle, the electric light and the ocean cable, more humble perhaps, but giving quite as much, if not more, happiness to a larger multitude.

The Furnishing.

But the house having been built, whether with piazza and vine, or without it, with what pleasure and zest do its owners move into it! There is usually a too goodly quantity of half-worn furniture on hand, and one is not in any such degree responsible for the taste and skill shown in the arrangement of the new house, as if everything had been to buy afresh, and there had been the opportunity to exercise taste and choice, and fit everything exactly to the place for which it is most suitable. If one, for instance, has old carpets, and can not afford to dispense with them, they must be ripped and turned and sewed over and made to answer in the new rooms and it is they, inanimate rags as they are, that settle the question of the color of this or that room, and not you, although you fancy yourselves ever so much the monarch of all you survey. There is, however, frequently the chance to show skill and taste in the adaptation of the old to the new, till it looks like design, and design that nothing could have improved upon; and there are many who derive the greatest satisfaction from this exercise of their ingenuity, like that good wife who trusted her husband never would be so rich that she should not be obliged to contrive how to make both ends meet and be praised for doing it.

Yet even if one has a purseful of money and no restriction or responsibility to another in its expenditure, the task of buying exactly what is best and everything that is harmonious is by no means an easy one, and in reality requires days, if not weeks, of considering and balancing the advantages and disadvantages, and of afterward regretting that the other thing had not been procured instead, and finally of being reconciled to the inevitable, and of adding some touch to it that shall make it just right after all.

The first thing to be determined on is to present a thought of solidity and comfort to the new-comer opening the hall door, and glad to step beneath the shade of the lintel. This can hardly be done if there is any patchwork in the appearance of things; if patchwork must needs be, it must be of the richest description and of such effect as an inlaid floor and warm and handsome rugs supply, and the carpets in the rooms opening on either hand in very brilliant contrasts, or else simply ascending in the same tone from the main groundwork of color that the hall presents. But, to be done well, this takes costly material, and those who cannot afford that would do better to cover their whole ground-floor with one and the same inexpensive carpeting, which gives an air of harmony to the whole of the house in the first place, while each room can be built up into its separate picture with its own upholstery and decoration. The inexpensive carpet is always the best, unless one can provide those of the costly and indestructible kind, for it can be replaced without ruin, and one is not obliged to become weary of it and still to keep it, till it shows the very threads on which it was woven and is an eye-sore of the worst sort. Nevertheless, the carpet should be one of which it will be difficult to weary, and to that end it should be as quiet a figure as possible, and in whatever color chosen that color should certainly be of pure tint. The pure tint is the only one that wears; the mixed and muddy mongrel tints become in a season utterly detestable.

Most people think that when they have set up a hat rack and an umbrella stand in the hall they have done all that could be expected; and if there is a little glass in the hat-rack, that then the effect is sumptuous, and the introduction of a chair or sofa seems almost too much luxury. Yet a slight reflection would tell them that the appearance of the hall is of as much importance as that of any room in the house, and not impossibly a little more so, for it is that which first strikes the guest and gives to him the key-note of the house. It stands to reason, then, that the hall should be an attractive spot at the first glance, giving the guest a desire to penetrate farther, and should never be suffered to remain a mere entry and passage-way. Here family portraits should be hung, like faces to make each comer welcome, your ancestors, if you have their likenesses, welcoming your guests with you, silently depicting to them your traits and characteristics, perhaps, and always looking down on your own going out and coming in. And here, too, should be hung any pictures particularly portraying the peculiarity of the ways and tastes of the family; here should stand the old clock; here should be a pretty table for chance objects to be tossed on, two or three quaint chairs, certainly a mirror, and if there is an alcove beneath the stairs, a lounge where an after-dinner rest that shall not be a nap may be taken while the summer wind blows through from door to door. The hall, in fact, may be made as inviting as any place in all the house, and if it is an empty and bare spot, one is very apt to expect the rest of the house to be in character.

It is the drawing-room, or parlor, if you prefer to call it so, in which the strongest interest of the furnishing usually centers. We will not say that it should be the kitchen, since we are looking rather at the æsthetic and artistic side, and will leave to every housewife her own kitchen. And, indeed, the drawing-room is, if not of as much importance, at least worthy of separate consideration, for everybody does not see the kitchen and everybody does see the drawing-room; and the opinion which our friends form of us by our action and surroundings is of real consequence in the sum total of our happiness, and the drawing-room depends largely upon ourselves, the kitchen largely upon the will of Bridget

The Parlor.

Not that we underrate in the least the vital part of the kitchen in the household, but we are speaking particularly of appearances. Moreover, since every day the drawing-room or parlor invests us with its beauty, or want of beauty, and is or is not delightful, it is for our interest and advantage to make it so, in order that our daily sights may not increase the disagreeable sensations that may be in our lot, but may rather ameliorate them. Little things will do this quite as easily as large ones. If the furniture is old, coverings of soft-toned chintz, of unbleached cotton cloth, trimmed at brief intervals with stripes of plain colored calicoes, will cover it and brighten the effect past belief. Little brackets, even home-made, but hung so that the rude manufacturing is concealed with pretty fancy-work, simple ornaments of no priceless material, but of some perfect outline, a vase, a candle-stick, a Pompeiian lamp, books, books in abundance, and flowers—all these, arranged with care and purpose, make up the cheerful, lovely aspect of a room, till it is as much a pleasure to go into it as if one should see the picture of some charming interior all at once take reality upon itself and surround us in still life with all the charm of art.

The first thing to secure in any room, and especially in any room bearing a peculiar home character, is the mantel—no mere slice of marble set on iron brackets, but the real chimney-piece going from floor to ceiling, growing out of the central part of the house, the protector of the fire upon the hearth. The room without a mantel is an atrocity, and has no right to be inhabited ; for the mantel always represents the altar of home. To the mantel, then, everything in the house should lead ; it should be either the white and culminating point of splendor in the room, from which everything retreats, or should be the body of shadow to which everything tends. It should be the one chief thing in the room which first salutes the eye ; in it centres the great idea of hospitality, for there is light and warmth, and should be space ; it stands for host and hostess to the guest; and it stands, too, for infinitely more, since in these days of publicity it is the one remaining representative of the old Lares and Penates, the shrine of the gods of home and the hearth, of domestic privacy and seclusion. If this one thing is remembered and attended to, there are scarcely any circumstances under which the room can be unlovely, and the result is tolerably certain, if care is taken to avoid a spotty effect by arranging the furniture and the pictures in masses with a view to equivalents in light and shade ; that is, if a table leads to a piano, and the piano to a lofty painting behind it, other

ITSELF DRAPED WITH VINES.

furniture in another part of the room shall be arranged to balance it with corresponding, even if totally different, effect.

The color of the parlor is a matter deserving more than a passing thought or an indulging fancy. There are reasons of complexion to be considered, of place, and of suitability ; for because one happens to love a certain color, one can not rush into it without reflection. There are few colors so rich and warm as the crimsons, for example ; but used in the steamboats and hotels, where the average American takes his splendor, they have unfortunately been vulgarized out of most houses. As lovely a drawing-room as we ever saw, in point of color, was carpeted with gray felt with a deep dull blue bordering ; the lounges and chairs were covered with chintz in the most delicate shade of robin's egg or gas-light blue, as the wool dealers call it, and the remainder was of wicker-work and black lacquer ; the heavy pieces of furniture were in black lacquer and gilt ; the curtains were of snowy muslin under lambrequins of the chintz ; and the rest of the room was made up of vases, tripods, cups, pictures, flowers and sunshine, till it seemed to overflow with harmonious color. But perhaps glory can go no farther in furnishing than in a yellow drawing-room ; there the splendor of color demanding splendor of material, lustre answers lustre, and you have a room where in the gloomiest weather the sun seems to be shining, and where the lovely yellow radiance of an October woodland is perpetually shed.

The Library.

Whatever riddle the drawing-room may read to its decorator, she finds relief from embarrassment when she comes to the library, for that is a room that may be said to furnish itself, since there is little place in a library for any but conventional treatment, and the rest remains almost altogether with the wealth or with the connoisseurship of the owner. The dining-room, however, is quite another thing.

The Dining-Room.

It has been far too customary, among those of us who have not unlimited bank accounts, to look upon the dining-room as a mere place to go and eat in and get out of as soon thereafter as possible. But the dining-room is the one place where, morning, noon and night, all the family come together, and are obliged to do so, at the same time. Certainly such a place as that should be made as attractive as any in the house. Besides, it is the place where the burden of hospitality is dispensed, and certainly there should be nothing there to suggest to the receivers of that hospitality any poverty or pinching, any fancy that the table is differently served in their absence, any vexing hint that the family disturbs its equanimity on their account. Thus the dining-room should really be as sumptuous a room as it is possible to make it; here the rich color and the gilding should be lavished ; here should be displayed all the painted china and frosted silver and other objects of kindred luxury in possession, something less being paid for the piano-forte that something more may be paid for the buffet, and here should be warmth and light and all reminders of comfort and cheer. And if the young mistress of the house once looks after these matters with a view to finding the reason for all things, these hints may light her on the way to still further discovery of how to make house and home delightful. Still, a country house can be made as attractive as it needs to be with chintz and wicker-work, leaving all these splendors for the town house that is so much more occupied. How precious a house can be to one, whether of one's building or of one's grandfather's, in the city or the country, the story of the Rosillon House tells us, and here it is.

The Rosillon House.

If it had not been his father's house and the house of his father before him it would not have been so much a matter of moment to Mr. Rosillon. He remembered the place when he was a boy and when it had seemed no less than an ante-room to some heaven of warmth, rich hues and sumptuous material atmosphere. And then it had become his father's property, and the family had lived there together, and the life was gay and sweet, and he had gone from it to his studies in the Polytechnic, coming home on the short vacations, and leaving with his course unfinished at his father's death. Crucial time! When his father's estate was settled—he never knew just how it happened, but there was little or nothing left for the family, and the house belonged to the executor.

The executor was the president of the bank where Mr. Rosillon had now been the cashier this twenty years and more. It is true he had given the boy a place in the bank and had steadily pushed him forward till he was cashier. But Mr. Rosillon had always looked upon the old house with the feeling that it was his and not another's, and vaguely formed but deep the resolve had always been in his will that some day it should be his indeed.

And now it was to be sold, for the president had stretched out his arms like an octopus, grasping this and that possession, and a palace had been slowly rising on the hill, inclosed with marble walls and wrought-iron grilles, and the old house, still furnished save for the modern additions, the old house that was no longer equal to the president's tastes, was in the hands of a real estate broker. But it was quite equal to the taste of Mr Rosillon, and he felt that if he failed to obtain possession of it now he never would obtain it. Yet how was it possible? He had not five thousand dollars in the world, and the place was worth twenty-five thousand. It had taken nearly all his income to care for his sick wife and to keep his boy in college—his sister Sylvia had the girl kept in Europe. They were coming home now, Harold and Angela, and he had been looking forward to it with a boyish eagerness. But if it were only up in the old Rosillon house that he was going to receive them! He was not a man that indulged in day dreams; but sometimes as the smoke curled up from the evening cigar he had pictured the home coming of the children, to him and to their mother, in that ancestral house, with a sort of ecstasy.

He had been up there only to-day on an errand for the president, and the quaint old tapestry, the rich, blue-green of the worn rugs and curtains, the massive mahoganies, the hammered brass, the huge vases as tall as he, all the spacious and tarnished splendor of the rooms, even the disjointed old portraits that had been banished to the upper passages, had filled him with an indescribable sort of homesickness, and he had pictured the place with the two big Copleys that he had, restored to their places, with the old silver and china that was still his and Sylvia's, with the grace that his wife would add to it, with his beautiful Angela roaming through it, with the voice of his boy back from college ringing down the halls. And if he could not buy the house now it was useless to think of it any more; for the Jerseys—people that seemed to him even more of a desecration to have in the house than it had seemed to have the president there—would be its owners. Paul Jersey had already made an offer for it, and he had a comparative fortune at his command.

Mr. Rosillon had spoken to the president about his wishes that day when he came down from the old house

"Why, I'd like to help you out, Rosillon," said the president. "I am always glad to oblige you. But, upon my word, I don't think it would be a friendly act on my part. That house would eat up your salary."

"I have been here a long time, Mr. Thursden, and have given the bank faithful service," said Mr. Rosillon, tentatively, "and my best years. Perhaps the directors might think an increase of salary"——

The president opened his eyes and mouth with a strange wrinkling resemblance to a jack-o'-lantern.

"Yes," he said, as soon as he had taken his breath, and losing no time in turning the tables. "The bank has given you employment for a good many years, Rosillon, and has let newer men with newer methods go by. But I don't think its interest in you will let it do more than that."

"I suppose not," said Mr. Rosillon, lowering his handsome head with some depression of manner. "But there is the house I live in now. With that and three or four thousand cash I might arrange a mortgage for the balance that would let me take possession."

"Now look here, Rosillon, what's the use? You know the condition of things as well as the next man. You know I'm in enterprises where I need myself every penny the bank can spare—enterprises before which this paltry affair of an old house has got to step out of the way. Good heavens, man! There's two hundred and fifty thousand cold cash, or as good as, in the safe now, and it's only a part of the money I've got to have to make the 'Pipsissewa' go through. And I don't know, I say, that I would help you buy that house if I could—Jersey offers me twenty thousand spot cash, for it; but it's worth more; there's a large garden to cut up in lots. It would only saddle you with a mortgage worse than a millstone round your neck. No, I advise you as a friend not to think of it. It's a mere matter of sentiment. And you can't let sentiment have anything to do with business. That's my rule, and you see it has met with some success. No, it can't be done, it can't be done," said the president affably. "And it isn't for any want of good will: you'll bear me out in saying I've always been ready with a helping hand, Rosillon, and I'm doing so now in refusing to let you act against your own advantage here." And the great man rang the bell and closed the interview.

It was very evident that Mr. Rosillon acted upon this rule. Mr. Rosillon returned to his desk and added his figures, but his thoughts were up in the dark, blue-green shadows of the old Rosillon drawing-room. They came back with a shock when he saw Paul Jersey pass up the place and go into the president's room, and his breath was hot between his teeth. He felt that he could never endure the fact of Paul Jersey in his father's house—the man who had married the girl he loved, gained the position for which he had fitted himself, kept him out of the land speculation he had seen the first, who, indeed, had got the better of him in every relation in life. To be sure, the girl had proved but a poor piece of humanity, and the wife he married later had been, for all her invalidism, a fireside blessing; but that did not hinder the main proposition. The thought of Jersey's getting that house now was like a cup of gall and wormwood at Mr. Rosillon's lips. It made him shiver with physical repulsion. Jersey's wife—the woman who had broken faith with him—queening it at his father's fireside! Jersey's daughters—the bold, apple-cheeked beauties—in the place that belonged to his little Angela! It could not, it should not be! And then he groaned in his helplessness. And Angela might be at home now or any day, and he knew as well as he knew his interest table that it had been as much the wish of his girl's heart as it had been that of his. And what a vantage it would have given the boy to have such a home as that to which to bring his mates—in time he would have helped his father pay for it. And the more Mr. Rosillon thought of it the bitterer the moment was. Jersey came out of the office, his hands in his pockets, his head a little bent ; he spoke to a man near the door as he went out—one of the clerks, and shook his head. Perhaps the clerk, who dabbled in outside things, was interested with him in the sale of the garden lots, for Mr. Rosillon's ears, preternaturally quick, heard a muttered oath. "And a couple of hundred thousand lying idle in the safe !" the man said.

A half-moment after he had caught these words, Mr. Rosillon glanced about him, with a sudden, half-scared look. Then, as suddenly, great drops started out on his forehead. The figures ran into a straight line. Everything was black around him. "No, no, no," then his stiff lips were forming to say, "I am an honest man!" And his fingers were holding the pen like an iron vise.

"What's the matter, Rosillon?" asked Jersey, pausing a moment at his window, "come out and have something. The air in this beastly place will kill a strong man at sight—sight draft," he said, and went out with half a laugh, half a grimace, as Rosillon shook his head.

Slowly the color crept back into Mr. Rosillon's face, till as he bent it over his ledger the purple hue might have been terrifying had any seen it. He had a quick notion that every one might hear his heart beat like a drum, far away, coming nearer, and bursting with shocks of sound upon the ear. He sat there calmly, as if cut out of stone—stone that inclosed a chaotic fire. At length, however, he looked around him again, to see if any observed the convulsion of nature that had been going on. But everything was the same as if he had not been absorbed into the atmosphere of another and evil world. He looked at the clock, and dipped his pen into the ink, but he did no more work that day. He sat on his high stool, his eyes downcast, but his whole being alert and sparkling from point to point of the scheme that rose before him.

It was so simple that presently he laughed. The bonds were unregistered, the bags of gold were not impossibly heavy, the packages of bills were of no great dimensions. Something like a quarter of a million in all. Perfectly safe. Then he laughed—he was afraid the president's great deal would not come off. And why should it come off ? Were there no equities to hinder it? Was not the man rolling in money now? Was it not unrighteous for him to go on adding millions to his million? And, after all, this little obstruction would be merely a rock in the river of his success; the stream would take a new direction and go on flowing over its golden sands.

Mr. Rosillon left his desk as the president came out of the inner office.

"May I ask," he said, "if Mr. Jersey made an acceptable offer for the place?"

"What place? Oh, no, he didn't. Come now, Rosillon, get that bee out of your bonnet! I don't know that I would sell it to you if you came cash in hand. You're too good a fellow to be ruined by a place that will beggar you with its expense. I shouldn't want the best man alive in the bank, with your opportunities there, and with such temptations as you would be under if you owned that house. I wouldn't trust myself!"

Mr. Rosillon's eyes flashed. "Do you mean to say," he exclaimed, "that after all the years I have served you "—

"With unquestionable integrity. Yes. I only mean to say that when one of the twelve apostles yielded, no one, no one can be trusted to handle another's money who is in great need of it himself. And that is just what I don't want to expose you to."

"You are very good," said Mr. Rosillon, his eyes on the ground. It smote him at that moment that it was the first time he had ever been unable to look a man in the face. He threw back his head and gazed squarely at Mr. Thursden.

"Why, what ails your eyes?" said Mr. Thursden. "Those cursed figures will be the ruin of all of us yet. You'll have to have some glasses. You're not looking at me. You look as if you saw a ghost behind me!"

Rosillon laughed. "No," he said, "it is you that see the ghost. I suppose my eyes are a little tired. I've been going over the expert account in Kane's case—we have the accounts, you know. No; I'm not afraid of the ghost you have raised, Mr. Thursden. I see my way to keep up the place if I can get it. And what I want is that you should keep the matter open till my sister comes here. You know she married a wealthy man, and is a widow—she has had my little girl in Europe with her, and she may be here now on any steamer—she likes surprises. And I think I can make an arrangement with her that will be satisfactory to you, Mr. Thursden."

"Well, well, well; I'll think about it, Rosillon. I'll think about it. But I don't advise it, I don't advise it, you know."

The president pattered away in his big overshoes, and one by one the occupants followed, and at last Mr. Rosillon was left alone at his desk, still poring over the expert accounts.

The watchman came up and lingered.

"What is it, Murphy?" asked Mr. Rosillon, struck suddenly by the circumstance that in his calculations he had forgotten Murphy.

"It's the little gurl, sor," said Murphy, longing in his sore heart for a word of sympathy. "She's down with the fever."

"Very ill?"

"She wor that bad when I came away that I misdoubt me an' she'll be there when I come back, I do. An' me wife's all broke up—ye do be havin' a gurl of your own, Mr. Rosillon"——

"Well, that's too bad, Murphy. Look here—I'll tell you what I'll do." Mr. Rosillon paused, half frightened. If he had forgotten Murphy in his calculations, here was fate playing into his hands. "Yes," he went on, "I shall have to be here, I can't say how late, with these condemned accounts. You go home and stay with the child and be back between one and two to-night—well, say one. I'll see that it's all right." And he ran his fingers down the column before him to escape the thanks that made him feel as if he had picked poor Murphy's pocket.

It might have been ten minutes, it might have been an hour, before Mr. Rosillon looked up again; he could not have said. The lamps were not yet lighted outside. What he had to do must be done now, for the great plate-glass windows were always left bare and a gas jet burned all night, for the better inspection of the place by the street patrol.

What he had to do did not take him long. There were some empty wooden boxes in the basement; there were two or three wax candles that had been used in sealing documents; there was a can of kerosene with which the char-woman now and then rubbed the woodwork, and then there was some powder that awhile ago had been confiscated from one of the messengers who had meant to celebrate too lively a holiday. His hand shook, but it answered for the work. When Mr. Rosillon had left the bank, turning on the gas and locking the door behind him, he knew that two fires were so arranged that they would smoulder for some hours, get headway and break out only in the dead middle of the night, when sleep was deepest, and just before Murphy's return, and that only when so far under way that the work was sure and the explosion was not premature, a trail of powder would explode the powder left in the safe and spread the flames in new directions, destroying so much that no one would be able to say whether the rest had been destroyed or not. The president would not perhaps make his deal, but he had made one deal too many when he had robbed the Rosillons of their father's estate; this would be hardly more than their right and the interest upon it; nothing at all more than he would have made if he had his own twenty years ago. Why should he not take his own? It was not that Mr. Rosillon put his thoughts into deliberate words—but all this was somehow in his consciousness.

A parcel of bonds disposed about one's person, some bundles of bank bills distributed here and there, some small bags of gold dropped in the capacious pockets of a great coat—it was heavy, to be sure; but wealth always carried weight, he said to himself rather grimly, and when Mr. Rosillon left the bank and went up the street, whether it was for a long or a short time, he was a wealthy man.

* * * * * * *

As Mr. Rosillon drew near his gate that evening he looked up and saw the little house blazing with lights above the tops of the spruces. He knew at once what had happened. Angela had come! And his heart almost leaped from his breast. For Angela, this beautiful young girl who was his own flesh and blood, and whose sweet existence had been a marvel to him ever since her birth, was the very darling of his soul, and the one more than any other for whose sake he had found life worth living.

But in another moment he saw how extremely uncomfortable it would be to meet her with the pockets of his great coat sagging in this manner, with the bulging of the hard packets of paper about his breast. He opened the door with his latch key, as quietly, the thought flashed over him, as if he had been a thief, and stepped softly to the little room at the end of the hall which was called his den, and divested himself of his new possessions, not staying, however, to put them away. When the house was still again he would take care of that.

Then he stepped into the hall and slammed the front door, and as he did so and although his mind was full of Angela, the sight of his father's portrait made him think of how well it would look in the old house—there was something stern about that face he had not seen in the light that usually fell upon it. And then in an instant a silver cry, a glad ringing silver cry resounded, and Angela came flying down the stairs. Her boxes had not yet been delivered, and she had taken off her traveling dress and wore a white wrapper of her mother's, and her hair had fallen, one long curl of fair dead gold, upon her shoulder. Her face was pale with excitement, her blue eyes blazed with joy—she seemed to her father in that instant like a spirit of light, an angel of the Grail—but he knew it was his little daughter, and he held her close, close, with a sense of the fulness of life, and with a more breathless sense of the dearness of this perfect being. She was half laughing, she was half crying and flinging her arms around him again and again, unable at first to speak. "Oh, it is so fine to be where you are again, dear, dearest papa!" she cried. "You are so good, you are so strong, you are such a comfort!" And she laid her head on his shoulder and was crying softly, and Mr. Rosillon was crying, too. But to be sure his nerves were a little unstrung. And then Harold was towering behind her, and there was more outcry and embracing; and the mother, pale and thin as a sweet shadow, was coming down with a radiant look on her face; and they all went into the library, where the firelight was the only light, and sat down to enjoy the rapture of being together again.

Angela with her arm about her father's neck, Harold standing on the rug, tall and straight as a young pine tree, the mother on the lounge, breathing now and then a long sigh of happiness.

'Oh, I haven't seen anything so good since I've been gone," said Angela. "This dear old room, the books, the oleander tree—just think of its being in bloom for me! Cathedrals and palaces and pictures are all very well and I'm glad I've seen them. But they're not to be spoken of beside being here and finding you all alive and well, and so dear, so dear!" cried Angela, pulling her father down so that she might put the other arm about her mother.

"I say," said Harold, "where do I come in?"

"You," said Angela, looking up and laughing, "never went out. I used to pity the girls over there who had no brother, the strongest man in his class, the stroke in his boat, and just A1 in his mid-years."

"I'll be content with a B," said Harold.

"When there is an A!" cried Angela. "Why, if he is going to be content with B I shall have to go to the Annex, just to keep him up to A!"

"Sort of a guardian angel," said Harold. "Well, I need one. Every fellow needs one."

"Now, Harold, darling, you know you can't be content with anything less than the best. Papa never was. Why, I can remember papa's saying, 'No, no, the best is good enough for me,' when he used to carry you around on his shoulder. How proud you were of him, papa!" She was standing now on the rug beside Harold, the fire behind her glowing rosy through the edges of her white gown. "And now it is his turn to be proud of you. I used to be when I saw other girls with fussy fathers, and tyrannical fathers, and ignorant underbred ones, and fathers who had made money in strange ways. There was a girl I saw in Algiers—she was dreadfully homesick—and Aunt Sylvia said her father could never come back to this country. I did pity her so! And do you believe," continued Angela, talkative with excitement and pleasure, "there was a man—he seemed quite a gentleman—coming over in the steamer with us, and it seemed he was in charge of officers—he was an embezzler or something dreadful; perhaps it was forgery—and they were taking him home for his trial. And people said his daughter had died of a broken heart on account of it. And when I heard about it I just went into our stateroom and knelt down and thanked God that my dear father was upright to the very core of his being—the very soul of honor. That poor girl," said Angela wistfully, still standing and twisting the long coil of hair about her fingers, "I don't wonder; I should have died, too, if I had been in her place. Because, you know, it must have seemed to her as if the sky itself had fallen—your father does seem to be something next to God. It would be like waking some morning to find there wasn't any sun—there wasn't any God."

'But suppose," said Mr. Rosillon, "that he had never been found out?"

"Well, all the same she would have lost her father! O papa!" she exclaimed, "I do believe that one reason I am so happy is because you are yourself, because you are my father, and I feel so safe! I said to Aunt Sylvia that it seemed like selfish exultation to think that I should never die of a broken heart with my father the best, the truest, the most noble, of the most inflexible honesty—Why, papa!" she exclaimed, she and Harold springing forward together. "What is it? Is anything the matter? You are ghastly"——

"Nothing, nothing," Mr. Rosillon managed to say, waving her off. "The air is a little close—and I have been—perhaps—excited—your coming—your panegyric"— and he laughed uneasily and rose somewhat blindly and reeled and fell backward into his chair. For at that moment the maid, bringing in the lamps had turned them up, and Angela crying out her joyous words, white and tall in the sudden glow of the light, seemed like some sweet but terrible accusing angel standing before him lost in the blackness of hell.

Mr. Rosillon recovered himself in a moment or two, but through the simple dinner to which they were presently summoned he was like one half-dazed.

"My dear," said his wife, "you mustn't let the children's return move you so. You're not eating a morsel."

"He's wondering how under heaven he is to clothe this angel he has drawn down," said Harold. A swift exultation filled Mr. Rosillon that this peerless girl of his would wear purple and fine linen the rest of her days, and that he could give it to her. "I suppose he'll say," added Harold, "that this particular angel is already clothed with righteousness and won't need a bank account."

"Indeed she will," laughed Angela. "And what's more, she'll earn it herself! She is going to do all sorts of good work, and she wants honest money for it, and that won't be money her father gives her"——

Mr. Rosillon started. Why not? What did she mean? What did she know? And then he laughed at himself. Who could know anything? What was there to know?

"For then it would be his gift while she pretended it was hers," Angela went on. "And so you see"——

'You lay great stress on honest money," said Harold "For my part, any money that I can get is honest money enough for me."

"No, indeed!" Angela cried. "A curse would go with it if it wasn't honestly come by. I should be afraid of it"——

"Do you mean, Angela," said her father, "that if I, for instance, gave you money that I had not acquired in an—an honorable manner "——
"What an impossible idea, papa! You of all people! I can't even dream of it"——
"The governor," said Harold, "who is so straight he bends back!"
"Well, we won't dream of it," said Mr. Rosillon. "When is your Aunt Sylvia coming? I wan't to see her about some business. And what is this delay with the trunks? Harold had better go out and telegraph about them." And so Mr. Rosillon held himself together till dinner was over and Angela had brought him his pipe and a light, and Harold having gone off on his errand, they sat around the library hearth again till, the clock outside striking nine, her mother carried off the girl to her own room for an early rest, and left Mr. Rosillon among the falling shadows. A moment he stood up and lifted his arms as if he threw off a burden—a burden, some subtle consciousness told him, that he was always to feel in his child's presence. And then he fell back in his armchair and lay there, so many thoughts whirling disjointedly through his mind that he could seize none and was practically in a sort of stupor. Through the bewilderment of these thoughts whirling with that speed which is so swift that it seems motionless, one figure kept recurring—it was that of a young man whose face burned with shame for his father—it was that of a young man who inherited the quality of a thief and brought all his splendid promise to dust. All that then disappeared only to be followed by another, Angela dead-white and still as clay, and looking at him with great bitter eyes that searched his soul, and he seemed to shrivel before them with a physical agony.

Through the blackness of his mood, far, far away, fell the tone of a bell—a clock was striking ten. Directly afterward a fire alarm sounded, booming close upon his ears, and then he heard the horses dashing by, and every hoof seemed to strike a spark of fire inside his train.

The alarm was for quite another portion of the town; he knew it had nothing to do with the bank; but he dragged himself up mechanically to go to an upper window, as his wont had been upon an alarm. But as he reached the foot of the stairs and glanced up, there stood Angela looking down at him, pausing on the way from her mother's room to her own; and whether she had been saying her old prayers at her mother's side, or whether it were just the whiteness and sweetness of her own spirit, the look on her face appalled him, and he turned suddenly without the good-night for which she was waiting, plunged into his den, and two minutes afterward the door had slammed behind him and he was running for the bank as if he were running a race for the prize of his own soul.

SUCH A PLACE SHOULD BE MADE ATTRACTIVE.

It was a mild, spring night, with an immense sky, through which the wind drove the clouds, and now and then the moon ran out on a long rift and sailed away again into cavernous darkness. Fragrances of blossoming willows and springing grass came in long puffs in the squares where the trees tossed on high and beat and swept the sward and sent strange shadows shifting across the sward. But rushing on with a breathless haste, except, mechanically, when he chanced to meet any one, Mr. Rosillon knew nothing of wind or weather save for some unconscious formula that it was an awful night for a fire. Three or four thoughts ran over and over each other as if his mind were a treadmill— that he must get there, there was a train of powder to be scattered, to be wet, there were some things to be put back in the safe, and there was Angela. Yes, yes, he must get there, he must scatter that powder before the fire reached it, he must get the things into the safe and then give the alarm. Angela's father was an honest man ! He must never see the look on her face and be afraid to meet it ! There was to be no shame and anguish for Angela. And he quickened his steps till he was almost running, and reached the bank door just as a policeman came sauntering up the street on his round.

It seemed as if he never could drag out that key, never could fit it to the lock. His heart was beating in the tips of his fingers—he feared he was too late, he smelled the smoke, he thought he saw light through a chink of the basement—oh, to get in before that policeman caught sight of him ! He was on fire himself from head to foot. And then the bolt turned, the door gave way, a cloud of smoke poured out as he dashed in, gathering as he went the parcels that he carried. He made three strides toward the safe, turned suddenly with a blinding flash in his eyes, heard a report like the crack of doom, and fell, face down, unconscious, with the gold, the bonds, the bills beneath him.

Murphy, who had been unwilling to impose on good nature, and so had hastened back before the time, arrived at the moment the policeman came running up, and together they dragged Mr. Rosillon and the packages he still clutched in a death-grip, out of the smoke of fire and ruin, and turned in the alarm.

"Oh, holy Lord !" said the policeman, as they put him down.

"Do be looking at him !" said Murphy. "He's given the life of him to save the bank money."

"He's done that !

"He's been in it this one and twenty year, an' it wor the same to him as his own childer, more betoken."

When Mr. Rosillon again became conscious he hesitated to open his eyes— his first idea that he was dead, changing to the assurance that without any doubt he was in prison. Yet there had been familiar sounds—and then a quick, wary glance showed him his wife and Angela and the accustomed things of his own room. His lips moved, but he could say nothing.

"It is all right, papa, it is all right!" cried Angela. "And, oh, we are so glad and thankful; we are so proud of you, papa!"

This was a new revelation. And as all things come to him that waits, Mr. Rosillon waited. From time to time in his drowsing, and as he lay silent, he gathered that the fire had been extinguished with but little damage to the bank, and that he had done something heroic. He took the drops and the nourishment that were brought to him and fell off again into deep sleep. He had, of course, been stunned, and there had been some fear of concussion of the brain; a doctor and a hospital nurse were busy about him for a while, he was vaguely aware, and then by slow degrees full consciousness came back to him.

But he said nothing. He was thinking, thinking, feebly at first, and then with all his might, that if he were really to get out of this clear, and all could by any possibility be as before, the cost of the safe and the expenses of the fire could be paid back to the bank in small sums and excite no suspicion, and he could account for his presence there. How could he account for his presence there? Oh, yes, it had slipped his mind—he had let Murphy go. He ought not to have let Murphy go. But the child was sick. And he had felt uneasy and had gone back. That was the truth. If it was not the whole truth, if it were a lie masquerading as the truth, he would have to live under the shadow of so much of it as was a lie all his life. That would have to be his punishment. It seemed to him that it would be an unspeakable relief if he could believe that for that little while he had been mad.

Mr. Rosillon was past all danger, lying back among his pillows, pale and weak, and with hardly any hold on life ; it seemed as if, indeed, it were something loathsome that he dreaded to take up again, when Mr. Thursden came in. Angela opened the door to him, standing up straight and tall like a young silver birch, in her pale green gown, her face rippling with sunshine and joy.

"Well, Rosillon," said Mr. Thursden, "glad to get you back, by all that's good! We thought we were going to lose you one time."

"Mr. Thursden," said Rosillon, his great hollow eyes dark with shadows, as the president's big, warm hand closed around his feeble fingers, "I have been down to the gates of hell !"

"I should have been down there if it hadn't been for you, you mean ! I swear, Rosillon, I haven't any words to express my sense of what you did. never heard, I never dreamed of such devotion to' duty as that ! Why, it's superhuman, such courage! Going to the safe and getting out the valuables for us in the face of that fire and that explosion. I wouldn't have done it for all the gold in Christendom, or the whole plant of 'Pipsissewa.' And I tell you the directors feel just as I do about it. And we've had a meeting and cast about in some way to show our appreciation for your act, and we have decided— I confess the proposition was mine, knowing your wish—that the old Rosillon house shall be a testimonial of our gratitude. And it won't tell the half of it. Where the deuce is my handkerchief? And now, shall we have the deeds made out in your name or in the name of your wife?" And the president, whose voice a moment before had been trembling quite humanly, began to swell visibly with his magnanimity.

"Mr. Thursden," said the other, "if you think I have done my duty"——

"Oh, duty! Duty carried to the highest point! Duty"——

"Then I can take no other reward. I want no reward for doing my duty."

"But, Rosillon, my good fellow"——

"No, no. I have been doing some thinking while lying here. I have turned over what you said—it seems a year, a lifetime ago—that the house would be a millstone around my neck. I don't want it. I can't take it. I am sensible of your goodness, of the generosity of the directors, but it must end here. I will go back to the bank when I am able if you will allow me"——

"Allow you!"

"And all shall be as before. But no reward, Mr. Thursden."

"I see, I see. By George, Rosillon, you're the noblest fellow—no, you're the most foolish, the most quixotic I ever met. Just think twice about the house. Why, if you don't want to keep it you can sell it"——

"Sell that house! No—I—I mean let Jersey have it, if he wants. I will stay here. This house where my wife and I set out the trees and planted the garden, where my children were born, where I have come up out of hell to find —not deserving it—this angel waiting for me," the gloomy eyes resting on Angela, the lips breaking into a smile, "this shall be the Rosillon house, and I will have no other."

CHAPTER NINTH.

In a Dangerous Place.

Thou treadst upon enchanted ground,
Perils and snares beset thee round.
—*Anon.*

Eternal vigilance is the price of liberty.
—*Adapted from Curran.*

O Rose, thou art sick!
The invisible worm
That flies in the night,
In the howling storm,
Has found out thy bed
Of crimson joy,
And his dark secret love
Does thy life destroy.
—*William Blake.*

If the germs gave the fever, why didn't they have the fever? How could they give a thing they didn't have?—*A Child's Story.*

The river Rhine, it is well known,
Doth wash your city of Cologne,
But tell me, nymphs, what power divine
Shall henceforth wash the river Rhine?
—*Coleridge.*

Better to hunt in fields for health unbought
Than fee the doctor for a nauseous draught.
—*Dryden.*

Health is the second blessing that we mortals are capable of—a blessing that money cannot buy.—*Izaak Walton.*

The Health of the Home.

In obtaining this house which is to be so dear a shelter, be it on the asphalt or under the green bough, we have of course been particular about the site, for it may be "writ large but the country is healthful only when it *is* healthful," and this sanitary condition is not to be taken for granted. Rose-bushes in the door-yard in too frequent cases supersede drain-tiles under it, and the cupola too rarely holds a ventilating shaft. In the city there are many houses that are built over old water courses, and the would-be occupant is wise when he procures an old map of the city, which will let him know whether or not he is subject to this danger.

It is the houses built over these old choked or diverted water courses, whose occupants are the sufferers from malaria. In the country house the chief risks to health come from the pollution of the water supply, and of the air, by contact with waste matter. Owners of property are left to build or not to build their drains and to bestow them perhaps as ignorance and indolence prompts, with no official supervision, and the consequence is, that sometimes the loveliest spots are nests of low fever, diphtheria and dysentery.

UNABLE TO LOOK A MAN IN THE FACE.

Rock and Gravel.

In choosing the location of the country house, it is to be supposed that we have given preference to a region of gravelly or sandy soil, or where we could have founded it on a rock, clay soils holding the surface water too long, and making the air damp and chilly.

Wherever the waste could contaminate drinking water with putrefying organic matter, we shall have found it the safer way to substitute rain-water for cooking and drinking purposes. If the roof and gutters are kept clean, and the rain water collected and stored in cisterns, and then filtered, all which can be easily done, the supply will be sufficient, and perfectly healthful. It is, however, wiser to boil it for drinking, then cool, and afterward aerate it. If filters are used for purification, they must be taken apart and the strainers carefully washed and dried at least once a fortnight. Otherwise they become useless, the sand and charcoal retaining organic impurities, and imparting a disagreeable taste to the water.

No kitchen slops, either from wash-tubs or dish-pan, must be thrown upon the ground, or into that open drain too often found at the back of the usual country dwelling. Organic waste festers in the hot sun, and the saturated ground gives forth incense fit for Beelzebub, god of flies. All household waste should be removed as fast as it gathers, and lightly buried. In the dark laboratory of the earth noxious matter is turned at once to sweet and wholesome uses. Lawn and garden thrive on what is fatal to man. But if this can not be done, then the kitchen waste should be burned two or three times a day. No standing pails of garbage should be allowed to tempt flies and defile the fragrant air.

The Cellar.

The condition of the cellar is far more important than that of the parlor. In light rooms dirt is comparatively harmless. In dark places it is a lurking danger. No old wood, no vegetables, no rubbish of any kind, should be allowed to cumber the cellar, which should have a water-proof and air-tight floor, to prevent ground air and soil moisture from rising to the living-rooms. Whether the floor and walls be cemented or not, it is necessary that all cellar doors and windows should be daily opened for free circulation of air.

The water from the eaves, if not saved in a cistern, should be carried so far from the house in well-laid pipes that there will be no contiguous surface dampness or wet foundation walls. Dampness is a ready vehicle for disease, as well as a fruitful cause of it. Another source of danger is decaying vegetable refuse in garden or grounds. Careless servants leave rhubarb leaves, prunings of vines, or weeds wherever they fall, instead of taking them to the compost pit or burning them. If they are out of sight they are out of mind, till they recall themselves in visitations of headaches, aching bones, or irritable tempers.

In short, eternal vigilance is the price of liberty from disease, as from other usurpers. Voltaire said that incantations would destroy a flock of sheep —*if* administered with the proper quantity of arsenic. But if we put a superstitious faith in country air, to the neglect of constant scrutiny and intelligent precaution, it is likely that our last state will be worse than our first. It is when the early autumn weather sets in, bringing cool nights, treading close upon the heel of hot days, that the demon of fever and infection is most apt to walk abroad, and our house-holders will find there is no time so good as the later autumn weather, just as the black frost falls, for exorcising the being that makes such destruction. Then, in the safe chilliness of the nights and days the places that he has haunted can be barricaded against his return, and the nests in which his evil attendance has brooded can be cleared of their presence for once and all.

The Prevention that Is Better than Cure.

It is when pickling and preserving and house-cleaning are over that the good house-wife will turn her attention to these affairs, more vital by far than anything that conduces merely to the pleasure of the eye, or of the table, and will look about her to see if her drains and sinks, her well and water-pipes, are in good order, and if her cellar is what a cellar should be, underlying as it does, the whole life of the house, and capable of sending, from its position in the sub-structure, bane or blessing, pure air or fetid, through every crevice of the dwelling. And there is no circumstance, by-the-way, that points more plainly to the wisdom of making every exertion to own one's home, of foregoing luxury and display and all other gratification that can be foregone with safety to soul and body, and laying away the wherewithal to purchase the place with which one can do as one chooses, and, uprooting what is already wrong, plant wells and dig drains where it is best: wisdom, since although the expenditure of the same money in choice food, in fine raiment, or in costly equipage may be even more delightful, there are no delights that are equal to those of health, and health can only be permanently secured when we are masters of our own situation. If the drain that receives the outflow of the house connected with the refrigerator be too near the well, or if the conduits from the sink, apt to be made of wood, and frequently leaking on the way, are equally near, there is no human power that can bar out the infectious fever from that house except the removal of the drains and conduits to a safe

STEPPING STONES TO HAPPINESS.

REELED AND FELL BACKWARD.

distance; for, inappreciably to taste or scent, atom by atom, drop by drop, the well is poisoned, the milk in the refrigerator is poisoned, and life is surer and better underneath the dew of the upas-tree.

But the position of these things it is not always in the housewife's power to determine, and she must make the best of things as they are, and the best is to have them cleansed yearly in the frosty weather, when the evil germs set free at their opening perish of the withering chill before they can reach the stomachs and lungs of the inmates of the house.

A thorough cleansing of these spots every fall is not so expensive as a course of doctor's visits, and does not mount up like the druggist's bill; and if it is disagreeable, it is one of the prices we must pay for enjoyment of comfort and health, remembering that there is no such thing as immunity from the trouble of this oversight while in a state of civilization; that this oversight, in fact, is the groundwork of civilization, and that in matters of sickness and suffering, as in matters of politics, the old adage holds equally true, that "eternal vigilance is the price of liberty."

But if it is ruinous to poison the water of the well from which we drink, it is quite as ruinous to poison the air which we breathe, and that is the part in the house which the neglected cellar has it in its power to play. Wherever vegetables have been stored, there some have run over the bins and been trodden on the floor, or have run into the dark corners of the bins and been overlooked, till they have decayed and transmitted their decay to others; there has been a "sup of milk" spilled on the floor, a bit of butter, a few drops of the drippings, some greasy brine from the barrel, some festering stuff from a broken bottle; there is a bit of mould here, a fungus there—in short, the witches' caldron is as ready as when the witches danced round it on the heath of Forres, and threw into it their horrid ingredients. Let now a wet season arrive upon this condition of things, let a hot and humid August come, or let a January thaw of snow and slush set in, let some water trickle into the cellar, or let the stones of the wall merely absorb the dampness and suffer it to ooze through there, and the putrid air that steals up through the studding of the walls, behind every partition, up beside every chimney, and through every door and every crack, brings disease stalking in with the death's-head behind it, only to go out of the door feet foremost.

The Only Curse on the House.

"There's a curse on the house, sure," said an old servant once. "The children all die as sune's they're born. The first of 'em went with the dysentery; then Miss Ellie, the darlint, follows, with—what's this ye're afther callin' it?—the dipthairy; the twins have gone, too, with the scarlet faver; and there's the master down himself now with the typhus."

"Perhaps the fault is in the house," we suggested.

"Dade a bit of it, thin!" cried the faithful woman. "Wasn't it claned in the spring, and, as ye may say, scraped? And wasn't there bushels of the wet dirt, such as you niver see, carried out of the cellar and spread over the garden, till the corn was that splendid the one ear was big enough for two?"

There surely was a curse on that house—the curse of carelessness, uncleanness, and unthrift; and the hands that would have been thrust into fire for those dead children had dealt them their death-blows.

Throughout the world's history everywhere this subject of pure air in the dwelling has received the attention of the thoughtful, and been laughed at by the ignorant. Certain of the ancients had a fancy that various plants of pungent odor prevented infection, and they set them in the way and about their homes—a practice at which while we of to-day smile, the camphor bag is carried in our pockets whenever small-pox or cholera prevails. When the plague raged in Italy, all the people who were able left Rome and flocked into a little town round which the laurel grew in luxuriance. We imagine there could have been nothing in it, or else the growth of the laurel would have been fostered round that Italian city into which some friends of ours once strolled and found the stone and sculptured houses, the deep-rutted paved streets, the churches and market-place and stalls, all intact but overgrown, and forsaken by every living soul. The fever had been there before them, and had desolated it.

LOOKING DOWN AT HIM.

Yet physicians have thought that a fearful cholera season was caused by an absence of ozone from the atmosphere, that bracing and life-giving principle which we seek at the sea-side, and which is largely generated by electrical and phosphoric agencies. And as many plants—notably, it is said, various laurels, lavender, hyacinth, mignonette, and the bergamot orange—evolve ozone in the oxidation of their aromas, and as in our own day the eucalyptus has been found to be of such immense value in malarial regions in absorbing and converting the poison, it would seem as if there were some spark of reason in the idea of the ancients just mentioned, and that they did not plant the most aromatic flowers and offer the richest balsams on the altar of the pestilence for nothing.

But this is at best somewhat fanciful and experimental, and at any rate none of us can rely on such uncertain aid in securing the safety of our daily and nightly breathing should we try it. Let us plant as many odorous flowers as we will about our dwellings, it will be none the less necessary for us to purge those dwellings of all accumulated foulness whenever the season arrives in which it can be done with safety to ourselves and others, and whitewash our cellar walls and sprinkle their floors, and all other equally dangerous spots with copperas, or with that guardian of domestic life, the ill-smelling but beneficent chloride of lime. Only by such provision can we hear the dreadful names of the autumnal diseases without a shudder, and only when we have exercised it have we a right to consider the load of responsibility lifted from our shoulders.

We or Providence to Blame?

When we read of great natural calamities, the floods, the freezings, the fires, or of the great unnatural ones, the murders, and wars, and famines, we class them under the head of Acts of Providence, forgetful that almost every one of them is within our own control. We read that a distant city is little better than one great pest-house with the small-pox; that diphtheria is seen to be moving—by the reports that come into the physicians' offices, and are jotted again on the map—with the slow but sure tread of an army on a march, through the midland country; that the scarlet fever is rampant like a terrible fiend in the North. The only one of these things that we make any positive preparation for is the small-pox; we secure ourselves from it, as far as may be, before it comes, by vaccination, and society puts us in quarantine if it should reach us, and demands fumigation and disinfection when it has left us. For the others, they always seem less tangible and possible; they are far off, and they may not affect us; we seldom dream of any preparation to hinder their fell visits, and society laughs at the idea of extra precaution to prevent the diseases from spreading, or of much attempt at purification after they have passed and left us for fresh prey. So much is this the case that we have even known patients in diphtheria to be incensed at not receiving the kisses customary in health; have seen fine ladies making calls in a house where two or three children were down with scarlet fever, quite careless as to whether their next call was to be made in one where the children had not yet received the dark guest; and have met with the servants of a house as yet safe chatting cozily in the kitchen with the servants of the house where the nursery was a hospital of contagion; and this when that especial disease is the most dreadful in all the known category of diseases; both at its height and in its results, and when the germs of its contagion live for weeks, and are so subtle and powerful that they have even been carried hundreds of miles in a letter.

We fear the small-pox, it would appear, chiefly because it robs us of what beauty or comeliness we may possess; because it isolates us from neighbors and condemns us to some weeks of solitude; because it occasions so much more fuss and inconvenience in the house than most forms of illness do. It can hardly be anything else that moves us particularly in regard to it, since it is not more loathsome, not more painful, seldom if ever more deadly,

HE REMEMBERED THE PLACE.

than the other diseases named. To be sure, these other diseases are the particular foes of children, while the former attacks ourselves as well, and so brings a more selfish element into play when we are people who have no children; but when we are people who have children, there is no suffering we would not take upon ourselves rather than have scarlet fever and diphtheria come where our children are. But every physician will assure you that he prefers to deal with the small-pox rather than with the others, for that has a plain and open course, and he always knows where to find it day by day; but the fiend of its kindred fever burrows in the dark, and sometimes undermines the whole foundations of life before its deadly presence is suspected. When there shall be abroad among all people, as there is now among intelligent and well-informed people, the same wholesome horror of scarlet fever and diphtheria that there is of small-pox and of leprosy and of typhus, the world will begin to make some headway in the effort to be rid of these cruel desolators.

Children's Diseases.

We all love our children as we love ourselves; it is, in fact, an instinct rather than a virtue; and we would protect them at the sacrifice of our own lives. But let there be an epidemic of this nature in the town where we live, and, heroic as our will may be, with what discretion do we exercise it? In the first place, we shut the babies up from the free air lest a whiff of the sickness should enter at the window or door, and so we force them to breathe, to large extent, a vitiated atmosphere that makes them the easier prey if attacked. Then we allow them to play with the cats and the long-haired dogs which have access everywhere, running up everybody's back-yard at all hours, and prevented by nothing known from carrying the contagion of any disease in their convenient coats. In the mean time, if a stranger comes to the house, ignorant though we may be of what he is and where he came from, we never think of such a thing as hindering him from petting the children if he pleases. We keep no disinfectant in constant use after we know the epidemic exists; and finally, we let the children have as much as they wish of the companionship of the maids, who, by reason of their crowded church-going, are so very likely to gather the contagion in their garments.

Look a moment at that last statement. Disease finds its favorite food in the region of poverty, bad air, narrow quarters, and in the unhealthy blood made by poor and insufficient diet. It is universally acknowledged that such spots are the hot-bed and propagating ground of everything of the sort. The unfortunate people whom the disease thus victimizes, frequently going through the trial without a physician, knowing nothing of fumigation or disinfection, and laughing to scorn what they happen to hear of it, seldom denying themselves the pleasure of free going and coming, can not but be the means of sadly spreading the evil from which they suffer. If there are half a dozen families in a house, as not unfrequently happens, and the sickness be in one of those families, none of the well members of that family would think of staying at home from church, and of course none of the members of the other five families who do not feel themselves to be affected; and what is there, then, to prohibit them from taking out with them and scattering through the congregation the germs of the disease, and the maid from innocently and ignorantly bringing them home in her shawl to the ruin of the child whom she also loves in common with the rest of the house, and whom she would do her utmost to save? It seems then as if it were not at all too much to say that it is no act of Providence by which we are smitten when such disease invades us, but only our own neglect and that of others.

Disinfectants.

It would be a simple and easy thing to keep a dish of carbolic acid or other better disinfectant, exhaling in the house in order to kill, or to make the effort to kill, and, at all events, weaken, any of the poisonous germs that might effect an entrance on the air; to dissolve a little chloride of lime; to burn a pinch of coffee every now and then, or some sugar or vinegar: if it is disagreeable, it is safe; and no one can positively assert what prevention it might not prove to far worse trouble than a slightly offensive odor ever is. We are told that it was given to man to "reduce the earth." When in some distant era that shall be effectually done, it is to be hoped that the germs of many of these terrors will have no breeding-place left there. But till then it is our duty to assist in the great work; and we venture to believe that if every house where such contagious and heart-breaking disease is found were to be quarantined by the yellow flag as small-pox is, and if it were fumigated with sulphur smoke, purified with atomized disinfectants during the reign and on the disappearance of the trouble, the ravages of the malignant monster, desolating households as it goes, would be largely checked, if the monster itself were not thus finally destroyed from the face of the earth.

The Scarlet Fever.

We can need all these precautions for nothing so much as for the scarlet fever, which, although like death it has all seasons for its own, nevertheless seems always to rage with more vehemence when the mercury gets down among the small figures.

Unlike their habit when the measles are in question, which many mothers think it desirable for their children to have early, there is almost no pains which wise mothers will not take to avert from their children this evil of scarlet fever, than which no other disease is so much to be dreaded. And it is justly that this dread is felt; for the scarlet fever, even if the little patient escapes with life, is likely to poison the blood, to injure the brain, to destroy the hearing, or to affect to deadly purpose some vital organ with long and slow and painful decay. Poe's terrible story of the *Masque of the Red Death* had in it some elements of the horror that belongs to this pestilence that walketh by noonday—and I have known an aged physician who never could speak of this especial form of fever without tears springing to his eyes, so much misery to child and parent and household had he seen it bring about.

When we see a disease which, even on recovery, drags after it in most instances long sequelæ of other ailments, often veiled and obscure and not easy to reach and treat—kidney affections, lung troubles, glandular difficulties, idiocy, and the rest—we can judge of the virulence of the original thing itself. And if by any chance we see the child itself enduring the first distress, the final agony, crying out in blind wonder at its own suffering, yielding up its brief life perhaps in delirium, perhaps in faintness, with the pangs of suspense and despair of the mother bending over it, and the desolation of the home it leaves so empty of its sweet presence, till it seems as if there were nothing but suffering in the world—when by any chance we have seen all this, have fought our own fight with a disease capable of working such woe—then it seems to us that we would almost give our own life rather than be the means of diffusing such trouble, of increasing the suffering of the world, of bringing such pain and sorrow upon another person who loved a child.

Yet it is an almost universal thing for families—every individual of whom would feel all this shrinking from increasing the sorrows of the world—instead of doing their utmost to prevent the spread of the terrible infection, acting with an almost criminal carelessness in the matter, and that, of course, with no intention other than good ones, but partly from ignorance and partly from thoughtlessness and partly from a general trusting to luck. There is a case of fever in the house; they isolate it, and then they think they have done their whole duty; they themselves, if not needed in attendance, go and come, here and there, in and out, as they please. "Oh, it is only a slight case!" they answer you if you question their action, forgetful of the fact that the most malignant form can be developed from the contagion of the very slightest case of scarlatina, scarlatina being the generic name of the disease in any form, and not merely of its slightest development. The doctor goes and comes unavoidably through the hall and up and down the common stairway between the door and the sick-room; nobody knows how many germs of the disease clinging to the woolen fibres of his garments to be scattered in the hall and on the stairs, over which the rest of the family pass necessarily many times a day, to gather them up in their own clothes, and have them ready to disseminate whenever they go out among people. The nurses, too, and those in attendance on the sick-room, go up and down into the kitchen and elsewhere about the house, carrying with them more or less of the atmosphere of the room and all that belongs to it, again to be possibly caught up by those who have never gone near the patient; and, as I have said, the very dogs and cats about the place, to say nothing of the flies, are liable to gather the dangerous unknown force in their long fur, and bring it to the other members of the family. If then these other members of the family, thus virtually contaminated, go out freely on the street, what deadly work is it they do, all unintentionally and unconsciously, what seeds of death and sorrow do they scatter with every wave of their garments as they walk and as they encounter people on the streets or venture into houses!

Doubtless it is hard and unpleasant, a sort of imprisonment, indeed, for people not immediately concerned in the work for the sick to shut themselves up when such a trouble is in the house; but there are always ways for them to get enough fresh air to keep themselves in health. And for the rest of it, if the thing comes, it should be received like any other dispensation, and borne with becoming strength and self-denial, even if that requires abstinence from church and concert and call, the foregoing of the morning shopping and the afternoon stroll. For fully three weeks after the patient is out of danger and convalescing a process called desquamation—a shedding of the scarf skin—goes on with the little person, and every flake of that cuticle wafted abroad is but inoculation of the disease wherever received. Isolation, then, can not be too much regarded; every one in the world must now know the value and necessity of disinfection, in its most extended form; but many forget or are not aware of the need of this complete isolation. There is nothing fine in the courage or bravado of those who would visit or go errands to the dwellings where this sickness exists. It is very easy to be courageous for other people, and it is other people, and not one's self, that the grown person endangers by going into the way of the disease, and those other people helpless little children. Grown people are seldom in much danger of receiving the contagion for themselves, but they can carry it in their clothes; and knowing this, and knowing the alarming vitality of the germ, and how long afterward it can maintain this devastating vitality with unimpeached power, they would be acting with total want of principle, and even of decent human charity, if they did not avoid going to the house where scarlet fever exists, and did not also avoid those who come out of that house. When people who are aware of the danger do avoid those who have come out from these fatal doors, it is not for themselves, it should be remembered, nor indeed always for those dear to them as life itself, but quite as often for the sake of those dear as life to others; and no one has a right to be offended at this avoidance. It is not the people themselves who are thus avoided; it is the terrible trouble whose companionship lurks about them. The very individuals who avoid them, or who feel compelled to condemn their want of consideration and care in going abroad, would, it is very likely, go to their houses and remain with them, helping and cheering them as long as the necessity lasted, but not daring to go out into the world again while the least danger of communicating the evil remained. Instead of being offended at the avoidance, all persons, on the other hand, would do well to prevent the necessity of such avoidance by keeping out of the way themselves and by voluntarily and spontaneously, with noble even if Quixotic regard, for others, maintaining themselves and their house in a sort of quaran-

tine, which, uncomfortable as it may be to them, is infinitely better than sickness and death and the sorrow of vacant houses to others.

The Children of the Poor.

When all has been done that can be done to secure sweet air and surroundings to the family, whether in town or country, the heads of the household have reason to congratulate themselves on the immunity that their own darlings have when contrasted with the condition of the children of the very poor, especially of those in the worst districts of the city.

Often when people who have loved and cared for their children to the last degree have at length lost them, they think that if their children had been allowed to run at large, unwashed, unkempt, unfed, all but undressed, in the wet and in the sun, they would have been left alive; and they look with envy at the washerwoman's sturdy babies rolling in the gutter as they go by, while their own dear ones, on which they spent such cares, are laid away in silence.

Their complaint and their envy, however, betray simply an ignorance that is widespread concerning the very great mortality among the children of the poor in cities. With these poor it is only the sturdy and the hardy that do not die in infancy; those are examples of the survival of the fittest. When they, in turn, have children of their own, those children inherit a great deal of their parents' hardiness, and live through nearly everything but murder. But murder comes to them; and the community allows the murderer to stalk boldly unchallenged at broad mid-day, while he decimates the ranks of those that can not afford houses by themselves, with light and space, pure air, pure water and dry floors.

Of all the children rolling in the gutters only a mere fraction endure the rough treatment and live. In damp dwellings, pervaded by the foul smell of countless sinks and deposits of filth, with fever already, doubtless, in more

than one of all the many rooms of the tenement, with little to eat, with no
cleanliness, with unhealthy beds, with insufficient warmth in winter, with
terrible heats in summer, what an amount of strength does it not need in order to meet such ills and conquer them! The mother who nurses these
children in their babyhood is half starved herself. As soon as they are old
enough to be left, and sometimes before, she is obliged to let them look out
for themselves while she is away at her daily drudgery, from which she returns to them heated and tired out, and all unfit; a little older, and they are
out-doors in her absence, fighting with the great Shanghai for an apple-core
or with the neighboring bulldog for a bone, or in-doors setting fire to their
clothing; and woe betide them, at all times, if they fall sick, for then the
whole grand army of noxious things marches into the breach, and it is found
almost impossible for very sick children of these quarters to recover, if left
in the place where they fell, as any physician will tell you who has had the
pain of seeing these children mowed down. What the effect of their surroundings is may be judged from the following instance: "About the year
1767 it was ascertained that not more than one in twenty-four of the poor
children received into the work-houses in London lived to be a year old; so
that out of two thousand and eight hundred, the average number annually
admitted, two thousand six hundred and ninety died. This alarming mortality induced the Parliament to pass an act obliging the parish officers to send
their infant poor to be nursed in the country at a proper distance from town.
After this measure was adopted only four hundred and fifty out of the whole
number died annually, and the greater part of those deaths happened during
the three weeks that the children were kept in the work-houses." Human
nature—at any rate, its physical portion—has not changed during the century
sufficiently to weaken the force of such a statement, and no broader commentary can ever be made on the way in which every country wastes its bone and
sinew in permitting such a state of things to continue, and in not making the
purification of its by-ways and alleys a matter of public economy. Of course
more than air is needed—water, time in which to use it, and food—but clean
air would go a great way toward obviating every evil, and would doubtless
vastly decrease the bill of mortality. Air that is unvitiated is positively essential to the health of children in dwellings and out-doors; it is by its means
that the blood is oxygenated, purified of ill elements, and kept bounding
along the veins; and it is through the medium of bad air that a fearful throng
of diseases are admitted to the tender system. And meanwhile, however it
may be with the poor, there is many a mother among those by no means poor
who thinks her own dead darling wanted for nothing, when, if she but knew
the truth, it wanted the air of heaven, and the air with which she so carefully

surrounded and shut it in, the air of her foul cellar and unpurified sinks, was its murderer.

When we have abolished all our nuisances, we will find that we have abolished with them one almost as bad as many of the others, that of the omnipresent fly, the little wretch that makes life in town or suburb equally hard to bear, but who will not live in multitude unless he has foul provender on which to batten. I remember seeing at an entertainment of one of the many minstrel troops of old times, whose members, by the way, a friend of the colored people declared were blacker inside than outside, for all their "quips and cranks and wanton wiles," a performance, known as the "Lively Flea," which always elicits roars of laughter and rounds of applause, as the play-bills have it. It is a very simple performance, a mere monodrame; for it consists solely of one rather ragged colored person sitting in a chair and playing his banjo—the other performer being invisible, not to say imaginary. As the player dreamily picks the string and hums the strain, he just as dreamily pauses to fillip his ear, as if something had disturbed him there, but it was not much matter, and goes on with his tune. But before the end of another bar the right hand leaves the string again to give a heartier fillip on another spot, and still the tune goes on; when suddenly the left hand, flinging the neck of the banjo to the right, gives, no fillip, but a good sound slap on a fresh portion of the person, and the music resumes its course again, as if that thing was settled. But hardly has another stave of the sweet song been sung—so sweet that the audience begins to be as much annoyed by that lively flea as the sufferer more directly concerned—when up goes the right hand dreamily again and seems to rub away some slight thing on the cheek or in the whisker, and no sooner is that done than the left is obliged to explore the back of the neck, and the right picks a string and darts off to the sole of the foot, picks another and flies to the left scapula, picks another and deals a blow at a knee-cap, suddenly catches the banjo by one string as the left hand in an agony flies to the distracted forehead, and the melody of the banjo and of the song breaks up incontinently in a sort of double and treble shuffle dance, in which hands, feet, head, shoulders, hips, and banjo all join in pursuit of that lively flea, which is caught and cracked to the satisfaction of the spectators, in order that the singer may calmly and sweetly conclude his song.

Well, we all laughed at the poor plantation hand and his flea, some of us in spite of ourselves, and all of us without the least idea that scarcely would the summer come before we ourselves would be as laughable objects, figuring in just such a drama, with the simple difference that the place of that invisible lively flea would be taken by the only too visible and just as lively fly—that nimble wretch that the moment we have finished proclaiming our July independence, surrounds us with his legions, is in our bread, in our tea, in our ink, in our cup generally; that gets crushed in our books, lost in the labyrinth of our hair, tickles our eyes, grudges us our flesh and blood, makes our life a burden to us!

The Lively Fly.

Yet what an innocent being the little creature seems when in his single blessedness he hums about the wintry pane! A cheerful and companionable soul left over from the summer, and managing to exist on what sunshine he can find in our window. If we do not hold him really in affectionate regard then, yet we would no sooner harm him than harm a household pet. We put a bit of sugar in his path, we brush down the spider that waylays him and we feel flattered if he deserts his luminous retreat to pay a call to the wax in our work-basket, or ramble round the margin of our inkstand, or stroll across our hand. But when at length the summer comes we realize in ourselves all the difference that exists between the calm inhabitant of temperate zones and the fiery and cruel native of the tropics. Ruskin tells us that the modification of the curve of the drip-stone in the Lombard architecture, as seen in the North and seen again under Italian skies, marks the whole round curve of the earth between those distant parallels; and just as broad a curve of the earth is shown in the difference in our feelings toward the fly in December and in July, and we pursue the little innocent of other weather as vindictively as though he was some wild beast out of his lair; as vindictively as he in his turn pursues us.

It seems impossible to us then to believe that we were once so weak as to regard him as harmless and show him mercy. If we really did, we anathematize the folly that in saving one saved the mother of millions. That little being, so busy, so blithe, so much occupied with his toilette, is no longer a friendly sprite, but has become foul and unclean, singly impish, and in multitude demoniac. His pleasant song has changed to a bagpipe drone, save when it gathers in a shrill alarm of attack. We hear it faintly across our dreams, sounding the signal as the first flush of the aurora runs before the dawn; and from that dead hour of prime till at last we rise, haggard and unrested, and driven from our stronghold, we are engaged in a hand-to-hand strife with him for the possession of our nose or ears or eyes, whichever it is that he may have taken a fancy for, and we feel like that dull book-magnate that Mr. Browning threw into the puddle of the hollow tree, where the little live creatures "tickled and toused and browsed him all over." We descend to breakfast. Be the safeguards what they may, we find two or three of him in the cream jug, a swarm of him in the sugar bowl; he hovers over the chops, gets mired in the butter, watches his chance for the morsel on the way to our mouths, and we feel a sort of surprise on breaking the eggs or the baked potatoes that he does not tumble out of them. There is not a point of the rest of the day that he fails to dispute with us. There is a mould in the inkstand; we fish it out— it is a raft of flies. We sit down with our sewing;

he comes and sticks needles and pins into us. He is up our sleeve, down our neck, between our lips. He grows aware of the charms of the baby in her warm and rosy nap, and eats her up alive. We go for our bath, he is there before us; we go to dinner, and he has rendered us suspicious of every object, and taken the zest from appetite; while at tea he mixes himself with the blueberries, and turns plain cake to currant. We brush him off, and he returns, with a defiant and insulting buzz and threat, nearer than before; we aim a blow at him, and inflict a fatal one upon ourselves. We hail a spider as a bosom friend. And at last we grow tired of the unequal contest, and resolve upon getting sleep while we may, and forgetful of the morning's rout, we ascend to the cool seclusion of our respective rooms. Already half asleep we open the door, and the instant the light enters up starts from their own slumbers on every coigne of vantage a cloud of witnesses, filling all the air with that hot and hateful hum; and we close the windows, and set down the lamp, and tie a knot in the end of a towel, and go to work and slay like Samson.

C'est le premier pas qui coû'e. After that we feel like the Malays, or the Berserkers, who run with their big knives, crying, "Kill! kill!" With what vigor we prosecute destruction, and are almost destroyed ourselves in the effort! We set dishes of water, in which the patent poisoned paper is soaking, about the house, and the flies drink and die, and the kitten, beloved plaything, and the Spitz, the baby's faithful guardian, eat the fallen victims of that poison, and die, too. We procure cruel sheets of a viscid preparation and lay them in tempting spots, and the flies alight never to extricate themselves from the toils again, and a gust of wind blows those sticky sheets over our sewing, upon our best book-rack, upon our new silk, and the flies avenge themselves in dying. Finally we buy a cage, where a wire cone fits inside of a wire cylinder, a tiny aperture in the top of the cone admitting the prey to the cylinder but not appearing very obvious to him again, and we observe with eagerness the adventuring fly as he slowly explores that cone and approaches that aperture. What a dramatic interest attaches to the moment! He is the hero of a tragedy—he is David in the cave's mouth—he is Jean Valjean. He nears the opening of the trap: will he mount? will he descend? He thinks better of it; he goes down, and our hearts go down with him; he wheels, he puts his head over the brink—for ourselves, we palpitate—he considers, he crawls boldly in, he is lost! And wretches that we are—with but little difference in all these centuries between ourselves and those Roman women who watched wild beast and gladiator fight in the arena, and turned their thumbs down at the end—we feel paid for all our vexation, and we watch fly after fly passing through the fatal aperture, and we go off to sleep, secure in the slaughter of Patroclus and his men—to wake up and find Achilles and his myrmidons in the field, fell avengers.

For it was only a momentary victory, a mere *ruse de guerre;* and we are half inclined to abandon ourselves to fate and the fly, and to believe that coming into the world before the extermination of vermin we came an æon too soon, till we remember a happy possibility, and at every window we have a screen of wire gauze, better than the Chinese wall against our enemy, and a thing which the least ingenuity can devise and shape, and we make that place a desert so far as the fly is concerned, and breathe again in peace, sure that we are not going to be tickled wide awake out of our pet nap, and that we are not going to be inoculated with all sorts of diseases from that little proboscis that fed last one knows not where. And yet fools that we are, we find ourselves in the end regarding the one fly left over and humming in the window-pane as we did before—as a cheerful and companionable sort of cherub, who reminds us of summer and its vanished glories.

At Autumn Time.

And when we have enjoyed our screens all summer, and have seen to sink and drain and spout and cellar, and to all the work necessary to health which we find it best to do in the fall, whether our lives be cast in town or country, we have time to look about and enjoy a world of small dramas still going on about us, and at which we may assist if we will as spectators. One observes then, for instance, just as much in the city park as in the rural field, the way nature works in her laboratory, the way in which the plants prepare themselves for their wintry term, and in which the little wild animals, even the squirrels and their kind in town, make themselves ready for that great general enemy, the cold.

The Birds When the Days Shorten.

There is nothing more interesting to watch than the birds and their habits, at the time when the days begin to shorten; the manner in which they congregate and confabulate in daily increasing numbers; the swarms on swarms of them that suddenly rise from some low meadow as you drive by, and for one beautiful moment darken the sky, while their multitudinous wings quiver and beat and separate; the trial flights in which they seem to be practicing for the long migration; the wonderful music that their innumerable shapes seem to dot along the bars made by the telegraph and telephone wires where they alight; the vast chattering and humming wherever they are; and the profound indifference of those birds that have no idea of making a journey, but that intend to take the winter as they find it, notably the town sparrows.

How much charm these bright beings have added to the year, when one

has been where one could observe them, it would not be easy to compute; for who can tell the value of a lilting measure, or weigh the worth of a flash of color? The thrill of gladness one feels when, almost before the ground is bare of snow, a robin's pipe is heard; the sweetness that fills the dead prime of the day when one awakes before the dawn sends his flushes up the east, and hears the world alive with music—who would forego these that has known them, or change them for other rapture that out-door nature gives? What amusement they make when, fat and saucy with all the stolen cherries, they skip along the grass at your side, and presently are disputing with your fingers the very pear and plum as they ripen! And what heartsome pleasure they give in their first and in their second nesting, as they steal the thread from your spool on the window-sill, the string from the baby's toy and even alight upon the old horse himself to pluck some good strong hairs from his tail for the better security of the new cradle—anything exceeding their sturdy impudence never having been known. Then come the excitements of the brood to the on-lookers—the amazement at the tremendous greed of the little ones, and the untold lives sacrificed at their shrines; the admiration of the show of fondness and industry by the father, who is fabled to share the labors equally with the mother, but who brings, comparatively speaking, very few worms to the young Molochs, and sings only when he thinks it is about time that his wife was done with this business; and the horror and anxiety when one of the fledgelings falls from the lofty nest—out of which it is a wonder they did not all fall at the first—and can not be returned, and Grimalkin is known to be ranging abroad. A friend of ours living in town once found an almost featherless member of one of these little broods peeping in the grass, and neither nest nor parents being in sight, took the little orphan into the house, and placing it in a soft nest of cotton-wool in a cage, fed it with the yolks of hard-boiled eggs, put down its gaping throat on a pen-handle, making herself a slave to that throat by rising long before day to light her spirit-lamp and boil her egg. As the little creature thrived and grew, she felt it must have stronger food, and stifling her repugnance, procured earth-worms with her own delicate fingers, and proceeded to mince them for Master Rob's dinners. By this time the little creature was as round and feathered and shining as a bird could be, and skipped from room to room after his mistress, stoutly resisted the cage, and visited her pillow every morning to pick her eyes open when it was time for his breakfast. At length he was able to live upon the same fare as the family had, and took his regular place at the breakfast table, the moment that the bell rang flying to the sugar bowl, helping himself afterward to his favorite dish, and always perching on the morning paper, and fighting for his rights upon it, having the advantage of the other children in his wings, which bore him off at a signal of danger, and kept him out of reach till his offenses were forgotten. Anything like a racket delighted his little soul; any noise was as good to him as the piping of Pan; in the putting in of coal he flew to and fro through the cloud of black dust, enjoying himself with song and chatter; while the manœuvres of the laundress and the iridescence of the soap-bubbles of her "suds" gave him such peculiar pleasure that once when she left her occupation for some other he gave battle, and nobody knows with what result, if his mistress had not been called to the scene by the woman's screams, as she had often before been summoned by the indignant cries of the cats that held him only in terror, by no means regarding him as an object of prey, but as a monster that had invaded their domestic peace. Finally, one day, this little imp that so took the world for all his own, slipped out of an open window, was heard of once at the windows of another house a couple of blocks away, and then, like a bird that flew through the Northumbrian king's palace from one darkness to another, was seen no more. But our friend would not have been without the excitement and pleasure of his summer's visit for anything you could name.

And not only are such little romances afforded us by the tiny creatures, but there are the epics and heroics of their skirmishes and deadly fights, to watch which, if old Greek poets could condescend to describe the battles of the pygmies and the cranes, are not entirely beneath our notice. In fact, to the last of the bluebirds that, when we walk abroad in the country or come to the end of our trolley-ride from town, we see fluttering in crowds about the berries of ash and elder and woodbine just before the robins go, to the flocks of chickadees that suddenly appear with the snow, to the long strings of the wild-geese that go clanging through the heavens with their wild music, to the witch-like crows that never go at all, if one uses one's senses there is hardly pleasanter amusement to be had than is found in following the habits of these little actors on the boards of summer, with the human passions repeated in a miniature mimicry, and in a grand theatre where the blue sky and the waving boughs make the painted scenery and properties, where the winds and waters are real, the orchestra, seen and unseen, pipes from the leafy screens of the summer that is over and gone all too soon, and whose departure makes one impatient for the next, that, among all the other problems to be solved, it may be seen if the empty nest will be refilled again, and if the same bird will sing again to his mate, to his brood, to the universe, that song to which, as Michelet says, he himself is, after all, the most delicate auditor, but which may even give pleasure to that creating power "*qui regarde tendrement un brin d'herbe autant qu'une étoile.*"

Light-Hearted October.

And while all this goes on, we seem to be breathing new life, and sure that all is right in our home we enjoy the invigoration of early autumn with a clear conscience. It seems strange that we associate with this season the idea of cheerfulness and mirth and light-hearted labor.

One might suppose that exactly the opposite effect would be produced upon us by all the threatening tokens. The dreary time of short dark days, gray weather, and storms is approaching, the imprisonment of the snow, the bleak winter cold. The flowers are gone, the leaves are going; frost is already upon us; the summer's sauntering is over, the moon-lit stroll, the sunset sail; the winds are keen and nipping, the ground is damp and sodden, and one might suppose it debatable whether it were best to keep alive or not, instead of rejoicing ourselves over the circumstance of life, as if, under such conditions, it were a boon worth the having.

And yet such is the perversity of human nature that not when spring rustles all her promise of perfume and blossom, of warmth and ease and beauty, when the sap mounts and the blood bubbles and the year opens with renewal of youth's freshness, are we half so cheerful as when this red autumn hangs out his banners. We take no heed then of the future, and we forget that all the splendor of his array changes presently, like fairy money, to ashes.

> "Bright yellow, red, and orange,
>   The leaves come down in hosts,
>   The trees are Indian princes,
>   But soon they'll turn to ghosts"—

ghosts whose apparition does not give us an apprehension. The dazzling color is enough for us now; and with the golden sunshine of the elms and beeches, the royal purple of the ash, the dull crimson and brown of the oak, the superb and scarlet flaming of maple and tupelo and sumac, the whole atmosphere is full of splendor, and we catch the spirit of jubilee—perhaps a battailous and triumphant jubilee—as we march out to conquer the coming hosts of winter.

> "Red leaves, trailing,
>   Fall unfailing,
>   Dropping. sailing,
>   From the wood
>   That, unpliant,
>   Stands defiant,
>   Like a giant
>   Dropping blood.

Autumn Cheer.

How much of this cheerfulness is due to the bracing influence of the air, which is apt to work like iron in the veins, and how much to the effect of light and color upon the nerves, it is not quite easy to determine. By the bracing atmosphere of the sea-side or of the mountains, however, we are not always made particularly cheerful, but by that of the sunny fall days, other things being equal, the happy change seldom fails to be wrought, and we may proudly imagine in ourselves an unguessed and unconscious susceptibility to beauty that is able to work miracles and turn even dead leaves into the brilliant jewels of the trees of the Arabian's garden.

There is such an illumination present everywhere, such an airy splendor lifting the woods themselves, such a field of the cloth of gold set among all dead ferns and brakes and stubble, there is such a lofty soaring of the lighted sky above us and around, that the will of beauty must be wrought unaware upon the veriest dolt and clown among us. Far off, too, on the horizon such hazes brood, with their soft deep violet tints, now and then letting a sheet of sunlight through to sift upon the scene, leading into the unknown, and borrowing of the infinite, and giving a certain satisfaction in the view; for wherever any suggestion of the infinite is given, comfort is to be found by those mortals to whom the idea of mortality is heavy with gloom.

Thus it is not impossible that out of the mere affairs of the fancy, the hues of leaf and sky and landscape, a positive happiness is wrought quite equal to the happiness usually given by what are reckoned more substantial things. It is well known that among the most cheerful sensations produced by externals are those produced by the various degrees of red, especially the shades of cherry, carnation, and deep crimson. The coquette understands this as she knots a red ribbon in her hair, and the beauty, too, whose damask blush is her chief ornament; the crimson-carpeted room is the one which instantly reminds us of warmth and pleasure, and in which any great fall of spirits from a high temperature seems impossible; it is the gray sea picture into which Turner thrusts the vermilion-colored buoy, and transforms it; it is the russet-colored autumn that nature enlivens with the scarlet leaf. And yet these reds are the color of blood, the signal of battle, the exponent of slaughter and of fire; and why a color that is the very flag of war, and the representative of cruel wounds and death, should give us pleasant and comfortable sensations is only explicable by the supposition that in itself the rosy ray acts as a stimulant upon the nerves, exciting these comfortable sensations. There is, indeed, something rather flattering to our vanity in the belief that we are thus strongly affected by such æsthetic forces; but if it is supposable that the most of us have souls, the idea is neither very extraordinary nor fantastic.

But quite apart from this merely intellectual or nervous action upon our batteries in this matter of the autumn cheer, is the much more earthly and solid content occasioned by the completion of harvest and harvesting, the knowledge that the round world over the laborer is reaping his reward, that the earth has again paid her dividend to the race, that nature has done her duty and kept her promise, that the Great Guardian still sees that neither seed-time nor harvest fails in its season. Indeed, if the bursting of the leaf and flower makes one feel that God is alive in His world, then the ripening of the broad fields from east to west of the planet, the filling of the vast granaries, the gift of the year's food to man and beast, give one even firmer assurance that the great pulse is beating through the days and nights, and that the eternal life and the eternal love go hand in hand. What wonder, then, that, although we do not pause to consider it, the consciousness that we are so surrounded by the Divine care that no malice of the fierce elements can reach us should make us light-hearted enough to go forward gayly to meet the icy darts that winter slings, secure in our power of protection, and delighting to turn old Januarius from an enemy to a friend? Who, indeed, can be anything but gay, unless there are some facts of actual care and sorrow and pain to supervene and strip away all the bright glamor from life, when the world around is so gay that nature seems to make holiday and to hold him a churl who refuses to join the revel—the revel where the noon sun hangs in an azure sky, and soft breezes curl, and resinous balms inform the air, and splendid colors set the scene? And then, as twilight hangs in the heaven, ready to fall, and a soft solemnity of that hour takes the place of jollity, it seems rather a sacrifice of praise and thanks, on whose altar has been shed the heart's blood of the year. And in that who is it, whether full of bliss or full of pain, that has no part?

Thus we see that, after all, there is nothing so singular in this autumn cheerfulness, and that, indeed, a contrary spirit would be the singular thing, while few follies could be greater, having this charming present, than to ignore it through fear of to-morrow, and that it is wisdom as well as pleasure to enjoy this bright day while it lasts, since

"before to-morrow's sun
Cold winds may rise, and shrouding shadows dun
Obscure the scene; yet shall these fading hues
And fleeting forms their loveliness transfuse
Into the mind, and memory shall burn
The painting in on her enameled urn
In undecaying colors."

By the Hearth.

And when the heavier chill does come, and the keen wind and cold dews announce the end of out-door freedom, with what lively pleasure do we light the first fire, whether it is for the many-colored flame of the driftwood fire at the shore, or the branches and cone of the wood-side place, or the sea-coal of the grate in the back parlor of the city house!

No one ever feels that summer is quite long enough, that it is quite time for it when the early dark draws down and cuts short the once long day; and when the cool autumn dusk appears, most of us sympathize with those who speak of heaven under no other name than that of the Summer-Land. For whatever pleasures of its own there may be in the coming imprisonment of winter, they are still in strong measure, the pleasures of imprisonment, while summer, on the other hand, is one long freedom. One hardly tires of the large out-door life in its infinite variety, the going and coming at will, the liberty of costume, the abounding verdure and bloom, the unrestricted enjoyment of breeze and bird and stars; of the warm nearness and friendliness of the moon in opposition to its wintry cold remoteness; of the water-life in skiffs and yachts, in the surf and on lily ponds—of all the prodigality of air and sunshine. And we do not wonder that in all the myriads of human beings no one has ever pictured heaven as any place of rugs and lamps and fires, or as anything but a land of everlasting summer.

We make the most of winter; we are happy in it; we see an immensity of beauty in its vivid contrasts of sparkling snow and azure, its web-like tracery of bare boughs and purple sprays, its frost-ferns on the frozen pane; its ice blocks riven by restless tides, its white whirl of storms, and we think of the round earth then as a winged dazzle among the stars. But when we have admired our most, we can never make any idealization of it into a heavenly state, but the majority of us, on the contrary, agree with *Dante's* ideas in making ice and snow and freezing blasts the inner circle and pivotal point of the last place of punishment. Yet for all that what a singular charm there is about the first fire of wood laid on the hearth, herald as it is of the cold imprisonment, laid there not any more for its heat than for its necromantic power of dispelling gloom when the weather begins to shiver, and its depression begins to overcome ourselves. How we welcome it, as if it were an old friend long gone and just returned! How we gather about it, and rejoice in it! How late we linger about it, how we open our hearts over it, as if thoughts and feelings were thawed out by its genial spell! and how heedlessly we assist, as its sacrificial flames wallow up the chimney, at the funeral rites of summer! Still after all, that first fire, tumbling wave over wave up and out into the darkness, is the concentrated essence of the spice and sweetness of what countless summers! What years of sunshine and dew have gone to the growth of the wood whose embers crumble from the andirons as we bend over them! The spirit and being of how many mornings of brightness are condensed there in stem and branch, and of what moon-lighted evenings! what red sunrises have glistened in the dark dew that fed it! what bird-song has measured the rhythm of its increase! what gentle evening winds have swayed it! what lovers have leaned against it! what storms have bowed and bent it! And as it burns before us and drops away into white ashes, what comprehension and memory of all this sparkle in every fresh burst of flame, in every dying coal, and diffuse themselves about us, and make that first little autumn fire for us the expression and ideal embodiment of perpetual summer. And yet greater is our delight when it is the first fire of all on our own hearth and in our own house.

CHAPTER TENTH.

The Light of the House.

A mother is a mother still,
The holiest thing alive.
                        —*Coleridge.*

                        Happy he
With such a mother! Faith in womankind
Beats with his blood, and trust in all things high
Comes easy to him.   —*Tennyson.*

His first love? Yes, I knew her very well—
  Yes, she was young and beautiful, like you;
With cheeks rose-flushed, and lovely eyes that fell

If people praised her overmuch, but true
  And fearless, flashing out as blue eyes can
At any cruelty to beast or man.

His first love? Oh, you do begin to see
  That he might love her dearly, and that yet
His manhood's love to you might guerdon be,

Upon your woman's brow its coronet.
  Dear girl, accept the gift. There is no other
First love so holy as she gained—his mother!
                        —*Margaret E. Sangster.*

Her children arise up and call her blessed.
                        —*Proverbs.*

Rock me to sleep, mother, rock me to sleep.
                        —*E. A. Allen.*

What will not woman, gentle woman, dare
When strong affection stirs her spirit up?
                        —*Southey.*

The light of love, the purity of grace,
The mind, the music, breathing from her face,
The heart whose softness harmonized the whole,—
And oh, the eye was in itself a soul!
                        —*Byron.*

She gave me eyes, she gave me ears,
And humble cares, and delicate fears,
A heart the fountain of sweet tears
And love and thought and joy.
                        —*Wordsworth.*

> Me, let the tender office long engage
> To rock the cradle of reposing age,
> With lenient arts extend a mother's breath,
> Make languor smile, and smooth the bed of death;
> Explore the thought, explain the asking eye,
> And keep a while one parent from the sky.
> —*Pope.*

Not a house as fine as Aladdin's palace will give us the stepping stone to happiness that we have expected it to be if it is not inhabited by certain fine and sweet spirits. And first of all these is the mother. It is one of the time-honored beliefs, old enough, those observers who have but a poor opinion of the modern society mother are saying, to have reached a foolish dotage, or old enough to know better, as you please—that there is no love like mother's love, as a modern poet phrases it; and it is true in so far as it implies that there *ought* to be no love like mother's love; but as mothers are as fallible as wives and daughters and sisters, we too frequently meet specimens of them that make us think that if there is no love like mother's love, we are glad of it, and we should think that children would be, too.

A Mother.

Of course these observers are not intending to deny the great fact of maternal devotion, of the self-sacrifice that bares its own breast to protect its young, that dies for it if need be. But there are mothers and mothers, and whenever we see an inherently selfish woman we see also one who, if she is a mother, is of the sort that, if there is any dying to do, lets her children die for her. Although occasionally this mother is of the description that makes you wonder how she ever happened to be chosen to preside over a home, usually she is the tender and petted pretty woman, gentle and sweet and incapable, whose children ride over her, as the word goes, not because she loves them so that she can refuse them nothing, but because she loves herself too much to undertake the trouble of resistance, and without saying it herself exactly, her actions say for her that she would rather the children came to grief than that she should be obliged to make an exertion or forego a pleasure to prevent it. This is the mother who lies at home reading a novel while the nurse-girl, fresh to our fashions and full of her own interests, drags the baby out in crowded thoroughfares, often with its eyes in the sun, or just as often among horses' heels, with her own head turned the other way, and so busy with her gossips and flirtations that the child might be stolen under her hand and she know no more about it than the nurse of the child who replaced Pomona's baby did; the mother who sits on the seaside piazza with her crewel-work and her friends while her child is in danger of drowning, or is off about her pleasure while the servant has her children sweltering in the neighbors' kitchens, and eating whatever they can lay their hands on. When, knowing their mothers' whereabouts and behavior, we see these neglected little beings, and find their pulses fevered, their digestion disordered, and their whole state just what it should not be, we say to ourselves that that mother's children ought to be taken away from her, and usually Providence seems of our way of thinking, and they are taken away.

It is well for one's opinion of one's own race that there is another sort of mother in the world—mothers whose lives, unlike those of such cuckoo mothers, resemble more the lives of the domestic hens, lives which are one long act of maternity. It is fortunate that one can remember the self-forgetfulness of one's own mother, listen believingly to the story of the sacrifices of one's husband's mother, see daily the argus-eyed care of one's wife's mother, feel sure that no dumb creature ever excelled in watchful provision the efforts of one's friend's mother, remember the great mothers in history, and not suffer the selfish short-comings of this incapable and worse than worthless mother to outweigh them all.

The Ideal Mother.

There are mothers in the world who feel that they are responsible for the sprits called from the vasty deep and for the bodies that clothe them, who do not know how to rest unless every condition of health and safety has been fulfilled. They would scorn the suggestion of the shiftless mother who takes no pains because she may have no thanks, for to them the thanks are in the deed, the reward is in the doing; they would be wretched if they failed to do, and they are happy in their endeavor. What an amount of good is it that these mothers render the world! To them more than to any other single and separate influence is due the health that follows the race up out of savagery, and attends it perhaps to unguessed development of strength; and to them—their hands upheld doubtless as the prophet's were on the mountain, by the help they have—is largely due that improved moral excellence, to prove the reality of which, if casuists deny its existence, one needs only to point to the difference in public and private life between the mass of people in the nineteenth and that of the fifteenth, the thirteenth and the eleventh centuries, and as much farther back as undoubted history can take us. And if the development of the brain of the race is not directly due to these or any mothers, it is, at any rate, to their watchful help that it owes the opportunity of development. For oftener than any one else it is the mother who spells out the lessons with the child, even after it has escaped her tutelage, and is in the hands of masters, up betimes in the morning, and bending over the book in the evening. It is she who denies herself the money, that the price of the education may be had, and the clothes for pride or for decency, if there is any denial to be done; and she who by her own exertion spares the tired little student in every way when studies and classes are over for the day; and it is she who fires the ambition and fans it with daily and hourly breath; and she who looks out for the play-time and pleasure between the tasks. Yet we would not take any credit from the fathers in allowing so much to these mothers who are mothers and fulfill their destiny. In the greater number of cases where there are such mothers there are fathers who encourage them by leaving no duty undone on their part, wise men who know how to choose wise women to wife, and whose exactions do not make life so hard to them as wives that they have no heart to do their work as mothers. These are the mothers whose love there is no other love to equal; and it will never be from them, or from any like them, that radical disturbers of the peace will talk of taking their children to be reared by the State, thinking that even the artificial mother, like the false incubator of the barn-yard family, is better than the mother who neither broods her young nor scratches for them.

There is a great deal of sentimental cant, one must allow, in the common talk about the beauty and glory of motherhood, but very little practical appreciation of that beauty and glory among the talkers. The accepted formulas would lead one to believe that the whole thing was a mere exhibition and enjoyment of loveliness and tenderness, without responsibility, or work, or weariness; without a moment of terror, or agony, or despair. Art has so far taken up the fancy and helped it forward that its perpetual presentation of the motherhood is either the blissful young being aureoled with happiness, and holding her baby in her arms, or else the saintly old woman who, with her silver hair and serene smile, sits down for a placid breathing space at the end of her labors.

But with the intermediate mother, the real mother, the mother of many cares, of constant effort, of daily and nightly anxieties, neither Art nor Poetry occupies itself; and though her children may some day rise up and call her blessed, yet for long and weary years her virtue is its own reward.

Indeed, there is little about her that is picturesque enough for the painter or the singer to use. The heavenly Madonna smiling from the canvas, all calmness and strength and joy, is available as the image of utter perfection in the idea; the daily drudge attending to prosaic duties and relieving ignoble wants, is not sufficiently gilded by the beauty of her self-denial and her love to give her the conditions that pen and pencil find desirable and requisite; she is, in point of verity, too near and too commonplace for Art. For the young mother with her baby, the old mother with her accomplished life, have, so to speak, a sort of aerial perspective, as if the one were an object among the dreams of the future, the other among the memories of the past. The present is seldom poetic; it is only when leagues of blue and misty distance intervene that the hard, bare path we climb to-day becomes the vision of a beautiful and ideal ascent into heaven.

The Every-Day Mother.

And yet this artistic beauty is a merely superficial one. The true beauty lies with the commonplace mother—the mother who not once in ten thousand instances fails in the fulfillment of all that routine, so seldom estimated at its worth when performed, so surely bringing condemnation if in any iota neglected. The true beauty, we repeat, is with this mother who rises in the middle of the night to see if her children are covered; who springs from warm and comfortable and needed rest at the hoarse breath or the restless toss; who lies awake plotting and planning, in these early years, how to get two articles of dress out of the cloth meant for one—in those later years, how to divine the bent of this child's genius, of that child's inclinations; who perhaps kindles the fires, perhaps prepares the breakfast, certainly sees the children contentedly off to school; who toils and moils all day long, endeavoring to have the home what it is desirable it should be for husband and children; measuring this way and that to make both ends meet; never glancing aside at the enticing romance; forbidding her feet to follow the pleasant path to some neighbor's gossipy fireside; denying herself sometimes necessaries in order that her children may have luxuries; foregoing social outside pleasure that the evening lamp may always be trimmed and burning, and the best-loved spirit of the bright fireside never wanting; bearing her pains and her sorrows with silent composure, that no thought of them may darken the young lives about her, and when all is done, and while all is doing, finding perfect recompense in the happiness afforded by the opportunity of the sacrifice and devotion.

The compensation seems to come to every real mother in every moment. She forgets her suffering from the first in the joy of her possession; and as the bird strips her breast of down to warm the nest for her young, so there is no self-abnegation that is too great for a mother to make, and none that does not bring with it a satisfying joy.

"Wearie is the mither that has a storie wean,
A wee stumpie stoussie that canna rin his lane,
That has a battle aye wi' sleep before he'll close an ee—
But a kiss frae aff his rosy lips gies strength anew to *me!*"

MOTHER'S DEVOTION.

It will only be when we understand, in gazing on the beautiful picture of the young mother, that she is so lovely because all this exertion and devotion and sacrifice are before her, in gazing at the old one, that she is so saintly because trial and labor and love have refined her in their furnaces, that our talk about the beauty of maternity and the sacred name of mother will cease to be poetical cant and become realized truth.

The Story of Old Margaret and Her Boy.

Let me tell you the story of Old Margaret, who was one of the self-forgetting mothers.

There are certain feminine instincts that assume in many eyes the character rather of virtues than of instincts, and the manifestation of which in any individual seems to touch all other women nearly.

Among these instincts, so to call them, is that maternal one which causes the year-old baby to hold her mother's needle-book or roll of work on her little breast and hush it off to sleep, which causes her half a dozen years afterward to wake up in the night and see if her doll is warm enough, and which, a score of years later yet, knits a tie between herself and every tender little child she sees. A strange tie, without the immense joy of a mother's love—that joy which overflows the inner cells of the most desolate heart with vital warmth, which is fulfilled with satisfaction and with that ineffable yearning where earth touches close on heaven—a barren tie beside that divinely complete thing, and with more pain than pleasure in it. It is as if the bitter lot of women in this world caused them to feel the pathos of the fate of every child born into it, and gave them a pity that is all but love. "Little butterfly in the sunshine and among the flowers," it seems to say, "by-and-by night is coming, darkness and heavy dew and the night-hawk. If only I could protect you!"

Whenever I used to see a little bent old woman go by my window with a child in her arms, these and kindred thoughts would follow her. I did not know her name, and I could not see her face; but she interested me far more than the bright-cheeked and golded-haired young creatures that tripped by on their way from the finishing school. Her clean but utterly faded calico was so short that it showed the clumsy village-ties and drab stockings of her knobby and rheumatic feet; her shawl was a threadbare black blanket; her bonnet was a rusty poke; an alpaca apron was her only vanity; her poor old hands were bare and bony and misshapen, but they seemed to me fairer than any idle lady's in the land when I saw the way in which they clasped the child she held; the way in which, as she walked, she used to pause and lift the child higher, and lay the little face against her own, and step off again as if she were young and happy. Day by day I saw her pass. As the child grew, and sat up in her arms and looked about, she would straighten her bent form to bear him more erectly. Often she would kiss him rapturously as she went along, and she was always crooning some low tune to him, or talking a loving gibberish that he seemed to understand. Evidently the child had no mother, perhaps no father, either, for he was clothed in odds and ends; a great sacque and hood wrapped him for a long time, and when the spring came his head emerged with the short yellow curls crowned by a hat that seemed to delight him, so often he tore it off with his little hands to look at it, and set it on again awry, but which she must have rescued from an ash-barrel, and have scoured and trimmed with scraps of cambric from her rag bag. I longed to ask them in while they were slowly

(250) SITTING AND PLAYING HIS BANJO.

going by; but I have an uncomfortable reverence for reserves, and I fancied she was one of those who had rather suffer than be seen to suffer. But when the baby grew so heavy that she had to rest every little while, she sat down one day on my garden step, and then I opened the door to go out, and stopped and made friends with the child, and gave him a cup of milk and a cake, and began with her an acquaintance which if I do not in another life resume, it will be because I am not fit.

Years and years ago old Margaret Ewins had been young; it seems as though no one could guess the fact were it not plainly stated, so gray and wrinkled and seamed was the face with which she looked up at you. "Years and years ago," she said once. "It's hard to believe it now when you see me, child; but every wrinkle is a care, and every furrow is a tear. There were no wrinkles nor furrows, no cares nor tears—it was all fresh and blooming—when I married Stephen."

When she married Stephen! That was full forty years ago. And thirty years he had been under the sod. Doubtless his image had grown dimmer than once, but he was still to her the fine and noble fellow that won her heart. She forgot that she was a withered crone, that he was a handful of dust; she set her love beside his inmortal youth, and looked forward to the end.

Stephen had left her with an only child, born on the day he died. Other children had come and been laid away before, but this girl was last and the dearest of all. In her the father seemed to live and breathe again; for her the mother lived indeed. She was a pretty thing as she grew into womanhood. Perhaps her mind was not altogether of the strongest; but one would have to be fastidious who paused to think of that in gazing at the red and white of her face, the clear blue of her great eyes, the gilding of her chestnut hair, her sweet and innocent mouth. Of course she had lovers, and of course there was a favored one—the least deserving of the whole, but the son of a family of vastly superior circumstances to her own.

For poor Bessie's circumstances were those which belong to the children of poverty and labor the world over. Her mother owned the little house in which they lived, and the larger part of which they rented to others; and for the rest they did sewing, nursing, clear-starching, whatever came to hand. But needy as they were, Bessie always had on a clean print dress, though she had to rise before day to wash and iron it; she always had a bright ribbon for her throat; she always looked as perfect as a rose.

And old Margaret's pride and joy lay in seeing her so. She wore her own brown gingham till it fell apart, so that Bessie might have a bishop's lawn for summer Sundays. She pretended dire dyspepsias, and lived on crusts so that Bessie might keep her b'ood sweet and rich with the little milk and meat there was. Long after Bessie had come home from her moon-lit stroll with the handsome and worthless James Falconer, Margaret sat over her needle or her Italian irons abridging the morrow's work, that Bessie's pretty shoulders might learn no stoop, or else turning an extra penny, that she might surprise Bessie with the bit of trimming for which she had heard the girl longing. Poor Margaret! she little knew the crop she sowed, nor recognized the fact that Bessie was becoming to herself as well as to her mother the chief person in the drama; she failed to see the springing and ripening selfishness in the girl, the wilful spirit, the deadly love of finery, the lack of reason. She only saw her standing in the light and looking at her with her father's eyes—those burning blue eyes that seemed at once to revel in the brilliance of the world and scorn it, too—and she felt that all she could have was not too much for her.

Still as she glanced from the window sometimes, and saw her by moonbeam or star gleam leaning against the gate post, with James Falconer across the little wicket, as tall and dark and glittering as Lucifer, a misgiving would cross Margaret as to whether she was right in letting the thing go on; as to whether it was possible for young Falconer to stoop from his ancient degree and his father's place to marry this clear-starcher. But then the child looked so bright and rosy and lovely as her mother gazed at her that she could but fold her hands above her beating heart and whisper to herself that all might be for the best, for stranger things than that had happened.

But the years went slowly wearing by, each one of them taking a degree of Bessie's bloom with it, and Bessie was old enough to know better, and still James Falconer followed her and did not marry her, and other lovers had fallen away, and the mother, through some hidden sense, was half aware that Bessie's name was spoken lightly. And one day Falconer had disappeared, leaving a defalcation behind him, and Bessie had gone, too.

No search was made for the defaulter ; a little of his father's wealth could repair the breach in the bank, and for his father's sake no suit was entered against him. Indeed, there were those who half excused him, and laid the blame on the shameless girl who had allured him, as they said, to his ruin. And certainly no search was made for Bessie. What could one feeble little old woman do ? Nothing in the world, nothing but pray—pray over seam and stove, by day and night! "What am I crying for?" she would say, dashing away her tears. "God is on my side, and with Him on my side, am I going to lose? No; Bessie will come back to me."

And so for five years she toiled and moiled, not for herself, but that when Bessie came home there might be something laid by to let rest and comfort greet her. And every night she swept the hearth and brightened the lamp for her, and every morning she made the place spotless, thinking it might hold

STEPPING STONES TO HAPPINESS.

Bessie before night. And her eyes longed and her heart ached and her hands trembled to see her. Her expectation was always at fever heat. She hardly knew that the tears wet her pillow at night, such comfort was there in the thought that Bessie might come to-morrow.

Five long, lonesome years! If old Margaret were sick, there was no one to soothe her; if she was cast down, there was no one to cheer her. But she clasped a sure faith; her hope brightened her days; and one night, as she had forefelt, Bessie came home. A weary woman got down from the stage, and tottered up the yard, and came in, and fell upon the floor, and in the night her boy was born, and in the morning consciousness seemed to come back an instant; for she looked up into her mother's face with those blue eyes and half smiled—Margaret always said it was a smile—and died; and all without one word! without a word! And if she could but have spoken—for there was no ring on her finger.

Five long and lonesome years—and just for this! Poor Margaret had no tears. A fierce, dry anger with fate burned them away at their source. Now, indeed, she was wretched. In those five years she saw she had been happy—happy with her hope. She took the child and cared for it mechanically; she laid it down between whiles as she went about her work, and suffered it to cry if it would. "Let it cry!" she said. "It's James Falconer's child. Crying's too good for it." But once as the little thing was sobbing, she went to it and saw the great tears shining in its blue eyes. "Ah, it is Bessie's child!" she cried. "I have been a cruel wretch!" and she caught it up and warmed it at her heart, and anger and grief went together; and thenceforth she was bound in the child. "I would have treated an outcast better," she sobbed at last. "Ah, my poor little lad, with such a life before him!"

And so she lived and strived, and had no other end in view than the well-being of little Steve, as she had named him. For him now she sat up at night,

as she had sat up for his mother; for him she denied herself as of old. That came natural enough. It seemed to her, she said to herself, as if she were doing still for Bessie. All she had laid by during the five years went in Bessie's burial. Anxious to have something beforehand again in case of her own illness, or in preparation for little Steve's future jacket and trousers, or schooling, she spared herself no pains. Her eyesight had failed so, what with years and what with tears, that she could no longer do fine sewing or starching. She was obliged to go out to the rougher labor of the tub, and another old woman from the other part of the house—too old, indeed, for anything but to hinder the baby from rolling off the bed—used to come in and keep watch for her while her poor old arms were in the suds. But people hardly liked to employ her, not only because she could not see well, but because it seemed as if they had better be doing the work themselves than imposing it upon that gray-headed woman. Her proud, keen spirit felt that it was more in charity than anything else that she was hired at all. And she hailed the fact, as if a miracle had been wrought in her behalf when rents grew so dear in the town that she was at liberty to receive twenty-five dollars more a year on the other part of her little house, of which she now reserved but one room and a closet for herself, and so was allowed to leave the wash tub.

Thus on one hundred dollars a year old Margaret lived and reared her child. It is that which seems the miracle to you; but her wants were very few, and she was not uncomfortable. She asked no aid of any for little Steve—least of all of the Falconers, who never knew from her that such a child existed. Her bread and milk was all he wanted as yet, and he wore, as I have said, almost anything The Old Ladies' Society of the town gave her a monthly allowance of good Oolong tea, and she accepted it as a public benefit of the same nature as the streets to walk on, or the use of the corner pump, or the ringing of the nine-o'clock bell, to none of which she contributed tax money. And now, with nothing to do but to keep her two rooms and her two people clean, to teach little Steve his first steps and first words, she abandoned herself to her first real bliss in years, and when I was pitying her most she was needing it least. Her first real bliss, for not a fear disturbed it. "God takes care of the sparrows," she would say. "And he will take care of little Steve."

"But when he is bigger," croaked the old grandam from the other part of the house, nearly as fond herself of the boy as Margaret was, though quite disapproving Margaret's devotion, "he will want different food from your bread and milk. He will need red meat, and where is he to get it?"

"Where the young lions get theirs," said Margaret, and went on joyously; and it was in the days that I first saw her, taking her morning and her afternoon walk with the child in her arms, talking gayly to him all the time, and kissing him at every other step. What visions she had of little Steve's future, and how she used to confide them to the child as they went! And the boy would lift his little head and pat her cheek approvingly, as if he understood them all, and give her now and then a great wet kiss of his rosy mouth in return—a kiss that knew no difference between her shriveled yellow cheek and the blushing velvet of youth.

How, after her hard experience of life Margaret could have had such a thing as a vision passes conjecture; but she was so light-hearted in her love that she believed in everything that another might have seen to be impossible and unattainable. The clothes which little Steve was to wear when he went to school; the errands he was to run in order to get the money to buy the clothes; the school to which he was to go—no common school at all, but one where her care of the rooms was to balance his term bill; the prizes he was to win; the day he was to graduate and speak his piece, and be applauded by the people and be mentioned in the *Morning Herald* next day; the apprenticeship he was to serve in a lawyer's office; the cases he was some day to plead; the lives he then was to save; the good, the glory; and by-and-by President—what a dazzling structure that she built up on the foundation of her little span of life and strength! And meanwhile, as she waited for the time when all these things should be accomplishing, she took her pleasure in her boy.

Perhaps Bessie's babyhood had been as lovely, her tongue as apt, her feelings as quick, as little Steve's were now; but Margaret had had no time then to enjoy any of it all—now she had nothing else to do. It seemed to her that no cherub slumbering in beds of amaranth and asphodel inside the sculptured gates of heaven could be so beautiful as little Steve was with the dew of sleep upon him as he lay on the old patchwork quilt. The day that the boy laughed heartily and intelligently she felt that she had assisted at a fresh creation of the human soul, and to her mind nothing more remarkable in the record of the race had ever occurred than the first articulate sound that little Steve uttered. His recognition of herself was an ever-recurring miracle; she snatched him up each time and covered him with kisses, as if it needed a special act of gratitude; the detestable old cat from whose back he pulled a handful of hair became a sacred being—she wondered that the cat did not like it; he was welcome to as many handfuls of her gray hair as he would take! "Do not talk about this earth's being a dark place!" she cried, to the old grandam of the other part of the house, "for it seems to me as bright as the sun itself! It must be bright when all the children that are born meet it with such a gay heart. I used to pity them all. But now—look at him! he smiles at everybody, all the world are friends—it is beautiful! The angels must feel just so. Oh, you don't think, do you, that he is too bright and good to live? Oh, my darling!" she would

(256) PRACTICING FOR A LONG MIGRATION.

cry, that single gleam of trouble bringing back the one dark thought of her life, "if I only knew that you had a right to the name you bear !"

And so the days passed on, each one a festival, each new one bringing a new feat of little Steve's to be shown and admired and praised, the child thrived and prospered, and more and more with each day the little old woman seemed to become a child with him. They used often now to come in and see me. I had the children's deserted toys for little Steve, that delighted him, and there were others which could not be taken away, such as the great music box, and the aquarium, and the fernery, over which he hung spell-bound, and I had certain innocent dainties whose whereabouts he early learned to know; and when he twisted his little lips into coaxing kisses on the air between, his grandmother, proud as she was, could not resist the child's insistence to be brought across the street to me.

The sight of age is always a pathetic sight to the young and strong, especially of age forgetting its miseries and the near grave in the love of others; but there was something exquisitely pathetic in the sight of this little old creature lugging the heavy child about, none the less so for her unconsciousness of it. Once, when she saw a shadow of the thought on my face, "Don't you pity me," she cried; "I am too happy for that! Keep your pity for the old women that are not grandmothers!"

"You set too much by the boy, Margaret," said the grandam, who had walked out with her that morning. "What if he should be taken from you?"

"What if he should be taken from me?" she repeated, opening her sunken eyes as if they had never seen the possibility before. "Well, then, I should go, too! It couldn't be for long. But no, no; he is as stout and healthy as he is bright and handsome. I only pray not to be taken myself till he can spare me!"

Poor old Margaret! It was well for her that she enjoyed herself while the sun shone, for the darkness was coming soon enough.

One day, just as little Steve came out of his bath, and, running away from her, was toddling about the room, his little body shining with water-drops, his curls dripping in wet, bright rings, there was heard a man's foot on the step and in the entry, a rap on the door, and the visitor had come in unbidden and stood before her.

It was James Falconer.

"I have come for my boy," said he.

Margaret, risen to fetch the child, staggered and fell back upon her seat, and caught little Steve and clutched him closely. She trembled from head to foot; but she glared at her enemy like a lioness defending her whelp.

"I suppose you do not deny that he is my child?" said the visitor, no longer the dark and handsome youth, but a worn and haggard man.

"He is his mother's child," said Margaret hoarsely; "and so mine. There was no ring on Bessie's finger!"

Falconer paused a moment and gazed at the boy; and the boy, full of roguish glee and kindliness, looked archly up at him, and kissed the air after the pretty fashion that he had. "Yes, he is Bessie's boy fast enough," said the man. "And he is mine, too, you will have to understand. And I have come to get him!"

"Go away, James Falconer!" cried Margaret, "or I will set the law on you!"

"There is no law to set on me," he said—"there is no law for me, except the law that gives a man his child, born in honest wedlock."

Margaret blanched as she heard him. Her heart rose and sank, and sent a pulse over her in hot waves. To clear Bessie's name from stain! But at such a price! Was it—was it possible? She looked at the vanishing ambro-type that, framed in its wreath of dead roses, hung beneath the clock—the bright, beautiful face with the smile.

"Was he," she whispered presently—"was he born so? Was my Bessie a lawful wife?" He nodded. "Do you swear to it, James Falconer? Will you publish it in the *Morning Herald?*" She ran and brought her Bible, over which she had sat so many a night spelling out the big type that promised blessings to the widow and the fatherless. She held it out at arm's length. "Kiss the book!" she exclaimed, "and swear it all." James Falconer bent his head and kissed the book. "Then you can take the boy," she said. "But take him quickly, before it breaks my heart!"——And the man went his way with his own. "O, Bessie, Bessie," she cried, as the door closed and left her all alone, "you bright and careless girl, what an awful price have I paid for your good name! I have sold my little Steve, his hopes, his future, his life and soul, to that man—to that man and to evil."

That night the old grandam fumbled at Margaret's latch to come in, according to her custom, for a social gossip in the twilight—Margaret did not answer her. She opened the door and saw her lying on the bed.

"I've had a stroke!" was all that Margaret said, as the other old woman bent over her—"I've had a stroke"——

"God bless me! The palsy! We'll have the doctor here"——

"Oh, no, it's not that," murmured Margaret, slowly. "But just the heart is dead within me."

The next day the poor soul did not attempt to rise. She lay there with the *Morning Herald*, in which at last was printed the day and date of Bessie's marriage, nearly seven years ago, spread out upon the pillow, as if in little Steve's place. To them that would have ministered to her she seemed in a stupor till she lifted her eyes, as wild and suffering as those of a dumb creature in mortal pain. She did not listen to what anybody said; she did not speak herself; she tasted the nourishment that was brought and turned away—the  tide of life was ebbing out, and she was letting go her hold upon the earth that had grown worthless to her. She lay in that half dream, and whether we came in or out she neither knew nor cared. Once only she spoke—sighed rather than spoke. "That is right," she said. "Punish me! punish me well for ever having dared to doubt my Bessie!"

But Sunday morning, just as the great first flush of the dawn came into the room, and all the air rippled with the tumultuous music of the birds, Margaret sat up in bed, and looked at the morning star sinking back into the rose and glory. It cast the shadow of the window sash in a long dark cross upon her bed. She glanced at the shadow and faintly smiled—the brighter light would soon efface the shadow, soon she would lay her cross aside! And the cross paled and faded, and was gone; and then, as a child's voice somewhere in the distance sweetly and shrilly joined the chorus of the birds, she shivered and her head fell forward and dropped upon her breast—and the dawn came slowly and softly up and shed a silver splendor round the poor old head, and showed us that Margaret had passed into the fuller day.

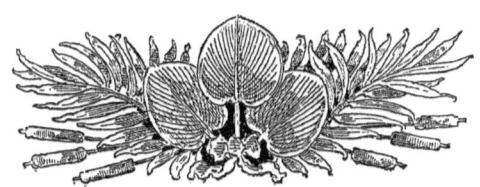

CHAPTER ELEVENTH.

A Well-Spring of Joy.

> God's child, with His dew
> On thy gracious gold hair. —*Browning.*

> The merry merry lark was up and singing,
> And the hare was out and feeding on the lea,
> And the merry merry bells below were ringing,
> When my child's laugh rang through me.
> —*Charles Kingsley*

> Happy is the man that has his quiver full of them.
> —*Psalms*

> So build we up the being that we are.
> —*Wordsworth.*

> A mither bairn who had never known
> Aught save the tenderest care,
> She had fared to the heavenly land alone,
> As the souls of all must fare.
> —*Margaret E. Sangster.*

> The children gather the table round,
> And this is rosy and that is fair,
> No dearer group in the land is found,
> With their laughing eyes and their golden hair.
> —*Margaret E. Sangster.*

> Among these latter busts we count by scores,
> Half emperors, and quarter emperors,
> Each in his bay-leaf fillet, loose-thonged vest,
> Doric and low-browed Gorgon on his breast;
> One loves a baby face with violets there,
> Violets instead of laurel in the hair,
> As those were all the little locks could bear.
> —*Browning.*

But one house will be only half peopled if there comes there no new life in the little child to carry on and enlarge the old.

When the first whisper comes to the young mother's heart which calls to her, "Blessed art thou among women," which tells her that the strength of her love has kindled a new being, it is not of the great gulf of death that she must cross to win her treasure that most she thinks, but of the field of her past years, and of the influences that have made her what she is for good or ill.

> "There are two moments in a diver's life:
> One, when a beggar he prepares to plunge,
> One, when a prince he rises with his pearl,"

she may perchance repeat, but not until she rises with her pearl from the black depths into which she plunged more bravely than any man ever went to battle, not until that most awful of all moments when she has felt the presence of the Lord of Life beside her, not until that sweetest of all moments when the little face lies near her own, when her tired arms clasp that which yesterday was not and to-day is, does she penetrate the secret and burden of those past years to its full meaning, and in the cup of her joy find a bitter tang, the sting of her own sins and errors, the effect of which the silent work of nature has passed over to her child, and made him in great degree that which she has made herself. Every mother knows something of the bitterness of this regret, unless she be immeasurably centered in the sphere of her own self-conceit; and from the instant of the experience her life is bent toward undoing any evil the child may have inherited from her or from another, and toward bringing all good influences to bear in developing his being symmetrically and in making him a blessing to his race, something lovely in the Eternal eyes, it may be, something worthy of the full receipt of that life which is love. She may be the sternest disbeliever in religious doctrine and dogma, finding no satisfaction to reason in the substance of any creed, but in this moment a sterner doubt will possess her: the doubt if this little spirit can be anything less than immortal; and she finds herself proceeding on that supposition, and, in the peradventure, doing her best to give him a good start in immortality. When those die whom, living, we adored, it seems blasphemy to them to doubt of their continued existence; when those are born of our love, as we know that love is everlasting we are assured that they partake of the nature of that which gave them existence.

As the mother lies quiescent in the long days, in the still watches of the night, more often than otherwise her mind is busy with the great verities; she is rehearsing the child's future for him; she is weighing and judging his possibilities; she is thinking how this one fault that is his father's may be brought to naught in him, those noble qualities be brought to light, how those boundless faults that are her own may be exterminated or rendered abortive, how the moral and spiritual inheritances from his ancestry may be handled, how best shall be developed this last flower of the race. She sees that **growth** is the unfolding of life; that there is in it something of the divine; that it must not be hindered; and that possibly all she may be able to do is to keep off injurious influence.

If she never prayed before, she prays now; if she never suffered before, she suffers now; if she was never glad before, she is glad now; glad with a sweet awe that she and the Eternal Powers of goodness are to work together in making this child worthy not only of his mortal, but also of his immortal, parentage.

The Baby.

The helpless morsel of humanity and flannel that has come into the house and has presently through his imperious necessities turned it upside down and made all its people slaves, is not three days old before he has found out who is master. When this little immortal being yells, he yells with all the force of his immortality behind him; the household prostrates itself as if before the vast outside agencies of the unknown. A kitten might squeal, a puppy howl; we would relieve it; but it would not be that matter of vital concern and effort that the relief of the baby becomes; and although we are not conscious of it, it is not our sense of selfish possession that prostrates us so much as our consciousness of this new being's identity, with the first groping of his hands, the first wandering of his eyes, and of his being the latest manifestation of this vast unknown, the finest and last result of a long line of generation, the crown of our own existences, the thing we love as a part of ourselves, and perhaps as a part of heaven, too.

Be that as it may, the little child has not learned to focus his eyesight, when, lying on his face across his nurse's knee, he may be seen to lift his head and survey his surroundings. In that survey he has made up his mind about many things and evolved the germ of his self-will. The problem that presents itself is not to break that will but to direct it; never to awake it in contradiction to the superior will, never to let the child know the need of screaming or insisting, or the possibility of any gratification following such screaming or insisting, to let him find that, strong as his will may be, the superior will is stronger, and it is profitless to resist it; that there is to be no yielding or changing after refusal or command, no playing fast or loose, but wise determination in the first and a firm hold of that determination afterward, no matter under what pressure of the child's wish or of a personal desire to the contrary. And with that the child is led to see that neither one will nor the other is of any use in contest with the facts of the universe, that fire will burn, that water will drown, that blows will hurt, and that there must be accommodation to the truth, and he will have taken then his first conscious step into the world outside his own narrow periphery, the world of law.

If one asked the young mother what was her first duty, she would reply that it was to establish habits of health in her child. Undoubtedly she is right. But if she has fed her child at such regular intervals that he has never had to exercise lungs, stomach, or temper in demanding food; if she has put him to sleep alone so early that he has never known any other way, and has never had to have his nerves rasped or his terrors excited by the unaccustomed fact, then she has already established some habits of physical health, even while attending at the same

WHAT A SINGULAR CHARM THERE IS ABOUT THE FIRST FIRE OF WOOD!

time and in a small way to matters of the higher nature. Of course it is a self-evident fact that no thoroughly harmonious nature can be expanded from an unsound body; and that the work calculated to achieve or to maintain the sound body must be coincident with other work, and must be unremitting.

The Physical Care of the Baby.

It is almost presumptuous to say to the mother that her child must be watched from the first, in order that it may be known how well or how ill his food agrees with him; that if he is obliged to resort to artificial food it must be prepared with the greatest care and cleanliness, with no long tubes and coils in his drinking-vessels to nourish the deadly ptomaines, and that the child must never be allowed to become so hungry as to gulp down greedily more than can be disposed of healthfully instead of such amount as the stomach can handle with slow and gentle satisfaction.

Constant care is the price of everything valued in this world, and the bodily habits must be made a matter of close observation, and if in any way they fail, the physician must be summoned and obeyed.

That the child must be kept dry, that chafing must be prevented by the use of home-made unguents pleasantly scented, or of finely sifted starch rather than of the possibly dangerous and highly perfumed powders to be bought, that a few drops of oil, a soft sponge and soap and water must be relied on to cleanse his head, that his hands and feet must be always warm, that the sleep must not be made restless by too much clothing, creating a heat that weakens, all these again are so self-evident facts that one feels like apologizing for mentioning them.

The mother herself must judge whether the child, if puny and delicate, shall sleep alone or have the warmth of her arms; her mother-wit will tell her that he must be handled as little as love can allow, must be fondled and breathed over no more than is indispensable, must be excused from promiscuous kissing from all sorts of lips, must not have his brain excited by too many faces, too much talking, too much going and coming about him. This same mother-wit, too, will abolish the long picturesque skirts loaded with finery that bear and deform the baby's legs and feet, and will shorten all skirts at the first moment in which the growth of the baby and the temperature of the weather act together, and will, moreover, cover the neck and arms, so lovely to look at and to kiss, with high-throated and long-sleeved slips, if indeed it does not keep the baby in little night-dresses for many weeks rather than in embroideries, laces, and ruffles. Mother-wit, too, will make the bath in tepid water a daily habit and joy from the first; in the early days, washing and wiping and covering a little surface at a time, and the full plunge bath when the little bather is able to splash the water with glee and comprehension; but even then the child will not be left in the water long enough to become blue or to receive the least chill.

Much of all this is such intuitive knowledge that many mothers may consider even the suggestion an impertinence. Nevertheless, the mother who follows these hints, whether naturally or otherwise, and further sees to it that her house, her drinking water, and the drinking water of her cow, as well as all her own habits, are healthy, will be rewarded with the possession of such rosy wholesomeness, such beaming intelligence as only a thoroughly comfortable baby can show, and with such joy as only the possession of such a treasure can give a yearning and a tender heart.

The Moral Growth of the Child.

From the healthy animal being made sure, by circumspection and solicitude, we may hope to see the healthy mental and moral being evolved. Mental and moral being will be evolved in some way, since that is an affair incident to all in the process of the opening out of that integral germ of individuality which belongs to each child as much as the development of seed and flower belongs to the plant. Out of its own mysterious sources will come the unfolding of the sturdy oak from the acorn, of the butterfly from the worm, of the storm-sweeping eagle from the egg, of the sage, the hero, the Saviour, from the first feeble morsel of humanity. But the determination of that unfolding, of the quality and direction of that mental and moral being, are very lovely in the power of the child's environment, and thus in that of his mother and father. Resting in this germ of individuality, it has been widely proved, lie many of the capacities of generations of ancestors, although certainly not all of those capacities; for some have been annihilated by intermarriage with contradictory and stronger ones, some have been atrophied by disuse. Those remain by re-inforcement and accretion either from the remote or recent past, while others are dormant but not yet withered, and capable under re-animating circumstances of being brought into use whether for good or evil. We see in almost every family some one person in whom have survived the traits of those dead and gone this many a year, traits long ago dropped by all the rest of the connection. The careful parent will not allow the possibilities these thoughts suggest to be forgotten; and in this view, knowledge concerning one's lineage is always to be desired. If among these dormant capacities there are any of value, it is the parent's part to vivify them, to stimulate and strengthen them in action, and if there are any noxious ones, to use every endeavor still further to asphyxiate and destroy them.

This recurrence of traits is seen so surely in the physical life that we might know the natural corollary of it all is in the moral. In certain households a peculiarity of the eyes will re-appear from time to time till it is known as the family eye, and it will be seen in old portraits, where they exist, for ten generations back. Where there has been a hunch-back, it is tolerably sure that somewhere in succeeding generations there will be another; it will be thought and declared then to be the result of accident, but investigation will probably discover the congenital weak spine in some shape all along the line, and knowledge of the liability will tend to make us overcome the cast in the eye and strengthen the weakness of the back. The same thing is familiar to us in the moral world; certain families are known to be of jealous and vindictive natures; certain ones to have parsimonious qualities; of these one is

STEPPING STONES TO HAPPINESS.

as sure of their benevolence as of their name; in others a scholarly habit has existed since they were known as a family at all.

Thus the work of the guardians of the child is plainly set before them; to repress here, to forward there, to increase existing power, to nullify wrong tendencies. It looks like a vast task; but when it is remembered that it means but a word at a time, day after day, one recalls the discontented pendulum, and is not so much appalled. The carrot, some one tells us, has to have twenty generations of culture before it is edible; but, on the other hand, let it be left alone for five generations and it is again worthless.

Still, although so gradual, this task of directing the child's growth is an unceasing one; for going along at the same time with the destruction of evil inheritances and the stimulation of good ones, there is usually also the implanting of other distinct and positive characteristics as they are seen to be necessary. It ought not to be a difficult one, however; for some of the desired traits are but the revival of those originated or taught by our earliest Aryan fathers, courage, truth, and worship, and much of it is done in letting our children see the noble qualities in our own lives and conduct. There is a sort of creative happiness in the work, meantime. We have seen a young mother who experienced deadly fear in a thunder storm, her heart sinking with every flash, hold her little child up to look at the lightning with smiles on her face, as if nothing were more to be admired than the blue and rosy splendor of the flash, and lift her finger the while inclining her head to listen, as if the reverberations of the thunder, the house shaking with the concussion, were music in her ears, because she was determined the child should not be the heir of the tremors and sufferings of others. It may have been an ordeal to her, but it would have been a worse ordeal to have her son a coward; and she was but repeating the lesson the first Aryan mother taught her son far away in the abyss of past ages, and she has a joy in doing it that more than compensated her, for she was creating a hero.

Deny the existence of original sin, as we may, the survival and appearance of these ancestral traits, whether rudimentary or full-flowered, which we shall constantly see in our children, if we look for them, amount in practical dealing to the same thing. Selfishness, fear, falsehood, cruelty, sensuality, will be the ghosts coming to revisit the pale glimpses of the moon, vastly modified, it is to be hoped, but still the same as in the mother of all the Jukes, and some one of them probably to be contended with by any one who has the care of the last inheritor of all the virtues and vices gone before, the last heir of all the ages, the child of any household. Yet it is not to be forgotten that good has been inherited with the evil, the good of all the struggles against temptation, the effort toward the better and higher, the refusal to surrender to sin, till that effort, that struggle, that refusal, till, in short, virtue becomes an hereditament. Hence to stultify the evil, to foster the good, is the burden that the parents take up with their first-born's first breath. It is a burden they have no right to lay down for a day. They are responsible for the child's existence, and so for what he does with his existence. It was they who called these spirits from the vasty deep; it is they who must lead them as Solomon led the genii in a leash.

When a child commits its first theft of apple, or cake, or what-not, the mother may well feel a horrible fear of the apparition of the original cave-dwelling savage, of the foraging marauder, the highwayman, the thieving borderer, the vassal or serf who attended the high-handed raider who knew no other law than that of might. When the child strikes its first angry blow, she sees all that old original savage rising in him. "'Opy the door!" cried a two-year-old child. "When I say 'opy the door,' opy the door!" And the mother knew that the time had come for her to obey tremblingly or to resist to the death the domineering spirit that had never been laid to rest with bell, book, or candle, capable of ruining the peace of a family to come as it might have ruined the peace of those dead and gone. "You said I would feel better when I had given away some of my caramels," said another little re-embodied trait. "I don't feel any better. When shall I begin to feel better?" And this mother saw something appalling as any old family ghosts, the old miserly spirit of one strain of his ancestry rising to contest, not with the desire for a peaceful conscience, but with the spirit that loves luxury and ease so much that it never does right, but only with the slothful dislike of the consequences of wrong; and while others smiled at the naivet of the urchin she saw a problem before her as intricate as one in the calculus of imaginaries. Perhaps it would help her to remember that one of the fairy fancies of science has been that owing to the thinner and lighter atmosphere of the planet Mars, the birds got the start there, in the matter of evolution, making the intelligent being of Mars, the human being there, a winged creature. It is her art to make his moral atmosphere that which shall develop the winged being in her child's nature.

Help in the Problem from the Great Educator.

In the solution of the mother's problem as to the right way to develop the minds of her children many great minds have come to her assistance; but none of them more practically than Pestalozzi, Rousseau, and Froebel, the latter with a patient working out of system that was creative. It is Froebel's

268   STEPPING STONES TO HAPPINESS.

ROCK ME TO SLEEP, MOTHER.

ideas that now govern nearly all primary education, even where his whole plan of teaching is not carried out. The intention of his work is to evoke a universal and all-round development of the nature and the faculties, and this is done by turning the natural activities of the child to use, by developing the body through gentle and rhythmical gymnastics, and the soul through the simultaneous action of the senses and of the social sympathies and instincts.

Froebel.

It is by the slow process of many years that the excellence of Froebel's ideas has been proved, and the process was accompanied by ridicule and obstruction till it triumphed. But the wonderful man had stanch adherents and powerful friends in his life-time. When some one spoke of him as an old fool, a learned professor replied that

Socrates was that sort of fool; when he died, his grave was filled with flowers by children whose lives he had developed as those flowers had themselves been developed from wildlings.

His work beginning with one school—a school of whose pupils Prof. Fichte, the son of the great philosopher, declared that they showed exceptional intelligence in the Universities and elsewhere—is now the compulsory system of Austria and of several other European countries, and is on the way to be widely adopted in the United States, very notably in the schools of Boston—an interesting fact because it was toward us that Froebel looked for welcome.

Among prominent people who have interested themselves in the work is the Empress Frederick, who had her children reared according to its plan, and who is the patroness of certain institutions in London, where Robert Owen introduced it; and the Princess Pauline of Lippe-Detmold, and the Duchess Helene of Orleans have made use of it, in forms somewhat modified for the very young and the very poor. It is even used among those having most success in the schools for the blind, and it is undoubtedly to become the one and only method of educing and training the intelligence of children the world over. "The most delicate, the most difficult and the most important part of the training of children," writes the Baroness Marenholtz-Bulow, in quoting Froebel, "consists in the development of their inner and higher life of feeling and of soul, from which springs all that is highest and holiest in the life of men and of mankind; in short, the religious life, the life that is at one with God in feeling, in thought, and in action. When and where does this life begin? It is as with the seeds in spring; they remain long hidden under the earth before they become outwardly visible. It is as with the stars of heaven, which astronomers tell us have shone for ages in space ere their light has fallen on our eyes. We know not, then, when and where this religious development, this process of re-union with God, first begins in the child. If we are over-hasty with our care and attention the result will be the same as with the seedling which is exposed too early and too directly to the sun's heat or to the moisture of rain. If, on the other hand, we are behindhand, the consequences will be equally fatal. What then must education do? It must proceed as gently and gradually as possible, and in this respect, as with all other kinds of development, work first only through general influences. As the child's physical condition is healthily or injuriously affected by the badness or goodness of the air which it breathes, so will the religious atmosphere by which it is surrounded determine its religious development."

Music, gesture, expression, love, are the first agencies which Froebel would use in his work; and in taking advantage of the intimate communication between the mother and the child, he would have all the mother's moods fine, and in the school those of the young teacher or kindergartner, the mother for the moment, because the child shares these moods. And while he makes the kindergarten a miniature world for the child, he makes its system a school for mothers. Indeed a school for mothers has been established on this basis and with this name in Prussia, and it is much to be wished that we might have the same thing here. Something of the sort, to be sure, has been attempted, but one class of mothers had no time from their work, and the other class from their play, and nothing has as yet resulted.

In the modern system of training children the work begins at the earliest moment; for as there is no moment too early for the implanting of evil, it is to be counteracted and prevented at the outset. "A tender young leaf pricked in the spring-time with the finest needle will show a scar of continually increasing size, till it withers in the fall." If one were to condense the system to a few words, one would merely repeat Froebel's own intention of satisfying the child's demands as much as possible, of being wisely indulgent, and of allowing the child, so far as consistent with safety, to learn by experience. By this means when the child attains his seventh year and leaves the kindergarten, character has been expanded, habits of discipline, obedience, exactitude, niceness, and unselfishness have been formed, the will has been trained through the exploitation of wise motives and reflection on the result of action, the intellect and the emotions have been exercised, while all the social instincts have been fed and strengthened to demand yet more food, instincts that are our joy, and, so far as much of the happiness of this life is concerned, are almost our salvation. And in the mean time the child has learned something of his relation to inorganic nature, to nature even in the iron in his blood, the chalk in his bones, to human nature, and, it is claimed, to God, and to God in nature.

At seven years the child has attained one-half his stature, one-third his weight, and his brain, save in exceptional instances, is as large as it is going to be. But although the brain has attained its size, it has not made much progress toward differentiation; its structural development is still very embryonic, but has been given tendency and direction, for, in the words of an authority, "all brain activity reacts on the particular structure engaged, modifying it in some unknown way, and bringing about a subsequent physiological disposition to act in a similar manner," establishing thus a habit, perhaps a faculty, as a gardener establishes a new variety. It is during this plastic period before the seventh year that Froebel puts in his work—the period that used to be thought of small account, in which the child was dealt with as a little animal, or not much more, and in which he has been, until lately, left to the care of nurses and ignorant servants, where there were nurses and servants to be had, and left to run wild where there were not. To deal with this period now, all the intelligence, learning, moral culture, and civilized graces, are not thought too much; and the work may be done in the preliminary school, or it may be done in the home nursery.

The Kindergarten.

All the methods of the kindergarten work are the result of the most exquisite study and elaboration. They go so far as to analyze the character of the child's pleasure, in the game of bo-peep, for instance—the willing surrender of the sight of the mother's face for the sake of the fresh joy of seeing it again; and in the later game of hide-and-seek, they show that the hiding is for the instinctive delight of being found, and that in carrying this play too far, or in leaving the child unsatisfied by expressions of pleasure at the finding, there is danger of letting the interest degenerate from the social and unselfish pleasure into the love of hiding for its own sake and so into love of concealment, into slyness and deceit. How many years ago is it that Plutarch said that children should be taught to avoid all that savors of secrecy, which tends to lead them away from uprightness and to accustom them to wrong!

It is through the child's play that all this study of his nature and effort to meet his necessities proceeds. For play is the expression of the child's nature, it is the way in which he attacks life, in which he reproduces his experiences, classifies his tendencies, and exhibits his inmost being and all its outreaching. In this play the child acts over again all that he has seen and would fain comprehend, and in this play he individualizes the inner spark which is himself and which is to be the agent of good or evil in him. One of Froebel's chief interests was in seeing the progression of the whole race from its savage days in the play of the child. "He draws a parallel," says Miss Blow, "between the child's love for running and wrestling, and for all games of physical prowess, and that first stage of human society when all men were hunters, warriors and athletes. He connects the child's love for digging in the ground with that agricultural instinct which transformed nomadic tribes into nations of husbandmen. He shows us the germ of rights and prosperity in the boy's love of ownership, opens our eyes to see in mud pies a faint straggle of the plastic instinct, persuades us to hear in the rhythmic cooing of the baby a prophecy of music, and bids us reverence the dawn of science in the eager habit of investigation. But he lingers most lovingly of all over those manifestations which reveal essential human connections, and never tires of following the soul as it struggles from darkness into light."

As it has already been said, the very beginning of Froebel's system lies in his deep intimacy with the hearts of mothers, his knowledge of them, and fellowship with them.

He has for the mother almost a divine tenderness; he educates her while he shows her how to make her child a symmetrical and a spiritual being.

As the kindergarten is the next step from the mother's arms, it is continued in the mother's spirit; and as the smile is the first expression of love between mother and child, in the spirit of that smile is a subsequent training to be given and received. In the kindergarten book of nursery songs and games, with every song for the child there is a motto for the mother, to show her the feeling in which the little game would best be played or the song sung. Froebel went about among the people studying mothers and babies; and it would seem as if he had caught and preserved every emotion of the little being in its first taking hold of life, and he taught mothers what their own natural play with their babies meant, and how it might be made yet more effectual. In this way motherhood is formulated into a science, but all so naturally that one sees, as it were, an apotheosis of pure family life in every household where these ideas are adopted and their leading followed, that of "father, mother, child, of light and love and life." It is through the mother that the child reaches that self-knowledge which is also self-reverence and self-control; it is through her instant sympathy that his instinctive activity compasses all culture; it is through the mother that the world of self, of others, of all the outside universe is first reached by the child; but it is all under a process not of forcing but of self-development.

Love is to call out faith, needs are to demand fulfillment, as in the instance given by one of his exponents, of the little child who being abused by her nurse, and wishing to complain to her mother, who was absent, exclaimed desperately, "Father in Heaven tell her!" and uttered her first cry for spiritual help that way. "Can you tell, O Mother," Froebel asks, "when the spiritual development of your child begins? Can you trace the boundary line which separates the conscious from the unconscious soul? In God's world, just because it is God's world, the law of all things is continuity—there are and can be no abrupt beginnings, no rude transitions, no to-day which is not based upon yesterday. The distant stars were shining long before their rays reached our earth. The seed germinates in darkness, and is growing long before we can see its growth. So in the depths of the infant soul a process goes on which is hidden from our eyes, yet upon which hangs more than we can dream of good or evil, happiness or misery."

In raising mothers to this height, it is recognized, even if unconsciously, that until now the race has "received its stamp from the male half only," and in teaching mothers how to turn even their instincts to account in educating their children, a new era is opening, in which the children of the race will have the benefit intellectually of mothers as well as fathers in a way they have not known before, and which must be enlarging and elevating and ennobling. In this light it is not so much matter whether mothers talk babytalk to their children or not; indeed Rousseau says that words are of almost no consequence in the early months, and that accent is all-important. It is the harsh sentence, the sharp emphasis, the unmusical tone that must not be given by the mother. It is quick and absolute sympathy that should be shown by her; for as Froebel says, "The whole after life of the human being, with all its deep significance, passes in dim, shadowy presentiments through the child's soul. But the child himself does not understand the importance of these presentiments, these dim strivings and forebodings, and they are seldom noticed or attended to by the grown-up people who surround him. What a change there would be in all the conditions of life, of children, of young people, of humanity in general, if only these warning voices were listened for and encouraged in early childhood and apprehended in youth in their highest meaning." It is because the mother guides and governs intuitively that she is peculiarly fitted to translate and to illumine these intuitions, intimations, or presentiments, and if she is the mother that she should be, to glorify them, and demonstrate the inner meaning of the universe through the experience of love.

It being to the mother, then, that Froebel gives his first assistance, it is out of her caresses and endeavors at entertainment that he builds up his system in a logical sequence of games that are satisfying, delighting, and developing to the child. adding little more, only enlarging and illumining the old. The child's first movements are made contributory to certain expansive gymnastic exercises, especially those for the hand, the most valued member of the body—the weathercock being the name of one of the earliest games, since, after light, the child oserves motion, which is life, and by holding the hand out flat with the thumb erected, a weathercock is imitated, and by the movement from north to south, from east to west, the connecting muscles of the wrist are brought into action, the action being accompanied by a little song which arouses a spark of thought. The next step is to make the child look for the wind, the invisible force behind. In another game the fingers represent father and mother, brother and sister, and the children are named and counted and put to bed. Another game is called the sun-bird, and consists of the vain attempt to catch the reflection of the sunbeam flashed to and fro by means of a piece of glass. "The child thus learns at an early age that it is not only material possession that gives pleasure, that beauty has the power to penetrate to the soul and to produce greater happiness than mere

SHE SPELLS OUT THE LESSON WITH HER CHILD.

enjoyment of the senses can afford." With this the little household pets and animals, pigeons, chickens, cats, whether real or imaginary, are to be called around, exciting observation and friendship, and tempting the child's desire for further knowledge. He is taught family-life by means of a nest of birds; in one hand-game he rounds his hands into the likeness of a nest, and he is taught then that every little bird is taken care of in a special way, how it builds its nest, where it is safe from danger and where the food it requires is within reach, and that it builds this nest and hatches its young ones at the time of year when the unfledged little creatures will be protected by the warmth of the spring sun. And then the mother drawing the child's attention to the fearlessness with which the little birds lie quietly in their nest, waiting for the return of their mother who has gone to fetch them food, repeats these words:

> "The heavenly Father's glorious sun
> Warms thy home, too, and makes it bright,
> He shines on thee and every one—
> Look up, and thank Him for His light!"

There is another hand-game, called the watering-pot, in which the child is taught the pleasure of doing for others, in imitating the action of giving water to the flowers, while his intelligence is awakened to the fact that all things require care. The child thus is taught, first, love for the father and mother, then for mankind, and then for the Infinite. He discovers for himself that he is "the child of nature, the child of humanity, and the child of God," even although he does not put his discovery into words; he is led to perceive later, and his parents are led to perceive with him, that the laws of the mind and the laws of the universe are the same; and those parents, in beholding the soul grope for and grasp the organs of the body, and use their hitherto unspiritualized substance, so far from doubting the existence of the immortal part of their child, will, under the light that Froebel gives, see it blossom and unfold before their eyes.

It is now evident that the office of education is that of assisting and guiding natural development, that the beginning gives a bias to all the rest, that the spiritual and the physical go on together, that the child's intuitions furnish a natural basis, and by using the physical wants we reach the spiritual, the senses being the slaves of the soul, the will, and the intellect, that instinctive notice is to be led into conscious action, that as only through physical impressions is the soul awakened, so those impressions should be the object of care, and not be left to chance, and that, as the last springs from the first, the process by education is to be continuous. Thus it will be seen the simple

BEAUTY AND GLORY OF MOTHERHOOD.

gymnastics for the hand, advised by Froebel, contain the seed and essence of all later instruction.

That the comprehension and practice of this require a good deal of study on the part of the mother is not to be denied, but it is simple, so gradual, that it is not to be feared, and it is all the time accompanied by the unfolding and perfecting of the flower of being in the dearest and tenderest thing on earth.

The Gifts in Froebel's System.

Froebel wisely begins by recognizing play as the absolute business of a child's life; and he utilizes the fact by leading play unawares into work and the business of the maturer life. He accomplishes this largely by the intelligent use of certain toys that he calls his "gifts," wholesome to handle, not easily injured, thus repressing the destructive tendency; toys of lovely suggestion, and most of them not so complete in themselves that they cannot afford the opportunity of doing something more with them. They can be used illustratively in later periods than that for which they were first given; and they are chosen to teach form, color, and distinctive qualities like weight and size, to teach also the love of law and the comprehension of unity in the each and all of the universe, each set of "gifts" preparing the way for the next. These objects, and the brief drill accompanying them, teach obedience, promptness, industry, facility, arouse imagination, quicken originality, and strengthen the body. In order that they shall be intelligently and faithfully employed, an educated and grown-up teacher is necessary, the child having left his mother's arms; and it is thought best that no class shall number more than fifteen children.

The first gift, which, indeed, belongs to early babyhood, consists of six woolen balls, three of the primary and three of the secondary colors, "the six children of light in the rainbow, the symbol of highest peace." These afford the child the means of judging of form, of color, of direction, up and down, to right and left, each ball having a string so as to be under control, afford exercise, and lead to the second gift. With any one of these balls begins the application of the law of contrasts, the first contrast lying in the object as one opposed to or outside of the child's self or identity, and afterward coming that of the varying colors, that of one or many of rest or motion, of the latter in straight lines or curves, given in tossing, or belonging to it in rebounding. Then, too, it is seen that the ball is always the same, equal in all directions, is a representation of all concentered force; it gives the child's first impression its own roundness and completeness.

The second gift is a wooden ball, and with it a cube and a cylinder. The ball carries on the lessons of the first gift; it represents motion and life, the cube, rest and inertia; the cylinder combines both; standing, it has inertia, rolling it has life.

"Thus the three appear as representatives of the vague essence of the three kingdoms of nature; in the cube, life sleeps as in the mineral kingdom, and the cube moves only when placed on edge or corner, to return again to sleep; in the cylinder, the type of the vegetable kingdom, axial life in certain directions begins to manifest itself; and in the ball, as in the animal kingdom, all-sided life, life in all directions is reached. Again, the second gift presents types of the principal phases of human development; from the easy mobility of infancy and childhood—the ball—we pass through the half-steady stages of boyhood and girlhood; represented in the cylinder, to the firm character of manhood and womanhood for which the cube furnishes the formula."

By revolving the cube, we find a cylinder; by revolving the cylinder, a sphere; by which we learn, "not only that each member of the second gift contains each and all of the others, but that whatever is in the universe is in every individual part of it; that even the meanest holds the elements of the noblest; that the highest life is even in what in short-sighted conceit we call death. And when, on the other hand, we revolve the sphere, and see that, try as we may, it will ever remain the same, we learn that all-sided animal life is, indeed, the highest manifestation of existence, that death means decay, and that only all-sided development can keep us from this."

The third gift, or the child's joy, as it is called, is a larger cube, cut so as to divide into eight equal cubes. This makes a step in development; for hitherto all has been whole, indivisible, and complete, all impressions have come as units, and now analysis and synthesis begin, of course in the simplest forms, and the most easily to be digested and assimilated, that of taking apart and putting together, of dividing, changing, and joining, of using will and inventive faculty, all in the exercise of the first glad activity, and all under that control which the shape and nature of the small cubes make inevitable, so that destructiveness and rude vandalism are impossible; and in the mean time number is taught by this, and the idea of the fraction. The child cannot re-create the toy he has shattered; but let the big cube be broken, and, "Oh, wonder and joy! each of its parts resembles the whole, the original; he has not destroyed, he has not killed his own joy, he has more, *more* of the same delightful playthings. . . . And, behold, when they are put together again—when the synthesis is made—what a wealth of new forms, what a store of new playthings grow as by charm out of the parts. . . . All the while, the child is gaining and fixing new cognitions; new relations of position, direction, shape, number, motion, life; acquiring ever fuller and clearer control of language, ever greater, higher, manual skill, bringing ever more unity into his thoughts, feelings, and expressions. Can we fail to see," adds Mr. Hailmann, from whom these sentences on the soul of Froebel's gifts are quoted, "that with such playthings, judiciously presented and managed by a mother whose wisdom is equal to her love, the child's instinct for activity, his awakening consciousness of power, grow, not in the direction of destructiveness and cruelty—but toward skill, to imitate, to reproduce, to invent." The fourth gift is again a cube made of smaller oblong blocks. The fifth gift, another cube made of twenty-seven smaller ones, introduces the oblique line, aids in the study of angles, and later in the comprehension of square and cubic measures. The sixth gift is another cube of twenty-seven oblongs, designed to help in building and in arranging symmetrically. All these impress upon the child the principles of unity and universality in their like and unlikeness. These six gifts are the most important; but all the others are of untold value in their various uses.

With the seventh gift come what are called tablets, slices of wood or of thick cardboard, from which the element of thickness is withdrawn so that only the element of surface is left, with which the child constructs representations or flat pictures or what he may, and the use of which is thought to mark an important point of his mental growth. The eighth gift is of slender wooden sticks of various lengths and tints, for making rude objects preparatory to drawing, the shapes of the letters of the alphabet, for interlacing into spaces for the multiplication table, for acquiring perception of length apart from breadth and thickness, and for similar uses. The ninth gift is of half and whole wire rings, for instruction in curves, leading to elementary science, to botany, astronomy, and geography. The tenth gift is of slates and papers netted in squares, by means of which both drawing and proportion are taught, and later the drawing of maps "in the net" is thus made exceedingly easy. The eleventh gift is paper and cards to be perforated, a needle with a handle, and a pad to lay beneath in this elementary form of drawing. The twelfth gift is made of perforated cards, and silks, and needles for simple embroidery. The thirteenth is of papers folded and cut in many ways that produce interesting designs and afford the delighted child the lawful opportunity to use scissors, thus turning his mischievous propensities into charming interplay of fancy. The fourteenth gift is strips of colored paper to be woven together in any pattern, wonderfully exciting to the inventive powers. The fifteenth is of hard wood slats which are to be interlaced into all sorts of figures. The sixteenth is of slender slats joined together, representing innumerable combinations of angles. The seventeenth is of colored paper strips, eight or ten inches long, to be folded lengthwise and bent into shape, according to rules given with them. The eighteenth is again of paper in squares, triangles, and circles, out of which many other objects are formed. The nineteenth is of pointed wires, corks, and peas—the ends of the wires to be united in the corks, or in the peas soaked and softened, and so erected into skeleton designs. The twentieth gift is of potter's clay, with a modeling board and tools.

Of all these gifts, perhaps none are made more useful than the last; for it can be made to take the place of almost all the others. Of clay, the child delightedly can create the ball, the cylinder, and later on express his perception of all other objects, and even can approach the threshold of art, although all unaware and as unconscious as Raphael's two cherubs that overlook the battlements of heaven. And in the modeling, a use of the hands has been acquired hardly to be had in any other way, an acquaintance with natural objects and laws, and an opportunity for the expansion into ideal artistic life for those in whom the artistic nature predominates. We are told that "the moral effect of this occupation is special, the yielding nature of the clay seems to develop conscious power, to prophesy the dominion over material nature commanded in the morning-hymn of creation that begins the Bible; while the indestructibility reveals the inexorableness of law; truths which are opposite but not contradictory."

The uses of all these gifts can be grouped into exercises with solids, with planes, with lines, with points; and with their employment comes a series of physical games, such as the drill, singing, ball-throwing, a change from manual to vocal work, and the rest to be found in calling upon other organs and muscles.

School Another World.

That school is important for the evolution of the social nature is apparent. "He who learns to swim must go in the water"; he who is to be happy or useful in the world must mingle with his fellows; and so in his first social experience the child should have a society as near perfection as it can be made, a society of the innocent, a society where personal liberty is supreme, where each has all his rights and chances and no interference from another. "Such a society does all it can to aid each member in the attainment of his individual ends, while he, in return, finds his highest aims in common purposes; such a society thanks the child cordially for his successful activity, and he gratefully acknowledges as his greatest triumphs those in whose attainment he played only a part; such a society enjoys the result even of his individual activity with full, unfeigned pleasure, and he again soon learns to seek his greatest joy in the joy of others, his highest ideals in the welfare of the whole. . . . In the kindergarten Froebel would provide a pedagogic society which answers to these requirements. Here the child finds a number of others of similar age, as nearly his equals in power, capacity, and scope as individuality will permit; a number of social elements with whom he can fully sympathize, and who sympathize fully with him in all manifestations of growing life, among whom he finds nothing inexplicable, unattainable, unenjoyable; playmates, associates, fellow-beings in embryo, with whom he can assimilate, coalesce organically without giving up his self. Here the child becomes familiar with the high value of union with others. Heretofore, self was the main center of his desires; now he begins to find aims beyond self; the germs of love, of devotion, of a widening humanity swell in his soul and burst into life; he is aroused to a consciousness of his worth as a part of the whole."

At school, then, it is evident the child is stimulated by others, pleased with companionship, and all his social instincts—that is, his relations to his kind—are developed at the same time with the rest of his better nature. Here the mental work, or sport if you please, is for fifteen minutes, and then the physical game, the song, the dance, the pretty play, is taken up for change and relief for as long a time. The child sees that it is a privilege to join the game, and that it is punishment to be unemployed.

In building with the blocks, the natural destructive element is restrained by the obligation of taking down instead of knocking down any and every structure, and of putting things away in place. The learning of the alphabet, which was once a dreary effort of memory, becomes a pleasure when the letters are fashioned with the sticks of the eighth gift; the first group of the letter I, and the figure 1, being made of the single stick, the next of X, V, L, by two sticks, and so on.

Among the effects of this system of preparatory education, at the end of which the child is found to know thoroughly much that used to be taught through that wearisome memorizing which makes the world a desert for the time, are many purely moral gains. Thus the child has been given, first, perception of absolute truth and of reverence for the fixed laws of the universe in the mere handling of his blocks, and, later, love for his little fellow-mortals, and the spirit of true democracy.

The old system of mnemonics may have its value, the mechanical and the ingenious systems, such as that artificial way by which we of an older growth were taught to remember, for instance, the year of the death of Charlemagne, 814, because the figure 8 resembles the hour-glass, the symbol of war;

the figure 4 a ploughshare, the symbol of peace. But here all the child's knowledge is firsthand knowledge, that has come out of his own experience, and is thus a part of himself and not to be forgotten. And with all the rest of his moral gain he has learned that self-control which calls into exercise those among the higher brain-centers.

All his toys, while they have taught him inductive reasoning, have been archetypes of nature; in the ball he has the earth and stars, the ideal of perfection in shape and motion; in the cylinder he has growth in trees and in animals, and further along he finds there the foundation of pottery; in the cube he has the mineral kingdom, crystallization, and by and by architecture; he himself in any childish experiment of play may see salt crystallize into cubes, and alum into octahedrons; everywhere he has been led upward in the way in which only geometry and geometrical forms lead; and all without a text-book he has been made master of much that text-books give.

In Visiting a Kindergarten.

One can find by personal observation the value of the Froebel system much more exactly than it can be comprehended by reading. If one visits a kindergarten watches the children building any object with their blocks, each one alone, and each one individualizing his work; hears the teacher tell them all a story concerning that object afterward, helping them by the details of the story to see if they have done their work correctly; listens to them then singing the song appropriate to the exercise; if one watches them unite and contribute to build a village, learning the while a new lesson of association; or if one only follows them in their playtime, one will still observe that with every chance for individual effort there is always the joy of united effort, of co-ordination without subordination, all in an atmosphere of joyous love and sympathy.

"Do you not see," asks Hailmann, "the gentle, steady impulse for growth, the abundance of food for development, which each and every individuality gains from this intercourse with nature? Do you not see that the full and respectful consideration, which the little society awards to true merit in every direction, teaches these little artists, discoverers, inventors, thinkers, to feel and to appreciate? . . . Do you not see that it is not in the power of a single home, no matter how great its wealth, material and mental, to supply the mighty influence for all-sided growth, individual as well as social, which is wielded by the free and full appreciation of individual worth and the just and moderate demands upon individual powers on the part of a society of equals? And do you not feel that it would be a crime to keep the growing human being from this influence, when his nature calls for it? Do you not feel that it would be sin to let it be exerted without proper guidance?"

Physically, morally, intellectually, and artistically the methods of the Froebel system, it must be seen, we think, are those which will soonest lift the child to those levels from which the great, perfect race to come shall take its departure.

When children emerge from the kindergarten their whole being is in a condition which renders them susceptible to the loftiest sort of instruction. Their faculties and their conscience are all alert, and they are ready to take hold of the great world of knowledge after the technical fashion and make it their own. Much yet remains that they may be taught experimentally, as, for example, in the woods the growth of trees, on the shore the structure of shell and sponge and seaweed, in the open country the movement of stars and planets. "What shall be attempted," asked Mrs. Hopkins, one of the supervisors of the Boston schools, "for the child who comes from the kindergarten all ready to learn, but as yet unacquainted with books? I answer, all, and more than all, that may be found in elementary treatises in every department of natural science may be given him in object-lessons, in a comparatively short time, with what is of vastly more importance—an enthusiastic love for these studies, a habit of careful observation, and a training of the senses which shall be a great addition to his power in science, art, or practical life. He may at the same time lay up in his memory the ground facts of written and spoken language and mathematics. Then, by natural stages, he will turn with avidity to records of the observations of others, until a conception of arrangement, generalization, and inference will grow up within him, the dawn of a higher epoch in the harmonious education of the mind."

Mrs. Hopkins goes on to tell of a year's work with a class of children some ten years of age, in which for history they studied that of the United States with Mr. Higginson's text-book and the help of the pictures in Lossing's Field-books and Catlin's North American Indians; Dickens' Child's History of England, with an examination of many illustrative prints; and a good portion of Greek and Roman mythology. With this, they studied also the geography of the United States, drew maps, made imaginary journeys, and traded products of the different portions of the country till they were tolerably familiar with the whole of it. Instead of a drill in grammar, they were shown that they already knew grammar in an elementary way and could parse simple sentences; while they had exercises in dictation and composition with constant reading and spelling and recitations of poetry. In arithmetic they mastered fractions, decimals, compound numbers, and the metric system, having treated all these subjects as variations of the rules of numeration, addition, and subtraction. In botany they analyzed flowers, learned the properties of tendrils, the propagation of the orchid, the multiplication of cells, studied forest trees, a first book in zoölogy, besides reading several elementary books on natural science, and making drawings of birds, all as if a new world were opening to them, and with delighted and eager apprehension. They drew, under a special teacher, learned to talk simple French with a native teacher, could play a French game, and in German could read Grimm's Tales. In all of this, learning seemed to be simply a delight.

For example, says Mrs. Hopkins, in that invaluable little book for mothers and teachers, 'How Shall My Child Be Taught?' "One day last spring, to reward those who had braved the storm to come, I took a dry account from a compendium of general history, and attempted to teach in an hour or two the lesson of the Crusades. The children had had but a glimpse of the matter, in connection with their lessons in English history, the previous year. Reading to them in some such way as I have described (that is, interrupted with questions and answers and brief conversations, using the skeleton of the book, and making, as it were, an impromptu translation of the text), writing on the board a schedule of names and dates as they occurred in the reading, in order to make the outline clear before their eyes; tracing the localities and movements on the map; reading verbatim passages from 'The Talisman,' also showing with it the engravings from a rare illustrated edition of Scott, and with pictures and a little of the text from 'Ivanhoe,' I found at the close of the session that, in the glow of the whole theme upon the clear mirror of their minds, they had received a comprehensive as well as a particular knowledge of the subject, a perfectly orderly outline of its facts, a vivid apprehension of its purpose, philosophy, connections, and results, as well as a strong scenic impression of the drama of the whole epoch."

But not only the method of study, but the matter given in the desultory reading of the child is a subject demanding serious consideration. This is no new idea; for, more than two thousand years ago, Plato said, in substance, that we must be scrupulous about the stories our children have; in them there must be nothing derogatory to the dignity of the gods; they must not mislead by false statement; they must not present the characters of the great in an unworthy light; they must inculcate courage and self-control; and they must be written in a simple style.

We see now how much depends upon the teacher, and how vital it is that the mind which imparts should be full and strong and replete with overflowing thoughts, and how unfortunate it is if resort to books and statistics and dry repetition itself is found necessary.

STEPPING STONES TO HAPPINESS.

We are in the habit of thinking that the teacher of the advanced classes of later years has the higher rank; but when we more fully understand the office of the teacher of these early years, see that a whole generation is clay in her hands, that her work "covers the most impressible period of life, it demands the most earnest enthusiasm, the clearest wisdom, and the most varied experience in one who undertakes it; in particular it requires intense sympathy with children in their tastes, in their outlook and ways of thinking, as well as in the singleness of their moral nature; it requires, moreover, a capacity of child-likeness which is the attribute only, of harmonious maturity or of genius.

"It is the unspeakable gift to become as little children . . Sympathy—not indifference, antagonism, or hostility—should be the medium of the teacher's influence. Desire for the pupil's advancement will awaken desire in him for that end, courage arouse courage, determination evoke determination; joy in the teacher's heart will communicate its stimulus and lead to victory; enthusiasm will kindle enthusiasm and create a vital atmosphere in which the child's being expands almost unconsciously. Intelligence should precede memory; imagination should accompany recollection; nature never set a child to learn by rote; those things which must finally be subjected to an act of memory should be approached as a discovery, as the symbol of ideas. Respect for the common-sense of mankind, faith in its formulated experiences will grow out of an intelligent attention to results of thought and conduct, will be accepted as guides for action."

A famous instructor some years ago, who said that he spent his days leading jackasses up Parnassus, would not be of much use to-day in this view of his duty and this exemplification of his love for his work. Another requirement of the teacher in the modern treatment of children is the ability to exalt and increase the strength of the will. "A culture of the will is a necessity of right culture for body, mind, and soul," continues Mrs. Hopkins in the wise and wonderful pages from which extracts have been given here. "It must be remembered that the fundamental law of growth by exercise is as applicable to the will as to any other power of man or nature. The will must be kept active in the child by leading him to determine and work for himself. If he is driven blindly to the accomplishment of the task set for him, he will never develop the power to set tasks for himself and put himself to work, which is his only chance for real achievement of either power or result. Give motive and stimulus sufficient to arouse the will until it commands the faculties successfully. It is immediate, clear, and decisive action which best defines the mental and moral ideas, executes their purposes, and evolves the will-power. Children should not be advised when they are competent to ad-

HELPLESS MORSEL OF HUMANITY.

vise themselves, but thrown upon their own resources for determination of aim and means as far as possible."

John Wesley's Mother.

The mother of John Wesley would have disagreed with this, for she once declared that the first thing to be done is to conquer the will, and while the improvement of the understanding is a work of time, the subjection of the will is something to be done at once, and the sooner the better. But if Mrs. Wesley were unwise here, she had some regulations in relation to her children that were worthy of remembrance. It had been observed in her family, she wrote, that cowardice and fear of punishment often led children to lie until the act became habitual; she therefore made laws that whoever confessed his fault should not be whipped, that no child should be punished twice for the same fault, or upbraided for it again; that every instance of obedience or self-denial should be praised or rewarded; and that good intentions should be respected. Certainly by these rules, or in spite of them, Mrs. Wesley had a measure of success with her children. There are some things in the old methods, it would seem, as useful and as good as anything in the new. But, on the whole, the old methods treated a child as if he were a piece of mechanism; the new methods treat him as if he were a living, growing, and unfolding soul. The old methods attend upon that which he knows; the new methods upon that which he is, regarding chiefly that most marvelous of all the phenomena of life, the capacity for growth, and seeking to bring about an intellectual and spiritual transubstantiation of the facts of the universe. By this new method, if we had not already a soul, we should develop one.

Slöjd.

Perhaps as potent a factor as any other in the new methods of rearing children is the adoption of technical instruction or manual training, in the manner commonly known as slöjd. Experts are still discussing whether we shall leave dead languages and go forward to that which is new, and whether the moods and declensions and analyses of grammar shall deaden and stultify the nervous centers much longer, whether arithmetic shall be simplified and much of it abbreviated and passed over to algebra, whether we shall leave the old wasteful ways, wasteful as regards life, time, and intelligence; but they are beginning to be of one mind as to slöjd. No such advance in mentality can be imagined as that god-like one which demands that the child shall not

THE CHILD WILL HAVE A LOVE OF WORK.

only observe and describe an object, but that he shall create it. The handling of tools, the manufacture of articles, however trifling, begets a habit of mental precision, of concentration, of clarity, of truth, that is precious; it breaks up brain-destroying monotony, gives relief from sedentary occupation, and vitalizes the effect and result of study. The ethical influence, too, of this manual training is immense; the child will have a love of work, will have acquired dexterity, patience, perseverance, practicality, invention, force of will, command of body, will have seen the beauty and virtue and need of order; the self-conceit of the merely glib memory will receive a paralyzing shock in the presence of the clear intellectual vision trained to exactitude and perception of right relations; and that will introduce true democracy which shows vivid intelligence, refined habits, a cultured family line, sharing the stains of the hands of toil.

There are economic views of the benefit of slöjd, moreover; it has been said, owing to the tyranny of trades-unions, that an American child can learn a trade only in the penitentiary, yet any finished student in manual training —it being remembered, too, that the intellectual training is coincident—has learned the use of tools so that he needs but a few months to make himself master of any trade he will. But there is a greater economic view of the matter in observation of the effect of the system on the child's brain, body, and soul.

But when school and lessons and master are done with, or very nearly so, the result of all that has been done is to be evident in the home. It will then be seen, if knowledge of the eccentricity of Mercury's orbit, if the skill to calculate eclipses, and acquaintance with the most ancient or the most modern tongue, has developed faithfulness in the young student's orbit, if the moral and emotional qualities have been as well rounded and perfected as the mental ones, and if an intellectual monster has been produced, instead of a loving and sympathetic being. Surely the answer will be a favorable one, if from the beginning the mother has given her child that full sympathy which creates both return of sympathy and unfettered confidence; has held before it the standards of honor and of truth, has taught it the joy of brotherhood, the love of humanity, and far from being the tyrannical ruler of days and doings, has been the sharer of studies, hopes, fears, joys, and dreams; and if the father has been in himself the fulfillment of his child's ideal of him.

The daughter of that mother, of the mother who deserves her, will not have been trained merely to books, to the pencil, the piano, belles-lettres, but to all the virtues of home as well. She will know the kitchen arts, at least elementarily; she will be able to take the charge of a younger child's wardrobe off the mother's hands, the care of the drawing-room, the arrangement

THE LITTLE FACE LIES NEAR HER OWN.

of flowers, of table decorations; and she will know enough of the arts of the hospital, of bed-making, of bandaging, of the dressing of wounds, not to be half heart-broken at her inability to give relief to the suffering whom she loves. She will remember that we are all alike the children of life; she will be a sister to the beggar within her gates; she will be incapable of small deceits. And the son of that mother will reverence her as the visible expression to him of heavenly power on earth, will have learned from her how to famish his evil passions, to nourish his loftier ones, will have acquired self-control, self-abnegation, the strength of his father, the purity of his sister. And if there is any further beauty to be known than the relations of such a mother and her son, of such a father and his daughter, it is to some other sphere that we must go to find it.

At the Hurricane Light.

The children of the Hurricane Light are not examples of the kindergarten methods—rather of Mrs. Wesley's plan than of anything else. But I think that neither Jack nor Emeline would have been as fine characters if they had not been reared on the true kindergarten principle, that of love.

The summer hotel stood alone on a point of rock in the sea, the narrow peninsula that led back to the mainland, washed over by frozen tides till, long before midwinter, there was no peninsula to be seen, only something like a broad floe of broken, tumbled blocks of ice full of crevasses and water-streaks and danger, although there was a sort of way along it. But the father of these children had some idea of frosting the malaria out of their blood, and thought staying there would be a novel experience, doing them good in many ways, while giving him the very chance he wanted for investigating some scientific matters in relation to ice and snow, germ-life and sea-currents. And so he had proposed, as long as somebody must stay in the hotel where they had passed the summer, to keep it from burning down, as summer hotels are apt to do if left vacant, that he would remain and attend to his studies there.

If Clara had been older she would have seen a world of poetry in the unusual life; for, when they were established in the big dining-hall, nothing could be quainter. Their father had put a heater in the basement, and the air from that, together with the fires in three huge stoves and in the open chimney, gave the room a summer warmth. At the lower end was the kitchen stove; and here were temporary shelves for the bright tins and the pans of milk skimmed by the pretty Swedish girls, whose long yellow braids made one think the serving-maids of the middle ages looked just that way. On one side of the room the windows were full of Aunt Marion's plants, and on the other were a tall book-case, a secretary for papa's papers, scientific tables, trays, and cabinets, and his charts upon the wall; and at the upper end was mamma's table and easel and work basket, and the piano and mirror and open fire, soft rugs and lounges and arm-chairs. And, as Aunt Marion said, it was the old hall of the primitive castle over again, with the lady on her dais at one end, and the maids and their spinning at the other. Their sleeping-rooms were just overhead; but they were in no hurry to go to them when, through the wide windows and through the glass doors on every side, they could see the sun set over the sea and the moon rise over the land, and darkness gathering on the waters, and storms coming up, and now and then distant sails slipping by like dreams, catching the sparkle of the light-house lamp that for an instant brought them into life and light.

After all, the days—however long they may have been to Aunt Marion—went by without seeming of appreciable length at all to the children, what with lessons, and practicing and watching papa's experiments, and climbing about the broken ice near the house, and skating on one of the broad piazzas that had been flooded and frozen for them. And presently, indeed, the days were far too short for Clara's and Nell's mysterious preparations for Christmas, which at last was close at hand.

When this all too sudden twilight came, Tom and Clara used often to conjecture about the children over at the Hurricane Light—the great white tower that loomed over the blue sea, the tower from whose summit they had so many times seen the light tremble and grow strong over the purpling waters of summer eves, with its narrow wooden causeway across waters always foaming between the tower and the rest of the island rock. They fancied all sorts of things concerning them; for they had heard there were two children there—little Jack and Emeline—with their father, the sturdy keeper of the light, and his assistant, Dan. But that was all they knew.

"Do you suppose there is any mother?" asked Will, with his nose flattened on the glass, as they watched for the light.

"No," said Clara. "Of course not."

"Oh! How can they do without a mother?"

"I don't see, I'm sure. But Emeline takes care of their clothes, I guess; and the man helps her do the work and lifts the heavy things. And sometimes—I shouldn't wonder—she sews at the little windows and looks out and thinks about how many children there are here. And perhaps she watches for our lights just as we do for hers, and wishes we could go over and play there of an afternoon. And sometimes her father lets her go up with him when he lights the lights. There they are now! Red and green, ruby and emerald—just a blaze! Oh! isn't it like Providence? Sure to be there the moment the twilight thickens; always there; I never thought about it in the summer."

"Yes," said Tom. "And don't you know, I'd rather keep a light-house than do anything else on earth; or water either"—stopping to consider if a light-house belonged to earth or water.

"What! Rather than be doctors, like papa and Uncle John, or be in business, or preach"——

"Anybody can preach. Aunt Marion's always preaching; and besides, I've heard mamma say a person should be sure he can preach well before he takes charge of folks' souls. But the light-housekeeper saves men's bodies every time he lights his lamps." And Tom felt like a preacher himself.

"What would happen," asked Will, anxiously, hugging his kitten closer, "if he didn't light the lamps?"

"The ships at sea wouldn't see it, and they wouldn't know where they were. They wouldn't say 'Hallo! Here's old Hurricane Light! Now we've

THE HURRICANE LIGHT-HOUSE.

Wreckers' Reef to keep clear of on the larboard and Drowned Man's Ledge on the port, and the Tushes to give a wide berth to'"——

"Larboard and port mean the same thing."

"Oh! you know too much, Clara!" continued Tom. "It doesn't make any odds. The ships know there are all these dangers 'round the spot where this light burns, and they luff and bear away."

"And so, if the light shouldn't burn," began Will, tearfully——

"And so, if the light shouldn't burn," said Tom, solemnly, "first a red and then a green flash, first a red and then a green, all night long, the coast would be strewn with wrecks from Maine to Mexico. I heard papa say so."

"Do you suppose," asked Nell, pushing Will aside for her own better view, "that Jack and Emeline ever go ashore?"

"No. Everything's laid in for the winter; and so they don't need to go," said Tom. "And they couldn't go easily if they did, papa says. It's all anybody can do to get over from here."

"They could come across that strip of water in their boats."

"Now look here! That strip of water is black as ink. A man might maybe. But what boy, the size of Jack, would be crawling down those slippery sides of the icy rock to get into a swinging boat sliding away from under?"

'I would," said Will.

"Folks always would do what they can't," said Tom, with grandeur. "I guess Jack and Emeline don't do it very often. I wouldn't."

"And if they could," said Clara, "and could get on our headland, the ice changes with every tide, and the blocks are too big to climb over, and there's deep water in between. If Uncle John does come to-morrow, I don't see how he'll ever get out, or ever get back."

"Uncle John," said Tom, "can do everything."

"I should think Aunt Marion would be so worried!"

"Do you suppose Jack and Emeline will hang up their stockings?" asked Will, not interested in sentimental matters.

"How is Santa Claus going to get out there with his reindeers?" answered Tom, loftily.

"Why, of course they will," said Clara. "Emeline has knit Jack some mittens, and Jack "——

"Do you suppose," said Nell, "that they know there's Tom and Clara and Will and Russ and me here?"

"Perhaps they don't call us Tom and Clara. Perhaps they call us Dick and Bell, just as we call them."

"I tell you," said Will. "Don't you think it would be nice if we made some Christmas for them?"

"But we couldn't get it out to them; don't you know?" said Tom.

"Uncle John could get it out to them when he comes," said Russell, with the general faith in Uncle John. "What would you make for them?"

"Isa could bake a cake early to-morrow morning"——

"With plums in it!"

"And frosting!"

"And Aunt Marion would pick a bunch of her flowers, roses and violets, if you ask her, Tom," said Nell.

"And a calla-lily."

"And papa could give them a silver dollar."

"But that wouldn't be us," said Clara, on whom it dawned that they were very generous with other folks' things "They can have my Girls' Own Book."

"And my 'Robinson Crusoe.' "

"And my 'Pilgrim's Progress,' " said Tom.

"I would give them my top, if I had another," said Russell.

"You always were a stingy!" exclaimed Clara.

"I'm not stingy! I don't want to give it to them if I want it myself; do I?"

"Well, perhaps they have a top. There's your parchesi-board."

"We like to play with that sometimes, you know."

"Or the kaleidoscope."

"Why, of course I'm not done with my kaleidoscope!"

"I guess Russell won't give anything," said Nell.

"Yes, I will, too! I'll give the transparent slate."

"'Tisn't yours to give," said Nell. "It's mine. But I'd just as lief. And Emeline may have my doll Queenie; that is, if Queenie would like to go."

"And her cradle?"

"Ye-e-s."

"Well, I guess I shall have to give Jack my box of tools," said Tom, with a fine air, "and trust to luck or Uncle John for another."

"And they might have the little camera that doesn't belong to anybody, and the second-best box of colors, with the old geography to paint over."

"Do you suppose they'd like a kitten?" asked Will

"Pshaw! They have half a hundred, very likely, now."

"Half a hundred kittens! Oh! how I wish I lived in a light-house!"

"Well, you do; the next best or the next worse thing. Though I never dreamed we should have neighbors. They really are neighbors, you know, if we don't see much of them or anything of them," said Clara. "There, if Aunt Marion will make a lot of her cider-candy to-morrow, to put in, I think that will do for Jack and Emeline. Don't you? The question is, how ever shall we get it out to them?"

"Wait for Uncle John. He will," said Nell.

"I'm glad they don't want the kitty," murmured Will, hugging his pet, as they went off to bed. . "It's only one more day now. If there isn't a red collar on the tree for my kitty I shall be awful cross!"

"I really think," said Clara to her Aunt Marion, when they said goodnight, and a broad ray of the light-house lamp came skimming into the room, "that it isn't so bad as I thought it was going to be here, seeing we have some neighbors."

Every few moments those great rays went sweeping by and bridging the darkness between the lonely hotel and the white pillar of the light-house in the night. Perhaps it was on that bridge that Jack's and Emeline's fancies traveled across the water and the long tongue of ice-wrapped land, to these children, with their pretty heads huddled together in the window-panes of the vast empty hotel.

"There's children over there," said Emeline. "I saw them through father's glass. They were playing on the long piazza."

"I wish we had a piazza," said Jack.

"Our causeway's just as good, in calm weather."

"No, it isn't. The ball bounces off into the water, and then I have to swim for it, and sometimes it's too cold, and sometimes there's a sea on and I can't go for it."

"I always make another, you know," said the motherly little body beside him.

"And we can't play marbles there, because they all roll off."

"We can play catch."

"Well, sometimes it's too wet with the breaking sea. Shouldn't you like to live, Em, where there isn't any sea?"

"The Bible says there isn't any sea in heaven. But I don't believe we should like it there. I guess we should miss the sea. Not to hear it, not to see it—it would be like not having any mother over again. It always sings us to sleep."

"Mothers don't make such a noise as this old surf does some nights, when you can't hear yourself breathe. Say, Em, do you remember mother?'

"A little. Not much," answered Emeline. "Only just that her eyes were the color the sea is far out under the sky in soft weather. Dove's eyes, that it tells of in the Bible."

"Hard on father to do without her; aint it? But he says you're just mother over again, any way. Only not your eyes. For yours are the color of the pools where the sun shines through the brown sea-weed. Do you suppose mother knew when Christmas came? Father doesn't."

"No matter. We do. Father has so much to think of. It's so awfully important to keep the light all night. - It would be so terrible if the light went out and the ships and people went down; and only think, so many fathers on them, too; with children waiting for them at home. Oh! it's awfully important, you see; and he can't think of everything."

"Well, if I had a little boy, I'd think of Christmas, I know. I'd give him a plane and a saw and chisel, any way."

"Perhaps he will. He'll think of it when I give him the comforter I've made."

"I know what he'll say. He'll say just what he did last year; that you're the best little comforter."

"Oh!" said Emeline, with her cheeks glowing: "We have to be very good to father, he's had so much trouble. It was dreadful for him to lose mother, and have us babies to bring up. And he's real good to us. Some fathers whip their boys."

"Whip their boys! I guess so. How you talk! Father never whipped me. He shook me once. I thought then I'd run away. Any way, I don't mean to stay here when I'm a man. Days when the sea is gray and black, and the rain is driving by, and the waves go off like great guns, I think I'll get away any time."

"And leave father and me?" said Emeline, pitifully, "when you're all we have?"

"I'd send for you. I couldn't do without you, you know. Oh! There's their light! The children's over on the reef. Now let's get father's glass again and look at them." And Jack fitted the long spy-glass to his eye with expedition. "There's ever so many of them. I should think there was a dozen. And one of them has a kitten. Oh! say, Em, I wish we had a kitten! And one has pushed the kitten boy away. I guess they're talking, by the way their heads go. What if they are talking about us?"

"Oh! they wouldn't be. I don't suppose they know of us. Maybe they're watching the witches make tea. I used to like to watch the witches making tea, before I knew it was only the picture of our lamp in the window pane, dancing out there. See the long rays of the tower-lamps wheeling about there now; one of them made a bridge clear way over to the children. They always make me think of that Bible verse about God's laying the beams of His chambers upon the waters."

"Things always put you in mind of the Bible. Does it say anything about Christmas there?" And while he still used the glass, Emeline went to the table and read him the story St. Luke tells about the shepherds keeping their flocks.

'I think of it often," said Emeline, 'summer nights when we are all sitting up outside the tower, and the Milky Way seems a road right into heaven, and the stars are spirits—great shining spirits—sweeping along. It will be splendid, oh! it will be splendid, after we are dead if we are just such great spirits, sweeping and shining with stars on our foreheads."

"I'd rather be alive," said Jack.

"Yes," said Emeline, half regretfully. "Of course; so should I; with you and father."

"But I suppose," said Jack, "we might just as well be three spirits all alone out there in the night as three people all alone here in the light-house. Only it's warm here and light. Say, Em, what do you suppose those children are going to have Christmas?"

'Oh! everything. They may have a Christmas tree. And if it's clear weather we may see it through the glass to-morrow night."

"To-morrow? Day after to-morrow's Christmas."

"But to-morrow's Christmas Eve. Folks always have their trees, I guess, Christmas Eve. We always hear the bells ringing from the towns, if we listen, you know."

"Oh!" said Jack. "I suppose we could make some molasses candy with nuts in it, any way," he added, presently.

"And father will tell us the story of when he was a little boy"——

"It doesn't seem as if father ever was a little boy; does it? There, they've gone to bed, now," as he shut up the spy-glass. "I say, Em, it's first rate to have neighbors, ain't it? They're just as good as deaf and dumb neighbors anyhow. We can see 'em if we can't talk to 'em."

"Yes; we never did have neighbors in the winter before. I wish we could send them some of our nut-candy," said Emeline. "Yes, it's real nice to have neighbors."

And before long, while the light-keeper toiled up and down his winding stairs to attend to the clock-work of the lamps, the children were asleep, while the broad beams went on their way through the darkness, leading the great ships by with the green and crimson rays glancing on their stiff and frozen sails

There was enough frost in the gray air next day for Christmas weather, certainly; but the blue sky and sunshine, that go with the last Christmas errands, were not to be seen. Indeed, the atmosphere was full of frozen spiculæ of snow too chill to fall. Nor was there any of the clear, night sparkle, where the stars seem to join crisp tones with the glad ringing of the bells.

In the mediæval hall, as Aunt Marion called it, the children were prancing about the screens that hid the unlighted tree, and wondering why Uncle John didn't come, and if he wasn't coming at all, and if they would have the tapers lit before he came, and adding something every little while to the parcel that was to be gotten over to the light-house by hook or by crook, when Uncle John came, if he ever did come.

And in the light-house home, Emeline had the spider on the stove, and the molasses bubbling, while Jack was picking the meats out of the nuts, and their father was up busy with the lamps; for the night was going to be so cold he feared it might congeal the oil; and the dim day was growing dimmer. The nuts were in at last, and with one more boiling up Emeline's platter was buttered, and the compound that had already made Jack's mouth water was set out to cool in the twilight.

"Oh! if it isn't cold!" she said, with a shiver, shutting the door. "And I declare I believe I've upset the trough that father has those frozen sea creatures in to find out if they'll come to life when they thaw out in the spring. I must see. And it's dark, so dark! How I pity children without homes on such a night as this! How quick it grew dark. I didn't notice it."

"Nor I," said Jack, still picking at a nut-shell.

"I can't bear the dark," said Emeline, bustling about for a candle.

"Nor I," said Jack again. "It—it always seems like a great—a great—thing—out there, you know."

"I suppose it's because we've always had the light, the beautiful great beams of the tower light. And—Why, Jack! where is the light? Oh! where is the light? We never were this way before! Can't father light it? O, father!" and she opened the door, to dart up the tower stairs, and tripped over something lying at their foot.

It was her father lying there. He had fallen—from what height who could tell, or whether stumbling, or whether with a stroke! He lay cold and unconscious. He might be dead. She did not utter another syllable; but she used all her strength and dragged him over the threshold, and stopped and pulled a little way again, till Jack sprang to her aid, and between them they got him across the room to his bed. It had taken almost a half hour to do it. Emeline threw herself beside him, her mouth on his, her tears raining over his cold face. "He's breathing! He's breathing!" she cried out. And suddenly she was on the floor again. "The lamps! The lamps!" she exclaimed. "O, Jack, you know how. You must go up and light them!'

'I can't! Oh! I can't, Em," he said, between his sobs. "I can't go up there in the dark!"

"You must!" she answered. "I can't leave father yet. Oh! do go, Jack!" she cried, in an agony. "Just think of the ships, of the wrecks, of the other children's fathers drowned and dead, if the light isn't burning; if you don't go!"

"I—I can't," he said.

"But if you don't, I shall have to. I shall have to leave father; and perhaps he'll die if I do. He may never come to if I don't get the mustard on! Do, Jack dear! Do go, Jack!" She was already hurrying about for clothes and hot water.

"I—I can't!" said Jack again. "But—well, I'll try." And he lighted the lanterns slowly, and left the door open, and began to climb the stairs, stopping at every step. And Emeline was binding the mustard plasters on her father's feet and neck, and filling jugs with hot water to put on either side of him, and holding his rough hand and kissing it, crying and trembling and frightened; for now he was breathing, indeed; breathing in such a fearful way that she thought every breath must be the last.

But why didn't the beams sweep out? Why was it still so dark out there? Couldn't Jack light the lamps? Hadn't he gone? She ran to the doorway. There he sat crouched half way up. "Oh! haven't you gone, Jack?" she cried in despair.

"I—I told you I couldn't!" he replied. "I feel as if all those dreadful things that will happen if the lamps ain't lighted are up there now."

She glanced back at her father. She could do no good if she stayed beside him. Up she dashed, caught the lantern from Jack, who meekly followed her as she almost flew on her upward way. One glance when well within the tower-chamber, and she saw that the clock-work which turned the wheel about was broken; and it was in his anxiety and haste for some necessary tool with which to mend it that her father had fallen. "Oh! what made us let Dan off for his Christmas?" she groaned. "There is nothing but to turn the wheel with our hands." And she lighted lamp after lamp and began to drag the wheel about. "And one of us must do it all night long; and one of us must go for the doctor. Which shall it be?"

And Jack, in the bottom of his cowardly little soul, felt that it would not be he. It was impossible; he could not do either. Stay there alone in that place, dragging the wheel around, with his father dying, perhaps dead—stiff and cold and dead—and the horrible vacancy where he had been? Oh! he never, never could. He would rather die at once, himself, here, with Emeline beside him. And he didn't want to die; he wasn't like Emeline; death was something unspeakably dreadful to him. But then, on the other hand, to go down into that black water underneath the causeway in the pitchy dark, and try to climb those icy shores opposite, and make his way in the night across those heaps of ice with the deep channels between them, and not a star, only the black, monstrous dark all about; and he would be lost and drowned and frozen. Oh! he never, never could.

"But father will die if we can't get a doctor; and he would rather die than have the lamps go out," urged Emeline. "One of us must go. It's nothing to stay here and turn the wheel, that's a good boy, dear, and I will go for the doctor. I can do that as well as you, you know." And so she could; for she could handle a boat as easily as other girls could trundle a hoop.

As Jack gazed at Emeline aghast, her face seemed to be shining and smiling on him like an angel's. She already looked like one of those white shining spirits she had spoken of the night before. He felt as if it were a sort of sign—if she went she would become one of those great shining spirits, not his little loving, living Emeline. His little Emeline out there in all those icy horrors and the blackness! The tears spurted out at the thought. He said something seemed to snap in his head or his heart, he could not tell which, and let him out, let him free from all his fear and shrinking. "Good-bye, Emeline," he called out, choking. "I'll go. And if I don't come back"——

"If you don't," she cried, stopping to throw her arms about him, "father will be dead, and I will, too, and it will be all the same; for we shall be together somewhere else!" And Jack took the lantern and came running back with her cloak and hood; and then his step rang on the stairs again, she heard the tower door slam, and nothing more, while she kept on her weary way dragging the lamps around, and out there the sea made its cry.

Poor little Jack! As he plunged into the night Emeline's white look seemed stamped on the darkness, together with the fixed and suffering face, livid and purple, on his father's pillow. How could any fear, he thought now, keep him from bringing help? He did not stay to untie the painter of his boat, cased in ice, as it was; he cut it with his jack-knife when he had dropped into the boat, and dipping his oars into the blackness, ferried across, guided by the flashing of the lamps that Emeline dragged round, in which everything started out one moment, and then was lost in blacker shadow.

I can't imagine how he climbed those rocks of the headland, mere sheets of ice; but he did. Boys can do almost anything. And he caught the rope in a cleft of the ice, knowing it would freeze there and keep the boat waiting for the doctor. He never doubted the doctor's coming through all the danger; for it is a way that doctors have. Behind him now the lamps kept up their flashing. Far, far off on his left glimmered the windows of the hotel where the children were; far, far ahead the town lights flickered. On he ran; swiftly wherever snow lay frozen and smooth; climbing and slipping, down and up again, where the ice-blocks had been piled. Now there was a streak of water only two yards wide, he saw by his lantern; he jumped, and the ice-cake tilted and rocked; and he jumped again and clung to solid rock. Up and down, sliding, falling, rolling, but always moving on, on through this hideous gloom, with only the eyes of the glancing lights in it. What a horrible noise there was everywhere in the grinding, griding, crashing of the ice. It seemed as if the whole cruel North moved down in a body on him. He thought of people caught on ice floes, of packs of wolves racing and scratching along them, of some polar bear protecting her cubs there; and he ran all the faster. But what was there in all out-doors, then he thought, which would be allowed to hurt a boy encountering such dangers for his father's sake and Emeline's? And he waited for his breath, his heart palpitating furiously, his lungs like red-hot brass. As he stood there, a little fellow in his pea-jacket, with the dull lantern in his hand, it was like some hero defying the powers of cold and darkness with the might of his holy errand.

He went on slowly; for the way grew more difficult on this narrow neck of the long peninsula, where the tide pushed the ice about and jammed it in mock icebergs glinting to the light-house beams which, fainter though they were with distance now, strengthened him, every time they came, with thought of Emeline at the wheel. He was scratched and bruised and bleeding; his clothes were torn, and his cap was gone; but he was conscious of nothing except that he must get on. He climbed laboriously a huge, sloping block of ice tipped over the way, slipping back half its height; and all at once he felt it move with him, pushed by another block, keep moving. And with a thrill of terror he realized that the tide was coming in, would shove and jam and heap and sweep across the neck of land, and if it did not crush him between the great pieces of ice, it would take him out to sea on the other side, do what he would!

Just ahead, Jack knew, must lie the old road that took people to the hotel in summer, raised a little from the level, and so offering a barrier that it might take the rising ice some little time to surmount. If he could only gain it! He dashed forward with redoubled speed, bumping, splashing, tumbling on his knees, on his back, on his hands and feet, cutting himself on sharp corners, clutching his lantern all the time, and all the time making progress, when suddenly the darkness came down like a heavier pall, unrent by any rift of light, impenetrable. The long beams of the light-house lamps had ceased to flash. There were no more of them. He gazed behind him, and about him; he could see nothing. The lamps had gone out.

The piled-up ice-drift hid the windows where the happy children looked for their Uncle John, where the beautiful dark eyes so often looked over their shoulders; hid the sparkle of the town as well. He did not know which way to turn; there was nothing but unbroken blackness, blackness and cold about him; he was getting numb with standing still and wondering; the ice was crunching like great jaws at work; the snow was beginning to fall over it all. He was lost.

Back in the mediæval hall, the children peered through the window.

"I don't believe Uncle John means to come at all!" cried Clara.

"Perhaps he had some sick patient that he couldn't leave," urged her mother, coming to her side, a little anxious lest Aunt Marion were anxious. "Besides it isn't time for him, quite."

"You don't suppose Uncle John can be lost?" whispered Will, as he felt Aunt Marion's hand tremble.

"No, indeed," said his father. "My dear," turning to his wife, "hadn't you better light the tree? It is already late."

"Oh! stop! stop! stop!" cried Tom and Clara then in one breath. "Something—something has happened to the light-house! Oh! the world is coming to an end! The light has gone out!"

"And how will Uncle John ever see to get here?" cried Will, as Aunt Marion suddenly clasped him in her arms.

"And what do you suppose has become of Jack and Emeline?" exclaimed Nell, bursting into tears.

"Light the tapers, and divert the children quickly as you can," said the father hurriedly to anybody in the universe. "I will get the men and see what can be done about crossing over there!"

"Oh! you never will try that!" exclaimed his wife. "You know it is impossible!"

'If it is, I shan't do it," he said, smiling.

"But what could you and two men do? Wait at any rate, for John and his man. You will be lost and drowned! I know you will!"

"Nonsense, my love! I will run no unnecessary risk. But that light out to-night, snow thickening, and storm coming, means shipwreck that I can't have on my conscience. Hands off, dear! It must be done. But first of all have half a dozen of the lanterns lighted and tied to a pole and thrust out of the cupola window for John's direction. Hurry now!" And then one was getting his long boots, and another his coats, and another the lights; and in the midst of it all, the screens slid away and the tapers blazed out, and one of the doors burst open with much stamping and outcry, and there was Uncle John and his companion and the burden that they bore among their other parcels. "A little lad half frozen," said Uncle John, staying to greet nobody, and laying his burden on a lounge. "Lucky the train was late. I heard him, and saw his lantern, just beside the old road. Bring some of that snow, and be quick about it! Now rub for your life!" And then Uncle John had turned and opened his arms and the beautiful brown eyes were hid upon his breast.

When Jack was well tucked away in bed, and the people had made their way to the light-house, they found the oil in the lamps congealed and Emeline fainted beside the wheel. But Uncle John knew how to right all that; and what to do for the father, too. And while the rest obeyed directions in the tower, he attended to the light-keeper's concussion of the brain, and spent his Christmas with Emeline.

"How glad I am we stayed here," said Clara, afterward. "If we hadn't, you know, the ships would have been wrecked, the light-house keeper would have died, and Emeline and Jack would have frozen to death. It's the nicest Christmas Eve I ever knew! Everybody ought to spend Christmas Eve out in old seaside taverns, I think!" And one would suppose Clara had done so purposely.

"I thought I had really died and gone to heaven, you better believe," said Jack, telling Emeline his adventures for the hundredth time, "when I opened my eyes, and that Christmas tree was twinkling, all lights and colors, with the children, and those women like angels! And I don't know but what I did! For it's like heaven to think father's going to help these doctors about their experiments and things, and you and I will live with the children, and grow up with Tom and Clara, and never lay eyes again on old Hurricane Light!"

CHAPTER TWELFTH.

Other Children.

> Wax to receive, and marble to retain.
> —*Byron.*

> I remember. I remember
> How my childhood fleeted by—
> The mirth of its December,
> And the warmth of its July.
> —*W. M. Praed.*

> With the smile that was childlike and bland.
> —*Bret Harte.*

> We pardon in the degree that we love.
> —*Rochefaucauld.*

> Use three physicians—
> Still first Dr. Quiet;
> Next Dr. Meryman
> And Dr. Dyet.
> —*Regimen Sanitatis Salernitanum.*

> Nature fits all the children with something to do.
> —*J. R. Lowell.*

> How cruelly sweet are the echoes that start
> When memory plays an old tune on the heart.
> —*Eliza Cook.*

> There was a place in childhood that I remember well,
> And there a voice of sweetest tone bright fairy tales did tell
> —*Samuel Lover.*

Themostocles said: The Athenians command the rest of Greece; I command the Athenians; your mother commands me; and you command your mother.—*Plutarch.*

It is not all children that are reared in the love lines of the kindergarten methods, or in any other method that makes them a blessing to themselves or to the community. Often circumstances master the parents, and the children shift for themselves and are in reality reared by their hereditary traits, and sometimes when the young mother has little knowledge or skill and no assistance, and proceeds with the old fear of sparing the rod, she is half beside herself by reason of the development of those traits before her eyes, and finds that, labor as she may to bring about happiness in her home, the very things that should make for happiness, the children, themselves, are growing up to precisely an opposite result. But since it has been discovered that homesickness is a disease, that laziness also is a disease,—apt to be incurable—that an inclination to petty thefts of things not wanted, and sometimes thrown away at once, is a mania, often inherited, and no more within the power of the patient to control than any more violent mania is—it is to be imagined that many other emotional matters may come under the same head, and gradually reach a similar classification as ailments to be medicined rather than wickednesses to be punished.

Medicine Rather Than Punishment.

In no way will this theory be of more useful application than in the rearing of children, who, from having been regarded since time began as full of the old Adam, which is to be chastised and whipped out of them, will now be seen as victims of the diseases of their tender years, and be untiringly diagnosed and medicated therefor.

Not that the maternal rhubarb bottle will take the place of the maternal slipper, but that divine patience will be more frequently invoked to fill out the measure of human patience, and it will be comprehended that naughtinesses are no more to be whipped out of children than spots out of a leopard, or evil desires out of grown people; and that if you can not "reason with a mule," you can with a child, even but just escaping babyhood, if you are willing to curb your own temper, to forget yourself, and not to fail in exhaustless gentleness; and that only those that can so curb temper and exercise self-forgetfulness have any business to be about children at all.

How many people do we see who are punishing children for their own faults, inherited and repeated without choice in the matter, administering the punishment all in good faith, and because they know the trouble those faults have given themselves, and are likely to give the little victims as they increase in years and find themselves in the toils, and because they think it best in pure love to drive out the evil spirit, as if the very process of such sweeping and garnishing, in exciting enmity and rage, and heating blood and brain, did not invite the other seven worse than the first to enter and take possession!

Heredity.

All parents are happy in viewing themselves when repeated in their children, as if it were a sure pledge of immortality that this line of face, that breadth of temple, this curve of eyebrow or of lip, were to be handed down

(308) THE LOVE LINES OF THE KINDERGARTEN METHODS.

the generations; and pleasant as they find all that, just so bitter do they find it when unfortunate traits, that previously might have been repressed in themselves, but that have not been, and that only afford misery, are brought into action through inheritance, and they see their own sins finding them out again. Yet although they may have reason to doubt if any rod ever hindered their lying, or did anything but drive them to concealment; if any deprivation of desired things ever made unselfishness in them, or did anything but aggravate avarice, if any ridicule ever made the difficult problem easy of comprehension, or if any of the compulsory and primitive methods wrought any but momentary and superficial gaining of an object, and lasting harm and hurt—still they go on with these methods, the rod, the dark closet, the make-game, the robbery (to call it its true name), and hinder the mental and moral growth of the generation by just so much unwise action in treating children like criminals.

That children have always been regarded as delicious and delightful things, when giving nobody any anxiety as to their real welfare, is quite undisputed; but when this anxiety arises, whether they are criminals or have been but too often the victims of criminals is a question that might be considered to their advantage. Meanwhile even our treatment of criminals grows to partake less and less of the punitive character, and more and more of the hindering and curative.

Sparing the Rod.

If we look with condemnation on the whipping-post for grown people in the full possession of all the faculties they ever had, how can we approve of the slipper used on children with faculties but half developed? The general sense of all civilization now seems to be that we shall not revenge ourselves for crime, but shall simply prevent its further commission; how, then, can we treat tender little beings, without the power to help themselves, with any less consideration? Assuredly the time is not distant when duty in this regard will be seen from a different point of view from that from which it has been regarded in the past. The half-opened blossom will not be made to suffer unnecessary pain for the worm at its heart, nor shut up away from the sunshine that the worm may be left to eat in peace, but gentle forces will find the blight and remove it, and let the bud bloom to what perfection it may in all the sunshine it can have. That it may take almost infinite patience to bring up children as children, and not as criminals, is not to weigh in the least against the necessity. Infinite patience is the first fruit of all true love, and no mother, no aunt, no guardian of children, has a right to be without a

310 STEPPING STONES TO HAPPINESS.

NOT TO FAIL IN EXHAUSTLESS GENTLENESS.

goodly supply of it, and while attending to the good of the children otherwise, to be busy besides in the active cultivation of this heavenly plant in themselves. There are numberless ways of repressing evil without exciting it, and of cutting off sin, not by lopping the little branches, but by gently digging round the root, and exterminating as much as can be reached at once in the yet imperfect system, which is to grow more perfect as each generation regards its successors as something, if not already superior to itself, at any rate to be made so, and not to be kept inferior by the lash of tongue and rod.

But it requires love to repress evil gently and firmly, to rear children with the tenderness that condemnation of rude methods requires, and every one does not naturally possess this love. That is a bold person who confesses so flagrant a fault as an absence from the composition of the love of children, not one's own merely, but all people's children.

Loving Children.

For that love has become universally recognized as a necessary feature of a worthy nature, as something by the absence of which one is indeed unnatural, not to say monstrous. Owing to this fact, it is very seldom that one admits, even when feeling it, that children are a nuisance, and more generally people consider it wise to pretend interest and affection whether it is genuine or not. Of course, as everybody knows, the politic person, the electioneering man, the woman with an object to gain, always begins by kissing the children; and the behavior of many young ladies in regard to the matter was long since caricatured by Dickens in one of his sketches, where he represents them crowding round the nurse who brings in the baby to the christening, and asking, as if with innocent ignorance and a reminiscence of kittens and puppies, if the dear little thing can open its eyes yet.

But there are many people who honestly think they do love children, and would be mightily indignant if told that they deceived themselves, that children annoyed them, and were on the whole rather disagreeable than otherwise to them. These individuals do love children for a little while, as an amusement when they have nothing else to do, and to caress when the child is sunny and pretty and sweet and clean. But let the child be ugly, and it does not attract them; let it be neglected, and of a dirty face, and it repels them; let it scream, and they can't for the life of them see why people bring their children on journeys, or to church, or into the drawing-room, or at the table—according to the situation of the particular annoyance at the moment.

But they who surely and absolutely love children do not stay to see whether their faces and frocks are clean and pretty or not—the child is a lovely thing to them under all the mask of the dust of which we are made, the soil, the wear and tear; they do not much care whether the child screams or not; often, indeed, to them, as to the old miner in the California theatre who, when a baby set up its pipes, called out to the orchestra to stop their strumming and let him hear the baby yell, the sound is a sort of music; and like the man who considered being beaten at whist the next pleasure to beating, they had rather hear a baby yell than not have one around at all.

Those who love children are not those who merely love the pleasure they can get from children; those love, not the children, but that pleasure, and the moment it ceases to be pleasure, then farewell to the children. Those who really love children, love all about them, the troubling and the

LITTLE MERCHANTS.

teasing that they make, the washing and wiping and worrying; they do not tire with their fretting, they are not disgusted with their care, they are not annoyed with their questioning, they are not made nervous by their bawling; they take them in their entirety; it never occurs to them to say that these things are disagreeable, for, in reality, the agreeable things, the loveliness, the velvet cheeks, the exquisite mouth with its little pearls, the perfect eyes, the opening soul, the charming intelligence, the constant sense of the creation of a new human being going on under the eyes, the receptivity of love, the thing for love, all so far overbalance anything that is not in accord with them as to put it entirely out of sight and mind. To those who love children it does not occur to wait before giving love in order to see if they are willful and spoiled, whether they cry too much, whether they are going to give trouble or not; they only say, "Here is a child; let us love it." They are ready to get up in the night with it, to walk the floor with it, to tread on tiptoe if it sleeps, to abandon themselves to its amusement if it wakes, to sing to it, to talk to it, to obey all its little tyrannies, to stay at home from other pleasure for it and think it no sacrifice, to forget themselves in its existence, and when it is the most trouble to be thankful that there is a baby in the house.

They Who Really Love Children.

These are the people who do love children, not merely they, it may be seen, who love the peachy cheek which yields to their kisses with pleasant sensation, and the fragrance of the sweet baby breath; not merely they who like the tickling that their vacant or tired minds receive from the action of the young expanding intellect of the tiny creature, who are entertained by the stammering of the first thoughts and the effort after the first syllables, who are pleased in fine weather and run away in foul. These latter are the summer friends of the little people, and full soon do the little people find it out; for, as a general rule, one needs no better criterion as to who it is that loves children than observation of the fact of whom it is that the children love. It is true that children will be amused and pleased for a while by the summer sort of friends; but let a tumble, a grief, a pain, come to them, and the summer friend is discarded unerringly for the one whose sympathy is steadfast, and who does not ask whether it is a good child or a bad one, a pretty or a plain one, a rich or a poor, but only whether it is a child. "Frank, I love *good* little boys," said a worthy parent, trying to do his duty to an obstreperous young son. "Yes, papa," came the reply of the four-year-old, "but Uncle So-and-So loves little boys whether they are good or not." And that, it seems to us, is the only way to love them; for is it not the way in which we hope we ourselves are loved, not only by one another, but by the power above us? It is also, indeed, the only way in which to obtain lasting pleasure from the little beings; for it is only when we have surrendered ourselves, without thought of what we obtain in return, but because we can not help it, and would not help it if we could, that we find out what they have done for us, the light and joy that they have brought into the house, with all the labor and confusion and care that they have brought there, too; for more than once has it chanced that into a tumultuous and hating household the advent of a little child has brought peace and harmony, and love, too, not only for itself, but for all around it, till it has made lives dear and desirable that before it came seemed impossible to live; for there are few such peacemakers as a baby; none such, if we may believe the poet, as a baby's grave.

Yet, while it is to be believed that all people love their own children, even if their love for the children of others is questionable, it would be a wise precaution on the part of one living or visiting in a house where there are children to learn something of child-love beforehand, if they wish to have any enjoyment of their life or of their visit, or to be a welcome member of the family. For unless there is our ideal mother in the house, and sometimes it must be confessed if there is, the children will be apt to run riot.

It is not every one who knows how to entertain and to take care of children properly at the same time. The little people are to their authors and owners astonishing and delightful circumstances, revelations of wonder; it is a marvel tnat they exist at all; and how much greater marvel that they are so lovely, so bright, so precocious, that they know black from white, that they can count three; how sweet the little syllables drop from their lips! how charming is the assertion of their will! how charming that they have a will at all! is all this possible? and is all this theirs? And the child is not only worshipped as a part of themselves and a possession, but as a subject of delightful awe and mystery in the very fact of its being.

Troublesome Children.

Of course this is quite right and pleasant with our own children; but somehow or other it does not seem half so right and pleasant with other people's children; and they are not half so charming in the assertion of their wills when they dispute the seat or the book with us, while politeness to their elders makes it rather difficult for us to assert *our* wills; and they are subjects

THE YOUNG EXPANDING INTELLECT. (315)

of no delightful awe and mystery at all when they are tumbling all over us with sticky fingers and daubed faces; when they burst into our sleeping-rooms in the morning; when they insist on crowding into the carriage already full; when they set up a bawl in the middle of an interesting conversation, and instead of being scooped up and swept out of the room are expostulated with; when they disturb the peace of breakfast, dinner, and tea; when everything is interrupted by the demanding of these cherubs, and everything is so in abeyance to their wishes that elderly people seem to have no rights in the world at all, and the whole pleasure of one's visit to the parents, or the parents' visit to one's self, is destroyed by their presence and behavior, till we are inclined to believe that the correct definition of the word cherub is that other word imp.

Of course parents owe an undisputed duty to their children, and it is necessary that the little things should be made happy; that their proper pleasures should be unrestricted; that their questions should be answered; that they should not be grieved or outraged; that their lives should be one long remembrance of happiness as far as their parents can make them so. But these same people owe, also, an undisputed duty to their guests, when they have guests, and if they can not perform it, they certainly should not put themselves in the way of failing in it by having any guests, and it is just as right that the guests should not be grieved and outraged as that the children should not be.

Only those people do that which is either agreeable or decent who regard their guests as wards, for the time being, if not actively to be made happy, yet to be allowed to be happy if they will, and who take into consideration whether or not these persons, who are thus at their mercy, can be happy with other people's children tyrannizing over them in the manner that one may so frequently see them do. It would seem as though plain common sense must teach people that their children are not as lovesome to all the world as to themselves; and that even if others find them very attractive, yet they may weary of what the natural ties of flesh and blood make it impossible that they themselves should ever weary; and that it is to be taken for granted that certain things are disagreeable, and that it is not to be left to the guest to complain, or else pretend politely that it is all as it should be, when trodden and trampled on by a parcel of little people without fear of man. One, indeed, may be as fond of children as the next person, but, it is always to be understood that that means children in the right place, and where the guest is concerned the right place is never the first place. And if we happen to be the guest of the occasion how swiftly our thoughts run, and how much to the purpose.

REPRIMANDED.

The Guest with Children.

How differently, we say, we would bring these children up if we had them, and how badly they are being brought up by those that do have them! In what cold blood do we look at them! They are not always children to us—the lovely blossoming things. They are little men and women, our neighbors in miniature, having the traits of their ancestors, of which traits we are apt through our family gossip to know more than the descendants of those ancestors do themselves, repeating this uncle or that aunt, or the old grandfather long gone, and exciting our animadversion, or, not so often, possibly our admiration, by the fact. Moreover, we forget in looking at them that we were ever children ourselves; we speak and think of them as of beings of a separate species, not quite of a lower order perhaps, and not quite cherubs certainly. But we expect of the little creatures whom we are unable to class the virtues and often the behavior of the grown folk, and we in our loftiness are capable of ruining their reputations, and giving them a name that it will take years of right living on their part in the future to overcome, if their little vagaries do not suit our own whims, while the high animal spirits of their happy years lead them into pranks that are not in conformity with our own staid and quiet way of life, in which the fermentation is over; and, stern critics that we are, we sit in judgment like those that break butterflies upon wheels. They would never conduct themselves in this fashion if we had them, or if we had had them in season.

Keeping Silence.

It is a question whether these views are not better hidden in the depths of our own consciousness than given to the world of friends and neighbors. They certainly do no good to ourselves, to the children, or to the parents of the children. On the contrary, the expression of them only serves to exasperate the parents, and to irritate ourselves to still further expression, till one listening would suppose from our conversation that all the children we knew were candidates for the gallows. The encouragement of these views may have, besides, a hardening and injurious effect upon ourselves, which would be a pity, when they arise from so evident a desire to improve humanity, for they must lead us all the time into the habit of seeing more evil than good—a habit whose aim is easily transferable to objects of more advanced years and equal terms, and they must cause us to yield as unlovely an appearance as those do who do not care for children at all, good or bad, and do not criticise their behavior, not from any want of hostility, but from complete indifference; people to whom children are like flies and night-moths, evils to be en-

THE OPENING SOUL OF CHILDHOOD.

dured, since there is no way of being rid of them if the lamps are lighted. For our own sakes, then, as well as theirs, if we can not praise them, it might be well to pause before letting ourselves get into the habit of condemning other people's children.

Yet in some respects, if we make no loud expression of it, this critical mood of mind may serve our own mere personal comfort in the long run as well as another which is quite at variance with it; for if in the other, or counterpart of it, we might be of some benefit to the little people, it is usually at considerable cost to ourselves. It is then not the case of condemning, but of loving other people's children too much. Of course there is no such thing as too much love in the world, and, if there were, few children are in the receipt of too much of it; it is not often that they are injured by its possession so much as by its lack. There is love, to be sure, that does them more harm than good; the love that follows them after parental correction and tries to soften the effect of it, for instance—a poor sort of love, more often self-love than pure love of the little culprit for whose better good the correction was administered. But the love of self-sacrifice that forgets itself in the child, the love of effort that takes trouble for it, remembers that the atmosphere of childhood is carried along to make the whole atmosphere and temperament of later life, and sees to it that it shall be a roseate one; the love of patience, that stops to think of the reason why before saying nay, and strains a point against the nay; that uses all preventive power to hinder wrong-doing or temptation to wrong-doing, instead of reserving itself to punish wrong-doing when done—that love, indeed, can not exist in too great quantity or force. Yet that is for the child; for ourselves, at first glance, there would seem to be no question that there is such a thing as giving too much love to other people's children for our own selfish ease. Our love may help to make the way smooth for them, but how is it going to work with us? It is an ignoble way of feeling, it must be admitted, as all views are that dwell simply on the light cast on our own future; but there are laws of self-preservation, and if there is no instinct to warn us, then experience must discover that whatever we do for other people's children we must do for love of them, and not for love of ourselves, for in the end the likelihood is that we shall be forgotten in the matter, and our love return upon us in bitterness.

Of course we are not speaking of simple liking and pleasant sufferance, but of the intense and yearning affection that the lonely heart extends to clasp round the little child in the house, in the family, or in the neighborhood. Yet with all that yearning affection, one to whom the child does not belong will have, as a general thing, reason to figure less and less in the life and thus in the thoughts of that child as the years pass, till one dwindles at first into

NECESSARY THAT THE LITTLE THINGS SHOULD BE MADE HAPPY.

insufficiency and then into forgetfulness and the oblivion of all but temporary presence. Nor does one always have to wait long for that fate—which, if possibly it may not come at all, just as possibly is sure to come—for no sooner may we have poured out the fullness of our tenderness about it, and made the child a part of our heart's blood, than the owners of it can take it from our sight and grasp, and put seas and continents and lifetimes between us. It had become all but our own child, and is snatched out of our arms; and, so far as we are affected it is in its grave, for it is dead to us in just the degree that the unloving, the indifferent, the disliking, or the cruel parent chooses.

What are we to do, then?—love nobody's children? It would be a dreary world for most of us in that case and a hard one for all the little people who are helped along their way by love, no matter whose. It is a necessity of some natures to love that would leave a great gap in life if unsatisfied, and if they have not one thing, they will have another, and will give the love that should have made the wilderness blossom like a rose for some child to weeds and stocks and stones, or what amounts to the same thing.

Feeling with the poet, however, that it is

> "Better to have loved and lost
> Than never to have loved at all,"

it would seem, on the whole, the best thing even for ourselves, and our own selfish ease ultimately, to forget self in the affair, and love other people's children wherever we find them, since one is so much the happier for loving, for having loved, for having love to remember, and since our small quantity of love may do its share in the elevation of all the world, however slight that share. It may give us more real happiness to close our eyes to those things in children which show that they belong to an imperfect race, and to take our draught of the infinite pleasure of loving as we go. And perhaps even that love may be retroactive in the end, nothing being lost in the universe, and soften the hearts of those round whom it was shed; and as the dreaded and fateful years go by, these so loved children will look back with love as we have looked forward with it, and feel for the old all that indiscriminate tenderness which we have felt for the young, and we ourselves come in for our portion.

Amusing the Small People.

But much of the annoyance that other people's children give the sojourner and wayfarer in the house might be hindered by that person's taking a little pains to give them amusement or entertaining instruction.

If, for instance, the guest should take out some drawing materials, how soon would every noisy child become a quiet spectator of the magic of the working fingers. And still greater quiet may be evoked by giving these children paper, or cardboard, with pencils, and showing them how to use the new tools. Many people have a notion that it is useless to instruct a child in any art for which no particular talent has been shown—the art of drawing for example. But every child, no matter in what condition, even the child of

LOVE OF THE CHILD FOR DRAWING. (323)

the savage, loves to make a picture. To these unbelievers unless the child is found making his own colors, and cutting hairs from the cat's tail for his brushes, after the fashion of Benjamin West, and securing wonderful effects with chalk and blackboard, red lead and barn door, it will not seem worth while to cultivate his talent; and even if it should seem worth while then, it will be thought it can be done only by means of a teacher who is himself an artist.

With Pencil and Paper.

But in reality it is well to teach every child certain of the rudiments of the various arts, and the very effort may burst the shell inclosing the germ of some capacity for them, especially in this very matter of drawing, since an impulse toward the imitation of shapes, the representation of outlines, and the expression of thoughts by means of a picture, is instinctive with us all, and an inheritance from the primitive man, whose only writing it was; and it is a further whim of ours that, strange as it may at first appear, a great deal of preliminary instruction may be given by the mother or teacher who can not herself, perhaps, draw either straight line or circle. Every child has some inclination in this direction; the margins of all his school books are scratched over with his favorite designs, and if he has been so fortunate as to possess a shilling box of colors, the pages of his atlas and of his history bear witness to his aspiration, and perhaps not only to his aspiration, for it is to be doubted if Turner's "Carthage" ever gave the artist such joy as the well-daubed prints of the "Landing of the Pilgrims," or "Georgian Girls in the Slave Market," in the geography book, have given to most of us in our childhood. It is no instruction, now, to take the pencil and paper and draw the line for the child to see and then to copy; he would be copying the line, not representing the object to be drawn. But it is real instruction to make the child actually see the object, and then set down on paper the lines that answer to what he sees. William Hunt used to say that the reason we do not draw an object correctly is because we do not see it correctly, or see it but partially; we think we see it, and see the whole of it; but if we do, there is nothing in the world to hinder our setting down its fac-simile. And thus the first thing to do is to teach the child to see, to see shape, relation of lines, shadow, mass, relief, dwelling first upon proportions and not till afterward on details. All that can be done before the child has taken a pencil in hand, and his eye may be in process of training a long time first, and a long time afterward, even while he is practicing on simple strokes and free lines before an object is put up for him to copy; but when his eye is somewhat trained, and one is satis-

MONUMENT AT NEW PLYMOUTH TO THE PILGRIM FATHERS.

fied that he has seen the shape of a thing, its projection and its proportion, and its light and shade, there is no reason why he should not represent it if there is any skill in his fingers, and he then will learn by his mistakes, each one of which to the right gazer is a step on the upward ladder. There are some, it is to be acknowledged, who have no finger knack, who can but copy, and that laboriously, by line and rule, for whom form has no attraction, who can not interpret color in black and white, and can not be drilled into the appreciation of masses and values; who, caught early, may be enlightened to some extent only sufficient to show the futility of the effort so far as any great results are concerned, yet doubtless the instruction relative to shape, proportion, and shade has opened their eyes to what would never have been seen by them without it, while within a limited degree the effort to do more has been of real benefit

Whether or not one is going to make pictures that will stir the heart with dreams of beauty, and live when the hand that created them is dust, it is exceedingly desirable from a utilitarian point of view, that one should be led to look carefully and see clearly, leaving imagination out of the question. A drawing is but a report of what one sees, hand and eye working together; if one can execute it, so much the better; but if that is not to be, even the verbal report will be the more accurate for any such early training as may have been given to the eye. Just as a matter of business the advantage of the instruction is easily seen; the traveler, whose eye has been early taught its functions and who would write the story of his sight-seeing, needing no other hand than his own to illustrate his work, doubles his profits; and if unable to do so much as that, is yet able to write with a sharpness of outline that bites into the memory, while the report of the traveler who sees all things but vaguely and pleasantly is blurred and forgotten; and so of the mechanician who needs no duller brain with apter fingers to stand between him and the model of his machine, and is able to sketch his own ideas as they come to him; of the naturalist whose specimens can not evade his pencil and vanish altogether, and of countless others. Thus in the light of the relations of money-getting, of science, of convenience, apart from any considerations of a possible genius to be developed, of a talent not to be wrapped in a napkin, it were well to give every child instruction in the art of drawing, encouragement to his endeavors, and praise to his success; not that unjust and indiscriminate praise which, not being deserved, makes a fool of one, but that praise which obliges a person to live up to its standard, remembering the while if the talent really exists, it is there for a purpose and to be fostered toward an end, and that, not existing, it would be a forgery upon nature to pretend that it was there.

But besides the pictorial way, there is many another fashion in which the children can be beguiled from noise and mischief. Let the person who wishes to bring peace out of their little pandemonium provide herself with a blackboard, easily procurable anywhere, and provide the children with slates, and tell them they are going to have a play with the round world on which they live.

A New Game.

Every one remembers the tears and struggles which the really simple and delightful study of geography used to cost; but there is a way of making it a charming amusement. Let our friend in question take chalk crayon and make a map of an island on the blackboard, not at all, however, out of his or her own head, but according to the instructions the children shall give. This map is then to be transferred from the blackboard to the slates. It was easy enough to measure the table by a chalk and string, and order a line of that

A WAY OF MAKING IT A CHARMING AMUSEMENT.

length to be measured and drawn on the board; but it is a different thing to transfer that line to their slates, and thus learn at once the significance of the "scale." This done at last, though, a map of the school-room is made; then one of the way to school, with the streets and paths diverging from it. From this arises the necessity of knowing the points of the compass—nothing being taught till its need is felt—and the instruction is given in a calisthenic exercise, in which the children are formed in a hollow square, facing outward, and the sides of the square are marched to their respective points till they are understood and remembered, upon which their application to the map on the board is mere play. When sufficient elementary knowledge has thus been acquired, intelligence is called more positively into play, and the children are told, for instance, as one way of doing this, that they may colonize an island. A rough sketch, a sort of land in the distance, being made on the board, every point in the shape of the island is left to be arranged by the children, who are to give reasons for their decisions. Some would have it a smooth plain, such as a hoop could be trundled on all day; some are for mountains and adventures. Mountains carry the day, and determine the nature of the shores. The reason assigned for the choice of mountains is that they are places for mines; iron and copper, if not silver and gold, will be wanted in the colony—mines will afford them; pasturage will be wanted for cattle, too —the mountain-sides will give it; rain will be wanted—the mountain-tops arrest the clouds and produce it; lastly, as the teacher suggests, rivers will be wanted. Shall the rivers flow from the sea into the mountains? Criticism is invited. Who ever heard of water's running up hill? The teacher draws a river, starting nowhere in particular and going anywhere in general, and requires the pupils to say why it is not right, till they see that nature does nothing at haphazard; and rivers, as well as other things, always run from some cause to some end, so that in this island they must rise among the hills in the springs that the rains and vapors make and swell, and then flow downward to their outlet where they feed the sea. And here, if the teacher is able, a digression explains the dead rivers of California and the rivers lost upon the desert. But why do they want rivers at all on the island? For roads, one says; for fishing, says another; to drain the lands; to water them; to turn wheels; to carry merchandise. As voice after voice resounds, a zest springs up, till the scene is as eager, if not as clamorous, as the gold room. And what kind of rivers is wanted for these things? is next asked. For carrying merchandise, let us say. A stream full of eddies and rapids that a vessel must skirt and struggle with, or a deep and quiet one that upbuoys the vessel which the wind carries along? And for turning wheels—shall it be a slow and sluggish current, or a swift one full of falls? All these things having been settled, the map of the island drawn in a satisfactory manner, and the colony being supposed to be on the way to it, the teacher asks if it is desirable to plant the colony in the interior or on the sea-shore; and the subject being well weighed, and the opposing reasons given, it is resolved to have it on the sea-shore, on account of the unexplored and uncleared nature of the interior, and from considerations of safety and of accessibility—all of which the children appreciate quite as much as they would the exploits of Hans or the escapes of Gretchen in their story-books. In this method the colony being established, so far as its geographical condition is concerned, it is proposed to send off a second colony to a point farther in the interior. Shall they strike out at a venture? Follow the river, cries one. Follow the river, by all means, and have your way open behind you. But how far?—to the source?—to the falls? To the falls. There they are, to move machinery, to saw lumber, to grind corn; ships can go up no farther; the tide rises on farther. The falls, then, are at the head of tide-water.

Another Game.

Sometimes this kind of exercise alternates with one which affords as much pleasure as the old game of "Dr. Busby." This is a game played with cards, evenly distributed, and on the back of each of which is written the name of a town or city, and on the face, in double rows, a statement of the usual imports and exports of the place. Any one can prepare these cards by the help of a school gazetteer. The scholar who begins the game, examining the cards allotted, finds that Rio Janeiro, it may be, has rose-wood and diamonds and tapioca to export, with other tropical staples, and is in sore need of linen for her ladies, cotton goods for her slaves, cordage for her ships, and straightway demands these articles. Liverpool can furnish them, and take Rio Janeiro's goods in payment. If, then, the scholar having the card Liverpool does not immediately cry "Here!" the Rio Janeiro merchant can take that card without further ado. If, however, the possessor of it does cry "Here!" then Rio Janeiro can not take it unless able to give its name—Liverpool. But supposing it taken, the Rio Janeiro merchant then looks at the Liverpool card and sees hardware to spare there, and cutlery and cotton goods; an immense business to be done, in short, in all sorts of exports and imports; and if Monrovia, glistening like the lady in the dentist's chair with gold, gums, and ivory, does not answer at the call for them, or for palm-oil and feathers and spices, then Monrovia also goes to swell the stock of the first merchant. But if, on the contrary, Rio Janeiro, having asked for the Liverpool goods, or for the Monrovian or other, can not give the name of the place furnishing them—Liverpool or Monrovia, or as the case may be—then the Rio Janeiro card is forfeited to the owner of the card with that place on the back, who then proceeds to make exchanges until brought up with some round turn which affords opportunity to the next.

Thus a knowledge of the world and of its balances and counterbalances is gained that books could hardly teach, and that is usually only half learned in the maturer life of the man of business. It is play that takes the place of experience; and not only have the thought-producing qualities been early strengthened and ripened for service, but the little people have had almost as much pleasure as if they had gone campaigning and playing pirate, and peace has reigned where they made racket and riot before.

It is only a boy that needs the best of interest and amusement at home that can furnish such a record of misdeeds, of good inclinations and bad results as Laddy did when all unintentionally he played the burglar himself.

The Story of Laddy's Burglar.

The great shining wheel, shod with silence and swiftness, sweeping on like a spirit—a bicycle—was that which, of all created things, Laddy longed for most. He saw the club roll by, he heard their warning bells tinkle like drops of sweetest sound, he saw their tiny red lights flashing in the dark, and his soul was full of desire for this steed which bears one as the outspread wings of the Afrite Danhash carried Badoura to Camaralzaman, a sort of visible whirlwind. For Laddy to see one of these lofty riders on his giant wheel, whose spokes, now viewless with motion, now dazzling as the sun's rays, seemed to be parts of the living thing, here slipping out of sight along the road, here mounting a hill and outlined on the sky, was to experience the same ecstasy of pleasure that you or I might have over a picture or a poem. And he had made up his mind to become, by hook or by crook, chiefly crook, just such a poem himself, if his father, who could amply afford it, would listen to reason and buy a bicycle. Grass never grew under Laddy's feet, especially in the winter, and having mastered the unruly creature, by dint of hiring and borrowing, he had never lost a chance of presenting to his father such considerations as his tireless running of errands, and general good behavior in the family, to the effect that he had fairly earned his gratification.

Laddy felt himself a very important member of the family, and had no more conception of his real standing there than many of us have who, half unconsciously, wonder how the world would get on without us. It was a jolly family, on the whole, that which was thus indebted to him, and it was such a numerous one, that it could hardly have experienced stagnation had there been no Laddy. There were a father and mother and grandmother, of course; it would have been a queer family that did not begin with those. And then there was a great-grandmother, too—and it was not every family that had a great-grandmother, if she was so disabled that she could neither speak nor move, but only sit all day in her chair and look about her with a pair of little sunken eyes, that blinked as the stars blink in heaven, and gave

HE SAW THE CLUB ROLL BY.

you the idea of her belonging already to some other world than this. And then there was Aunt Mat, who did everything for everybody; and all the servants, particularly Michael; and the three older sisters and their two brothers; and the half dozen children, more or less, of the younger brood, who made noise enough for all the children that followed the Pied Piper of Hamelin. For when Sacie was not tittering, Katharine was singing, or Lucy was bawling, or Tom was whistling, or Johnny was playing his jews-harp, or they were all shouting—Laddy's shout being a roar. They banged on the piano, tramped up the stairs, slid down the banister, and would perhaps have swung on the chandeliers if they could have reached them. And every little while there was a fearful agitation all over the place, for Laddy was in the river, or Johnny was being brought out of the river, or the whole crew of them, with Tom for captain, were adrift upon the river. The elder sisters painted and embroidered and practiced, and went driving, and young Sylvester came to see them—came very often, by the way, and stayed very long, and always took Sophy down to the gate with him. Sometimes Rosy and Katharine were found rendered useless by meddling with the clay of which the three elder sisters had been moulding jars and vases; or Sacie and Lucy might be seen smeared from ear to ear with Laura's water-colors, or with their gowns sewed up in Eleanor's flosses and crewels; or half of Sophia's music would have been taken to make Johnny's kite, which had ended by falling into the water and going out to the sea. Yes, it was a jolly family, Laddy thought; especially when time came toward Christmas and Aunt Mat was helping the kitchen-girl pick over currants and giving any loiterer a good handful, and grandmother was showing them how to make sausage meat, and Laura, streaked with chrome yellow from top-knot to shoestring, was learning the mystery of squash pies, and the little people were allowed to slice the citron, and everybody was busy with a secret.' Nothing could be more to Laddy's mind than this state of affairs, unless it was the building of the Tower of Babel. He could think of but one thing possible in the way of making life still livelier, and that was possession of the bicycle which he had told everybody was to be his share of the Christmasing, and which he meant to ride down the front stairs, if not the banisters! "I like to see things fly round!" said Laddy, leaving one to guess whether he meant things in general, or only the bicycle. His mother used to say that it was no wonder she was ill; the wonder was that anybody was well in that house.

I suppose it is to be admitted, before going further, that Laddy was the bad boy of the family. Yet he was a taking little scamp, with the honest wide blue eyes in his sunburned face—a face where no amount of tan could obliterate a swarm of dimples that made his smile as sweet as honey. For all that, no one loved a bit of roguery so well as Laddy did. It was he that tied Lucy's and Sadie's long braids together, so that when they rose to go different ways he might enjoy the consequences. It was he that made "apple-pie" of Johnny's sheets and seasoned it with red pepper. It was he that scared the whole parlor by coming down with a candle in his hand and beginning to climb the mantel-shelf as if preparatory to crawling on the ceiling like a fly, walking in his sleep when he was really wide-awake, and laughing so gayly and sweetly when, like a bottle of medicine he was taken and shaken, that nobody could be very angry with him. It was he that emptied Rosy's doll of its stuffing and filled the body with red-cedar sawdust, leaving a little crack in one arm so that when Rosy saw the red sawdust trickling out she really thought her doll was bleeding to death. It was he that tied all the bells in the house with one string, and in the middle of the night woke all the sleepers with their furious ringing. And, in general, one might say it was he that cried peace, peace, when there was no peace! And there was nobody like Laddy for getting out of a scrape. He never looked guilty. When on Sunday he was bringing the pot of baked beans, suspended on a string, from the baker's, and met the people going to church, he accidentally hit the pot against a lamp-post, and knocked out its bottom, so that the steaming beans poured in a mortifying mess over the sidewalk—mortifying to any one but Laddy; but Laddy never once glanced down at the ruin; he simply opened his fist and dropped the string and passed on as if they were anybody's beans but his; he had nothing to do with them, and didn't know there was such a thing as a baked bean in the world, in fact. *Ex pede Herculem.*

Perhaps the worst thing Laddy ever did was—— But I hesitate to tell you. It really was too shocking. Still, I don't know—if you will promise never to speak of it—and then I hardly think he realized what he was doing. If he and Johnny had not been left alone that day—but they were alone with great-grandmother, and had been told to take care of her, and see that she didn't fall into the fire, till grandmother came back. Grandmother herself seemed almost a young girl in comparison with poor old great-grandmother, who never stirred from the moment she was put into her arm-chair in the morning till she was taken out of it at night. Laddy sat looking at her with I know not what strange fancies flitting through his mind. Possibly there came over him such a sensation as one might have when looking down the crater of a burned-out volcano, or over a picture where the painting had been wiped out. For all at once he whispered to Johnny, "Larks, Johnny, larks! let's do it!" How far the little wretches would have gone in their wicked work nobody knows; for they were interrupted by grandmother, who had thought matters were too quiet to be wholesome in there, and who seized them both and shook them till they did not know whether they were on this star or on several others. And then the little torments ran back to their mother at last, saying they couldn't stay with great-grandmother any longer, because grandmother was so cross! Laddy was a good deal younger then than at this present writing, but I am afraid he had some reprehensible beginnings in him.

Yet, after all, I suppose I could find as many good things to tell of him. I remember that once he gave his own shoes to a beggar, and would have gone barefooted all summer if he had not known of a pair of Tom's that fitted him; he was always polite to the cook, and she, at any rate, did not believe it had anything to do with sly turnovers now and then; he never robbed birds' nests—he had business with his marbles, indeed, at birds'-nesting time; he never called a boy names behind his back, and he always gave away the core. In spite of everything, he was an affectionate little fellow, and loved his people as much as he tormented them. If his mother sternly called him "Lawrence!" it hurt him more than a whipping from his father did.

Laddy had been busy several weeks with chips and tools, frequently running in from his place of seclusion to ask on what day of the month Christmas came this year, and forgetting again as soon as he was told. He had been fashioning a foot-rest for great-grandmother, having often exercised himself, since the enormity of his intended behavior on a certain previous occasion had been felt, in doing one little odd turn and another for the poor old lady's comfort. Now, by the help of the lathe, bright-headed tacks and varnish, he had succeeded in quite an effective bit of work. With his head first on this side and then on that, he contemplated it in satisfaction, as he thought of poor old great-grandmother's tired feet resting on its soft cushion, whose down he had himself plucked, last summer on the farm, from under the wings of the old gander, at the imminent risk of his life; and he found something a little touching in the contrast between the rest of this cushion and the soul of speed and motion in the bicycle for which he had such a raging desire. Bobbins, and sheaths, and various other small wooden trifles had his carpentry devised for the rest, and he only finished the last as the girls were hanging up the green and the bells were ringing for Christmas Eve. Having deposited his little accumulation in safe hiding, he went to bed, answering questions as to his gifts in rather surly fashion, in order to avoid having more of them to answer, and waited breathlessly, till every one in the house should be asleep, that he might steal down secretly and dispose of them among the array of the other gifts.

It had seemed to Laddy as if that Christmas Eve would never come. He had told his mother that he wanted new skates; and to his father he had been eloquent on the charms of that or any other bicycle. Grandmother would probably give him a little purse of money—and he wanted money sadly; Johnny, he knew pretty certainly, was going to give him his ball; and Rosy, and Lucy, and Sacie, and Katharine, had united their funds toward a knife with a pair of scissors at one end. What Tom had in store for him, what Laura and Eleanor and Sophia, not to speak of his grown-up and prospering brothers Will and Harry, had prepared for him, he did not venture to imagine —something very desirable without a doubt, for when Christmas came Laddy knew that all his sins were condoned and forgotten.

How long it took that red sunset to fade into orange over the snow! How slow the stars were about coming out, how long the folks were about getting through tea, and what a tittering fracas Katharine and Lucy and the rest of them had to make in putting their paper parcels in convenient places for their elders to distribute by direction! What fools girls were! And when up-stairs at length, what a splashing and chattering, what dancing about from room to room of the little night-gowned figures, and what choruses of glad giggles about nothing, till the hush of heavily-breathing slumber came and found him still waiting, waiting for the elder people to seek their sleep in turn. He watched the stars through the uncurtained window while he tried to keep his eyes open; they seemed to get caught in the huge pine boughs, and to make thin streams of white fire there; then came an aurora

LADDY SLIPPED OUT OF BED.

borealis, like a web of white gauze burning and shaking over the whole heavens; he thought of the dreams stepping about from pillow to pillow, and he was pretty sure that he had been asleep himself when he started with a ray of the moon in his face, to find the house so still that it was plain everybody, young and old, were in what he called the arms of Murphy.

Making quite sure of it, Laddy slipped out of bed, and gathered his footrest, and bobbins, and knitting sheaths, and brackets, and their remainder, into his arms, and tiptoed down the thickly carpeted stairs to the sitting-room, where everything else was already in place and waiting for the morning.

And what a scene it was! The fire was out upon the hearth, the fire that it was Michael's pride to build every morning, and the bulging stockings hung from the nails driven into a long board laid upon the mantel-shelf. Laddy knew of old that there were only jokes in the stockings, the candy mouse, the toy fiddle, the china dog. The real presents were laid out on tables at either side of the chimney place; Aunt Mat had seen to it all. There was the silver cream jug that mamma had wanted when these new æsthetic things made her tired of her old silver; there were the engraved onyx buttons for papa from the big boys, and the driving blanket, wrought by the fingers of the older girls; there was the sealskin sacque that Eleanor had been sighing for ever since he could recollect, and that now everybody had joined in giving her; and the brooch for grandmother of a braid of gray hair set in seed pearls; and there was Rosy's new doll, as big as she was; and a fur cap, yes, a fur cap for himself, for if L-a-w-r-e-n-c-e didn't spell Laddy, what did it spell? And there were some gold bangles for Laura—only Will and Harry could afford to make presents like that—he should himself, some day. And a lace-pin in the shape of a fan, made of something like sky-blue sealing-wax —Laddy was not acquainted with turquoises—for Sophia; and what was this for Sophia, too? A pair of great white diamond ear-rings, winking and blazing like the sun in the dew. Laddy started back, and then looked again in virtuous indignation. Was Sophia engaged to anybody without telling him? Was that tall, dark Sylvester fellow coming here to take Sophia away? And Sophia was his favorite sister! And here were presents from his people to Sophia, as their little labels said—a great pearl ring from the Sylvester mother, and a curious piece of paper, folded like his composition on the Four Seasons, from the father; he opened it—for he had seen bonds before—a United States bond for a thousand dollars. Well, that was a great go! Grandmother's gold thimble the smoked pearl pencil-cases, the silver pocket-knives, the slippers, and smoking-caps, and afghans, and silk socks, and all the rest, fell into insignificance.

And nobody had told him! As the thought recurred he began to feel exceedingly wide awake; he was of no account at all in the family; even Muff and Tippet, the cats, knew more of what was going on. And thinking it over he shrank back unconsciously into the yet warm corner of the fireplace, where he was quite in shadow, while the great moonbeam that had waked him fell into the room and lay over the two tables and all the beautiful objects glittering there, struck those stones sparkling like imperishable drops of dew, that pearl white as concentrated moonshine itself, the blood-red onyxes, the turquoises, blue as Eleanor's eyes, struck and glorified all that store where the love was even more than the treasure. By the merest accident, as Laddy looked along this display, his eye fell upon the mirror, and he saw the whole thing faintly repeated, with dim colors and dark flashes and the hoar frost of the moonshine. And in another moment he had seen something else; he had seen the figure, the shadow, the vague outline of a man in the doorway!

Laddy was a born fighter. To spring and grab the poker, and to confront the man, crouching, with the mouth of his bag just opened to sweep all the precious things into it, took him but an instant. "You clear out!" he cried, "just the way you came! Or if I can't kill you myself, I'll make such a noise that somebody else will! There's the man in the house, and my father, and my big brothers, and"——the fellow, who did not know Laddy had carefully closed the door leading from the stairway, lest his own proceedings should be heard, had turned and fled without waiting to hear the whole list of his enemies; the sight of Laddy, whose voice could raise the house, was enemy enough. He tried to hit Laddy a clip first, but Laddy dodged it and followed him, brandishing his poker with one hand, and tucking up his little nightgown with the other, and putting down and hasping after him the window through which the burglar leaped.

Nobody ever felt more like a man than Laddy did at that moment. The bed-rooms were quite remote, the inner hall door was closed, and people were tired and sleeping soundly, so nobody had heard him, or, if any one had heard, it was thought he was talking in his sleep, and thus he alone and by himself had put a house-breaker to flight! He had put a house-breaker to flight, and yet his father would not let him have an air-gun! He went back to the place of the presents, and there they still shone as calmly as if nobody had just tried to sweep them into a bag. Somebody would be trying again; it would never be given up so. He would wait a while, and see what would happen.

What a very imprudent thing it was, after all, to leave such valuables unguarded in this way, thought Laddy, as he again surveyed them all. What if somebody *had* stolen them;—it would have been a pretty how d'you do! People as thoughtless and careless as this really deserved to lose. But how that man ran—just fluking! And Laddy doubled up with silent laughter at the recollection. And, meanwhile, across all these reflections and this laughing, an awful shadow was stalking, for Laddy, still looking around, was slowly coming to a realizing sense of the fact that there was no bicycle anywhere leaning up against the wall for him!

No; no bicycle. After all that he had hinted and spoken outright, and even begged—no bicycle. And then he grew hot all over, and very angry. He had never known what it was before to be very angry, it seemed. He could not have told you whether it was a minute or an hour he stood there and ground his teeth, but when he saw more clearly, his mental articulation was repeating the last words he had distinctly thought, without acknowledging the reason of his anger even in his inner consciousness. Certainly people as careless as this deserved to lose. What if anybody—and then an idea struck Laddy—what if anybody gave this family a scare, and made them think they had lost their Christmasing! For his part he had lost all the Christmasing he cared for.

With Laddy a thing was no sooner said than done. There was still five or ten minutes of good light from the moon. He remembered that one of the old-fashioned white dado panels in the side of the chimney-place was a closet opening with a sunken ring, where a hearth-brush and kindlings were once kept, although disused now. He went and pulled at the ring. It was so long since it had been opened that it stuck. He took the new silver paper-knife that was to be papa's to-morrow, but which, in Laddy's mind, was nobody's just yet, and ran it along the cracks and pulled again. It opened with such force as to throw him on his back, although, owing to the spring in its hinge, it immediately shut again. But it had disclosed the most charming hiding-place in the world—all one side of it shelves made by the receding brick-work of the chimney-pier. Laddy did not lose a moment in hesitation, but setting it open again, he was scarcely longer than it takes to tell of it in transferring to this receptacle every article from the two tables, and every stocking from the mantel, woefully disturbed the while lest the clinking of silver and gold and glass and china should betray him.

At last it was done, although not quite to his satisfaction. He was afraid lest a scrap of lace, a thread of Kensington work, should protrude and tell the secret; the last ray of the moon had gone, and in the gloom he had to feel rather than see. He got farther into the closet than he knew, in arranging matters, and then his movement happening to push away the little prop that had kept the door open, it swung together, and shut him in with all the hidden gear and the dark.

For a moment Laddy felt as if there was no heart in his body. He groped about, hardly daring to move lest he should break something, and fumbled all over the place. There was no handle on the inside of that door, as the case is with most closets, and there it was plain he must stay till he was let out—unless he hallooed.

Should he halloo? What a time it would make if he did! Father and mother and the big boys and the little girls would all come rushing down—it would take more than his hallooing to get the big girls out of bed—and maybe great-grandmother would have a fit—and then, besides, everybody would be sick and cross to-morrow. No, he would wait a little while and see what would happen Perhaps Johnny or Tom would be the first to come in in the morning, and could let him out and they would enjoy the joke together and creep back to bed

So thinking, Laddy laid his hands on the driving-blanket for his father, and wrapped it round himself, for it was none too warm in that closet which, besides its other uses, had been part of an old cellar ventilating-flue. A fresh sense of injury in relation to the bicycle overcame him, as he folded the blanket—his father's pleasure was provided for. And then he chuckled to think how mad the folks would be in the morning' But it would do them good They wouldn't leave diamonds and pearls, and bonds and sealskins and purses of money round in that manner again, with burglars prowling about the house! He rolled up his eyes in a little sanctimonious virtue, thinking of the lesson he was giving his elders, and saw something overhead shining brighter than Sophia's diamonds—a star, like an immense jewel on the deep dark-blue velvet of the bit of sky above him, and then he realized that the place, running up in a hollow shaft beside the chimney to its top, was open to all the winter night, let the opening be ever so narrow, and he grew, perhaps, sixty degrees colder in a second Goodness, how cold he was His teeth began to chatter, he felt his throat tickling, his head stuffing, his back aching, and he was confident he would have a lung fever before daybreak. He put his bare feet against the chimney bricks; to be sure there was some warmth in those—but what was that in a place open to all outdoors? For some of the top bricks had fallen, weathering to storms of half a century, and made the hole larger than that crack through which the draught originally whistled. And what if it should begin to rain or snow! Laddy, in his mind's eye, was already buried in a snow-drift, and he began to think that he had better make a noise about it He was, perhaps, to be suffocated there in a drift that no St. Bernard dogs would ever find, nobody would ever know anything about it, and his mother would miss him in the morning—he was just on the edge of tears and cries.

But before the tears could gather and fall, a new thought flashed over Laddy.

What had he done? He had taken all those objects of value and made away with them. That was what he had done, and what anybody would say he had done. What difference, to all appearance, would there seem to be between him and that other house-breaker? What if they should hold him to be a thief? The awful thought made his pulse stop, and his feet turn icy cold.

The very hair on his head began slowly to rise as he pictured the scene to himself, when his father should take him by the shoulder and wheel him about to look in his face; when the constable should spring the handcuffs round his wrists, and march him down to the police court with a crowd of hooting boys following—and there the terrible old judge would be sitting in his chair! Laddy knew just how that court-room looked; for once, when the boys had been nutting in old Jacques's pasture, old Jacques had surprised them, and driven them all into town in front of him like a flock of sheep, and walked them up into the court-room, seated them on a bench, and left them there, cooling their heels, as he had called it, and gradually finding out, through their sobs, and gulps, and lamentations, that that was the end of it. But remembering his sensations of shame and horror then, Laddy had never been able to think of the place since without a shudder. And now if he were to be taken there in earnest—for here he was, with all his plunder about him, and of course his father, never dreaming that his own boy was the culprit, would be having the constables in to survey the scene and discover the thief's tracks. And, thereupon, Laddy resolved never to halloo, in fact to die in those tracks first!

As he lay there he saw the slow star overhead swim out of sight; a little thin cloud blew over the darkness; one by one, other stars came and looked down at him with their beautiful eyes; perhaps this last one was a comet speeding on her flight, with all her shining films around her—if it was, Laddy was the only person who ever saw it, and he did not see it long; for in the midst of his doubt, and fear, and misery, haunted by flashes of stars, and flashes of Sophia's diamonds, and flashes of the constable's brass buttons, he fell asleep.

How long he slept Laddy had no more means of knowing than if he had been a little stowaway in a ship's hold. But all at once he woke, woke to find himself overwhelmed with a feeling of unutterable horror, he knew not why. But as soon as he could collect himself and distinguish one sensation from another he was aware of a strange swift crackling sound, like the noise made by burning pine kindling-wood. With that, too, came a stifling choking smell, a smell of smoke, and a red glare through the mantel chinks. Ah, great heavens! the house was on fire, he thought, and he could not get out, and nobody knew he was in, and he would be roasted alive, he would be burned to death! "Let me out, let me out!" roared Laddy. "Fire! fire! fire!" and the sound sank in his throat, and he fainted dead away.

When Laddy came to himself he was lying on the bed in his own room, and the commotion was all over. For a commotion there had been, and a wild one. The screams, the kicks, the smothered cries of "fire!" and

Michael's single yell of terror, had brought almost the whole of the household down in wrappers and shawls, and anything handy, to behold the stripped mantel-shelf and the bare tables, and old Michael, who had kindled the blaze on the sitting-room hearth, as usual every morning before putting on his back-log, ignorant that everything was not as it ought to be there, standing and holding up both hands, his eyes and mouth wide open, and himself now voiceless with fear and amazement.

The others were not voiceless, however. A clamor that might have waked the faint-away rose from nearly a dozen throats; cries that a burglar had been there, that the house had been robbed, that all their presents were gone, that the police must be sent for, and suddenly, added to all the rest, cries from the mother, who lived in a wild fear that her children would be kidnapped, and then a swift calling of their names, and nobody answering to Laddy's! By that time, the father had arrived upon the scene, and looked about him, and partially begun to comprehend it. Perhaps his comprehension was assisted by the sight of Laddy's reels, and bobbins, and brackets in a little heap together where Laddy had left them, meaning to put them in last of all, perhaps by a tolerably thorough acquaintance with Laddy's peculiarities

"There is no burglar in the business," he said calmly, "and there is no need of so much noise. This is some of Master Lawrence's work." In spite of the wonder and alarm of the moment then, Tom and Johnny could not hinder a thrill of pride and envy that shot through them—Laddy to be the cause of all this rout! "Now, Michael," said his master, "what is the matter with you?"

"Begorra, sor," said the man, trying to hold his shaking chin on his face, "sure it's the ould boy, an' no other, do be in the chimney closet yander!"

"Humph!" said his master. "The old boy! I shouldn't wonder if it was the young one.'

And then a broad grin spread over Michael's countenance. "The spalpeen himself!" he cried. And he seized the sunken ring and wrenched open the door, and there lay the little wretch in his dead swoon among all those gay and precious objects.

In spite of their consternation and indignation and marveling, one and all they could not but commiserate the little fellow there. Indeed, Katharine and Rosy, unable to understand it now, were loud in their exclamations concerning the house-breakers who could be so cruel as to take their Laddy and shut him in there, while his father lifted him in his arms and carried him away.

And so, as I was saying, when he came to himself Laddy was lying on the bed in his own room, and his mother was on one side of him with cologne, her long black hair streaming around her, and his Aunt Mat on the other side with camphor, her nightcap all askew on her head, and grandmother was running with hot flannels; and Johnny hung over the footboard, as if he wanted to break his neck; and Lucy and Sacie and Katharine and Rosy were huddled in a frightened group in the window-seat. Opening his eyes slowly, and glancing from one to another, it gradually stole over him, as life stole back to him, that the house had not been on fire at all, and he had made a great fool of himself. He was sick, dizzy, faint; no drum-sticks, or mince pies, or raisins, or cranberry sauce, or plum pudding for him to-day! He knew just what they would do—they would keep him on gruel, perhaps they would give him castor oil, and when he got well they would scold him. "Pretty sort of Christmas for a fellow!" wailed Laddy.

"Oh, he's alive! he's alive!" cried his mother clasping her hands in thankfulness.

"He's breathing!" cried Aunt Mat.

"I'm talking!" cried Laddy.

And then, for a minute, the room seemed to turn upside down, whether because Johnny turned a somersault, or because Tom came riding in on a great silent bicycle that looked to Laddy's eyes, as he lay there on the bed, like one of the wheels in Ezekiel that grandmother read about to them on Sundays, sometimes.

"I don't think you deserve it," said his father, a little severely, following Tom in again, while Sophia shook her head at him in the doorway, with the diamonds sparkling in her ears. "But I bought it for you—and you have been already well punished—and so—as long as it's Christmas"——

"Is it mine?" interrupted Laddy

"Yours," but I want you to understand that he would not have had it if he had been my boy. "Yours," said his father.

"As long as it's Christmas," repeated Tom, grandly, from his lofty perch.

"Then, Tom," cried Laddy, standing up in bed, "I'll stump you to ride down stairs on it!"

"I guess he'll live," said his father.

"And we will have a pretty sort of Christmas, after all," said Laddy. "For there really was a burglar, and I really put him to flight. And it was mighty careless in you—and now I'll tell you all about it!"

CHAPTER THIRTEENTH.

Angels Unawares.

A happy youth, and their old age
Is beautiful and free.
—*Wordsworth.*

Therefore my age is as a lusty winter,
Frosty but kindly.
—*Shakespeare.*

Youth is a blunder; manhood a struggle; old age a regret.
—*Disraeli.*

His helmet now shall make a hive for bees,
And lover's songs be turned to holy psalms;
A man-at-arms must now serve on his knees,
And feed on prayers which are old age's alms.
—*George Peele.*

A lovely lady, garmented in light
From her own beauty.
—*Shelley.*

She is the lady who breaks bread
To those who suffer for the want of it.
—*Anon.*

Those graceful acts,
Those thousand decencies that daily flow
From all her words and actions.
—*Milton.*

And when a lady's in the case
You know all other things give place.
—*Gay.*

I am very fond of the company of ladies. I like their beauty, I like their delicacy, I like their vivacity, and I like their silence.—*Dr. Johnson.*

No house or home is quite complete when everything has been done without that presence in it which redeems the too sordid pursuit of present opportunities by the tender touch of the things of the past. "What is home without a mother?" the street ballad has it, but just as true and forcible a phrase would be, "What is home without a grandmother!"

Whether it is the brisk and bustling grandmother whose years set lightly, and who is more useful than any brownie in the house, or the dear old saint whose work is done and who can only sit with folded hands and show us how near heaven is to earth, it is the grandmother that is the real angel in the house, and every child of the family thinks so.

What one boy thought of his grandmother is quite apparent in these lines:

What a Boy Thought of His Grandmother.

A stitch is always dropping in the everlasting knitting,
    And the needles that I've threaded, no, you couldn't count to-day;
And I've hunted for the glasses till I thought my head was splitting,
    When there upon her forehead as calm as clocks they lay.

I've read to her till I was hoarse, the Psalms and the Epistles,
    When the other boys were burning tar-barrels down the street;
And I've stayed and learned my verses when I heard their willow whistles,
    And I've stayed and said my chapter with fire in both my feet.

And I've had to walk beside her when she went to evening meeting,
    When I wanted to be racing, to be kicking, to be off;
And I've waited while she gave the folks a word or two of greeting
    First on one foot and the other and most strangled with a cough.

"You can talk of Young America," I say, "till you are scarlet,
    It's Old America, I say, that has the inside track!"
Then she raps me with her thimble and calls me a young varlet,
    And then she looks so woe-begone I have to take it back.

But! There always is a peppermint or a penny in her pocket—
    There never was a pocket that was half so big and deep—
And she lets the candle in my room burn way down to the socket,
    While she tews and putters round about till I am sound asleep.

There's always somebody at home when every one is scattering;
    She spreads the jam upon your bread in a way to make you grow;
She always takes a fellow's side when every one is battering;
    And when I tear my jacket I know just where to go!

And when I've been in swimming after father said I shouldn't,
    And mother has her slipper off, according to the rule,
It sounds as sweet as silver, the voice that says, "I wouldn't—
    The boy that won't go swimming such a day would be a fool!"

Sometimes there's something in her voice as if she gave a blessing,
    And I look at her a moment and I keep still as a mouse—
And who she is by this time there is no need of guessing,
    For there's nothing like a grandmother to have about the house.

THE SWEET SERENITY OF SILVER-HAIRED AGE.

It becomes us to keep the old in reverence. While they are with us they seem to be a barrier against the dark unknown. The day they go it is we that take their places, and become in our turn the barrier for those younger than we.

Old Age.

If we live there is one thing before us all, and that is old age. And yet it is strange that what is so universal and so inevitable should be so dreaded, and that none of us desire it in the least degree, when we so frequently find it lovely in others. Perhaps it is the doubt, the uncertainty, that it will be found as lovely in us that makes us postpone it while we may, for "we know what we are, but we know not what we shall be." Perhaps it is the eager grasp which we are giving to the things of this world that makes us loath to drop them, makes us feel it impossible to stand contentedly empty-handed, our eyes dim to this world's brightness, and only the light of the city on the other side of the dark water shining in our faces. But on how many of the sweet old faces we see that calm, white light, till we might almost fancy that their angels are holding before them the refulgent crown of their good lives, and that they stand under the shelter of heavenly wings!

But near as the old must be to the other shores, there is too much of the awful and unknown in the thought for familiar use, and it is in relation to this life, this stir and strife, that we are the most apt to look at them, and thus there is to us much that is ineffably touching about an old man or an old woman who has laid down the weapons of the warfare, who sees all for which the struggle was made slowly slipping away, and who now is only waiting. Something of the innocence and holiness of babyhood gathers about these old people; we feel for them a portion of the same tenderness that we do for those who are just beginning life, while at the same time we recognize in them already the outline of the sacred thing they are presently to become. They are so helpless that all our helpfulness springs forth to support them, and are being made so destitute of those things for which we care the most that all our pity is theirs, too.

It is not with any selfish comprehension that as they are we, too, shall be, in the words of the old epitaph, that we feel thus toward them, but through the inherent graciousness and beauty that old age possesses. "There is one glory of the sun and another glory of the moon," the apostle says, and the velvet skin, the smiles and dimples of youth, do not monopolize beauty so long as the sweet serenity of silver-haired age exists.

It may be that we look upon the old with such a tender and admiring regard chiefly because of this serenity—the serenity of abnegation or of conquest;

THAT TENDERNESS FELT FOR THE OLD. (347)

we know they have gone through the trial from which we shrink, and that they have come out victorious and at rest; we wonder at them, and think of them in some measure as of a superior order of beings. They have surrendered the bloom of youth, and all its fresh strength and vigor—the bounding heart, the dancing step, the sparkling eye, the quick senses. They have laid their dear ones in the dust; they will soon be dust themselves; they know it, and yet they smile upon us and go on without shrinking. We might suppose, possibly, that a portion of this serenity was due to duller perceptions, if we did not sometimes see it accompanied by power of as vivid emotion as was ever shown by youth, by as strong love, as eager kindness, till we are forced to recognize it as an aura and emanation of age itself.

Growing Old Gracefully.

Still, for all the interest that attaches to age, most of us find it difficult to grow old gracefully. The first few whitening threads in our hair amuse us as a prank of nature. Other people may grow gray, but in ourselves we feel the bubbling of a fountain of inexhaustible youth. We hardly think of those white threads as a serious fact, never as spies who have stolen in to possess the land. But we have read of certain weeds foreign to a soil that one year appear here and there thinly, a struggling outpost, and another year the whole grand army has advanced, the possessor is dispossessed, and the weed reigns. And one day we are suddenly startled to see that ashes have fallen on our head, that ours is the common lot, that age—dark and unlovely it seems then to us, as it did to Ossian—has in reality begun. And at the same time, very like, we see the wrinkles round the eye, coming so stealthily that we had never suspected them till we were used to them; the deepening lines of the forehead; we see that the lustre and the smoothness and the roundness of youth are gone. Ashes are on our head indeed, and we are inclined to put on sack-cloth, too; for while we are still conscious of the buoyancy and hopefulness of youth, we find that we have lost its charm, and we cannot so resign it without a struggle; angry with our impotence, we declare ourselves old, wear old colors, adopt old ways, in a sort of satire upon ourselves, till, before we know it, that buoyancy has gone, too; elasticity has followed; in the relaxing of our muscles we observe the sinking of the eye, the sagging of the cheek, and if there is a sudden revulsion of our methods we do not strive to disguise it; we strive to ignore it, and are resolved to be young in spite of years and fate. We scrutinize those, then, who have already suffered this crisis, if, indeed, they cared as we have cared, with an ignorant marveling; their peacefulness seems

STEPPING STONES TO HAPPINESS.

stolidity, their cheerfulness seems but submission to the inevitable; and perhaps out of the dark a great helping hand reaches forth to give us strength, to lead us forward till we can gild the future with faith, and there has begun to mingle with our wonder a sympathy that, if it strips away some of the mystery from hoary eld, gives it a more human interest than we have hitherto allotted it; and we understand how the widowed grandmother relieves her gay days in the gayeties of her grandchildren, understand how she beguiles herself with knitting and netting and all the little domestic details of the house, and we find something more pitiable than we found before in the loneliness of the old grandfather, whose eyes have failed and whose mate has gone before.

GAYETIES OF HER GRANDCHILDREN.

The Satisfactions of Age.

But age must have some satisfactions of its own, independent of our care, or love, or pity, that are a compensation. There is hardly anything, for example, of the uncertain before it. All has been gained or lost—and what has been enjoyed is never lost. Sitting in the shadow with its thoughts, muffled from the outer world by torpid and weakening nerves, what bright and joyous phantasmagoria may move before it !—the laughing hours of a long-gone childhood; the tremors, the assurances, the transports of riper years, when all the world seemed made only to bring such happiness about; the successes of later life ! What merry memories and what tender ones blend together! How the forgotten starts to life like the sparks that run along a dying fire! And how, with one foot on heaven's threshold, it lingers to look back and get the last drop of the honey here !

And yet, full of fascination as the study of old age might be, both intrinsically and from constantly approximating interest, there are few who have been attracted to make use of it ; philosophy has not concerned itself with it, physiology has insulted it, sculpture and painting have slighted it, and poetry has shuddered away from it. To this day Tithonus stands as a model of misery ; and one poet only has, to my mind, touched the matter deeply, for the old gypsy who magnetized Browning's duchess to her flight alone seems to appreciate the whole meaning and purpose of this crown and sum of existence.

" So at the last shall come old age,
Decrepit, as befits that stage;
How else wouldst thou retire apart
With the hoarded memories of thy heart,
And gather all, to the very least,
Of the fragments of life's earlier feast,
Let fall through eagerness, to find
The crowning dainties yet behind?
Ponder on the entire past,
Laid together thus at last,
When the twilight helps to fuse
The first fresh, with the faded hues,
And the outline of the whole—
As round eve's shades their frame-work roll—
Grandly fronts for once thy soul!"

The Refinement of Old Age.

In some manner not easily or entirely comprehensible the aged have almost always, or seem to have, a singular refinement of manner and feeling. The grandmother, no matter in what condition of life, is felt by those that come in contact with her to have that quality about her which is possessed by those to whom we apply the term of lady. It is not because she sits still with little to do, if that so happens, but because love, suffering, sacrifice, and perhaps the near presence of death, have so refined her and given her those qualities of ladyhood which are a happiness to all about her and a boon in any family. For refinement is a contagious thing, and one lady in a family is apt to make another there in the course of time. Few terms, by the way, are so misapplied as this pleasure-giving title of "a lady." "Me last mistress was a leddy," says scornful Nora; "she niver putt the nose of her intil the kitchen door." With Nora, then, the element of ladyhood was the accordance of liberty to run the wheels of the kitchen without interference. "Mrs. Fitzgerald is a raal leddy," cries Bridget, "she niver asks me to set me hand to a dish on the ironing day." With Bridget, then, the element of ladyhood is consideration for the worker. And Teddy will speak to you of "the lady that do be doin' yer washin'," whether through fear of hurting the feeling of the laundress, or from a desire to assert an equality which you can not stoop to dispute but which, not being disputed, he may feel is in a way tacitly established.

Of course our democratic system and principles of government are responsible for much of this. Every woman between the Atlantic and the Pacific seas has the opportunity of becoming a lady, this technical lady.

The Term "Lady."

It is the height of the ambition of the newly arrived peasant; equal in rights before the law, she interprets the law as she would have it, and asserts herself equal in all else, the moment that she graduates from shopping at a dry-goods store; and it being in everybody's power to become this lady, she considers it an insult to take it for granted that one is any otherwise than all she could be.

The term "lady" had originally a signification that explains something of this ambition and pretense. It can claim either of two derivations; the one coming from the verb "to lift," meaning that a wife was lifted to her husband's rank, and in so far as she was made mistress of his house, had received a desirable elevation from her "previous condition of servitude." The other derivation is from the Anglo-Saxon words that signify the daily delivery of the loaf to servants, guests, and beggars, thus implying the features that generally distinguish the idea of the lady to the present day—supposed dignity of marriage or of years, the wealth that makes it possible to dispense the loaf, the gentle civility or charity that does dispense it. The recognition of a lady from the day in which this custom originated has been as the mistress of a manor, of revenues and retainers, one who followed the established manner of the feudal days in feeding them that hungered. The recognition of a lady now should only be changed by the progression of events and ideas, the abandonment of all thought of the necessity of manor and revenue, and maintaining only the necessity of possession by her of the Christian charities; for she who practices the Christian charities, and practices them with reflection, cannot fail to be gentle and well bred, and that is the whole of a lady. Certain small conventionalisms of place or fashion are of no account in the scale; to conceal vexation, to guard the unruly member—"for the tongue is a fire"—to give pleasure, to regard the feelings of others—can a lady do more?

One may, perchance, demur a little at this characterization, yet no other is at all practicable. To fix education and accomplishment and wealth as the criterions of a lady would scarcely be possible, owing to the very various degrees of these qualities, if for our purpose they may so be termed. The wife of the merchant prince who is taxed for a hundred millions may not know how to make a drawing of her teacup, or how to play a tune on the piano-forte, or how to tell a fine poem, a fine picture, a fine sonata, when she reads it, sees it, hears it. She may be an upstart, and look down on those less wealthy, and rudely show her poor disdain. It is possible that she may be rough and coarse, of low taste and ill disposition. We can not make her wealth one of our criterions. Or, again, it is credible that one may be educated in books to the last degree, yet know nothing of good manners; may wipe her pen in her hair and her fingers on her gown; may quarrel with her tradesmen, slap her servants' faces, insult her neighbors, brawl at her gate, and indulge in such peccadilloes as an inherited kleptomania or a spontaneous dipsomania. Her education can not be one of our criterions. The woman whose painting hangs on the Academy wall may not be worth a farthing in money, but then, in addition, she may not know how to sing a stave by note, and may be totally uneducated in everything but her special art. Her aptitude in painting can not be one of our criterions either. The woman whose accomplishment in music is extraordinary, who can delight you by the hour with her rendition of the choicest morceaux, who, if she appear in concert, will be half hidden from sight with the flowers flung for her taking, and whose songs yield a fortune every year, may be utterly unlettered, utterly ill-bred, unable to speak her mother-tongue correctly, almost ignorant of existence of any other art than her own, a vulgar glutton: we can not make her phenomenally sweet voice, her knowledge of counterpoint, her accomplishment in music, any criterion of the lady.

Thus we see that as neither wealth in the one instance, nor education, nor genius, nor the natural endowment of a warbling voice cultivated to its utmost, is to be admitted as the essential of a lady, something else must be wanted, and that something can only be the thorough high-breeding which is measured by

GENTLE AND WELL BRED, AND THAT IS THE WHOLE LADY. (353)

the length and breadth of the Golden Rule. To be a lady is not to live an idle life and have smooth jeweled hands; for the word lady implies some stage of civilization, and a barbarian may lead an idle life and have jeweled hands, and nose, too. It is not to trail silks and velvets after one; for a squaw may buy silks and velvets, if she will, with her husband's peltry, and can wear the imperial furs, since she catches the creatures of the precious skin herself. It is not to wear silver moons on one's shoes, as certain of the Romans did who wished to claim a preferred gentility. It is not to count earls and princes in one's ancestry, and trace the family tree back to the root of sturdy and heroic knights, unless their blood has blossomed into noble deeds in us, for otherwise we are their reproach, not they our glory; and one may be the descendant of a king, and yet sink, as descendants of kings have now and then been known to do, into the slums and waste places of society.

> "Christ, wol we claime of him our gentilesse,
> Not of our elders for their old richesse:
> For though they gave us all their heritage
> For which we claime to be of high parage,
> Yet may they not bequethen for no thing
> To none of us their virtuous living
> That made the gentilesse callèd to be,
> And bade us follow them in such degree,
> And he that wol have prize of his genterie
> —For he was boren of a gentil house,
> And had his elders noble and virtuous,
> *And n' ill himselven do no gentil dedès*
> *Ne folne his gentil auncestrie that dead is*
> He n' is not gentil, be he duke or erl,
> For vilains sinful dedès make a churl,
> Then cometh our very gentilesse of grace,
> It was no thing bequethed us with our place,"

says old Chaucer. And though he speaks especially of men, a lady is only the complement of a gentleman.

To be a lady, then, it is clear, does not depend on any of these factitious circumstances with which we have nothing to do, but entirely on ourselves. The woman who does the washing may, indeed, be as much of a lady in some respects as the woman who employs her, if, that is, she carries her self-respect into her work, and is that gentle thing from which the word gentility was born —gentility, which belongs only to those who strive to do what is fit and becoming; and if it is fit and becoming in her to do washing, it then being fit and becoming to do it well, in so far as she does it well, in so far she is a lady. Yet only so far. Other things than the mere routine performance of a coarse duty are requisite in this grand inventory; those gentle manners which offend none;

that consideration for the feelings of others which pleases all; that absence of anything which can produce a sentiment of repulsion or of disgust; that submission to the fact that the humblest woman in the street is a soul of equal value in God's eye.

One, in short, is the true lady in whom courtesy and tranquillity and trust are rightly mingled with discretion, with knowledge, and with the grace of God.

> "Wrong dares not in her presence speak,
> Nor spotted thought its taint disclose
> Under the protest of a cheek
> Outbragging Nature's boast, the rose!"

But be the grandmother as much a lady as you will—she has still—even if she has the possibilities of the angel in her—a good deal of the human about her also, and she is a little more than mortal if sometimes she does not try to impress upon others the advantage of her own experience. She does this more especially in the matter of attending to the health of the children, who are her idols, and it is a wise mother of those children who can reach the golden mean of having them cared for as they should be and at the same time of not displeasing the grandmother.

Ailments in the Family.

The grandmother who, having brought up a family of her own, thinks her knowledge well proved and her ways the right ways, and at every ailment of the children would have her advice followed, often without regard to any improvement that may have taken place in all the years of study, research, and experiment since her day. And what those years have brought to light is something hardly to be reckoned, and far beyond the poor old grandmother's knowledge, and almost beyond the appreciation of any but physicians and students themselves. As it is now, when we read of the immense discoveries and inventions in the practice of medicine, the discrimination and diagnosis of delicate differences of kindred disease, the chemical discoveries and consequent application of new remedies, the superb point of skill that surgery has reached, the microscopical examination of the germs of various diseases, and new light thrown on their possible extirpation, the beneficence of anæsthetics, we sorrow over the stupidity of those Dark Ages when the leech and the barber were one, and the trick of blistering and blood-letting and the administration of dried adders and pulverized angle-worms was the height of medical knowledge—knowledge that often called in witchcraft and divination to its aid.

Yet it is but a little while ago that remedies as trifling as those of the Dark

Ages were in vogue among us, and questioned only by those daring skeptics who doubted the fact that epidemics, traceable to and explainable by our own neglect and filthiness, were visitations of Providence. It is but the other day that the gouty were admonished to drink every day for a twelvemonth, a weak tea of the leaves of the holy thistle, made palatable by the addition of those of angelica—not less wise than the ancient Greek belief that eating ripe blackberries prevented people from becoming gouty, anyway; and at the same time it was held that a hysterical girl was to be cured by spreading her matutinal bread and butter with caraway seed, ginger and salt. These ideas, if they really reached the dignity of ideas, were hardly to be called improvements upon Hippocrates' notion that the brain was a large gland which absorbed the spare moisture of the body, or Galen's that the soul was composed of three parts, the vegetative in the liver, the rational in the brain, and the irascible in the heart.

There have been dogmas in all ages regarding the things that are to cure disease as instantly as the disease comes. It is still held in some of the English rural districts that a ring made of a sacramental shilling—that is, a shilling given in the alms collected at Communion—will at once cure the epilepsy; and by the same class of people fried mice are held to be a specific for smallpox, the more effective specific, too, if the mice are fried alive; and it is believed that the advice of anybody riding on a piebald horse will cure the worst case of whooping cough to be had. Mrs. Delany, in 1774, gave in all good faith the recipe of sealing a spider into a goose-quill and hanging it round a child's neck to cure the ague; and Dr. Graham in his medical work prescribes spiders' webs rolled into pills for intermittent fever. Perhaps some of our travelers who suffer from Roman fever—although in this country the same thing is called only the democratic "chill"—might try this spider's pill to advantage. Bishop Berkeley, who was wise enough to know the direction taken by the star of empire, was weak enough to see in tar-water a panacea for every ill; and for the cure of Lord Metcalfe, who died of cancer so late as 1846, a plaster and a powder were prescribed by a friend and well-wisher, the chief ingredient in which was a portion of a young frog. Yet how can we laugh at these fancies or dare to despise them when we condescend to carry a horse chestnut in our pocket to ward off the rheumatism? People who have listened to such nonsense have no right to smile even at the Egyptian who regarded the eating of a citron the first thing in the morning as an antidote and preventive of every sort of poison.

The truth is that we are all far too prone to dabble in physic without knowing anything about it, and had much rather take and give remedies of our own or the next person's conceit than call the doctor, whose business it is to know all about it, weakening or exciting ourselves usually in just the wrong way as a result. It might be better for us if we agreed with M. Monthyon, who, being forbidden wine in an illness, and prescribed large doses of cold water, returned the glass after one sip to his wife, saying, "Take it, my dear, and keep it for another time ; I have always heard we should not trifle with remedies." The French gentleman's precept, if not his practice, would be worth our attention.

Until our education in pathology is better attended to, it is playing with fire for us to undertake to "doctor" ourselves, as the greater number of us are fond of doing in our little ailments, and really rather as if we were glad of the opportunity, especially so long as there is a class in the community educated for nothing else than to take care of the little ailments with the great ones, and much better aware than we are how easily the little become great ones. Indeed, apart from direct and immediate safety, it would be better policy for us to call a physician in these small matters, because through them the physician learns our constitutions and the habits of our systems, and is better able to handle for us the larger troubles when they appear. The child taken in the night with the deadly chill of scarlet fever is dosed by the frightened mother till its power of sustaining itself is gone before the doctor comes, and another, seized with internal pains, has by the fondest love and effort a supposed remedy sent tearing and ripping a murderous way through its little body that should have been left absolutely quiescent. And the instances are multipliable almost to infinity where mistaken love has put the sick one beyond help because relying too much on family tradition and the wisdom of past generations.

Still, as the physician can not always be had, and one is loath to call him in the night unless the case be extreme, it follows that we shall go on administering the wrong dose, with the best intention and the worst result for some time to come. Much of this might be obviated if, instead of a good deal of useless knowledge taught in the schools, and expected to be learned, there were taught and obliged to be learned a sufficient preliminary knowledge of physiology for every girl to know the structure of her frame, and how wonderfully she is made. It would seem as if neither man nor woman should venture to undertake the management of a household and the rearing of children till they know something of what it is they undertake, with such issues of life and death in their hands. And whenever this shall be an absolute requirement of early education we may rest assured that the health of the community will be on a far superior basis to that in which remedies are used ignorantly, according to hearsay, or to the misinformed grandmother's well-meant advice, and we shall have heard the last of those household remedies, hardly beyond comparison with some of which was the former administration of bird-shot to an old person troubled with "rising of the lights."

And there is another thing in the way of health on which the grandmother will be very apt to interfere, and that is the amount of sleep the children (and for the matter of that the rest of the family) take. Old people, it is well known, sleep less than the young do, and it is a foible of theirs to insist that the young shall have as little as they find sufficient for themselves. "Early to bed and early to rise makes a man healthy and wealthy and wise," is a distich they love to quote, and they are often of the opinion of those people who plume themselves upon the fact of their early rising as upon some virtuous achievement.

The Right Sleep.

One might infer from their conversation and behavior that the taking of a sufficient quantity of rest was a sinful indulgence of the senses, and that the height of innocence and intellectuality lay in the involuntary nervous restlessness that will not or can not stay at peace, but, like the doubtless good and surely disturbing woman in Proverbs, has the maids up in the middle of the night for their tasks. All this is disagreeable enough when it occurs among individuals having no positive power over each other by which one may be deprived of the really needed sleep; but when it occurs among those that have either the moral or the material power to direct movements, as between parent and child, the old and the young, husband and wife, mistress and servant, the thing becomes a tyranny.

During all the hours of wakefulness the brain is in a constant state of activity—for it is impossible to be awake and conscious without thought and emotion—and therefore of waste so far as this activity is understood to use the substance of the brain. "Its substance," remarks a noted observer, "is consumed by every thought, by every action of the will, by every sound that is heard, by every object that is seen, by every substance that is touched, by every odor that is smelled, by every painful or pleasurable sensation, and so each instant of our lives witnesses the decay of some portion of its mass and the formation of new material to take its place. The necessity for sleep is due to the fact that during our waking moments the formation of the new substance does not go on as rapidly as the decay of the old. The state of comparative repose which attends upon this condition allows the balance to be restored, and hence the feeling of freshness and rejuvenation we experience after a sound and healthy sleep. The more active the mind, the greater the necessity for sleep, just as with a steamer, the greater the number of revolutions its engines makes, the more imperative is the demand for fuel."

Thus it is apparent that in sleep this waste of the brain is repaired, and during sleep, if the brain is at all active, but a small portion of it is so, as any one can see by the slight and superficial character of dreams. So long as the brain does not feel the strain, one is wakeful and alert; but when repair becomes necessary, it feels the amount of feebleness which makes sleep desirable, and produces irritability and torture without it. A person deprived of sleep has no resource but those drugs and stimulants and that enfeebled general condition which are the authors of much disaster, or else insanity in its various forms; for when that state appears in which it is impossible to sleep, then the overstrained brain is unable to make repairs, and disease is already there or impending.

When it so happens that one individual in all the house wakes betimes, either from habit or choice, or because the brain and body do not require so much rest as do those of others, what worst despotism could there be than the requirement that everybody else under the roof should conform to that standard of early rising, and be up and about, whether it is simple misery or not to rise just as the last sweet dregs of sleep make the soul heavy and the body a weight well-nigh impossible to lift. The hours of mounting morning are delightful—fresh and bright and dewy, what is there to exceed their cheer? But if you are drooping with unrested weariness, it is hard to see the cheer; and if you are worthless before the noon comes because of your early rising, and have to pay your way with a nap by the afternoon, what advantage is there in time? In truth, nothing that you do all day will be done well, and everything will drag, so that the difference in your life's accomplishment, if you rise early or if you sleep your sleep out, will be evident to any one that takes the pains to investigate, while the difference in your state of feeling does not need to be investigated by anybody, but is as apparent to everybody else as it is disagreeable to yourself.

The very aged, as it is well known, do not require so much sleep by a large degree as others do, for the less activity of the brain with them, of the nervous system, and in fact of the whole system, makes less repair necessary, and thus less demand for sleep; and this being so it is odd that they are so inclined to make a virtue of the fact, when, in addition, it is true that if they did not rise early they would be very uncomfortable in bed.

But children, on the other hand, require a vast amount of sleep, for in their case the constructive processes are lively, and it is a lesson which their elders can not too often repeat to themselves, that these little people must be let alone till nature dismisses them from the land of dreams back to the world of sunbeams.

Those in middle life, again, save for the exceptional cases, also need sleep in greater proportion than when more advanced, although in no such measure as children do. But one need only to think of the state of all but perpetual motion in which children's thoughts are, to say nothing of their work of receptivity when all the world presents itself in its varying phases for the first time to their apprehension—to be seen, to be wondered at, to be comprehended, to be enjoyed, to be remembered, to be generalized from—to understand that both the waste and the repair must be tremendous, and he is ruinously heedless, or else willing to mutilate the intelligence, who prevents a child from getting this needed repair in sleep, simply because it is convenient to have the family breakfast together at seven o'clock, or because the school bell rings at nine, or because it used to be so in grandmother's day, or for any other reason under the sky. As air is free to all, so should sleep be, that equally great requisite with air and food, and to deprive one of the due quantity is the same thing as to deprive one of food, and is a species of starvation perhaps more cruel than another, for it starves the brain and the body, too. "Sleep that knits up the raveled sleave of care" is sweet to all, a luxury to some, but to the weary and to children it is vital.. And if it were not vital, is not the world a hard place enough to live in ? and have not children who have the rule of three or the irregular verbs to learn, under the best of circumstances, a hard time in the future ? and is it well to call them back to all this hardness when they are in that rosy, dewy, happy world the gates of which are sleep ?

The Grandmother's Chair.

But when the grandmothers do not insist upon their too old-fashioned recipes in case of illness, and do not demand too early rising on the part of the children, and are, in fact, what grandmothers ought to be, what treasures they are in a family, especially at the twilight hour! It is they who have all the family traditions and know how to tell them, who keep the genealogical tables, and are wise in the family connection to the third and fourth generation. It is they who are storehouses of story and of song, song which they sing in quavering voices which to the hearers are infinitely sweet; and it is they who recite to us the old ballads and poems which first teach the love of poetry. And what greater gift could they give than the joy and comfort that through life come with the love of poetry ? We sometimes meet people who tell us they have little or no love of poetry; we always think they could have had no grandmothers.

Delight in Poetry.

To them the most exquisite images fail to convey an idea, and they see in sapphic or lyric nothing but a promiscuous whirl of smooth words, not unpleasant in their jingle for a little while, but rather tiresome in their monotony after a page or two, while sometimes the finest raptures of the poets seem to be only scaling, in their eyes, the heights of absurdity.

Such people, speaking literally, deserve a vast amount of compassion. They are shut out from a literal paradise of sound and sight and fancy, and at first glance are even more pitiable than those with no ear for music; for the one would appear to be but a defect of the body, the other of the soul. For surely they who receive no pleasure from

> "soft Lydian airs
> Married to immortal verse,
> Such as the meeting soul may pierce
> In notes, with many a winding bout
> Of linked sweetness long drawn out,
> With wanton heed, and giddy cunning,
> The melting voice through mazes running,
> Untwisting all the chains that tie
> The hidden soul of harmony"—

surely they lose a pleasure only less in kind than that lost by those who see no beauty in the words that describe those airs, nor in the ideas that they convey. Such people should find no charm in that most alluring, most mystical of sounds, the airy voice of the echo of the hills, "Sweet queen of parley, daughter of the spheres."

Poetry is the first blossom of all literature. Long before history was ever heard of, before philosophy began to think, before fiction had a fancy, the light-hearted of the race began to sing. It might seem, then, as if this art had had time to come to perfection that the other branches needed generations to attain. In fact, it has learned to interpret nature as no other art can yet do. What figure-painter, what flesh-painter, what painter of interiors, what prodigal of colors can equal the picture that Keats makes of Madeline :

> "A casement high and triple-arched there was,
> All garlanded with carven imageries
> Of fruits and flowers and bunches of knot-grass,
> And diamonded with panes of quaint device,
> Innumerable of stains and splendid dyes
> As are the tiger-moth's deep-damasked wings;
> And in the midst, 'mong thousand heraldries
> And twilight saints and dim emblazonings,
> A shielded scutcheon blushed with blood of queens and kings.
> Full on this casement shone the wintry moon,
> And threw warm gules on Madeline's fair breast
> As down she knelt for Heaven's grace and boon;
> Rose-bloom fell on her hands together prest,
> And on her silver cross soft amethyst,
> And on her hair a glory."

What landscape painter could spread more beauty on his labored canvas of many feet in size and many months in work than Tennyson has shut into four little lines:

> "How faintly flushed, how phantom-fair
> Was Monte Rosa, hanging there
> A thousand shadowy-penciled valleys
> And snowy dells in a golden air!"

What sculptor of marbles of world-wide fame, and for which kings contend, of Joves and Cæsars, can let us see any more statuesque sight than Browning gives us when he draws old Hildebrand:

> "See him stand,
> Buttressed upon his mattock, Hildebrand
> Of the huge brain-mask, welded ply o'er ply
> As in a forge; it buries either eye
> White and extinct, that stupid brow; teeth clenched,
> The neck tight-corded, too, the chin deep-trenched,
> As if a cloud enveloped him, while fought
> Under its shade, grim prizers, thought with thought
> At dead lock, agonizing he, until
> The victor thought leaped radiant up, and Will,
> The slave with folded arms and drooping lids
> They fought for, lean forth, flame-like, as it bids!"

And what piper playing with cunning pipes can let us see beauty and hear music at one and the same time as Swinburne lets us do in one of the verses of "Atalanta"—

> "The ivy falls with the Bacchanal's hair
> Over her eyebrows, shading her eyes;
> The wild vine, slipping down, leaves bare
> Her bright breast shortening into sighs;
> The wild vine slips with the weight of its leaves,
> But the berried ivy catches and cleaves
> To the limbs that glitter, the feet that scare
> The wolf that follows, the faun that flies;"

or as Dryden does in the sweet falls and returns and chimes ringing through every ode he ever wrote; or as Milton causes to move along all his heroic measures; as haunts the songs of Shakespeare; as blows like trumpet peels through all the Border ballads?

All these arts—the painter's, the sculptor's, the singer's—the poet combines in his own, and that all these arts are capable of yielding, provided only that his song does not fall upon a deaf ear, that his picture and his carving are not set before a blind eye. For in order to gather all the wealth that there is in a poem, one must be in some degree a poet one's self; that is, if not an executive poet, as one may term it, an appreciative one. We have to look in a mirror to see our own image reflected, and the poet can not paint his picture or call up his echo except upon an answering surface.

Nor is this enjoyment and appreciation of poets altogether a natural gift; it is capable of growing from a small germ and enlarging itself to full bounds, although undoubtedly the germ there must always be. He who is going to love music, hears his mother singing it beside his cradle, till, through sweet accustoming and tender memory, the strain becomes a part of his being and draws other strains to keep it company; and thus the imaginative faculty of the child, together with his love of melody, has usually to be stimulated by early usage, in order that this chief of all the pleasures shall be his in its perfection by-and-by.

"Next to the language of poetry," says Willmott, "is the tone of its voice. It makes love to the ear, and wins it with music. Certain passages possess a beauty altogether unconnected with their meaning. The reader is conscious of a strange, dreamy sense of enjoyment, as of lying upon warm grass in a June evening, while a brook tinkles over stones in the glimmer of trees. Sidney records the effect of the old ballad on himself, and Spence informs us that he never repeated particular lines of delicate modulation without a shiver in his blood not to be expressed. Boyle was conscious of a tremor at the utterance of two verses in Lucan, and Derham knew one to have a chill about his head upon reading or hearing the fifty-third chapter of Isaiah and David's lamentation for Jonathan. How deep is the magic of sound may be learned by breaking some sweet verses into prose. The operation has been compared to gathering dew-drops, which shine like jewels upon the flowers, but run into water in the hand. The elements remain, but the sparkle is gone."

Surely it is the last gift the divine powers can give, this love of poetry. They who possess it can be content with little else besides; it can bring palaces and the pleasures of palaces into hovels, it can make the Barmecide's feast a satisfactory banquet, and can play at all times the part of fairy godmother to any Cinderella's rags. It is, like virtue, its own exceeding great reward. Those that have loved it it never forsakes. It is eyes to the blind and ears to the deaf; it spreads morning and bird-song and flowers and dew on the dark field of the sleepless night; it is sunshine in the dreariest day; it lends to the old the blush and fire of youth again. Some young savage, blowing through his plucked-up reed, may have invented the first instruments of music; some idler, scratching the rude outline of another with a chance bit of red ochre on a rock may have invented painting; some uncouth genius may have imagined the god slumbering in the stone, and have cut him out and set him up to worship; all these arts men may have established; but poetry, that enchantment

DRAWING AND SCULPTURE DURING THE PALÆOLITHIC EPOCH.

where melody flows through all the mould of words, where every word is color and every modulation form, where the heart and the soul enter, where the tear trembles and the smile kindles—poetry, that union of music and beauty, is the gift of the Lord Himself.

And if the grandmother, when the children cluster about her, has succeeded in filling them with the love of this divine gift, this comforter and consoler, she has given them as firm a stepping stone to happiness as they will find in purely earthly things—I say earthly, and yet surely it is something close upon the heavenly, too.

But it is not only the children that find happiness in the grandmother; it is the grandmother that finds happiness in the children. And how our grandmother found it and made her life a blissful thing when she took the children into it, the story of Mrs. Penn instructs us. It is the story of a perpetual thanksgiving.

A Perpetual Thanksgiving.

It was certainly a dreary house, Mrs. Penn's, and never more so than when the autumn sun sent the shadows of the hills across it in the early afternoon, and cast a double gloom throughout the great solitary rooms and the long passages.

The servants went and came noiselessly; no foot in it fell more loudly than the autumn leaves, and Mrs. Penn trailed her widow's gowns through its solitudes, sometimes feeling as if she were buried alive, and with a listlessness that said she did not greatly care if she were.

On the outskirts of the village neighbors were few, and friends came rarely. There were almost no outside interests. Mrs. Penn read the books that came up from town, and sent the box back and had another, and did some endless embroideries. And every morning she opened her eyes with a dull sense of oppression and regret that the day was to do over again; and she always cried a little at twilight, and said to herself that her husband, who had been very much her senior and had indulged her with every desire of her heart, would have resented her loneliness and want of happiness.

The coming of the one daily mail meant but little to her, for her friends had their own interests and families; and, except in the midsummer, when the mountains were to be climbed, she had so little to offer them by way of entertainment that she had long ceased to ask them under her roof; her few letters were spasmodic and brief, and her sole regular correspondent was her husband's granddaughter by his first marriage, Eva Robson, who resided abroad with her babies, Mr. Robson having a small consulate and living much too luxuriously,

HER FEW LETTERS WERE SPASMODIC AND BRIEF

as Mrs. Penn thought, on his wife's inheritance from her grandfather. "No, Eliza," said Mrs. Penn, to the person who united in herself the functions of friend and lady's maid and housekeeper, and who had come in to see about engaging a certain monstrous bird for dinner six weeks off, the young girl, Sally Bowen, who had reared it, being then in the kitchen. "No. What should I do with such an affair as that—an overgrown, unnatural, unhealthy fowl! I don't see why we should have a turkey at all, if it comes to that."

"Because every one else does," said Eliza stoutly.

"We have turkeys often enough on other days," said Mrs. Penn, still looking over her silks for the shade she wished.

"But Thanksgiving Day," persisted Eliza.

"What is Thanksgiving Day to me?"

"Ma'am!"

"What is Thanksgiving Day to me? What have I to be thankful for?"

"Well, ma'am," said Eliza, who was on the intimate footing given by having lived with Mrs. Penn since she was born, "you're alive, and you're well"——

"I don't consider that anything to be thankful for," said Mrs. Penn. "I'm not at all thankful to be alive—I'd rather be dead. And being alive I've a right to be well!"

"I suppose Charity Bowen thinks she has a right to be well, too—bedridden for twenty years," said Eliza, in whom the ways of the household and the habit of years had fostered an easy familiarity. "And, perhaps, she would be better for the medicines if they could afford the difference between selling the turkey here and selling it to the middle-man."

"She can have all the medicines she wants, and you know it very well!"

"They're a proud and honest folk, Mrs. Penn."

"Oh, for goodness' sake, Eliza, buy the turkey, if that's what you want. But you mustn't keep it for any supposititious Thanksgiving Day. You can have it to-morrow."

"It won't be ready to-morrow. They don't expect to kill it till the last week in November."

"Well, do as you please. If you're set upon eating turkey by way of expressing any annual pressure of thanks, why, eat it! Only don't expect me to do so. I'm not at all thankful for the privilege of living in a tomb".——

"It looks like a tomb," said Eliza, gazing down the stately room, with its rich rugs, its old portraits, its china placques, its glowing fire, its flowers in crystal vases, its books and silken cushions and deep chairs.

"No matter what it looks like; it *is* a tomb. And I am just as dead in it as if the bells had tolled for me."

"You'll have to excuse me, ma'am, out if I talked that way you'd say I was tempting Providence."

"To what?" demanded Mrs. Penn.

"For my part," said the desperate Eliza, goaded by long series of similar outbursts, "where the Lord puts me I expect He puts me for something."

Mrs. Penn looked at her with almost a gleam of amusement in her eyes. "Oh, I'll excuse you," said she. "Anything by way of a diversion. One must have conversation, even if it's with an impertinent"—— But Eliza gently closed the door, and the opportunity for further conversation, too, before the word "servant" should offend her ears.

Mrs. Penn put away her silks; it was too dark to match the shades, and, gathering her threads to put in the fire, walked up and down the room. "One must do something to change the poles," she said. And then she paused to look out the window at the man plodding up the avenue with the mail, and then at the gray landscape—the hills already black with shadow, a dull rose in the upper air above the rising mists, where a couple of crows flapped heavily, all fading to dim, melancholy outlines and a promise of coming storm. "And one night just like another, and one day just like another," she murmured, as she turned and sat down before the fire, lifting her skirt daintily, for all it was no matter, she said, whether it scorched or not. "I don't know why I care," she said. "There isn't anything any matter. And as for me, I'm not as much use as the log on the coals—that is good for something." And she hid her face in her hands, and began to enjoy her favorite twilight diversion, the summing up of her misfortunes and injuries and miseries, and if she could have had a new one to add to them she would have had a pang of satisfaction. "My husband dead, my children dead, my people dead, shut up here because on account of my hay-fever I can't live in any other spot on earth; without a friend to talk to superior to a servant, without an object in life, without a soul to love, without a soul to love me—except—maybe—poor Eliza—why shouldn't I call such an existence a living tomb? Why should I give thanks for it? It's unbearable—the solitude, the dreariness. Oh, I'm so lonely; if I only had something I could love!" she exclaimed, the tears trickling through her fingers; "If I only had a cat to love—and I don't like cats—I'd as lief have snakes round"——

Eliza opened the door, and John brought in the lamps and went out again.

"The mail," said Eliza, rather loftily, but lingering over a lamp after handing Mrs. Penn the newspaper and a letter with foreign stamps.

"Mercy on us!" cried Mrs. Penn. "A black border! It's from Eva; who in the world is she in mourning for?"

"Some one out of the world," said Eliza, busying herself with the shade.

"And sealed with black wax—dear, dear, I wonder who is dead now!"

"If you would open it," said the irrepressible Eliza, "you would find out."

"Oh, Eliza, how unsympathetic you are! When you know it's bad news"——

"Shall I open it, ma'am?"

"Yes, Eliza, do. I don't know—I'm all of a tremble"——

"There. Here it is. Now you can read it. And you know that whatever happens to Mrs. Robson, you've been in the way of thinking it's not much matter to you."

"Not much matter to me? Oh, Eliza!" cried Mrs. Penn, whose eyes had been rapidly running over the unfolded sheet. "Not much matter to me? Just read that, and see if it's no matter to me. They're coming here!"

"My gracious!" said Eliza, taking the chance presented and reading a little more slowly. "Bag and baggage! The whole kit of them!"

"Every one."

"Oh, I don't know about that. Isn't it awful? And I never used to children."

"Eliza! You wouldn't leave me now?"

"Land sakes! Who said anything about leaving?" exclaimed Eliza, who, having played dolls and gone to district school with Mrs. Penn, had been her familiar and tyrant ever since. "How could I leave you—all the same as born and bred together! I wasn't talking of leaving; I was talking of this Bedlam upside-down."

"Yes, Mr. Robson dead, the poor soul! And the money gone—I always knew it would go! And they all on the way over. And Eva wants to rest here a little, and then leave the children with me till she finds work. And she has no one else to turn to. And that means—oh, I don't know what it means! Eliza, I see it all as plainly as if a messenger from Heaven declared it—if they come here, they never will go away! And they'll be here any day now! There's no time, there's no way of heading them off. A telegram can't reach people in mid-ocean!"

"The poor young thing!" cried Eliza, with a total change of base. "Alone in a strange country, and with four children—why the oldest of them isn't ten! And crossing the sea with no nurse, and seasick, I'll be bound, and without a penny in the world—I don't wonder it makes your heart ache, ma'am!"

"Oh, yes, yes—it's all very terrible! There's so much trouble in the world. It seemed as if I had enough of my own before this."

"And now you've got hers."

"And oh, Eliza, just think of it! A horde of children overrunning us. Only picture it! This room, this heaven of rest—what a den of confusion it is to become! The books will be ruined, the photographs—they will break that dear bust of the Baby Emperor all to flinders, just as sure as you live! Nothing will be safe. There will be finger-marks on the windows and on the paint, crumbs everywhere, crusts of bread and jam, and half-eaten apples on every chair in the place—and I don't dare think of the dining-room!"

"Then I wouldn't, ma'am."

"Oh, how can I help it? There will be cries and screams there and everywhere else—those children never can have had any bringing up, if I remember Eva."

"Oh, now, ma'am!"

"Yes, Eliza, children are children the world over," said Mrs. Penn, as if she announced a new fact in natural history. "They'll be having bad dreams in the night and crying enough to wake the dead, and they'll be carrying on with pillow fights before daybreak, and I'll lose all my morning nap—the very best sleep I have! And they'll be having croup and measles, and you'll have to keep the house still then, and you can't. Oh, I know what children are in a house! And, Eliza, I'll have the whole of them to clothe and feed! Eva Robson do anything to earn money! Oh, Eliza," cried Mrs. Penn, in a heartbroken voice, "what have I done to be punished this way? Wasn't it bad enough before, without having a tribe of little Mohawks let loose in m**y** house! Oh, I can't bear it—I shall have to go to bed, and you must bring me something hot to put me to sleep; and oh, it's in my heart to wish I might never wake up! It will be the death of me, that's what it will be!"

And Mrs. Penn tottered off to bed, and her tears fell into the unaccustomed refreshment of her hot dose; for Eliza made it, and she made it strong, and she dreamed that all the cherubs in the print of the Madonna standing on the moon had come out of the picture, and were flying through the room and buzzing around her pillow, and she could not get a netting stout enough to keep them out.

It was some days before Mrs. Penn, owing to the results of her unwonted excitement, and perhaps of her unwonted refreshment, left her room. The sunset that had been pouring over the valley had fallen into starry dusk, and the whistle of the mail train was sounding far off on its way between the hills. John was just lighting the lamps. "I've come down stairs for one last hour of peace," she said. "For they may be here any day, now. To think I shall never see this great lovely room again in any decent condition till those children go! And go they must! I will have my trustees get Eva something to do the first moment possible. And if they can't and worst comes to worst, she can take half my income and go away somewhere out of my sight, and I'll dismiss half the servants and shut up half the house. I *can't* lose all my rest! I will have some sort of peace in my declining years!" She rose hurriedly as she spoke, and set the cup of fragrant tea that Eliza had brought her on the mantel-shelf; for there was a sound of beating hoofs on the avenue, a crackling of gravel under wheels, a furious ringing of the big doorbell, an outcry of voices, and suddenly the children were swarming all over her, with cold lifted faces and clasping arms, and little Penn was raising his voice in tears, and some one was bringing in the mother and laying her on a sofa, where she quietly fainted away.

Mrs. Penn gave herself and her condition and her apprehension one wild hurried half moment; and then the woman in her rose triumphant, and she ran to Eva with her smelling salts, and she snatched the water from a bowl of violets with which to sprinkle her white face, and called for Thomas to drive post-haste for the doctor, and with the children exclaiming and wailing and tumbling about her, had John carry the insensible form up to the best room, that Eliza had already aired and warmed on a peradventure. And then Mrs. Penn and Eliza, between them, got off the prostrate woman's clothes, and bathed her with alcohol and warm water, and put on her Mrs. Penn's very best laced and tucked and ribboned night-dress; and that done, Eliza went to see to the children and give them their supper and put them also to bed.

"Just a spark of life left," said Dr. Thoms. "Danger of heart failure. A weak heart, anyway. She will have to owe her life to your care, Mrs. Penn, if she comes round. I'll be in again in a couple of hours."

And when, after midnight, he had done his best and left his further orders, Mrs. Penn did not even pause to wonder at herself for the eagerness with which she obeyed him, for the way in which all night she kept the bottles of hot water packed about the frame where the vital action was so low, administered the restoratives, and hung upon the faltering breath, and when at last toward morning she felt an answering pressure of the frail hand she held and saw the eyelids flutter, and a glance of recognition come and go, she went to the window, with her heart swelling in her throat, and she looked out upon the great stars flashing in the sky, with a sense of kinship she had never had before, as if she, too, were fulfilling some office in the universe· for the doctor had said this life depended on her, and she was saving it.

The doctor had telegraphed, when he first left the house, for a couple of trained nurses, and they arrived in the morning, and Eliza kept the children in a distant part of the house, and Mrs. Penn had a long slumber before she came down to tea, and found little Irene, the ten-year-old child, mothering the brood, as if she had long been used to it, and in a way that first made Mrs. Penn open her eyes wide and then filled them with tears. "I declare!" Eliza had said to her before she came down, "the way that child carries the load of all the other children is enough to break your heart, the little woman!" Mrs. Penn took Penn, the two-year-old baby, on her lap, and fed him herself, carried him into the drawing-room and warmed his feet by the fire there, and undressed him,

Irene hovering about to placate him if need be, and sang him to sleep in her arms, and carried him to his little bed at last, and went to her own wearied but full of sense of duty done that was as novel as it was agreeable. "I'm sure Mr. Penn would be pleased," she said, and fell asleep.

She was waked in the morning by a patter of little feet and a disturbance of the coverlet, and a little white-robed creature in the gray morning twilight was creeping into bed with her, and two little arms were round her neck, and a little rosy cheek was touching hers, and a silver voice was cooing in her half bewildered ear: "I love 'oo. I love 'oo vewy mush!"

"Bless his little heart!" she said to Irene, who had pattered in after him to hinder his waking her. "Here, here, you come round and get in the other side. You'll have your death o' cold! John hasn't shaken down the furnace yet." And the little adventurer lay between them, and she turned to stretch an arm over both of them, and they all fell asleep again together, and when at length Mrs. Penn awoke again and saw them, a sunbeam stealing in and kindling the two pretty heads to gold, she knew she had not been so happy since she used to wake and see Geoffrey Penn's head on the other pillow.

It was Mrs. Penn herself who slipped on a piece of half-eaten gingerbread on the stair carpet, and in her hurry to overtake little Penn, who had fallen down, forgot to remember the spot it made. And it was Eliza who gathered a select assortment of apple cores from the drawing-room tables and said nothing. And it was Mrs. Penn who sopped with her own napkin, before the maid could reach it, the contents of Penn's overturned glass of milk, and had to take him in her arms then for the remainder of the dinner time to quiet his frightened and repentant roaring.

"It's singular," she said to Eliza next day, "but I don't know when I've had such a good night's rest."

It was Mrs. Penn who found herself buttering bread at all hours of the day, taking a little company into the store-room to overlook the jams and cakes and goodies there, telling story after story when the dark came on, creeping in to look at the little sleepers in the middle of the night, and visiting the sick room with breathless and soundless caution, and crying over Eva at last when she had been lifted to the lounge and was able to hold one down with the embraces of her poor weak arms. "You are so good," sighed Eva. And at another time she murmured, "Oh, what should I have done if I hadn't had you to come to!"

"I am sure Mr. Penn would be pleased," Mrs. Penn said again, as she left the room.

If you had happened to be on the Pennfield highway any pleasant November afternoon, you might have seen Mrs. Penn, who had been in the habit of

THAT TURKEY WILL BE LOOKING LIKE A BIG HEATHEN GOD.

never setting her foot on the ground, walking with a little rabble of children, this one holding her finger, and that one her skirt, and investigating ants' holes and forsaken nests and seed vessels and the like; or you might have met her coming home from somewhere and holding at arm's length and by the nape of the neck a scrawny kitten that pawed the air, of which monster she was terribly afraid, but for which both Penn and Irene had chanced to express a wish.

"I guess I would let that go till regular cleaning day," said Mrs. Penn, as Eliza was going round with a wet cloth, wiping the finger-marks off the paint. "It might hurt their feelings, you know."

"That's so, ma'am."

"Do you mind it all very much?" asked Mrs. Penn, wistfully.

"Mind it!" said Eliza. "It seems as if we had just begun to live, ma'am."

"I don't know but it does, Eliza," said Mrs. Penn. "How short the days are growing! I don't seem to get anything accomplished."

"Except making these dear children love you, ma'am."

"You're as silly as I am, Eliza."

There had been three or four weeks of this when, one day, the door of the mother's room being left open, there poured in upon her an amazing sound of revelry. Of course poor Mrs. Eva did not know that Geoffrey was standing in his boots on the velvet sofa to better inspect a "Holy Family" with his lead pencil, or that Penn was drumming on a lacquered tray with a gold filagree spoon, or that Amy was meddling with the big Swiss music box, or that Irene was sitting with a strew of precious photographs around her, to which the others came with eager fingers and loud shouts every few moments; but she knew that Pandemonium was reigning there "Oh," she murmured, "you will be so glad when they go. It is a cruelty. Your quiet house! How can you bear it? Oh, I know it is an imposition!"

"What are you talking about?" exclaimed Mrs. Penn.

"But you see I am gaining so fast I shall be downstairs in a few days. And I think I shall be able to get a position in the Government; it has been promised to me, and then I shall relieve you. But I shall never, when I am gone—never, never, oh never, forget your goodness in taking us in so!"

"When you are gone! My dear child, you are talking nonsense. When you are gone with my consent will be the day after never. You wouldn't have the heart, now would you, Eva," said Mrs. Penn, the tears ready to start, "to put me back where I was before you and these darling children came into the house? Dead and alive—more dead than alive I was—just in a living tomb!"

"But the noise—the mischief—the confusion "———

"Oh, my dear, it is life! I used to think so much of my pimlico order, and now it is a positive pleasure to see a train of cars and a circus in the drawing room. Eliza and I were saying this very day we didn't know how we got along before you came. And I am going to have the big room in the wing fitted for a schoolroom, and the room between for a nursery, and have a nurse for Penn and Amy and a governess for Geoffrey and Irene."

"But oh, the expense!"

"Never mind the expense! It was their grandfather's money, and he would rather they had it, I know, than have it hoarded for a lot of societies in the end. And they shall! I am making you an allowance, Eva, and I shall see to all the rest. Oh, Eliza!" as a foot drew near; "is that you, Eliza? What have you done about that turkey? I wish you'd send down to the Bowens' and see if it's gone."

"It's hanging up in the cold cellar, Mrs. Penn," said the demure Eliza.

"Eliza, what a jewel you are! You always just anticipate me. Eva, darling, I think we can get you down to the table where that turkey will be looking like a big heathen god, and we will forget you have ever been away!"

And as they all sat about the table with the nuts and candy when the feast was over, "I haven't had such a Thanksgiving," Mrs. Penn said, "since my husband died! I was dead and I am alive; I was lost and I am found. I was a limp and useless nonentity, and now I am a part of the breathing world, with something to do, with people to love, and with a heart full of thankfulness."

"I wish we had Thanksgiving twice a year, don't you, grandmother?" piped Amy.

"I am having it now every day of my life, my little dear," said Mrs. Penn. "I am having a perpetual Thanksgiving!"

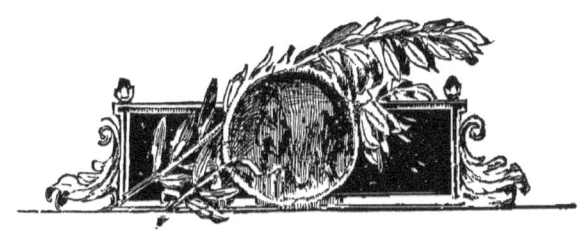

CHAPTER FOURTEENTH.

About Pets.

But think admitted to that equal sky,
His faithful dog shall bear him company.
—*Pope.*

Like a dog he hunts in dreams.
—*Tennyson.*

The house without a pet
Is a sad house, you know;
There all the trifles fret,
And every task is woe.
—*Anon.*

He hailed the bird in Spanish speech,
The bird in Spanish speech replied,
Flapped round his cage with joyous screech,
Dropped down and died.
—*Campbell.*

Let Hercules himself do what he may,
The cat will mew and dog will have his day.
—*Shakespeare.*

A harmless, necessary cat.
—*Shakespeare.*

When I play with my cat, who knows if I do not make her more sport than she makes me?—*Montaigne.*

A hardy mouse that is bold to breede
In catte's eeris.
—*Chaucer.*

The human members of our happy household cannot flatter themselves that they are the sole constituents of the family. There are certain other members whose affection and whose intelligence have a great deal to do with the happiness of the house. To be sure, in the city certain pets are impossible; it is difficult, for example, to have large dogs in town and give them the exercise needed for health. But when one is willing to take the trouble of giving them their frequent run, how much they add to our amusement and the liveliness of the family!

STEPPING STONES TO HAPPINESS. 377

NOT THE SOLE CONSTITUENTS OF THE FAMILY.

Poor Dog Tray.

There are many people who have an unreasonable fear of dogs, and especially so in the season known as dog-days. These days of sultry and humid summer have an ill repute which is undeserved. "Dog-day weather" is a final epithet of opprobrium when we condemn the temperature. Yet, curiously enough, the dog-days originally received their name as a matter of honor and dignity. The long-headed Egyptians, observing that the Nile rose annually with the heliacal rising of a certain brilliant star, called that orb of beneficent influences Sihor, the Nile. And as its coming warned them to their terraces out of reach of the flood they typified it as a dog, or a man with a dog's head. The Latins adopted the star as Sirius, but forgot, or never knew, its significance, while ignorance, mistaking coincidence for cause, ascribed to it a baleful increase of the heat. In time the popular belief declared that on its rising wine turned sour, dogs went mad, all other animals began to waste, and man to decline. The Romans even sacrificed a brown dog to appease its rage.

Superstition has a deep root. Macaulay's school-boy may repeat till he is hoarse that this slandered luminary twinkles at the reassuring distance of two trillions two hundred thousand billions of miles from our little sphere, while the illustrative cannon-ball, traveling four hundred and eighty miles an hour, must consume five hundred and twenty-three thousand two hundred and eleven years in the journey thither; and science may reiterate that rabies, whatever its nature or origin, is not exclusively a midsummer madness; every year, notwithstanding, panic terror concerning hydrophobia recurs, and walks hand in hand with wholesale slaughter.

Yet the patient, faithful, taciturn creatures thus despitefully entreated have been the unselfish friends and servants of man since the dim antiquity wherein that naked savage suddenly bethought himself to make a coat of his companion's skin. Indeed, your dog is your only unquestioning and free-hearted lover. Other animals return a vague attachment for benefits received. Humanity rigidly exacts its *quid pro quo;* to be loved of his kind, one must be lovable. But a man's dog clings to him through ill report and good report—suffers, starves, dies at his hands, and counts itself happy in the opportunity.

Famous Dogs.

Did not Plato the Broad swear by a dog? Did not the dog of Alcibiades cost seventy minas—a thousand dollars of our coinage? was he not even more esteemed for his sagacity than for his beauty? and did not his fidelity withstand the coarse caprices, the cruel indignities, of that brilliant master from whom all other friends fell away? Did not that greater general, William of Orange, love his dog as well, and honor him much more?

Charles the Second, who cared for neither man nor woman, cherished his dogs with a fondness bequeathed to him possibly by his grandmother, Anne of Denmark, who kept a retinue of those followers, and paid a very pretty annual bill to Master Heriot, the court goldsmith, for their gold and silver collars and emblazoned blankets, thereby contributing, no doubt, to the endowment of his famous hospital. It was that royal lady's successor, her present Majesty of England, who, inheriting the family taste, presented his ugliness of Skye to an obsequious court, and made him a fashion.

Who, among us, being examined as to the events of King John's evil reign, could remember one save the signing of the Magna Charta, and the death of Gelert, the hound? What a dreary waste of dates and bloodshed is the history of the Crusades; but at the name of Roswal, the dog of Sir Kenneth, how the hot sands of Syria, the splendor and valor of the legions, the fierce courage of Richard, the enlightened chivalry of the Sultan Saladin, the aspirations, the prejudices, the very image of the time, rise before us!

Barry, the famous dog of great St. Bernard, saved forty lives, and among others, carried on his back to the hospice, through towering snow-drift, a baby whose mother had been killed by an avalanche. If he stood for charity, Aubry's dog stood for justice, when, with whatever emphasis might lie in furious threatenings, he accused Richard of Macaire of his master's murder.

The Dog in Literature.

Literature has made the dog her own, and Art has loved him. Who thinks of Sir Walter without Maïda? Is not Flush beloved by Mrs. Browning's lovers? Can we separate heroic little Miss Mitford from her faithful spaniel? Is not Byron's Boatswain fitly sepultured at Newstead Abbey? Who can read without tears that perfect story, "Rab and his Friends"? Who has not a tender feeling for the invisible, beloved Schneider who comforts scapegrace Rip Van Winkle in his distresses? Who has not known and loved the dogs of Landseer? How many tombs of the old knights bear a sculptured dog to show that they followed their standard as a dog his master? On how many monuments of illustrious women his effigy symbolized fidelity and affection, as the lion's image symbolized courage and magnanimity! What innumerable records of fearlessness, self-sacrifice, patience, sagacity, devotion, justify that good saying of Hamerton, "I pity the man who can live a dogless life!"

It is true that in the cities there is no room for dogs. They must be crowded out, with some other good gifts of heaven. The dog is a natural rover. He loves free air, free ways, the smell of fresh turf. Shut in to alien pavements, scorched by the sun, pinched by the winter winds, parched with thirst, faint with hunger, the race deteriorates, develops strange diseases, and from man's safeguard becomes his possible danger.

But in their natural home, with water, shade, and kindness, the nobler

breeds of dogs, which alone should be perpetuated, are no more dangerous in August than in January, which is more than can be said of man, who too often develops a most uncertain, not to say ferocious, temper under these brazen skies. Let us, then, be reasonable. Banish poor Tray to the country, watch him if need be, slay him if need be, but let us not indulge in excessive apprehension of the whole canine species. We shall have gotten a step farther in civilization when dog-days cease to be an indiscriminate carnage of dogs of all degree.

Harmless Necessary Cat.

And if there is so much to be said for the dog, who appears to be capable of every emotion that human beings show—love, hatred, jealousy, fear, anger, courage, depression, sorrow and joy, patience and faithfulness and the rest— shall nothing in her turn be pleaded for the cat? The ubiquitous cat, found all the world over, and all the world over always the same, whose lovers claim for her an almost human perfection, and who everywhere, on sea or shore, in the parlor or in the hut, makes a place look like home! And yet no member of the family has suffered the abuse that the family cat receives at the hands of the world. We do not speak of those who starve her; who turn her outdoors at night, who go away for a season in the country and leave her to forage for herself, but of those who simply slander her by injurious report. According to these scandalous people the cat is without beauty and without affection; she is ungrateful, cruel, stupid, treacherous, and dishonest. Strange that on such a worse than worthless being should be lavished the religious worship of nations and so much of the household love of uncounted individuals as poor Pussy has received!

The Cat's Beauty.

But let us look at the charges. Without beauty? She is a being whose outlines are beauty itself; she is a succession of supple curves, and every curve obeys the law of the line of beauty, and all that beauty is heightened by the further beauty of gloss and movement. How brilliant are those eyes, likeness to which gives value to a precious jewel—the cat's-eye quartz, that otherwise were a worthless pebble! She is clad in furs shining with life, and which, while upon her, are incomparably superior to those dead furs which a princess is proud to wear. Every motion is grace, and whether she is black, or white, or gray, or tortoise-shell, every tint she assumes is a pure and charming one.

Is she without affection? When she goes to meet her chosen friends in the family and fawn about their feet, when she caresses them in their sickness, and sometimes dies broken-hearted in their death, it would seem to manifest love for them. When she suffers little children to lift her by the tail and carry her round by the heels, dress her up in caps and aprons as a doll, and inflict upon her a thousand well-meant pains, it looks as though she loved them. There are innumerable instances on record of the affection of cats for children, and entirely contradictory of the outrageous old notion of their sucking the breath of babies.

Puss, indeed, often makes her nest in the cradle, but not because she loves the little milky breath, nor because she loves the warmth, but because she loves the baby. She has been known to fly at the biggest and most ferocious dog entering the room where her little friend lay sleeping, to jump from the cradle when the child cried and run for the mother, returning and standing with her fore-feet on the cradle's edge, nervous and anxious till the mother took up the child; and one belonging to Mrs. Wilson, of Cults, near Aberdeen, Scotland, once accosted his mistress with piteous meaows, running repeatedly to the door, and endeavoring to fetch her with him, and finally succeeding, when the lady found her sick and feeble child rolled from the sofa where it had been left, and so enveloped in the rugs and wraps that it would presently have suffocated if help had not been brought by the cat.

When, moreover, the cat conquers her hereditary attachment to places, and follows persons about in their peregrinations, it cannot be because she loves to travel. Dr. Stables, a surgeon of the British navy, tells us of his cat which, although at six years old the mother of a hundred kittens, yet found time to accompany him on all his travels, having journeyed over twenty thousand miles in his company, usually bestowing herself, when she judged that it was flitting-time, in the little basket that carried her, but on one occasion, having taken so long an airing before starting that her master was obliged to leave without her, she hailed him, as he walked along the railway platform, from a first-class carriage that she had thought it best to take to save time.

The Cat's Virtues.

But when people say that Puss is cruel they forget that all carnivorous animals, and man among them, are cruel, too. Yet Puss is sometimes more virtuous than man in this regard, and will live for years with the tempting morsel of a bird playing about her, disputing her dinner, and alighting on her very head. Dr. Good told, long ago, of one that had lived at peace with a tame canary, suddenly, to the horror of the family, seizing it in her mouth, and springing to the top of a tall secretary, whereupon it was found that a strange cat had entered the room, which authenticated fact, from a scientific authority, must be held to dispose of the accusations both of cruelty and of stupidity if there were not other instances in plenty to do the same. There is certainly sagacity in the way any cat finds her way across miles of country to an old home, in the way she often sits by the cow, and asks the milkman to attend to her wants, in the way she as often goes fishing; it was sagacity in the cat which caught the escaping canary, and brought it back alive to her mistress; it was sagacity in the cat that absolutely baited a mouse-hole with part of her dinner, and sat and watched till she could pounce upon the mouse; it was sagacity in the cat that knew when Sunday came, as Mr. Whyte, of Dallfield Terrace, Dundee, relates; and the cats that, threatened with condign punishment, have suddenly disappeared and never re-appeared are legion. If one wants a study in philosophy, by the way, and an oppor-

CATS ARE A PART OF THE LARES AND PENATES.

tunity to discriminate between instinct and reason, he has only to observe any young cat on her first experience of a mirror, as she tries to put her paw behind it, pops back to see if the foe is still there, and ends by boxing the ears of the impudent creature confronting her there, and scampers away with her tail as big as ten, profoundly convinced of magic, whether or not she knows the word.

As for the treachery and dishonesty of Puss, which must be classed under the same head, that charge is simply libelous. The cat is naturally a hunter. If you take her away from her hunting-field and expect her to live the civilized life of the parlor, she must be fed regularly, as any other civilized being must be. The best of us, King David, for example, when famishing or when simply hungry, can be tempted to help ourselves. What credit to this little dumb creature, then, that she does not do it oftener ! The cook would have whipped Puss for eating some of the oysters. "And what for," said the table girl, "when he did the dacent thing to lave any ?" There are really few *honester* persons than a well-trained and well-treated cat. She is often the trusted guardian of property, as any grocer who keeps his pet parading on the counter can tell you. Why we should expect those little furry paws to keep themselves "from picking and stealing" any more than our own fingers, in like circumstances, is not to be explained by merely calling names.

The Cat a Fireside Ornament.

In the mean time, as it has been often said, there is about every cat a certain feminine quality that makes her an appropriate "property" of the hearth ; she loves her home and fireside, where she welcomes the wanderer, and seems to him a part of them ; she is gentle in her movements, and graceful as a court lady with a well-regulated train ; she cheers tired and dull moods with her pretty pranks, and sick hours with a watchful solicitude, always glad to sit beside your pillow when allowed. If she has some curiosity in her composition; if she loves a gossip with a neighbor; if she values praise, and brings you her first captive mouse to get it; if she has a little, ever so little, cunning—does not all that furnish further resemblance to the daughters of Eve ? And when you see her bring up her kitten, teach it its manners, and box its ears on misbehavior, does she do anything but complete the parallel ? Certainly cats are to every household where they are loved at all a part of the Lares and Penates, and to such households it is no matter of marvel that the Egyptians deified them and laid their poor little carcasses away at last with all the honor given to the royal mummy. But it was not merely as the friend of the hearth that this was done; for Egypt was the land of grain, and the enemy of rats and mice preserved it from incalculable loss. In our own country, where it can hardly be denied that such vermin cost many thousand dollars' worth of damage yearly, the cat is no less valuable an animal than she was in ancient Egypt, and if she is not deified, she should certainly be treated with indulgence and respect.

The Little Egyptian Cat.

They made a mummy of her, I say, over there in those dark old days. Did you ever hear the story of one of those little mummied cats?

"I was a little Egyptian cat,
And I lived in King Pharaoh's house, I did
The rats and the mice I caught with delight,
And I even ate birds, which I know was not right,
And instead of a fence I would sit out all night
And meow on the top of a pyramid.

One day I was greedy and ate seven mice,
And I had a bad fit, and I died, I did.
They hurried and made me this beautiful case,
Which covers me all excepting my face,
And they laid me away in a snug little place,
On a shelf inside of a pyramid.

And there I have lain all these thousands of years,
And hoped to lie buried forever, I did.
They hunted me out and brought me away,
And now isn't it awful that I have to stay
In this dusty museum, day after day,
When I want to go back to my pyramid?"

The Cat's Usefulness.

And if there were no more to say in the praise of Puss save that she is the destroyer of the small deer that infest the dwelling, and particularly the city dwelling, it would have to be acknowledged that she is a blessing past valuing. For although there are countless things that would seem to have been set on foot merely to try the patience of the housekeeper, and show her what a saint she could be if associated kitchens, and reservoirs of heat, and all the kindred household labor-saving machinery to be thought of were applied to her case, yet there are none of all her vexations that exceed in trouble that given by vermin in the walls of a house, and no vermin in diabolical maliciousness and intelligence equals the nuisance of rats, which, for excess of evil, may have been banished from Eblis itself.

The rat, in fact, is the housekeeper's worst enemy, always of course putting possibly her own indolence and procrastination out of the question. His boldness is only equaled by his cupidity, his cupidity by his cunning, his cunning by his courage. Her larder is invaded by him by day, her sleeping-room by night; her house itself is eaten up and reduced to sawdust by his teeth, and her only satisfaction in contemplating him is that if he lives long enough, the poor creature, those teeth will grow over each other so that he can not open his mouth to gnaw. She builds a new kitchen when he has riddled the old one, very likely, but she would have to line her closets with sheet-iron to keep him out of them. His sharp teeth may be heard filing and scraping all day long; they wake her out of sound sleep at night, and as she hears him tumbling round the rafters and behind the wainscots, she cannot tell in the dark if it be he, or tramps, or burglars, or fire, and he injures her nerves as much as he injures her house. She fears to leave the children alone in their beds in the evening, fears to leave the sick, and knows that even the dead are not safe on their biers. She dare not keep arsenic or strychnine in the house lest some one else get it, and worse trouble than that of rats follow; she hates to buy it, too, lest the sudden death of anybody in the circle of her acquaintance should put her under suspicion; she dreads to use it when it is bought, lest the house be made uninhabitable by the last vexation which the creatures that die of it can leave her to endure. If she lives near a piece of water, it is not only her house, but her yard, her garden, her orchard, that are infested, and fairly undermined by the pitfalls of the holes they dig; the roots of her apple trees are devoured; her hens are pounced upon when stupid with sleep; her chickens are snatched before her face and eyes; her eggs are carried off warm from the nest, and the food of the fowls is shared by the bold interlopers with ruinous robbery. She cannot fight them, for they will fly at her throat if attacked; she cannot drown them, for they swim like bubbles; she cannot catch them, for her traps are as good as laughed at by the wretches that figuratively snap their fingers at them—and if they were not, of what use would they be where the creatures multiply a dozen and a half at a litter? If her home is a rural one, ferrets, which are so valuable in the city, are not to be had; she remembers the old Bishop Hatto who was eaten in his tower, and shudders at possibilities; she would almost forswear her country for the sake of living across the sea in Aberdeenshire or Sutherlandshire, where a rat cannot be induced to stay; she doubts if even the Pied Piper of Hamelin could rid her of the pest for a wilderness of guilders; she wonders if, in the survival of the fittest, this strong, inexterminable brown Norway rat is not destined to destroy the human race and take the earth to itself; she does not see anything strange in the circumstance that people with shattered nerves, whether from delirium or other cause, see such things as rats—she is beginning to see nothing else in the universe herself.

The Norway Rat.

He is an intruder, this fierce little pest, at the best, and belongs to a conquering army. He came into Europe from Asia, he came to England from Norway, he comes over to America by means of every ship that touches our ports; he has destroyed our own rat, which, bad as it was, seems now a superior being in remembrance; he is all the more terrible that he takes care of his old and sick, and so swells his number; and the only mercy to be found in the visitation is that he frequently eats up his companions, taking care to turn the skin inside out with a nicety to the very toes.

And meantime a sort of nervous horror follows the neighborhood of these small deer; the housekeeper afflicted by them knows that they are the creatures of uncanny legend; that a certain awesome mysticism surrounds them; that they have unknown intelligences which warn them when a house is going to burn down, or a ship to sink, in full season to desert in safety, and be met marching away in platoons; that of old, if not now, they were wont to flee before rhyming anathemas addressed to them vocally, and quit the place where such were delivered, and instantly obey a letter written to them and sealed with butter, politely requesting their departure; that, in fact, every rat born is possessed of a little demon more untamable and vindictive than the armies of demons that went wherever Cornelius Agrippa did. She reads old accounts of the various methods of attempted extermination, and laughs bitterly to see how they have failed; she turns over prints of Annibale Caracci's Rat-catcher of Bologna, of Vischer's Dutch Rat-catcher, of the Chinese Rat-catcher with his cat in a bag; and while she feels that she could take them all to her bosom, as dear friends with one common purpose in life, would they only rise in the flesh and come to her rescue now, yet they only serve to show her that the trouble is universal and ineradicable all the round globe over. She marvels that the inventive genius of America has not come to her help, and she will regard the man who finds out and makes known some way of setting her free from the ravages of the rat as greater than he who invents electric lights and telephones, or he that taketh a city.

The Bird in the Cage.

Nor is it impossible, as some have thought, to keep a bird where there is a cat; for, as we have just seen, there are some cases where the cat is the bird's best friend. Always does that house seem delightful to me where, on the opening of the door, there comes a distant gush of bird-song. And those who have canaries and finches and mocking-birds and love-birds will assure us that the birds are their intimate friends. Surely that is so with that almost superhuman creature, the parrot. I myself have never been able to discover either common logic or common sense or common feeling in the old-fashioned fleer upon the love of the spinster for her cat and her parrot. If women condemned to solitary lives, denied the love of husbands, the caresses of children, the companionship and the protection, both for the present and the future, that family life affords—if such women can find in the love of cat or dog or parrot or any other pet any solace or compensation, however small, for the loss of the blessings that are the privilege of their sisters, what is there ridiculous about it or worthy of the least notice or mention? People must love and be loved by something; pity them if they have nothing better. Only vulgar observation and a low order of wit could have originated the idea that there was anything absurd in the business rather than something really touching and pathetic. The purse may not be sufficient for the adoption of children, the reason may not be convinced of the wisdom of bringing up the inheritor of unknown traits to break one's heart at last; but the bird and the cat are within the means of the poorest, and offer no suggestion of folly to the wisest.

Pretty Poll.

But although spinsters are beginning in this country, as they have long done in England, to hold a position of much more consideration than they used to do, it is perhaps still fortunate for them in this matter that there is a fashion in pets, a fashion by whose revolution certain others are banished, and the little marmoset and the larger monkey are brought into the drawing-room, and which makes paroquet and lory, long relegated to the spinster or the sailor boarding-house, now held as a charming addition to the picturesqueness of the modern parlor—the poor parrots that used to take from the original proprietor a goodly share of respect for daring to love anything not human and a man.

But how is it possible, fashion or not, for anybody to find, among all pets, one more interesting than the various individuals of the parrot tribe? Certainly as a pleasure to the eye they are remarkable—the comely shape, the wondrous colors, the fine poses, the beauty of expanded wings and tail. Every poet, every painter, one would think, might value this beauty, and find advantage in its companionship, whether it is exhibited in the little green love-birds, sleeping head down, who have nothing to say to any but each other, or in the Australian grass-paroquet, whose song is as sweet as the voice of the huge red and blue macaw, who measures a yard from crown to tail, and who lives all his life with one mate only, is strident, or whether it is seen in the great gray parrot, with his scarlet tail like a burning ember, who talks like a familiar for a hundred years, or in the purple-capped lory, who, unlike his lory cousins that can pronounce only the name of lory, adds language to docility and both to the charm of a scarlet and gold body, green wing passing into violet, a purple plume on his head, and an orange bill, or in the common, chattering, friendly, festive parrot of the Amazon, with all his bravery of green and gold and vermilion, or any other one of all the countless specimens that find their way to our shores and doors.

There is something picturesque in the very thought of the way the pretty creature does come to us, those that we see being seldom bred in captivity, but made prisoners when ravaging semi-tropical harvest fields, or swinging from bough to bough of the forests that lift their rank growth just under the equator. Some old Jack Tar, ashore on his holiday, captured it, or some negro or Indian child brought it down to the strand and the ships to sell, and it has been the pet of Jack over all the long lonesome seas between his port and its home, and has learned far more than it will ever tell, for all its talking. As it sits chained to its perch, what memories it has, and what strange hints it gives of groves with their gums and spices in distant archipelagoes glittering in the morning sun! Those weird eyes have seen Canopus and the Southern Cross; that black tongue guards the secret of night in the forecastle, and all with a grim uncanniness as if it were leagued with dark powers; and when it speaks, and when it bursts into peals of clattering laughter, it seems no less than the witch of Endor herself in disguise, or makes us believe in all the enchantments of the *Arabian Nights*. No one possessing a parrot can really be quite destitute of imagination, so much does it force upon any with the most meagre outfit in this regard thoughts beyond the bounds of the customary existence; the Black Prince of the Fairy Isles, one-half of whom was marble, is no longer a marvel and an impossibility; here is some cunning and articulate being who thinks our thoughts and talks our tongue, the whole of whom is feathers

The Children and the Parrot

And what a benefactor to a community is she who keeps a parrot, and is not niggardly with it, providing she has the sheltering cage cloth to envelop it for the benefit of neighbors, whenever he remembers its wild life of the woods and attempts its field cries. As far as the school children are concerned she is the one person in the village; it is about her garden and her window that they flock, and only a hand organ and a monkey are capable of rivaling it, and they not for long if Polly, stimulated by music, lifts her own voice and reclaims their allegiance.

She fills the gaps in conversation, too, does Polly, sometimes, as well as the shortcomings of Bridget, or the existence of the weather, entertains the uproarious baby brought on a visit, or scares him into quiet, keeps the cat out of mischief with her warning voice, frightens off house-breakers and tramps and book agents, and is a live and seemingly intelligent companion. And if it is but the simulacrum of a companion, somehow it is such a cunning simulacrum, helped by the unknown agencies that always seem to make its speech so pat and apropos, that, in a growing attachment, one never finds it out. Poor pretty Poll brings to us in our plain lives of the temperate zone all the richness of the tropics, although she is cousin to the great snowy owl of the arctic regions; and while that ominous bird and all its congeners are associated in our minds with scenes of desolation, of deserts and ruins and empty church towers, where the fallen bells no longer lay the ghosts of the churchyard, this bird seems hardly less than a patron bird of home and the home-staying spinster.

Famous Parrots.

Nor is the parrot a thing to be despised for any such superficial reason as that it has kept company with Jack Tar, and knows the dialect of the sailor boarding-house, and sometimes swears in Spanish. Alexander the Great himself brought one into Greece; undoubtedly that parrot was acquainted with both Hindostanee and Greek, if he did not pick up a Persian phrase or two. Ovid wrote an ode on the death of one belonging to Corinne, and of course that parrot spoke Latin. Those birds outweigh the forecastle. And both Aristotle and Pliny condescended to make themselves acquainted with the Southern stranger, and to observe and describe its habits. And we doubt if in their day there was so little superstition that even their great minds were exempt from a touch of awe in dealing with this bird so far the superior of its remote cousin and counterpart, that bird sacred to the great spinster of all, Pallas Athene.

Birds in general, it is true, belong more to the city house than to the country one, since all about the latter birds sing on every bough. But in the country there is another member of the family, so to say, which is one of great importance, and an immense help in every way.

A Kerry Cow.

It is a little remarkable that so many families in our large country towns and their surrounding regions have not more universally imitated the example of the poor emigrant, who on the moment that he lands looks about him and proceeds to get his potato patch and his cow into action. Of course in cities and their immediate neighborhood such a thing is impracticable if not impossible; but in towns built like the most, loosely and over large territory, and where almost every house has its bit of land about it or behind it, a dead waste takes place; and a great help is thrown away in failing to procure "the little cow," as the affectionate Irishman is wont to call this generous provider. And this was never more worthy of consideration than at the present, when, for some fortunate reason, the price of a cow is wonderfully moderate, and a good one can be procured without trouble for a small sum. A couple of acres of land will comfortably pasture the creature, once in possession, through all the summer months; or, if one has not the land, a small sum of money will pay for the pasturage elsewhere, and the winter feed is less than three tons of hay with a few bushels of meal. The work of taking care of her is so light that no man in any family of moderate circumstances needs to grumble if called upon to do it; but as he very probably will grumble, it is a blessing to know that a small boy, in consideration of fifty cents a week, and often for a quart of the day's milking, may be had, in the greater number of towns, able and willing to do all the service that the Dame of the Crumpled Horn usually requires.

As this is a subject which comes home directly to the housekeeper, we shall be pardoned if we dwell upon it a moment. It will be seen that the outlay is not large which procures and maintains this household comfort; and what a comfort it is it will not take long either for the purse-holder or for the mother of children, or for the cook distracted over her desserts, to discover.

Wherever there is a cow giving the usual quantity of milk, there need never be actual hunger; it supplies a score of deficiencies; and even where hunger is not in question, the bills of the butcher and grocer are very sensibly and healthily diminished by large rations of milk served to those that can drink it, which even the most delicate and dyspeptic can do with the tasteless addition of a little lime-water, especially if they remember the favorable action of "milk-cures" in many cases, which probably means nothing more than cure by means of a nourishing food easily assimilated, as other food may not be.

Advantages of the Cow.

Very few families feel themselves able to contract and pay large milk bills, and they are apt to go without more than just enough for tea and coffee, or perhaps the exact needs of the baby. But when the milk is in the pans and they are not feeling the cost of it, they find its advantage not only in the pleasure and comfort of bountiful draughts, but in the thousand and one varying dishes which it makes possible, and which were previously reckoned as too expensive for daily use. Thus in the more generous table made possible the well-being of the family is increased, as enriching and blood-producing diet cannot help doing.

What a comfort it is to the housekeeper to have her pans of milk ready to surrender their rich skins of cream, only those can tell who have been suddenly taken unawares by "company" without a satisfactory dessert on hand, or who are at a loss for something just a degree nicer than common for breakfast; since this cream is capable of being whipped and poured into a countless number of hurried forms, each more palatable than the other, and is delicious poured plain and untutored over the simple breakfast cake, while served with a common apple pie, or with even a dish of boiled oatmeal, or with old-fashioned "preserves," it gives a delicacy and daintiness that deceive one into thinking the dessert of the finest. Meanwhile there is left the "skimmed milk," for which the cook has endless uses, for which the poor are only too thankful, and on which, if one has a little pig as well as a "little cow"—although that I never will advise—the pig can be fattened royally. The good house-mother also may find that the men of her family who have a plenty of rich milk to drink will not seek anything much stronger or more hurtful, and it will always be a help to her larder, and a balm to the feeling that hates to dismiss a "tramp" without food, lest it should be the traditional "angel unawares," if there is a big bowl of milk to be handed out to him.

I do not mention at length the ineffable comfort, saving, and satisfaction of having one's own butter at command, for one can not do everything with one cow; and remembering the vulgar but veracious adage that one can not have one's cake and eat it, too, we understand that we can not use our cream and still have butter. There is, nevertheless, now and then some one cow which deserves fame, which gives a family all the milk they can drink, all the cream they can use, and furnishes enough cream besides for a good quantity of butter; and if I myself have never met with her, yet her report has reached me. But they that have ever realized the charm of "gilt-edged" butter, which once tasted makes those who used to spread the thinnest possible skin of butter on their bread, afterward eat as much butter as they do bread, will realize a still greater charm when the butter is of their own production, and will be willing either to keep an extra cow, or to be sparing in the use of the cream of the one cow, for the sake of having that luxury all their own, and will think nothing of the care that the necessity for purity and cleanliness occasions, which, after all, when the routine has become established, is hardly a noticeable addition to the house work. Nobody knows but those that have experienced it the pleasure and pride to be had in the giving, to less fortunate friends and neighbors, of little pats of dewy golden butter made and stamped by one's own hand, looking as if the cow that produced that butter were fed only in heavenly pastures.

To crown the whole, the pleasure to be gained in the love and admiration of the cow that adds all this comfort to our household arrangements is something more than money usually can procure for us—those sleek sides, those great moon eyes, those gentle ways, are almost as good in the yard as the daily sight of a Cuyp would be in the parlor; and there is something very humanizing in the presence and possession of the pretty creature. One grows constantly more and more attached to her; and we have seen the little half-bred Jersey, bought when a calf for ten dollars, increase her values in her owner's estimation at such gigantic rates, as month by month went by and that owner reveled in the luxury of boasting of her points and her beauty, that there was apparently not money enough in the world to buy her.

Pegasus.

And if one has a cow why should one not have another friend, especially a friend to the women of the family, saving them fatigue and throwing the world open to them, and making it a world of pleasure? Once in a while, and more often now than of old, we meet with women who really seem to have escaped from bond and thrall, in so much as they can drive a horse. Not only that, but they can harness him. And not only that, but, if put to the pinch, they can take the entire care of him, and not handle him at arm's length, either, but familiarly and easily as if he were a kitten, without constant remembrance that he has teeth for the sole purpose of biting them, and heels made for nothing else but kicking. There is a capable woman. She is independent of man. She waits on no one's pleasure. She begs and cringes, and is servilely polite for the sake of a favor to none. If there is no man handy, no man who can leave his work for her uses conveniently, she goes and does the thing herself, claps on the harness and claps in the horse, and is off about her business or her amusement with no one to say her nay. That which, by submitting to the trouble of subduing and training her natural timidity, she has gained, is something really almost inestimable in the comfort that the nag affords her, the excursions within her choice, the freedom and the variety brought into her daily life. When left alone in the vehicle, no horse looks round in the woman's face, and remarking to himself, apparently, that "it is only she," proceeds to tangle the reins, and snarl the traces, and get the breeching where the collar ought to be, or other antics as generally impossible; no horse starts off lame with her in hopes of loafing all the way; no horse dares to make the motion of taking the bit between his teeth if she holds the reins—he knows she has the bit between hers. That woman has, in fact, the freedom of the continent, of the round earth, one might say, when Behring Straits are frozen over so that she can drive across, for nothing but death and a lack of oats can interfere between her and any hostelry at which she chooses to put up.

The Woman Who Used to Drive.

Although there are more of this order of women in the world than one would think, yet among the whole multitude of married and single they are but few. To see the ordinary woman drive is to assist at an experiment in torture; the arms jerk in and out with as steady a motion as the fall of the animal's foot; first one rein pulls and then another; a tender mouth in any beast is ruined; a comfortable action is so broken that the good horse acquires more gaits, as some one has said, than the city of Thebes itself, and the driver, sitting far forward, with a terrible eagerness in her eye, especially if another team is coming, if there is a hill to descend, or if there is any likelihood of being obliged to turn about, looms on the sight like the vision the poet saw

> "Most awfully intent,
> The driver of those steeds is forward bent,
> And seems to listen

to the voice of fate itself, it may be, prophesying overthrow and death if the wheels deviate one line from the straight one, while ever and anon a fearful phantom looks over her shoulder of that horse down, and she herself sitting on his poor head, and the shuddering, heaving bulk suddenly at last shaking her off, and rising over her, a night-mare, if it were not in the day. To the apprehension of these women the horse partakes somewhat of the awe-inspiring quality of him with whom they are most associated; a portion of the power and authority of man himself surrounds him; he is, in fact, a sort of Centaur; they endow him, in the mind's eye, with an intelligence and with a commanding spirit that might belong to some mysterious hippogriff, and they feel when they hold the reins that the creature obeys as if they had not anything half so gentle as Pegasus in harness, but the horse of Achilles, or the steeds that Phaeton failed to drive. To them every horse is the superb and appalling creature that Job describes, whose neck is clothed with thunder; and in reality that extra strength and power of the beast, which he never uses, and of which he is unconscious, is the thing that they always expect to assert itself.

The Woman Who Drives Now.

But the woman to whom a horse is but a beast of burden, an intelligence entirely subject to her own, a thing to be well treated, a servant to be considered, the possessor of no mysterious attributes or of no malevolent inspiration, but to be saddled and bridled without any more concern than one has in making a bed—that woman has made life infinitely more convenient and comfortable than it was before, has created for herself and her companions a thousand independent pleasures, has enlarged her sphere almost as much as wings could do it, and is mistress of the situation in two-thirds of those cases where other women are "in the hands of their friends."

CHAPTER FIFTEENTH

The Household Conduct.

Begone, dull care! I prithee begone from me,
Begone, dull care! Thou and I shall never agree!
—*Playford.*

She who ne'er answers till a husband cools,
Or if she rules him, never shows she rules.
—*Pope.*

It is better to dwell in the corner of a housetop than with a brawling woman in a wide house. —*Proverbs.*

She looketh well to the ways of her household, and eateth not the bread of idleness.
—*Proverbs.*

And here's to the housewife that's thrifty.
—*R. B. Sheridan.*

From care I'm free!
Why aren't they all contented like me?
La Bayadère

Economy is the fuel of magnificence.
—*Emerson.*

The primal duties shine aloft, like stars,
The charities, that soothe, and heal, and bless,
Are scattered at the feet of man like flowers.
—*Wordsworth.*

And where Care lodges Sleep will never lie.
—*Shakespeare.*

You have too much respect upon the world;
They lose it that do buy it with much care.
—*Shakespeare.*

The cares that infest the day
Shall fold their tents like the Arabs,
And as silently steal away.
—*Longfellow.*

Care will kill a cat,
And therefore let's be merry.

If we would have perfect happiness in our house, one of the first things we will do is to arrive at a perfect understanding as husband and wife. There are two statements very frequently used concerning the married life which must always be peculiarly offensive to those who desire the good of the family as an institution of beneficence, and through that of the good of the race. One of these statements implies that it is given to the husband to rule; the other implies that without seeming to have her own way, the wife quietly manages the husband and has it.

Both of these ideas are as absurd and injudicious as they are harmful.

The Ideal Household.

In the ideal household—and every household should at least strive for the ideal, however unhappily it falls short of the standard before it—there is no such word as rule. Marriage is not a bondage. It is a contract, a partnership, an association, a union; and without speaking of it in relation to the decrees of the Church, to all those that enter it reverently it is a sacrament. The idea either of reign or of submission in such case is impossible. The partners are equal, and each has a separate course to pursue toward one end. Because the husband earns or possesses the means necessary for the family's subsistence he does not therefore inherently have any more right than the wife has to be the absolute owner and ruler of the house. When with the solemnity of an oath, and with the supposition that it was an oath, he said, "With all my worldly goods I thee endow," it could only have meant that from that moment the worldly goods alluded to were as much hers as his.

Being as much hers as his, morally at least, there is exactly as much authority vested in her by reason of ownership as in him, and he can claim no right at all to govern because he earns or owns the money. Moreover, the wife is supposed to be doing, and should be doing exactly as much in her paths of duty for the benefit of the household of which her husband makes one as the husband does; her services are worth—if a money value could be put upon them—as much as his, and so the matter is equal between them.

Managing and Ruling.

The only legitimate way for the husband to rule, if he cherishes the ignoble wish to rule, is to show his superiority to such degree and extent that the wife must needs admiringly see and confess that his opinion, his wish, his determination, is the best, and gladly advocate it with him, and follow its direction. But to say that the wife must give up her own cherished opinions and life-long preconceptions and plan of action is to say that she must be reduced to the condition of a slave, entirely unfit to be the mother of children or the guardian of their morals, manner, and health—the guardian that it is everywhere understood she has to be; it is to reduce her to a subordinate condition, the result of which is as injurious to her husband and to his children as it is to herself.

The husband who chooses to make the effort will find that when he accords to his wife full acknowledgment of her individuality, and accustoms her through all the routine of married life to the same gracious courtesy he used to practice at an earlier day, he will have a fearless companion by his side, a woman of reflection and judgment, who, having a sense of responsibility and accountability to herself, always the sternest of judges, is an actual helpmeet, a possible champion, a charming friend, a reasonable assistant, a woman with some other entertainment in her than the reflection of his own accustomed thoughts, with some novelty and interest; and so he will find his marriage a far finer thing than if he had always a sweet and tiresome little slave at command. He will find his own position, too, a something loftier one, for he will be the protector and shield and support of one of a nobler order than weaklings, and he gains even in his own esteem by the assumption of that loftier character.

Tyranny and Its Result in Cunning.

But, again, as detestable as tyranny is cunning; and it is the invariable and necessary accompaniment of tyranny. People, be they men or women, wives, or children, or servants—nay, even husbands—if they cannot have their own way by fair means, will have it by foul; and unless they are persuaded that what they wish is positively not desirable, they will continue to endeavor to obtain that wish if it be a possible thing, and by sly traverses and cunning methods. It is only in this way that a wife ever tries to "manage" her husband. And it is in this way that she makes herself as wily as the serpent in Eden, and develops qualities of deceit and craft that cannot help being transmitted to her children. The mother who desires to lower the human standard, who wants her children to be in the way of themselves becoming the parents of thieves and criminals, will only have to resort to managing her husband in order to sow the first seeds of that sort of crop.

There is something too base and servile in the idea of "managing," of obtaining a desire by the hidden and circuitous routes of cunning, for a woman who aspires to any worthiness of character to be willing to confess to it even in her own consciousness. Open revolt were better in the long run for her, for her family, for her race. The trick is on a par with lying, with stealing, with forging, and with all the low, small, slimy vices; it is degrading, not only to the woman who engages in the "management," but to the children, servants, and dependents who can not fail to see it done.

Working Together.

The only noble and honorable course for husband and wife, then, is co-operation, with frank admission of the individual rights of each, with the same course that would be followed in independent friendship, with repeated assurance of love, anc trust, and undiminished affection—assurance that every true wife wishes and longs for when she is seventy as much as when she is thirty, that ought not to pall upon any husband. The wife may be guided, but she is not to be governed, and when she is consulted, trusted. treated as an integer, and as a person to the full as honorable and powerful as her husband is, the home will be something very different from the harem, and very much nearer heaven than any place full of submissive *houris* could ever pretend to be. Let there be no ruling and no managing, and there will come presently the ideal household, a place full of joyous endeavor, of fortitude in suffering, of glad fruition and content the life long.

But even in the ideal household there will be household cares. In the variation of Blackmore's charming black-bird's song the strain goes,

"Whistle, father birdie, whistle household cares away,
Household cares would turn me soon from blackbird to a gray;"

and there is not a woman who reads it or hears it without in her soul saying "mother birdie" in correction and realizing that household cares are doing that discoloring work for her, and have been ever since she undertook them.

Daily Cares.

It makes little difference with her, either, in the matter, whether she is the wife of a rich or of a poor man, unless she is of the mind and estate of those who employ a housekeeper, and are themselves a sort of "lady boarder" in the house; that is, having shifted all responsibility, and having retained only the right to find fault, in which case the question only changes form and not nature, as the housekeeper is the one to turn gray under the ceaseless irritation of the household cares, instead of herself. But women able to hire a housekeeper in this country are numerically but one in ten thousand, if so many; and frequently those who are able prefer to have the charge of their own house, and to render account of their own stewardship; and others, again, do not desire the too familiar presence of a third party whom they consider neither quite equal nor quite servant.

The Hired Housekeeper.

Something of this latter feeling in relation to the hired housekeeper might be overcome if those who take the position—people usually who have

THE IDEAL HOUSEHOLD.

been in better circumstances, and learned how to do for others by ruling their own kingdoms—would take it for granted that it is understood they are as much "ladies," technically speaking, as their employers are; that the position and the duties of making a home comfortable are no more derogatory to their dignity than keeping a school or practicing any other profession—since we might almost say that fine housekeeping is one of the learned professions— and that being understood, it is not necessary to be all the time asserting it and insisting upon it, feeling hurt if a family prefer to be by themselves, or if morning visits paid to them and invitations extended to them do not also include the housekeeper. Every housekeeper who in taking her situation stipulates for her own little parlor and her own table makes herself a separate family in the family, with her own friends, visits, and interests, solves the question of equality and of intrusion, reduces it absolutely to one of business, saves herself the possibility of slights and hurts and becomes in the house the next valuable consideration to the strong-box.

The Strong Box.

It is the strong-box, after all, that is at the root of a good deal of the household difficulty; it is the perpetual grasping for the coin that eludes the fingers, the endeavor to make bricks without straw. Women have a natural pride in their homes, poor or rich, and in their administration of the provision made by their husbands. They think themselves culpable if they miss a point in the possibilities of that administration, in the wasting of a crust by oversight, in the breaking of a dish by carelessness, in the soiling of wall or carpet or garment by neglect, in the absence of the stitch in time that saves nine in the matter of clothes, in the use of the ounce of prevention worth a pound of cure in the matter of health and doctors. Perhaps their husbands think them culpable, too, in such case; certainly the neighbors do; and quite as often as because it is right, or as for the applause of the neighbors, is the work done from fear of the husband's reproaches. Yet it is to be owned that the applause of the neighbors has a world of influence upon these household cares that turn one from a blackbird to a gray. If this wealthier acquaintance has a "second girl" to aid her in keeping up an "apple-pie order," one must wear one's self out to get in one's own house with one's own hands the same apple-pie arrangement; if that too industrious neighbor has her house-cleaning over in March, one dares not be behind lest one be found a laggard, and accused of want of system, or ambition, or right feeling, even although it had been better to defer the cleansing process till the muddy season were gone, or till the dust of furnace fires, together with the old jollity of the open ones,

"Down that dark hole in the floor
Staggers and is seen no more."

And if a third equally forehanded one has made her currant jelly "before the Fourth," one must follow suit, although headaches hang in the air like trip-hammers ready to fall in one's brain, and although one has to run in debt for the sugar, and be harassed about the increased grocer's bill, till one is half sick from that also, and from all the kindred apprehensions, when that half-sickness is felt, of dying prematurely, and leaving the children to the care of some necessary step-mother, or of leaving them without a house over their heads, anyway, to wait by-and-by on those who have been wont to regard them as their betters. And if yet another friend has her woollen carpets rolled away in summer, and straw mattings laid in their place, and double windows put in in the winter weather, and fires kept everywhere, and numberless other luxuries that could be dispensed with, one trembles lest one's husband should be suspected of penury, or of inability to provide, or of indifference to the home comfort, and one goes without something necessary, and has the luxury out of hand, or so much of it as possible. The person who said, "Give me the luxuries, and I care not who has the necessaries, of life," unconsciously struck the keynote of some of the bitterest of household cares.

Yet none of these, literally speaking, are the genuine household cares. One need feel little interest in those which proceed from pride and vanity and pique. Those only with which we have a right to concern ourselves are the cares which are inherent to the average house, and have to be encountered whether or no. Perhaps even these cares are taken too seriously, and the household care-taker does not rely implicitly enough on the sense of justice that, seeing she does her best, will not expect of her the impossible. What if it is sweeping day, or baking day, or preserving day, if she rises in the morning with a headache it is headache day, and unless she wants another and a worse one in a hurry, she must give up everything to that headache, otherwise she is wasting health and strength, and her husband's and her family's substance, as well as her own, for the sake of a habit or a petty pride of routine. If sometimes she could bring herself, on seeing a spider's web, let us say, to suffer it to remain a while longer, against the next time the children cut their fingers, perhaps it would not be held as so very heinous an act as to deserve punishment in the final settlement. But the fact is, it would annoy her more to know that the cobweb was hanging there than it would to make the effort of taking it away. It is impossible for this natural care-taker to avoid fulfilling the object of her being, and taking care; and the only remedy is for her supposed protector, or whoever it is, that is, that has the power to do it, and to whom her life and brain are valuable, or who feels a pity for the overworked, to force upon her, if she will not take it otherwise, a month's yearly separation from her family, and every one and everything connected with it.

A Vacation.

She will come home from it a new creature; and even if she find a little additional work waiting to her hands, the strength of body and mind gained will make that work seem light, and it will pay in actual cost and comfort all but the most slenderly provided to try the experiment. After one or two of these yearly vacations she will herself so feel the worth of them that she will dispense with things to display before the neighbors for the sake of the healthy relaxation, will do her utmost to arrange a corresponding change for her husband, and will even come to think that if there is no other way of providing the outing, the need of it should receive the attention of the Society for the Prevention of Cruelty to Animals.

School for Cooks.

The chief of the household cares is always the cook. She is very seldom in the ordinary family, or in that of narrow means, what she should be, and her shortcomings do a great deal to bring about the change from the black bird to the gray. There is one way to overcome her incompetency that I have often wondered was not more generally pursued. There exist now in most of our larger cities good and effective training schools for servants of all classes and capacities; and, besides these, various persons of skill and renown in culinary matters advertise lessons in cookery; standing ready, on certain afternoons of the week, to impart to the class of the hour all that they know on the subject, even announcing in their advertisements the dishes to be prepared that day—fifty cents admission, and sometimes not so much.

Now it is possible that the mistress who complains of her cook—and complains not so much because she herself is disappointed in the toothsome dishes attempted and ruined in her kitchen, as for the sake of husband and friends— may know how to prepare every dish that these professors and advertising teachers do. But she may not have the time or the health or the disposition to go into the kitchen and teach their concoction, or other reasons may render it impossible. And just as likely she does not know how to prepare them; she was learning to play the piano which her parents wished her to learn to play, and was not taught kitchen-work; she was dancing, and receiving and making calls, and leading a gay life, never expecting to need the knowledge for which she should always be able to pay, and for which she may be able to pay now, if she can get it for money; or she chose the more congenial work of teaching what she had learned in school; of painting, or designing, or engraving; or she was obliged to earn her living in tending shop, in dress-making, and kindred employments—and with it all had no opportunity to acquire skill in the domestic arts. Whatever was the reason, it was supposedly a righteous one, or seemed righteous at the time it influenced her action. And whether that is the case or not does not affect the fact that her cook is a poor one, and that there is a way of making her a good one. For the professors of cookery have made it a business to inform themselves thoroughly; they know how to do the best thing, and they know the best way of doing it; they not only know all the flummeries and fancy affairs of the fine art of cooking, but the solid A B C of the common domestic dinner.

What then, is easier, if one's cook is not all in skill and information that she should be than to send her through a course of these lessons that she may become so? At the first blush the suggestion arouses, in some degree, a sense of injustice at being obliged to pay for the article and yet not to have it, and in order to get it, to do what seems like paying for it a second time. One feels that no cook, being a human creature, with knowledge of right and wrong, should engage to do certain work unless she knows how to do it, and should have a conscience about it all herself. We have known of some who did, and who privately took measures to attend such affairs as these class lessons. But it is self-evident that cooks cannot afford such extravagance out of their own pockets; and if you want a thing badly yourself, you will pay for it even if it does cost more than honor and justice warrant.

If then, every city mistress who feels the need of it in her kitchen will spare her cook on one or two afternoons of every week, and send her, not at the cook's expense, but at her own, to take at least one course of cookery lessons, and afterward such lessons as propose to teach other yet needed things, one part of the bad business would be mended.

A Radical Procedure.

It is a rather radical procedure, but, as radical things profess to do, it strikes at the root. The ordinary idea is that if anybody is to take lessons, it should be the mistress, and that, besides, no sooner will the cook be taught than she will demand higher wages or be leaving. But in answer to such arguments it is to be said that if the mistress wished to do the cooking she would not send the cook to learn, and if she does not wish to do the cooking, and does wish for the cook, it is for her interest to have the cook, and not herself, learn the art. It would be a foolish waste of material for her to learn it, and stay in the parlor. *Au reste* there is nothing usually to hinder her from taking lessons also, if she desires.

And for the other matter, that of the cook's demands for wages and threats of leaving, that would have to be arranged by agreement, and if the cook left at unreasonably short notice after having received the lessons, the price would have to be repaid from wages due. But usually a grateful servant and a pleased family could make a compact that each party would regard as sacred, and would agree to agree together as long as one needs a place and the other needs a maid.

It is scarcely to be expected that the great body of servant-girls should, of their own accord, rise and patronize the cooking professor in a mass. But one mistress would set the example to another; they would find themselves able to afford the extra expense by going without something else for the time being, in consideration of the advantages; and one servant would carry the tale to the next, who would hate to be outdone.

And as we throw a stone into a lake, and see the ripple spread through circle after circle, from centre to farthest edge, so the first mistress who denies herself some costlier whim or other in order to give to her cook, who, however faithful and willing, is at present but the modest apprentice, the full scope and compass of her trade, will have effected a revolution in that world which is founded on the kitchen, and will have turned the organism there from darkness and dirt and confusion to sweetness and light and order.

Old Cookery Books.

But if the mistress sets out to study the subject and art of cookery itself in all its bearings, she will find some interesting reading on her way. From any great library she can secure a collection of old-fashioned cookery books that will afford her amusement if not instruction. These books are not merely those full of "Mrs. A.'s this," and "Madame B.'s that," but such as the entertaining Dr. Kichener's, the wise and witty Brillat Savarin's, and the work of the famous Mrs. Glasse, with her descriptions of "a curious way" to concoct a dish, "a pretty way of stewing chicken," or others where you come across such phrases as "as mellow as marrow," or where directions to "pickle a buttocky beef," to make a "Carolina rice pudding," and "an approved method practiced by Mrs. Dukeley, the Queen's tyre-woman, to preserve hair and make it grow thick," are all huddled on the same page, and where the spelling is "salamongundy," "asturtion," and "camphire." One of the most amusing of all the old cooks, who called themselves "artists," is M. Ude. "Take," he says, "one or two live eels; throw them into the fire; as they are twisting about on all sides lay hold of them, with a towel in your hand, and skin them from head to foot. This is the only means of drawing out all the oil, which is unpalatable and indigestible. Several reviews," he exclaims, indignantly, in a later edition, "have accused me of cruelty because I recommend in this work that eels should be burned alive. As my knowledge in cookery is entirely devoted to the gratification of taste and the preservation of health, I consider it my duty to attend to what is essential to both." His indignation, however, is elsewhere equaled by his sense of any violation of the proprieties. "Remember that the word 'soup' is so vulgar as not to be admitted either in good company or on a good bill of fare," he remarks, probably preferring "purée" and "consommé." But, with all that, the little Frenchman has a certain democratic sense of his own dignity; he fully expresses his contempt for certain young British noblemen whom cooks are likely to encounter. "Do not be frightened by their repulsive manners," he says, grandiloquently. "Never mind. Do as I have done."

Another cook of a less original cast of mind is old Robert May, of the seventeenth century, a man who used musk for one of his flavorings, and all of whose recipes, of an era before any of the French refinements, were on such a gigantic scale that one might think him cooking for the lower gods, or at the least for an army of Goths feasting after battle. For the curiosity of it, the reader should glance over his way of preparing what he calls an "Olio Podrida." "Take," he directs, "Pipkin or pot, some three gallons, fill it with fair water, and set it over a fire of charcoals, and put in first your hardest meats, a rump of beef, bolonia sausages, neats' tongues, two dry and two green, about two hours after the pot is boiled and scummed; but put in more presently after your beef is scummed, mutton, venison, pork, bacon, all the foresaid in gubbins, as big as a duck's egg, in equal pieces; put in also carrots, turnips, onions, cabbidge, in good big pieces, as big as your meat, a faggot of sweet herbs well bound up, and some whole spinage, sorrel, burrage, endive, marigold, and other good pothearbs a little chopped; and sometimes French barley, or lupins, green or dry.

"Then, a little before you dish out your olio, put to your pot cloves, mace, saffron, etc.

"Then next have divers fowls; as first, a goose or turkey, two capons, two ducks, two pheasants, two widgeons, four partridges, four stock-doves, four teals, eight snites, twenty-four quails, forty-eight larks.

"Boil these foresaid fowls in water and salt in a pan, pipkin, or pot.

"Then have bread, marrow, bottoms of artichokes, yolks of hard eggs, large mace, chestnuts boiled and blanched, two colliflowers, saffron.

"And stew these in a pipkin together, being ready clenged with some good sweet butter, a little white-wine, and strong broth.

"Some other times for variety you may use beets, potatoes, skirrets, pistaches, pineapple seed or almonds, poungarnet, and lemons.

"Now to dish your olio, dish first your beef, veal, or pork; then your venison and mutton, tongues, sausage, and roots over all.

"Then next your largest fowl, land-fowl or sea-fowls, as first, a goose or turkey, two capons, two pheasants, four ducks, four widgeons, four stock-doves, four partridges, eight teals, twelve snites, twenty-four quails, forty-eight larks, etc.

"Then broth it, and put on your pipkin of collyflowers, artichokes, chestnuts, some sweetbreads fried, yolks of hard eggs, then marrow boild in strong broth or water, large mace, saffron, pistaches, and all the foresaid things being finely stewed up, and some red beets over all, slict lemons and lemon peels whole, and run it over with beaten butter.

"For the garnish of this dish make marrow pies, made like round chewits;" and the garnish goes on to an extent almost as elaborate as the original dish. It is a miracle that any one, unless provided with a strong brain and a sound stomach, should read this recipe, much less eat of its results, without an attack of indigestion.

A noticeable feature in the pages of these writers is the way they despise all the world that is not engaged in cookery. They make brief forays, every once in a while, into dominions foreign to their own art, as if to show their capability in other directions, and hence their right to speak; but they return to the matter in hand with a gusto that makes the mouth water, and they take care to exhibit the time-honored bad temper of a good cook, that is, as it were, a certificate of character, whether the heat of the fires or of the spices is so exciting to the nerves, or whether they are overcome by their thought of the habitual waste of good material by others.

The home-made cookery book is, however, often quite as entertaining as the antiques, and in itself as much of an "Olio Podrida" of recipes as old May could get up of comestibles. Nevertheless, it is an excellent plan for every housekeeper, old or young, to write out the formula of any dish that pleases her palate or the palates of her family, for cooks change and memories are deceitful, and once set down in black and white, there it is always to refer to, and much that would escape is put in preservation, and handed down from mother to daughter, till it becomes a part of the family archives, and substantiates the claim to the nice manner of life and generous table of one's ancestors. For it is plain to see that the family which made a practice of cherishing daintily compounded dishes for its table had occasion for them, and lived otherwise, most probably, in a style to correspond with them, taking hold of life in a different fashion from those families that had no table *répertoire* beyond the fried steak or the boiled cabbage, and knew nothing of the French science of dressing beans to imitate either roast beef or ice-cream at discretion.

As she goes on, the reader of these old cookery books will find that the

BANQUET OF VITELLIUS.

banqueting of her forbears was a very different thing frcm that of to-day. For when the table is set with lace and satin and damask and embroideries, with engraved crystal, silver and gold, candles, china as beautiful as jewels, with banks of flowers, and all the latest whims of decoration, the dinner-givers of the present think they have done the utmost there is to do in the way of ornate splendor, and the rest goes without saying and according to the prevailing custom, a rational and refined feast among dinner-givers costing from ten to fifty dollars a plate.

Ancient Feasts.

What would these worthy and generous hosts have said, then, at the feasts of Vitellius, who in seven months spent on his table a sum equivalent to thirty-five million dollars; at a time, too, when money was more valuable than it is to-day! Lucullus also must have been able to give them points in the art of banqueting, when he never had a supper in his room of Apollo at a less cost than eighty thousand dollars. And was it not Apicius—one of the three—who had a dish made of the brains of five hundred ostriches, and the tongues of five thousand birds that had been taught to speak? There was an old Roman cook in the days of these gourmets and gourmands who, with a vanity unrivaled by any other writer in history, save and except M. Ude, declared: "Assuredly I have discovered ambrosia. Had the dead but the faculty of smelling, the fragrance of my compositions should speedily restore them to health and strength." Doubtless this discovery of his was washed down with old Falernian or with smoky Greek wines; and in the eight or ten delicate varieties of bottled sunshine and dew, whose clusters of dainty glasses ornament the table as much as the flowers do, our later diners have the advantage.

But the mediæval banquet was a very different thing from the ancient banquet, which with all its prodigality, was a thing of art beside the other. For the mediæval banquet was a perpetual effort for the prodigious, and the men and women who feasted at it might have had something about them of the bestial and the god combined had their appetites really required any such feeding. The most poetical thing we have ever come across in accounts of their festivity, if it can be called poetical, was the pillar erected at the coronation of Cœur de Lion, a hollow marble pillar on steps, and on the top a gilt eagle, under whose claws, in the capital of the pillar, were divers kinds of wines gushing forth at different places all the day long, of which all who came, were they ever so poor and abject, were at liberty to drink. At another feast, that given at the marriage of Lionel, Duke of Clarence, the third son of the third Edward, to Violantis, the daughter of Gelasius II., Duke of Milan—a feast one of whose guests was Petrarch—there were thirty courses, and between every course wonderful presents were distributed. "There were in one only course seventy goodly horses, adorned with silks and silver furniture; and in the others silver vessels, falcons, hounds, armor for horses, costly coates of mayle, breastplates glittering of massive steele, helmets and corslets decked with costly crestes, apparell distinct with costly jewels, souldiers' girdles, and lastly certain gemmes by curious art set in gold, and of purple and cloth of gold for men's apparell in great abundance. And such was the sumptuousness of that banquet, that the meates which were brought from the table would sufficiently have served ten thousand men." Compared with this wholesale gift business, the presents, however delectable, distributed as favors at recent germans and dinners must make, after all, but a beggarly array.

The Peacock at Banquets.

At all banquets, both of the elder and of the middle ages, the peacock was a favorite piece of decoration. Sometimes it was quite covered with leaf-gold, as if that were an improvement upon its brilliant dyes, and with a bit of linen in its mouth, dipped in spirits and set on fire, it was served on a golden dish by the lady of highest rank, attended by her train of maidens and followed by music, and was set before the most distinguished guest. This was a performance of great state and ceremony, and the bird was held in so far sacred that oaths could be taken on its head. One of the old turnspit directors gives us full information as to another and certainly handsomer way of serving the creature, although one may be pardoned for querying how it was contrived afterward to carve him: "At a feeste roiall pecokkes shall be dight on this

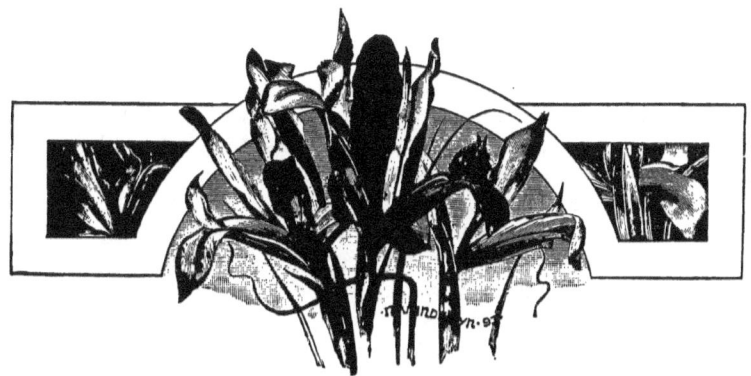

manner. Take and flee off the skynne with the fedurs, tayle, and nekke, and the hed thereon; then take the skyn with all the fedurs and lay hit on a table abrode, and strawe thereon grounden comyn; then take the pecokke and roste hym, and endore (baste) him with rawe yolkes of egges; and when he is rosted take hym off and let hym cole awhile, and take and sowe hym in his skyn, and gilde his combe, and so serve hym forthe with the last cours."

But whatever may be thought of the decoration of the tables as in comparison with those of our own era, or of the character of the prodigal squandering of food and drink, or of the manners and customs of the time in general, one rather amusing first course of a period as late as 1630 is reported to us by Robert May in his *Accomplisht Cooke*—a book dedicated to Lords Mountague, Lumley, and Dorner, and to the Right Worshipful Sir Kenelm Digby, so well known to the nation for their admired hospitalities, as the writer says, which interlude, as the writer further sets forth, was formerly one of the delights of the nobility before good housekeeping had left England.

A Battle at Table.

Among his *Triumphs and Trophies in Cookery*, this good-natured little author gives instructions for the manufacture of a pasteboard ship, with flags and streamers and guns, and little trains of powder added after it has been covered with a coarse paste and baked, certain portions of it gilded, and the whole planted in a dish full of blown egg-shells filled with rose-water and set in salt. Opposite this is to be a castle similarly manufactured, with turrets and battlements, and drawbridges and "percullises." Between the two is a stag, compounded in like fashion again, with an arrow in his side, and his body full of claret. Two pies then are baked, and after baking the lids are lifted, and one is filled with live frogs and the other with live birds. Then, all being set at table, the trains of powder are lighted, and the castle fires upon the ship, and the ship returns the fire, and the arrow is plucked from the stag, whereon the claret flows like life-blood from the wound. "All danger being seemingly over by this time, you may suppose they will desire to see what is in the pies; when, lifting first the lid off one pie, out skips some frogs, which makes the ladies to skip and shreek, and after the other pie, whence comes out the birds, who, by a natural instinct flying at the light, will put out the candles; so that what with the flying birds and skipping frogs, the one above, the other beneath, *will cause much delight and pleasure to the whole company*. At length the candles are lighted, and a banquet brought in; the musick sounds; and every one with much delight and content rehearses their actions in the former passages." Certainly people who were pleased by such tomfoolery as this would think very poorly of our tame and quiet manner of ministering to the senses, and were best regaled by mighty sides of venison, by oxen roasted whole, and by copious washes of strong beer; their coarsened palates could have seen no difference between Chateau Yquem or sparkling Moselle and any diet drink. We may not reach the mad point of luxury of Lucullus and Apicius, although we are fain to see no especial luxury in the brains of peacocks and the tongues of nightingales, but, on the contrary, a vulgar brutality; but we have certainly improved upon the ways of our own more immediate ancestors in abolishing powder trains and jumping frogs from the table.

But if we have not rivaled the prodigality of the ancients, we have in this country of ours allowed ourselves great latitude of lesser but almost as real extravagance, and we are only now beginning to comprehend the wasteful manner in which for a century and a half at least, we have been living, and to feel the need of an economy that shall make the most of such provision as we have, and carry it farthest. In the earlier years of the settlement of the continent the food supply was on a different basis from that on which it was afterward placed, and during that time the home traditions, those of Mother England, were in full play. In a few families these have descended, and are recognized as binding to-day, many a stern woman having tyrannized over her son's wife till she has in her turn felt the authority of the family tradition, and thanked Heaven and her mother-in-law therefor. But in the larger number of families the greater and still growing abundance of food soon destroyed the sense of any necessity to save and spare, and a prodigal carelessness and wastefulness was the result, which has been continued till to-day.

Some Economies.

Doubtless it takes very much more time to practice these economies than it would to let them pass, and continue to live with spendthrift ease; but it is questionable if in most instances the time would be any better spent, while the result is tangible and desirable. It is said that there is enough substance thrown away and squandered in American families to keep the moderate French or English family; and although that is probably an exggerated statement, there is a moral in it. The American marketer buys usually the best; it appears upon her table once, is sometimes warmed over for a second dish or for a breakfast, sometimes not, and Bridget does as she pleases with the fragments, either giving or throwing them away. An English woman buys, let us say, a roasting piece of beef; she, too, buys the best, because, as she will use it, it is the cheapest. The upper cut makes one day's dinner handsomely; the under cut, in thin slices, carved across instead of up and down, fried in butter, and served on mashed potatoes or on rice, garnishing the dish to make it seem like something choicer, and add to appetite, makes a second dinner; then the long end piece, which has remained untouched, makes an excellent stew with tomatoes or carrots and potato balls for a third dinner, being cooked and cooled so as to remove the grossness, and then warmed up again; the various fragments either make a pie, or, hashed and spiced or curried, answer for a fourth dinner, which will be pieced out, as one may say, by a rather daintier dessert than usual, as the case will be also with the fifth dinner—a soup of the bones that remain, made hearty with vegetables; and, after all, there is left a store of invaluable dripping. The American housewife in comfortable circumstances who should make five dinners for a moderate family from a roast of beef would, until recently, have considered herself a scrimping and shabby woman, and would fear being held by her neighobrs, well-informed through the servants, as a niggardly skinflint. Now, on the contrary, she is inclined to look about and see if she can not better instruction, and procure a sixth dish from the same source.

The English Woman's Economy.

But there are various other ways in which the Englishwoman can give us lessons in economy. It is safe to say that nothing is wasted under her care. Even her stale beer is saved to rinse her bronzes in, to boil with other material and make her old plate look like new, and to clean her soiled black silks; and the lemons whose outer skin has been grated off, and whose juice has been squeezed out, if they are not laid aside to boil in any compound, are given to the cook to clean her saucepans. If she keeps fowl, every egg brought in is dated with a pencil, and those of the earlier date are used first; if there are any to be spared, she lays them by for winter provision, usually by passing over them a camel's-hair pencil dipped in oil, which hermetically seals and preserves their contents; and where she uses only the whites in one dish, she contrives another in which she shall use the yolks. If the bread has become dry, she does not immediately throw it to the hens or dedicate it to a pudding; she dips the loaf in hot water, and sets it in the oven, and finds it sufficiently fresh for family use. Nor does she often indulge in the doubtful luxury of baker's bread, since she has learned that she thereby loses in bread just the weight of the water used in compounding it, besides running the risk of deleterious ingredients. And when the bread is really dried past freshening then it answers for stuffing, is grated for crumbs, or is soaked with milk and beaten eggs for puddings; none of it is thrown away. She is equally economical concerning the ham; when no more slices can be cut from the bone, there is yet a small quantity of dry meat upon it that would seem to most of our housekeepers as something rather worthless. Not so to this good woman; it is dried a little further, and then grated from the bone, and put away in jars, to be taken out and seasoned on requirement for the enrichment of omelets, for spreading upon savory dishes of toast which make a nice addition to breakfast or lunch, for stuffing olives, and making sandwiches, after which grating the bone serves to flavor soup. In the same way she grates her cheese that is too dry or near the rind, using it afterward as a relish, or as a dressing to macaroni or other substance. All bones, meanwhile, as well as the ham bone, are objects of care with her, or with the servants whom she has trained to her will, and are regularly boiled down to add the result to the stock pot for gravies and soups, by which means she procures the latter at almost no cost at all. Whenever she has a few slices of heterogeneous cold meats, she has countless palatable ways of using them—deviled, broiled in a batter, scalloped, minced into croquettes or mayonnaises.

As a general although not universal thing, among ourselves, when these stray bits and bones are not thrown away, they are given away; but the latter is not the English woman's idea of charity; she holds that the poor, unaccustomed to dainty food, find a coarser kind quite as agreeable as the leavings of her table; she prepares especially for them, saving all liquors in which meats have been boiled as a base for broths of barley and pease, that are regularly dispensed, with tea leaves and coffee grounds dried over, and from which a second draught can be made, with oatmeal, vegetables, and dripping. Dripping, by-the-way, forms no inconsiderable item in this sort of economy; it is skimmed from every pot and saved from every pan, and when a sufficient quantity accumulates it is clarified by pouring boiling water upon it, mixing it well, and putting it by to "set," the sediment going to the bottom when cold, leaving a hard clean cake, which is useful on domestic occasions where butter or lard would be used, as the "shortening" of meat-pie crusts and gingerbread. and for common basting and frying.

Saving on a Small Scale.

Some housekeepers, to be sure, who are able to live more sumptuously, abandon this to the cook, by whom it is claimed as a perquisite, and valued as an equivalent of large extra wages. Beyond this system of saving on a small scale and doing it so regularly and so precisely that it becomes second nature, and is done with as little extra thought as there is given to the paring of the potatoes, the English housekeeper goes further, in dealing out to her servants the week's allowance of sugar, rice, flour, coffee, and all other household provision that is kept in quantity, and requiring an account of it all to be rendered, the thing having been brought to so fine a point that she knows the exact amount of each article requisite for her family, allowing so much to each individual, and that quantity being sufficient, as she knows by experience; two ounces of tea, for instance, being regarded as a week's supply for each single individual, one-half pound of sugar, three and one-half pounds of meat for a woman and five and one-quarter for a man—facts which the housekeeper probably learned from her mother, and she from her mother before her—knowing, moreover, that the greater variety of food offered diminishes the quantity of the simpler kinds required. All of these stores she sets down in her housekeeping book as she gives them out, and she does not fail on the next dispensing day to consult her dates, and if anything be left over in the cook's hands not accounted for, to subtract that from the amount to be newly issued. And in England servants expect this; so far from being indignant with it, they would feel as if there were no guiding hand behind them were it left undone, and they given their head in an overflowing store-room, as servants are with us. In fact, there is no saving which the housewife across the water considers too small to practice, or as beneath her dignity; and when we shall have followed her example in her pet economies more generally than we follow it at present, we shall have more right and more ability to indulge ourselves in our pet extravagances otherwise.

Old Dishes.

And in addition to such economies there are others to be made in considering and possibly adopting a good many valuable dishes which are either in bad repute for no good reason as coarse articles of food, or are forgotten and only to be seen in those old families that have preserved their traditions. We should be able to increase our variety somewhat if we occasionally remembered them, or looked about us and made inquiries in the old mansions or hovels concerning them. Who can not call to mind some one of those old dwellings where the mistress does as her grandmother did before her, with her *potpourri* of rose leaves in the old china jug, in the one case in the parlor, and in the other in the kitchen, with crook-necks over the high shelf, and long strings of tiny savory onions hanging about them, only one at a time of the choice things to be used for adding flavor to some dish, and all of them, if one looked with the same eye to grace and tint, an ornament of beauty past buying? In among them will be the bunches of herbs—the pot-herbs of fennel and parsley, the sweet herbs that distil faint perfume on the air with every waft of the steam beneath them, thyme, sage, mint, marjoram, and sweet-basil, and all of them, though now but kitchen herbs, once parts of ancient song and verse. There, also, will be the dried bulbs of the purple orchis which in heat and thunder keep the milk from souring. On the fire, perhaps, a curious preparation will be simmering—greens, but tender and needing no vinegar or dressing, as they are the common sorrel leaves stewed in no water, but in their own juice, and seasoned to the fancy; or perhaps a pot of dhal will be bubbling—split peas with curry, bits of onion and butter, and "three cloves chopped fine." On this same fire it is not at all unlikely that a dish of sour-krout may be in preparation, sweet and odorless, and wondering at the bad name it has in the world, made with such care to renew its brine frequently, and its linen cover being so often rinsed that it has none but an appetizing smell; if it is in the summer, too, hop tops will be boiling in a little flat pan as a sort of substitute for asparagus, for however well-to-do in the world now the family may be, the traditions of a time when inventive genius had to apply itself to turn everything to account are still preserved with them. If you look in the store-room of any such house you will find an odd array of jars; there will be a pot of coarse "carrageen moss" picked up on some afternoon excursion to the sea-beach, and cleansed and dried for *blancmange*; there will be strange pickles, samphire whose little pulpy red reeds have been covered with hot vinegar and spices, gathered on the marshes, no longer with the dangers that accompanied its plucking in the time of the crazed old Lear:

> "The crows and choughs that winged the midway air
> Show scarce so gross as beetles. Half way down
> Hangs one that gathers samphire—dreadful trade!
> Methinks he seems no bigger than his head."

Here, too, are bottles of the nasturtium seeds that answer all the purposes of foreign capers, and cost nothing. There are pots of the Jerusalem artichoke, too, so called by corrupting its own pretty name of Girasole, because the plant producing it turns always toward the sun; and here are jars of East India sauces and pickles all made at home, but with such cunning disguise and deceit of raw ginger, red peppers, garlic, turmeric, and mustard that only the trained palate knows the difference. Preserves and sweetmeats, also, of unaccustomed sorts will appear here—a rhubarb marmalade, one of the red Malta orange, the blood orange that grows from a graft of orange on pomegranate, another of green orange peel that brings the whole tropics about the taster, mulberry sirup for sore throats, Normandy biffens, or apples shriveled in the oven, to be stewed in the winter days; jars of candied lemon peel, and of a foreign flavored jam made of the red lips of the wild-rose bushes, stewed and strained and sweetened and strengthened with a dash of spirit, something, perhaps, after the pattern of the old rose conserve of the Venetians; flasks of noyau made of honey and peach kernels; and another home-made cordial—a maraschino-like thing of beech leaves steeped in sirup, gin, and sugar—in fact, all manner of curious and strange little compotes and rarities that one would never see anywhere else under the sun, and memory of many of which has quite died from among us.

Different Kitchens.

Any housekeeper who knows how unpleasant it is always to be obliged to set the same round and routine before her guests, would be thankful for any thing that enlivens it, that varies it with a new sensation; and it has often struck us that it would be a good plan if our country tourists made friends now and then with some of the simple families of the old farm-houses, and learned where the arcana of their kitchen secrets differ from their own. We all know how good it seems to come home to our own table and the manner of cooking to which we have been accustomed, even after the most luxurious of hotel tables; and we all know how useful it is, when the appetite is poor, once in a while to spend a day or two away from home, and taste the customs of other kitchens and dining tables. Some little quaint thing that nobody ever heard of, or at any rate ever tasted, is a treasure to the tired brain of the provider, and even if it is not a complete success, it has changed the current of monotonous dishes; and, as in other things, it is sometimes better to have failed than not to have tried at all. Meantime, there is some reason for the self-satisfaction of noted cooks, even if not quite to the extent of the one who considered the inventor of a new sauce as the equal of a great general; for the one who puts together a new dish is certainly, to a larger degree than it would seem, in enlivening, in gratifying, in pleasing, a family benefactor.

And it is, indeed, still more becoming to look about us and do the best we can with all the material at hand, since there has been such a change in relation to income and outlay in the increase of prices of all the commodities of life; a change that has made it difficult for the master of the house not to do the small and pitiful thing, and has caused many a house-mother to groan in spirit seeing the quarterly bills mounting, and not knowing where the money is to come from to meet them. And yet all the time—all the spring and summer time at least—there is suitable and delicious provision at hand, waiting to be taken, asking to be eaten, receiving nothing but contumely, yet capable of making a third dish at every meal for absolutely no price but its seasoning—a bit of butter, a pinch of salt and pepper.

Undreamed of Dishes.

Some of these pleasant esculents are things dreamed of in the philosophy of very few of us. For the first of them—friends in need, as they will prove to those who adopt them—who would think of turning to the nettle, that hateful plant whose stings are a torture, and of which we make all effort to rid our land? This nettle is a plant of such a pungent and astringent nature that its juice, applied on lint, will stop the flow of blood from the nostrils and from any slight wound; there is a property in its seeds powerful enough to fight successfully against the dreadful goitre; and it is acrid enough, too, to give flexibility to a bit of steel that has been dipped in it. With such properties it is hard to imagine it an edible, and almost impossible to think of it as a choice edible. Yet, boiled and drained and chopped and served hot with butter and pepper on toast, it is an excellent substitute for spinach, and is preferred by many. If this seems strange to any of my readers unaccustomed to such aid in their bill of fare, they will perhaps think it stranger still that quite as palatable a dish is to be had from burdocks prepared in the same manner. A dish that is very agreeable, also, is made from certain of the very young ferns, a peculiar variety, boiled not quite a half hour and served with drawn butter or on buttered toast. Nobody, to look at the little downy, curled-up things, would ever dream of dining on them; but they are really medicinal, in addition to their other qualities, being a good tonic, and having some of the same properties that the dandelion has in relation to biliousness, and they are of some service to dyspeptics. They must be plucked very young, when still woolly and curled up; blanching improves them; they should be boiled a little over an hour, with some salt in the water, and will be found excellent as a change of diet in the early season to which they belong. We shall hardly be accused of helping to hurt the beauty of the natural world by assisting in destroying the kingdom of ferns in thus advising their use—loveliest of all shapes, as they are, which nature imitates in every crystal and on every pane—because the fern is so prolific that it would take the æons it required to bring the world out of that primeval condition when all growth was more or less ferny in order really to put an end to the pretty things.

Besides these uncouth vegetables which may be impressed into our service, there are several excellent "greens" not in common use, though growing everywhere. Among them is the much-despised purslane, the bane of gardens, the object of the farmer's loathing, and which the author of *A Summer in My Garden* has loaded with witty obloquy. Nothing sweeter nor more succulent and nourishing is known in the way of "greens," and those of our readers who see its pulpy sprays spreading from spot to spot in their gardens are advised by us to turn it to account and save many a half dollar at the green-grocer's. Five minutes' work will gather sufficient for a large family.

The Mushroom.

But perhaps nothing is quite so generally neglected as the generous and multitudinous mushroom.

It is true that very few people feel well enough acquainted with it to dare pick it, and there are as many various opinions concerning its distinguishing marks as there are mushrooms—these picking anything for mushrooms that grows with nothing between itself and the sky, those contending that the best mushrooms are grown in the darkness of cellars, some of the growth that we knock over in our pastures for toad-stools being the favorite mushrooms in the foreign market, for instance, and those that the English esteem as the best being considered poisonous by the Italians, and making the burden of one of their bitterest imprecations. It is worth the reader's while to educate herself in the knowledge of the varieties of this appetizing fungus, for, rich as a venison steak when broiled and buttered, with pepper and salt, stewed it gives a strong and juicy gravy, and minced it imparts a fine and rare flavor to any dish with which it is mingled, so that, as may be easily seen, it is no mean accession to the store-room; and as it can be dried and strung, it is one of the things that can be relied upon for the round year. Another article that is not often thought of among ourselves for its capabilities as food, however in its ultimate results of pumpkin-pie it may be valued, is the pumpkin blossom; though if one should see a market scene in some Mexican mountain town, with heaps of the great golden flowers all tumbled together and trembling with dew, one would understand that its capabilities were appreciated elsewhere. These blossoms, torn apart and tossed in a napkin to absorb the dew, and dressed like lettuce, make as tender and crisp a salad as an epicure—and a Spanish epicure at that—could desire.

These are but a few instances of the use of the things that are usually considered worthless, but which are lying all about us, and the moment that we observe them remind us of the beggar with whom St. Martin divided his cloak, and show that the humblest object is not to be despised.

The Story of Sylvia Dexter.

The mother of Sylvia Dexter was a woman who never would have dreamed of any of these out-of-the-way dishes, and would have scorned to use them had she known of them. But Sylvia, herself, would, I think, have discovered them, every one

"Yes," said Mr. Dexter, "honest poverty is nothing to be ashamed of."

"Nothing to be proud of, either," said his son John.

"And very disagreeable, anyway," said Sylvia, his pretty daughter

"Well, I don't know why we need to talk about it. It's something of which we have no experience," said his wife, "honest, or otherwise."

"Yes," said Mr. Dexter again—looking round at the breakfast room, whose walls were lined with Sylvia's vines and flowering plants that made it a bower of greenery, at his shining table, and the pretty, petulant woman with her pink ribbons at its head—"we have every comfort, and some luxury"——

"Papa means mamma for the luxury."

"No; he means her for the comfort," said John, who was her special care.

"Thanks, thanks," said mamma, bridling a little. "Comfort is quite lative."

"A very dear relative, sometimes," said John.

"John," cried Sylvia; "you really must go into politics!"

"Heaven forbid!" said his father.

"He has such a capacity for pretty speeches he would be invaluable in diplomacy," urged Sylvia.

"It is all he has a capacity for," his father thought. But he did not say so. "No, no," he said; "the less politics the better. His desk in the bookstore is the place for John."

"I should be well enough content with that if I owned the shop," said John. "But this spending the best of your days for others isn't what it might be."

"It is a great deal better than running into debt for your beginning," said his father, as he left them.

"Yes," said Sylvia; "save your salary and wait till I can help you."

"You!" was the contemptuous reply.

"I do think," said Mrs. Dexter, "that a little dose of poverty wouldn't be amiss for Sylvia. She always feels such immense capabilities that it might bring her "——

"To a realizing sense of her inefficiency," said Sylvia. "Well, mamma," she added presently, sipping her coffee—John having gone upstairs again to change his tie—"you speak as if that would give you pleasure.'

"No, I don't; not at all. But you are always opposing John"——

"Why, mamma!"

"Yes, you are. The moment John comes anywhere near proposing to your father to give him the money to buy out the stock of that place, you come in with your influence against it."

"My influence, mamma! As if there were such a thing!"

"Well, there is! You are so exactly like your father that he hears all you say. And he feels you behind him and laughs the whole thing off. Saving his salary, indeed! He might as well think of buying the crown jewels with his salary! A salary is a dreadful thing; it binds you down in chains. Yes; there is no doubt about it, a salary is a dreadful thing."

"But, mamma, do you think it is right, when papa has you and the little children on his hands—I don't speak of myself, because I suppose I *can* see to myself."

"There it is again! Your immeasurable conceit of yourself."

"But, mamma, there are quantities of young girls who do take care of themselves."

"Their name is not Sylvia Dexter, then."

"Well, if I can't see to myself, it seems to me there is all the more reason for papa's not crippling himself by giving his money to John and risking everything."

"There is no risk about it. You are a selfish and unnatural girl, Sylvia! You would let your poor brother toil and moil all his life, rather than make a little sacrifice yourself. And he has always been so good, so kind; he was such a beautiful child—I remember when his curls were cut off that Mrs. Dares said"——

"Mamma, dear, you sent Julia on an errand, and said you would make John's lunch"——

"Sylvia! And it's almost train time! Why didn't you see to it? So full of the good of the family theoretically—and poor John all day in town with nothing to eat"——

"And not a restaurant handy," said Sylvia. "Well, I have seen to it. And there's an egg-sandwich, and a breast of duck, and some celery, and some salt, and a buttered muffin, and a little tart, and a doughnut, and a flask of coffee. John has a better luncheon than we shall have. He has it every day.'

"I should think you grudged it to your brother!"

"No, indeed! John likes good things, and I like to put them up for him; so we are even. John doesn't think so badly of me as you do, mamma."

"I don't know what you mean, Sylvia. I never said I thought badly of you. You annoy me with your jealousy of John—poor, dear John; he was meant for a prince—and you uphold your father in his severity."

"Here, John—excuse me, mamma—here, John!" cried Sylvia, hurrying to the door as he went by. "Don't forget your luncheon."

"Oh, hang the luncheon!" cried John, as he took the parcel. 'My father's economies will be the ruin of this family yet. If there's any one thing that has a cheap and detestable look, it's this pulling a luncheon out of your desk instead of going out like a man with any independence."

"I'm sure you needn't take it, John, if you don't wish," remonstrated his mother.

'Yes, take it, John," interpolated Sylvia. "A penny saved is a penny earned. It means more than half a dollar toward your capital."

"Come, now, that's interesting! Work it out for me while I'm gone, and see if I will have enough at that rate to put out at interest before I die."

"There," said Sylvia to herself, "I shall say no more about it. If papa chooses to take the risk—poor papa! Well, it's fortunate that Aunt Jeannette has invited me to visit her just now." And she put on her jacket to go and call upon the neighbor whose cow pastured in her lot, and see if it would not be as convenient to pay the rent now as later, so that she need not ask her father to open his purse for her. And she came back with so bright a face that her mother declared she thought that cow-right was worth more to Sylvia than the whole place to them.

"Perhaps it is," said Sylvia; "for it's mine, mamma. And it isn't going to be absorbed and lost in John's business, if the rest of the place is."

For the little three-acre lot was Sylvia's. She had bought it and paid for it from her small savings, together with the two hundred dollars her grandmother had left her, when there was a rumor of its purchase for some unpleasant purpose, it being just at the foot of the garden. Her mother had never given her any peace concerning it, so to say. She ought to have lent the money to John, was the tenor of 'Mrs. Dexter's frequent remark; and doubtless she would have done so but for Harley Melton's influence, and for her part she wished Sylvia had never set eyes on Harley, undesirable and unsuitable as he was! But Sylvia, for all that, had been a proud and happy landholder and taxpayer ever since, and had enjoyed the sight of the neighbor's cow under the great trees, and drinking from the little brook formed by the spring that bubbled there as cold as if it had come all the way from Spitzbergen; and she had enjoyed quite as much the ten dollars a summer that the neighbor paid her.

She had had another pleasure in it, too; for often had she and Harley Melton laid out those three acres in their strolls across them; and here should be the house, and here the little lawn, and here the orchard; and it would be so pleasant, being near papa; and if Harley did not think it would be so pleasant being near mamma, he kept the thought to himself. Sylvia, with her great blue eyes, her lovely fairness, her sweet and sparkling brown-haired beauty, was so precious, that if the mother who bore her was not perfect, too, he was not sure that the fault was not in himself. He loved Sylvia beyond any words, the bright and busy little creature, alive to the tips of her hair with interest in all things and all people, feeling all things alive as well to her, the bird on the bough, the blossom there, too, the child playing beneath it. They had no idea of marrying, except far in the indefinite future; they had nothing to marry on; it was enough to love each other now; by-and-by they would build the little

LOOK AT THE JEWELS. OH, WHAT A GLITTER!

house, perhaps, in the piece of pasture. They used to wander over the bit of land as if it were an estate, with a joy of possession; and where the spring bubbled out of the ledge that cropped up beneath the group of great trees, they would sit and watch the water as if every bubble were a miracle.

"Just look down in it, Harley—how clear! Look at the jewels on the bottom; they are rubies, sapphires, emeralds, opals, topazes, beryls—oh, what a glitter! What color, what splendor! It seems as if I could put down my arm and scoop up a handful of the gorgeous things."

"The pebbles down there? It is the wonderful clearness of the water that makes them seem so near; and I suppose it is the vertical sunbeam that makes them seem so beautiful. They are really a dozen feet beyond your reach," said the young chemist.

"They can't be, Harley!"

"Yes, I sounded the spring last week; it is eighteen feet deep; and I don't dare to say how many gallons it pours out a minute that all go to waste through the Telassee River."

"To think that our brook makes part of a big river!"

"And I analyzed it, too. The river that went out of Eden could not be purer. One drinking this might think he was drinking of the water of life."

"Well, it will be Eden when we have our little house up there on the knoll. What a beautiful earth it is, Harley, when such freshness and purity pour out of its dark places! What a dear earth, to let us call this little piece of her ours!"

"I really should think," said Mrs. Dexter when Sylvia came in, "that that spring was full of diamonds by the way you and Harley Melton hang over it."

"It is, mamma—it is!" and Sylvia danced away with no idea of the truth in her words.

It was lonesome at Aunt Jeannette's, in the big town twenty miles away. Her father and John and Harley came in every day to their business, and for five minutes she saw Harley, who made occasion to go by the gate. Her father and John found time for few visits. Her first letter from her mother informed her that she would be glad to hear that her father had at last sold his bonds and given John the proceeds to buy out the business where he had slaved so long as a clerk. Sylvia knew, however, under what unbearable pressure her poor father had been brought to yield; and her indignation and pity for him made her feel at first as if she never wanted to go into the house again. Succeeding letters were very jubilant and happy; it gave his mother so much pleasure to see John taking his place as became him, a man among men. She thought the business must be flourishing, for John had a little naphtha launch on the river, in which he went to town now, instead of traveling with all the dust and jar of the railway. Of course, of *course* there had been opposition, the letter said, for his father was one of those men who never liked innovation; but probably he would soon be going into town on it himself. He was always prognosticating evil; any one would think John was committing an unpardonable extravagance in having devised a healthier way of going to business than they had ever known before. Mr. Dexter did not approve of John's new horse, either; and yet any one could see that the horse was as gentle as a woolly lamb, and he ate apples and sugar from the children's hands, and when he traveled he simply flew.

When Sylvia made an errand to her father's office, she found him as anxious as she had expected. But it would do no good for her to go home with him just now; she would show her disapprobation of the state of affairs too plainly; and she couldn't if she would, for Aunt Jeannette was ill with typhoid fever, and, of course, it was out of the question to leave her. There was really a pestilence of typhoid in the town. All the drinking water was drawn from a river that passed large polluting towns and tanneries, and every day a new case appeared, till there was almost a panic in the place.

Fortunately for Sylvia she was one of those creatures so full of vital strength and fire that fear was unknown to her; and so well had she nursed Aunt Jeannette that, when she was a little rested, the hard-pressed physician begged her to help him on another case. And so it chanced that she went from one sick bed to another, and presently came to be offered large payments for her services; and in view of her apprehensions concerning John and her father's unsecured loan to him, it seemed best for her to continue both earning money and carrying relief. Harley protested that she would wear herself out; but she protested in return that she was well and young and strong, and liked it; and that even if the duty had not been set so plainly before her in relation to the sick and her ability to help them, it would be a wanton waste for her to refuse to earn the money thus offered her. "Oh, Harley!" she cried; "I must do all I can for them. For when I think of the poor creatures dying for want of good water, murdered by bad water, and remember our spring in the pasture bubbling up fresh and pure every second, I feel like a criminal; as if I kept health and strength all to myself; as if I, and not the spring, were wasting what would be life to them."

"Such a morbid feeling shows that you are tired and in no condition to be nursing the sick," said Harley. But suddenly, as they went along together —for he appointed to meet her almost every day now in the hour's walk allowed the nurse by custom—his face flushed and flashed with a sudden thought like the passing of a sunbeam. "Will you give me permission to do what I please, to take all I want of the spring water, and in the way I think best?"

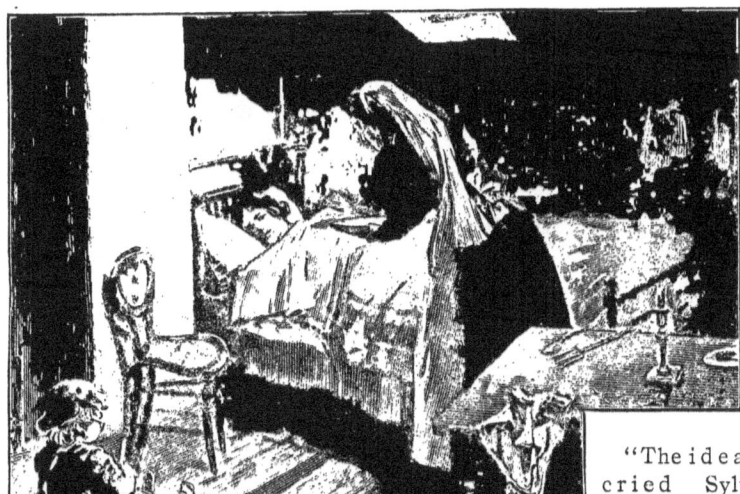

FROM ONE SICK BED TO ANOTHER.

"The idea!" cried Sylvia. "Permission, indeed! Isn't what is mine yours?" And they passed to more purely personal matters.

"I don't know if you are aware," wrote her mother, some weeks afterward, "that Harley Melton is meddling with the spring in your piece of pasture, as you call it, meddling in my opinion most unwarrantably. He has had men there scooping it out and curbing it; and he has rigged an unsightly derrick there, and men are filling great glass demijohns by the wagonful. And at this rate there'll be no spring there at all presently. I suppose it is to save himself the trouble of distilling water for his prescriptions—that is so pure. I'm sure if he has money enough to hire men and rig derricks and all that, and cares as much as he pretends about you, he had better lend it to John, who can't sleep nights for worrying about his notes."

Sylvia was too busy with her sick and dying people to wonder much about the burden of her mother's letter. She knew that whatever Harley did was likely to be right. She could not spare the time to go and see her father again; she could not get the time; but she felt oppressed with fear for him, and she laughed a little bitterly at herself to think she had supposed she could help him with her earnings, when a whole year of them would not amount to a thousand dollars. But, at any rate, she was glad that she was lifting any portion of expense from him, be it ever so small.

It was some weeks afterward that when she went out for her morning walk in a new direction, and saw great posters on all the fences and telegraph poles, "Drink water from the Sylvan Spring and prevent typhoid," she understood with a double thrill of joy—joy for themselves, and joy for the sick—what Harley was doing. And when she met him driving in with a load of the glass carboys filled with Sylvan Spring water, which he left from house to house, before going to his headquarters for fresh orders, she felt as if he were really an angel of the Lord in mortal guise. And he held out his hand for her to mount to his side, and she rode back into town with him, feeling as a devotee might do who carried holy water to the perishing and penitent.

Sylvia had gone back to her Aunt Jeannette's for a short rest after the hard and cruel winter, when, one bright May day, her father came to see her. John had failed; and all that Mr. Dexter had saved and spared in the long years had gone into the gulf with the money of the other creditors. There were no assets to speak of—a few notes, the remnants of an ill-chosen stock, the horse that had gone lame, the disabled naphtha launch. Slyvia felt as though her heart would break when she saw her father's despondency. "I don't blame your poor mother," he said. "Love is a good fault. It was her love for John, and her belief in me. She thought I was equal to any trouble that might come, superior to it; but even I supposed John had some capacity. It's hard, my child, to begin life over again at sixty."

"I don't think you will have to do that, Mr. Dexter," said Harley who, coming in just then, had heard the last words. "I am just making a return to my chief; and I am sure it will be a joy to Sylvia to replace a good portion of your losses by indorsing this check to you."

"Harley!"

"I have deducted all the expenses and my own commission," said Harley. "You will see by the schedules that we supply in this town and others along the route and on the further side—for the typhoid scare is widespread now—more than a thousand families with the Sylvan Spring water, at fifty cents a week. Of course the expenses are heavy; but then the net profit is heavy, too. It gives Sylvia and me enough to build our house in another spot at some distance from the water-works, a pasture of *mine*. And if you, Mr. Dexter, will take the management of the business in town—I think it need not interfere with your present arrangements; and John will oversee the teams—that is quite within his power; I can attend to the spring-house until the time, that is, when the towns take the works off our hands and pay us fifty or a hundred thousand for our plant, with permanent positions in the business."

"There is no more honest poverty in ours, papa," cried Sylvia.

"Harley!" said Mr. Dexter; "you are my salvation."

"Well, sir, you can reverse the thing and be mine by giving your daughter a command to become my wife here and now!"

"Without her mother?"

'Well, papa," said Sylvia, blushing rosy-red, but feeling obliged to come to Harley's help, "Aunt Jeannette would *do*. And you know that mamma has a great—a great faculty for obstruction. I think she will be so relieved about John that she will forgive us. And we will make her a wedding present of a paid-up mortgage of the house."

"You are a *nouveau riche*, Sylvia. Harley must not allow you to be too free with your money."

"Oh, it isn't ours; it is a trust the dear old Mother Earth gives us. We are to be happy out of it, and to make every one else happy. And, oh, what happiness it is to bring health to whole towns full of people! Don't you remember I told you the spring was full of sapphires and rubies and emeralds, Harley? And real ones, you see, papa!" for Harley had slipped a ring on her finger some little time before. "Papa, you are quite another person already," she cried, pinning on her hat and going out to the minister's with them and her Aunt Jeannette

"Oh, you dear, sweet, confiding old Mother Earth," Sylvia exclaimed, kneeling at her window that night, and looking out on the dark, slumbering, champaign country behind the town, "I love you so!"

"I think," said Harley, "you had better be saying how you love me!"

"That goes without saying," she replied, leaning back her head on his arm. "But this dear earth—she makes us so happy while she rolls with us about the sun that it seems to me now only a happiness to think of the time when we shall be a part of her—just brown dust together in her bosom!"

"Oh, but a long way off!" he cried, folding her still more closely in his arms.

It was at about the same hour that Mrs. Dexter, having inspected the released mortgage and the gratifying check, had coquettishly picked out the pink ribbons of her cap and was remarking to her husband:

"Well, it was the most thoughtful thing Sylvia ever did—to save me the fuss of a wedding. That piece of pasture! Is John to have a salary—or a commission? A salary is so comfortable. You always know where you are with a salary. It has to be paid. Oh, yes, a salary is the best thing; I have always said so. Harley Melton is turning out better than I thought. I never said there was any harm in him; only that he was so inefficient. Still, with the money coming in, Sylvia could have done better. She could have married almost any one. It is vexatious, say what you will, to have an outsider like Harley directing family affairs. It is just the thing for John himself to do; and it is my private opinion that John suggested the whole business in the first place. He always said that water was pure. John is so full of ideas!"

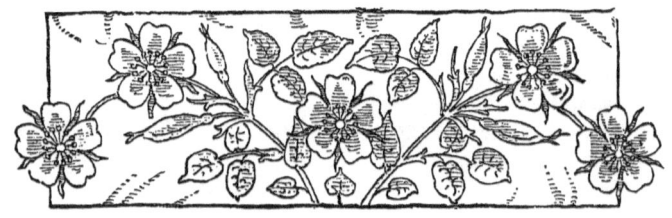

CHAPTER SIXTEENTH.

Work.

> Laborare est orare.
> Books or work or healthful play.
> —*Dr. Watts.*
>
> And blessed are the horny hands of toil.
> —*J. R. Lowell.*
>
> Men, my brothers, men, the workers, always reaping something new.
> —*Tennyson.*
>
> For men must work and women must weep
> And there's little to earn and many to keep.
> —*Charles Kingsley.*
>
> In the morning when thou art sluggish at rousing thee let this thought be present: "I am rising to a man's work."—*Marcus Aurelius.*
>
> If all the year were playing holidays
> To sport would be as tedious as to work.
> —*Shakespeare.*
>
> Every man is the son of his own works.
> —*Cervantes.*
>
> By the work one knows the workman.
> —*La Fontaine.*
>
> Man's work is from sun to sun,
> Woman's work is never done.
> —*Old Distich.*

As necessary a stepping stone to happiness as there is in the whole world is to be found in work—enough work, and not too much. When we murmur about our work, we seldom reflect how much more pitiful would be the condition of the most laborious among us if we were suddenly to be deprived of it. We often look upon it as a burden, when it is in reality a blessing in disguise. We picture to ourselves how much happier we should be without it, and envy those who are born to a heritage of idleness, when we should be, in truth, the most wretched beings alive could we exchange places with them for a day. What an angel of mercy has it proved to many! What a solace for vacant hours! What a panacea for troubles, sentimental or otherwise! Did not John Bunyan bless it, think you, in Bedford jail, where he beguiled the time with toiling over his *Pilgrim's Progress?* Has it not ministered to many a mind diseased, plucked from the heart many a rooted sorrow? Is it not the only sure antidote to ennui? a remedy against a host of ills to which flesh and spirit are heir? Has it not rendered us oblivious to injuries and neglect?

That the money value of work is not its ultimate charm is well attested by those who, having been hard workers for the greater portion of their lives, retire from business, expecting to enjoy themselves and their hard-earned wealth, but finding the weeks and months heavy upon their hands, finally resume their old habits of industry, having made the important discovery that they had been enjoying themselves all their days; that their true contentment was like the statue hidden in the marble block—something to be wrought out by toil; that work was the only talisman against low spirits and hypochondria. We rarely, if ever, hear busy people complaining of megrims; they do not often swell the number of suicides. They have little time to spare for their neighbors' affairs, since the sincere worker must pin his mind to his work, if he would accomplish anything worth dignifying with the name, and not some slop-shop makeshift. We sometimes feel that if we could only choose our work or exchange with another we should be better pleased and more successful; then we should become earnest in its pursuit; then should we cease to slight and slander it; then would our efforts be as spontaneous as the bird's song. But is it not wiser for us to do honestly that which falls in our way, if it be only to darn stockings or to scour knives, without waiting for anything more worthy of our strength or talents? Is it not a reproach to Him Who assigns it to suppose it a mistake and something beneath our abilities, as well as a vanity in us, to imagine ourselves capable of more ambitious tasks? And are we not assured that

> "Who sweeps a room as by God's laws,
> Makes that and the action fine?"

Mrs. Browning's Word.

Perhaps Mrs. Browning's noble sonnet says in small compass the best there is to say of this:

> "What are we set on earth for? Say, to toil;
>   Nor seek to leave thy tending of the vines
>   For all the heat o' the day, till it declines,
> And Death's wild curfew shall from work assoil.
> God did anoint thee with His odorous oil
>   To wrestle, not to reign, till He assigns
>   All thy tears over, like pure crystallines

>   For younger fellow-workers of the soil
>   To wear for amulets. So others shall
>   Take patience, labor, to their heart and hand,
>   From thy heart, and thy hand, and thy brave cheer,
>   And God's grace fructify through thee to all.
>   The least flower with a brimming cup may stand
>   And share its dewdrop with another near."

The Value of Work to Character.

In another consideration, one perhaps more selfish, there are few things of so much value to the character as work and the habit of work. This, the pleasure-lover, the idler, the very young and thoughtless may be inclined to doubt, but advancing years will teach them the truth of the statement. I remember having heard Emma Stebbins, the sculptress, and the friend of Charlotte Cushman—and both of these illustrious women had been ardent workers—once say to a young person who complained that she hated work, and would like to loll a year or two on rose leaves: "Ah, my dear, I hope the time will never come to you when you will be thankful for work!"

It may be a vastly more agreeable thing for a season to lounge in the sunshine, to sit half buried in luxurious ease, and read a novel that takes us out of our humdrum existence and into a life inviting as Elysian fields, to fold our hands, doing nothing but waiting for something to turn up; but all that sort of thing, pursued as a profession, grows infinitely more tiresome than the most tiring work. For there is occasionally an immense difference in the significance of the two words, tiresome and tiring, the one often implying a fatigue of the spirit which dissipates all its forces, and the other a wholesome fatigue of the body, to be refreshed by rest or sleep; no rest or sleep refreshes us when a thing is simply tiresome, for the tiresomeness is monotonous, underlying and always there. In fact, if we do not want pleasure and ease to fall on us so that we would at last find ourselves glad to dig or scrub for a change from the soft condition, we shall have to learn to take that pleasure and ease only as the reward of labor, as a relaxation really earned by effort, a something that has become ours by personal right; and we shall discover it to be then as much more delicious in its sweetness as the honey of the bee, with its wild-flower tang and flavor, is more delicious than the baker's treacle with its dull insipidity.

Nor is work, of whatever sort it may be, merely desirable in this way of exercise and sport to the healthy muscle and healthy brain maintaining sound condition or creating it; but it is a blessing even if in disguise by means of its taking us for a while as completely out of ourselves as the most enthralling romance could; for as we have seen we can seldom do our work without thinking of that work; that which can be done without thinking seems to have little of the sacredness of work about it and to be really only a hybrid between work and play; and if we are thinking of the work then certainly we are not thinking of the other matters that environ us or overwhelm us and by their monotony would furrow ridges in the brain were that possible. We come back to ourselves with the interest of those that have been away from home and we are better able to meet our circumstances by the new view we get of them through our absence and return. If we are of that great number whom sorrow has marked for its own, who are surrounded by an atmosphere of teasing trouble, or who have met with some great calamity, then how great a resource shall we find this absorbing work which we once so scorned! For the time, at least, the stinging throng of annoyances is escaped, the pressure of the great calamity is lifted; we find ourselves with a new anxiety, that of doing our work well, of expressing our thought perfectly, of achieving success in the direction we have aimed. Only those who have suffered may perhaps know the full extent of the blessing that work is when it comes to absorb them from their grief; yet they who are loaded with all the pleasures which the world has to give will usually find that it has one thing more to give in the enkindling and revivifying of work pursued in earnest.

All Creation Works.

But even if work comes not as a blessing *per se*, and has to be considered as part of the primal curse in which man was bidden to earn his bread in the sweat of his brow, and which the minority of mankind seem to think did not include themselves, what right has any created thing to wish to evade it? Is there such a thing known as absolute rest among all the powers and agencies of the cosmic universe, the very names of power and agency implying action? Are not the four elements constant at their never-ceasing, never-resting, always interchanging labor? Does one drop of water pause in the roll of the ocean, one tongue of flame hang suspended in the fire, one cloud stay motionless in the wide heavens, one atom of the brown earth cease to disintegrate, to moulder, to crumble and change for its new state? Is not the seed ever germinating, the flower ever blooming, the fruit ever ripening, the wind ever blowing, vapor rising, sunshine falling, rivers running? Do the planets rest in their courses, the earth in its revolution, the tides in their great swinging? All the atoms and impulsions of nature are constantly rendering their tithe of service; and why, then, should any one of us, as much an atom of nature as stock or stone is, and moved by nature's quickening as much as tide or sap—why should we halt at our work and bemoan our fate that we have our share of work to do? Even while we bemoan ourselves the work of the universe goes on unceasingly in our own bodies and the changes that bring on old age daily within us and about us. There is something marvelously strange in view of the industry of all the natural forces that the human race, or any portion of it, should be the only thing to rebel at the necessity of labor, in some degree at least.

But apart from all fancies of the kind it is a fact that there has never been anything of moment in the world accomplished without work. What an immensity of it must have been done to complete those conquests over the raw material of the earth in the ancient desert ruins, temples and aqueducts in the modern tunneling of mountains and stretching of railroads across continents! "The money that you pay us for our labor we send home," said the Chinese to some agitator against them, "but the work remains for you." And so the act of work remains in its effect upon the character of the worker. He is up and doing when others sleep, and not only winning his measure of success thereby, but keeping himself from rusting out, polishing every faculty, stretching every nerve, bright and alert for the next thing, whatever it be, the business of this world or that of the other—the other upon which he may some morning wake surprised—surprised to find work waiting for him in the new horizons, and himself all the better fitted for it that he did no shirking here.

It often seems a regrettable matter of concern when we observe the manner in which a large number of subordinates—we can hardly call them workers since they would avoid any reason for being called so—complain of the necessity that compels them to their daily tasks. One thing of their future is certain: no individual of those complaining is a person who will ever, as the vernacular goes, "amount to anything." For look at their chiefs and employers; there is no clerk in any leading business of the country who works as indefatigably as the head of his house does, so long as he remains in the business; up betimes in the morning it may be while the clerk is still stretching and yawning and hesitating on his pillow; and the last perhaps to leave the counting-room at night. It is quite possible that in such an employer's case there is too much business done out of the superabundance of activity; but it *is* done, the profit and reward of it is reaped; and while he bemoans himself that he must work, the subordinate will never be reaping any other profit or reward than his meagre salary, which he evidently works hard to get without work.

Conscience in the Work.

Whatever the work is, it is always to be done with a conscience. In the struggle not only for superiority, but for existence, and the making of existence comfortable if not also beautiful, with which this country and this age are only too well acquainted, it is said that workers have no time to take conscience into counsel, and to do their stent as if doing it to the stern judgment of the fullest light that might ever fall upon it.

Yet if all workers, and in that sense all individuals, realized the great doctrine of consequences, and the manner in which every circumstance is interwoven with every other circumstance that has gone before or is to come after, conscience would never be thrust out of sight, but would be the chosen friend, and given the place of honor at one's right hand.

The careless, happy spinner slights her thread; the rope spun with that thread breaks, and the man it held falls down the shaft; then a family is left fatherless and destitute children grow up to crime and shame; theft, murder and the gallows hang on those strands of thread, sighs, tears and agony, desolated affection, betrayed love, crime multiplying crime with the rapid growth of a fungus, a country its prey. If conscience had sat by that spinner, that contingent amount of harm, at least, with its far-widening and long-reaching circles, would never have been done the world. For there is no action that does not entail its consequences, not on the actor alone, but on all in contact with the actor, with the air one might declare that the lifting of the arm to do the deed disturbs, and all whom that air touches.

Work Here and Abroad.

We often hear complaints that this and that sort of work is not done so well here as in England, or France, or Switzerland; and allowing it to be true, one marvels why liberty and all the civilizing influences that surround the worker in this country should have the effect of making his work poor and slovenly and unfaithful. Yet, if the statement is really true it is doubtless because in the older lands the workman has no expectation of ever rising above his work, and his only hope is in its perfection; while here, on the contrary, every worker knows certain of his possibilities, and looks at the future through them and not through his handiwork, as he should do; he does his handiwork only in the interim before he carries out his possibilities

Perhaps the complainants have done their own work well in complaining; or perhaps they have been too hasty in demanding more than one century and a quarter of national life has had time to effect, and we may be just entering on the ripened fruit of those years of liberty. Nothing speaks better for our later conscientious endeavor than the appearance of much work at the various exhibitions, the fact that to-day many of our wares find more demand and better market than the foreign, and than so little a thing, as at first glance it may seem, as the discovery by a woman of the secrèt of the lovely Limoges ware, so that its foreign maker mistook her work for that of his own people.

Love of Art Equaling Conscience.

Sometimes, indeed, the European worker's love of art answers for conscience. Doubtless that old Demetrius of Ephesus who made silver shrines for Diana did his work faultlessly. But it was another sort of conscience that animated Yoshiaki, the sword-maker of Osaka, in Japan. "His idea was that having been bred up to a calling which trades in life and death, he was bound, so far as in him lay, to atone for this by seeking to alleviate the suffering which is in the world; and he carried out this principle to the extent of impoverishing himself. No neighbor ever appealed to him in vain for help in tending the sick or in burying the dead. No beggar or leper was ever turned from his door without receiving some mark of his bounty. Nor was his scrupulous honesty less remarkable than his charity. Whilst other smiths were in the habit of receiving large sums by counterfeiting the marks of famous makers of antiquity, he never turned out a weapon which bore any other mark than his own. Without knowing it Yoshiaki was a sound Christian." And there can be no doubt that this man did his work better, made his blades keener and lighter, because his conscience was so active that it caused him thus to atone for the making of swords at all.

But it is not only the makers of swords, and of ropes, and of artistic objects, that need their conscience in their work; the domestic worker needs it just as much, if not more. The child at her practicing, the girl who sets a stitch in her darning, the maid who trims the lamp for the night, the man who shovels the snow from the door, the mistress who directs the servants, and who ruins them as well as her housekeeping by neglecting to keep them up to the proper point in their duties—all these need conscience at their side as well as the weaver whose badly woven sail, splitting with the bellying wind, as the carpenter whose badly driven bolt, hurl a ship to her destruction. These stand in danger of hurling more than a ship to destruction, one might imagine—of ruining all the comfort, the peace, and happiness of a home, by the want of this conscience yoked with needle and brain, eyesight and will.

For this very "conscience that makes cowards of us all," once admitted to our company makes us afraid to slight our work, makes us feel the consequences that come from badly baked bread, from poorly aired beds, from loose buttons, from strings not renewed in season, from unwhipped seams in our sewing, from stitches dropped in our knitting, from children unreproved at the moment of a fault, from servants allowed to commit the second time the error they made before, since nowhere has this useful conscience greater opportunity for play than in the work of the housekeeper—work that begins with the first breath she draws beneath the roof of the home that she undertakes to care for, that ceases neither by day nor night till she draws the last breath, and is only made systematic, and thus as easy as the breath itself, by the aid of this bosom friend and counsellor.

Those Who Are Down on Their Luck.

But not only concerning his work will you hear the idle and the listless worker fret his soul, but of something that he calls his luck. He is one of those people who never are "in luck." These people feel that if they were not born under an unlucky star it was because a wandering comet, yet more baleful, was in the ascendant. They made at the beginning, they might suppose, some one of those infinitesimal errors which in the course of a lifelong calculation widen out into the logarithmic figures.

They came into the world behind time, they would tell you, and have always been in pursuit of it and never catching up. They were born just too late for a legacy, they die just too late for the life-insurance which happens to expire first. Their piece of bread is sure to fall and always on the buttered side; their dear gazelles are sure to die; if they think they can play comedy, a compelling fate thrusts them into tragedy; they would like to write poetry, but are obliged to make a living by plain prose; if they have a chance in an oil well, it runs nothing but mud and water; if they have a silver mine, it turns out a false lead; if they dabble in stocks, it is only to burn their fingers; all their bulls are beared, all their swans are geese, there are seven Fridays in every week of their lives, and all of them are black Fridays, so black that they are blue! On the wedding journeys of these worthies nobody has a slipper to throw after them; horseshoes never lie in their path; let them get up never so early in the morning to catch their worm, an earlier bird has been before them. The blind beggar on the corner always sees them, when their pockets are empty and a charming girl is their companion, before he sees anybody else; the confidence man always selects them for victims; if they travel, they are the Jonahs of the journey; if they stay at home, it is to see the folly of not having gone abroad; their brothers never learn to swim, and sail round the world in safety; they learn every trick of the water, to be drowned in their own bath-tub; regardless of the economies, other people may put bacon in the engine fires and sit on the valve, and nothing happens; but these people will not only be blown up by the steam of their own tea-kettle, but will have to eat their greens without bacon. No contagious disease goes a-begging for the want of them to take it, and always at the most inauspicious season; their good crop and their neighbor's famine never come together; if they make a corner in cream, there is always a thunder-storm on hand to sour it; in short, whatever they do, they will have reason to wish they had done the other thing; they are so invariably out of joint with the times and seasons of prosperity that if a fool's cap be thrown into the crowd where they are, theirs is the head it falls on, while they are led to declare that if they had been born hatters, other people would have been born without heads; and they are thankful for but one thing in the world, and that is that they were not born a pair of twins.

It may have been to this strangely infelicitous class that those wretched women of the French Revolution belonged who, when one tyrant went down and before another came to the top, were taken from the prison to the guillotine by mere routine. For such a fate as that would seem something to be avoided neither by wit nor learning, and only to have come through a natural alienation from luck, an inherent hostility to happiness. But if we admit the existence of luck or of ill luck at all, certainly these and such as these are the only ones who can claim any striking disagreement with it.

But the wretched individuals who pride themselves on being so invariably unfortunate never attribute any of their misfortunes to their rashness or to their procrastination, to their indolence or to their meddlesomeness, to their pusillanimity or to their overplus of pluck, to their maladroitness or to the element omitted in their combinations; they neither reproach others nor themselves—it is always and merely their luck. Luck is the divinity that shapes their ends; and if we will accept a new reading of the old passage, is the divinity that shapes their ends rough—hew them how they will! "Just my luck," is the shibboleth they use on all occasions, till other people adopt their own view of themselves, and leave them out of their schemes and out of their parties, as persons with whom it is not best to attempt fine undertakings, till the unlucky ones again cry out against their treatment as a fresh manifestation of the injustice of Providence, and against themselves as nothing but the fools of fortune.

It has sometimes occurred to us that a possible reason of many of the woes of these poor creatures is that they are completely out of time and place, they do not belong to this generation or to this era; they were unlucky at the outset, in that they reached this planet some thousands of years after all their kindred souls had passed away. They belonged to the times of the augurs; to the times when adventures were undertaken by the direction of the smoke of sacrifice or the position of the entrails of animals; to the time when Fortune had her altars, and men invoked good luck with burnt-offerings, and poured libations to prevent its opposite; to the epoch of superstition between those two great flights of birds, one of which directed Romulus to Rome and the other directed Columbus to America. They are still the devotees of small credulity, and certainly are foreign to the age and the latitudes of civilization.

It is not, of course, impossible that, in all the complications of the innumerable threads that hold the worlds in order, there should be some found running at cross-purposes through unwise human intervention, that there should be born individuals the currents of whose lives may run counter to the great currents of the universe; but since there is a deep and everlasting law to control the things of creation, and reconcile disturbances, and a wise disposer of events, such variations are, to say the least, unlikely; and it seems to us, after all, about time for a general declaration of disbelief in the existence of any such thing as ill luck. "It is not in our stars, but in ourselves, that we are underlings," the great poet of humanity tells us, and reason confesses the truth of the statement. The person who is in earnest is never unlucky. This is a world of equations and equivalents, and every serious effort has its balancing power of success.

Rest After Work.

And when one has worked all one will or can, there comes usually the recompense of toil, and then comes a measure of rest. To those whose toil has brought them the means to do so there is no more delightful rest to be had than in a short season of travel and of making one's self acquainted with the world. It is singular that there seems to be no such rest to the wearied mind and nerves as that which travel brings, although it may sometimes fatigue the body.

The Rest of Travel.

Perhaps it is on the same principle that a new attitude is often restful, bringing into use another set of muscles, and letting those that have been long exerted take a season of relaxation. For the mind that has fallen into a routine, and worked too long in a rut, finds itself flaccid as a string that has been stretched too far. and it receives benefit from another sort of exertion and in

INUNDATION OF THE NILE.

a different direction. One would suppose that all the rapid changes and novelties met and the bodily fatigues undergone in travel would themselves be exhausting, and that, if one wanted mental rest, one could secure it better at home. But it is well known that precisely the opposite is true, and that most physicians who have nervous patients, or those threatened with derangement of nerves or brain, order travel, as they might order a narcotic or a stimulant, sure of its beneficial result.

Certainly this is a delightful medicament; and how could one better harmonize the right and the delectable than in obeying such prescriptions, and taking up one's bed and walking, to the ends of the earth if need be, and not forgetting to reward the prescribing physician by seeing everything and enjoying the whole of it. One can stay at home and take nauseous doses, doubtful if one is to be better at the end than in the beginning; but who would not rather take a dose of moonlight in Vienna, city of mirroring, a dose of the ruins of the Alhambra, with a run over to Tangier to heighten the flavor; who would not make an exertion to see that there was no error made in the compounding of the prescription of a dahabeeyah on the Nile, and rest under the shadow of Philæ; would not gladly swallow such a bolus as a summer on the Ægean Islands, in the Engadine, in the Trossachs, at the North Cape—and feel that the old saying of "See Rome and die" in such case is transformed into "See Rome and live"?

The Mind in Travel.

But, besides rest and medicine to tired nerves, is there anything much more elevating and stimulating to the mental processes than well-conducted travel? Does it not enlarge the mind as well as the sympathies, and tend to give us a wider scope in every way, and more active intellectual energy than we had before? "To abstract the mind from all local emotion would be impossible if it were endeavored, and would be foolish if it were possible," says a great writer. "Whatever withdraws us from the power of our senses, whatever makes the past, the distant, or the future predominate over the present, advances us in the dignity of thinking beings. Far from me and from my friends be such frigid philosophy as may conduct us indifferent and unmoved over any ground which has been dignified by wisdom, bravery, or virtue. The man is little to be envied whose patriotism would not gain fervor upon the plain of Marathon, or whose piety would not grow warmer among the ruins of Iona." If this be true, it is no marvel that our wishes turn so ardently to that dark side of the earth unknown to us as the dark side of the

ASCENT OF MONT BLANC.

moon, since for all that books of travel may tell us, no imagination, even' by their help, is vivid enough to paint the whole picture as man and nature may have made it. Whoever pictured to himself the unseen home of a friend as it really is, on this side of the street, with this furnishing, this atmosphere, this character? and how, then, should all the travelers' tales of all the travelers in existence give us in our mind that clear view which our actual eyes shall have strike them like a revelation as we look at the Parthenon, at York Minster, at Freiburg spire, at Mont Blanc rosy in the sunrise, at the Campagna in an autumn morning, at Rome, and all the ghosts of the Old World rising with it to salute us? Let them content themselves with books of travel who can do no better than sit at home and turn the pages; but those of us whose kindly doctor orders change will be only too glad to borrow of Puck's wizardry, made matter of fact through electricity, and put a girdle round the earth in forty minutes in the shape of telegraphic messages from Land's End to No Man's Land. And when we come back to humdrum life again, and all its duties, what wilder wizardry shall we make every time we shut our eyes, and the picture, the person, the scene, starts up vividly as a fire in the night, drawn clearly on the brain, an everlasting wealth in the memory.

It is true that this kind of rest and change and medicament takes a great deal of money out of the country, and enriches foreign lands at our expense, and that the political economists strike and spare not a great deal of gratuitous growling in relation to the subject. But does it really do no more than enrich other countries to the loss of this? Does it really bring nothing back of as much value, to say the least, as the money it took out? Is there no wealth to a country in the experience of its citizens, in their education, their acquirements, their familiarity with the works of greatness of whatever sort? Are values only to be found in raw material, in so much wheat, so much gold, so much cotton? To my thinking, what the traveler brings home, stamped with fresh impression, is coin for currency, capable of being of infinitely more use to the country than the trivial dollars and cents that he took out of it. He has seen the best that art has done, if not the best it will do; he has seen the ruins of dead empires, and the workings of existing ones; he has seen this one and that of the famous people of the earth; he has learned, if he has wit, a part of the lessons that the Old World has to teach the New, and that are seldom learned except by actual contact. He brings home to a new land, with vast untrodden and untraveled tracts of country, almost without monuments, and with art, however high in individual achievement, but little beyond its infancy so far as the general public is concerned, tradition, knowledge, culture, and as good as all the rest, acquaintance with what it should avoid in its newness, since its two hundred and fifty years are but a babyhood beside

DRYBURGH ABBEY FROM THE EAST.

the years of the ancient kingdoms of the earth. Every traveler who comes home to us, still regarding the institutions of his own country as sacred things, and not denationalized by admiration of the admirable things of other lands, nor dazzled by the glittering of crowns and coronets, still remembering that of all good things liberty is the best thing, can only contribute to our real wealth by adding to us, as a people, appreciation of those advantages that come with later growth, each individual doing his share toward the leavening of the lump.

The Reader in Travel.

It is the reader to whom this travel is of the most account. How many are there who go to Scotland, for instance, for no other purpose than to follow out the fancies of Walter Scott's immortal music, who tramp over the Highlands to the memory of Rob Roy, see the purple Trossachs for the sake of Roderick Dhu, for whom Flodden Field would be barren of interest had "Marmion" never been written, and who would never see Dryburgh Abbey, or the ruins of Melrose, or Kenilworth Castle, but for the phantoms that rise to welcome them at the wand of the wizard of the North?

How many are there, again, who would never cross the limits of the Italian town that knew the history of Romeo and Juliet if Shakespeare had told us nothing of their love; whom neither the heath of Fores, nor Birnam Wood, nor Dunsinane, would ever tempt from the beaten path, had not the witches met the Thane of Cawdor on that heath, had not Macbeth seen those woods moving on his stronghold?

Who of the wandering band has not looked for Lord Steyne's mansion in London as much as for the solid stones of the Duke of Wellington's—does not glance for some reminder of the old Colonel and Clive Newcome among the Bluecoat Boys far more than for any of the real and famous among the long list of those boys?

And for whom is not London peopled with the beings created by the fancy of him whom Lady Bulwer—before his death, in common with the crew who busy themselves in hunting out only his follies and blemishes since his death—styled the Aristophanes of the Pot-house and the Plutarch of the Pave, but whom the world will know long after his defamers are forgotten, as the Lord of Laughter and Tears? What is the Court of Chancery to our travelers but as it gives them Mr. Jarndyce and Miss Flyte? Of whom of all that have entered the gates of the Marshalsea do they reckon but Little Dorrit? And do they not know the very house that will presently crack from top to bottom, the man whose mustache goes up and whose nose goes down when he

KENILWORTH CASTLE.

laughs, sitting in the window meanwhile? They walk through High Holborn to look for the shop of Poll Sweedlepipes and the lodgings of Mrs. Gamp; they follow Mr. Pickwick from the city; Brighton stands to them only for Paul Dombey and "What are the wild waves saying?" the dialect of Yorkshire has no other significance to their ears than that John Browdie spoke it; Dover is sacred to Betsy Trotwood and the donkeys; Yarmouth means the wreck of Steerforth: England and the English are, in fact, only Charles Dickens. And now they will be following the footsteps of Macleod of Dare, perhaps, or looking up the localities of the next story-writer who stamps his die with such vigorous action as to impress all hearts with the personality of his fancies or his portraits.

Do we not picture to ourselves and realize more clearly the domestic life of Egypt, better than the tomes of history can teach it, on reading Theophile

Gautier's "Romance of a Mummy," and have afterwards explored an Egyptian tomb ourselves? What should we reck of the barbaric tribes of a little peninsula in the Levant and its rocky islets, if Homer had not held up his torch to their struggles? Do we not all feel that Homer created Helen? and should we care a straw for all Schliemann's work if Homer had never sung of Achilles and the Xanthus? But Homer having sung we must go and see what Schliemann has dug up.

Travel in Our Own Land.

Yet great as I believe the advantages of foreign travel are, not to the individual mind alone, but to all others with which that mind is afterward brought in contact, I cannot but think that a little, nay a good deal, of home travel has its advantages, too.

Certainly in point of grandeur and picturesque beauty our own country confessedly carries off the palm, though we may have no cities so appositely placed as Rome in the circuit of her hills, or Venice on her isles; and if it has not the interest that tented tribe and caravan merchant and border baron have given to foreign spots, it yet has, as archæologists maintain, an unwritten and wonderful history that every traveler and explorer may help to bring to light.

When in the midst of an afternoon stroll in any sufficiently commonplace region one mounts a hill to find a lake on its top, and presently sees that the lake is an artificial basin fed by presumable adits from higher hills and by the constant rain-fall, banked up for some unknown purpose so long ago that trees apparently of the primeval forest have grown upon its edges, then one knows that there is a history written there which he who runs may not read, and that in its vast hieroglyphic is held the story of some old race whose very traces have hardly other recognition. Is it any more pleasure, we wonder, to read the hieroglyphics of the Rosetta Stone than, if it were possible, to read the burden hidden here? And to the careful eye the whole land, it is said, and particularly in the more picturesque portions, is written all over with as evident a script of its secrets.

To people who go abroad for the sake of the associations that foreign places have with historic names and identities, and for the sake even of general enlightenment, travel means much more than simply journeying from place to place, and sight-seeing by the way; but to people who go abroad merely for the sake of scenery, doubtless they might find as good at home.

We question if the falls of Schaffhausen, whose polished chrysoprase Ruskin loves, exceed the beauty of the falls of Montmorency, of Trenton, or Pas-

THE SWITZER TRAIL, SIERRA MADRE MOUNTAINS, CALIFORNIA.

saic, or countless other falls in which we rejoice at home; if the Lakes of Killarney are more wildly beautiful than Lake George, than Lake Tupper in the Adirondacks, than the Upper Mississippi at Trempealean Island or at Lake Pepin; if the Rhine has more positive loveliness than the Hudson, or many legends better worth, or has half the loveliness of the blue Juniata; if any single scene in the Alps is superior to the scene at the mouth of the Willamette where the seven snow cones of Oregon pierce the purple, with the black woods climbing their sides till the clouds drift through their tops; if any river in Europe at all equals either the Green, the Weber, or the Colorado, with their mighty canyons; if anywhere in the world a rival is to be found to the valley of the Yosemite, or of the Yellowstone, with the weird color of its rocks and waters, the very witch-work of beauty. And with Quebec, a remnant of the old French civilization, across our line on the north, and Mexico, with its Spanish cities, its cathedrals, palaces, and plazas only a few days' sail away on the south, who shall say we have not a mimic Europe on our own borders? It has always been a marvel that people should desire to go abroad and inspect other countries when they have not yet seen the most famous portions of their own. If it is on account of the need of study, if it is through some yearning to tread in the footsteps of those whose fame is enshrined in our love and reverence, if it is to see some battle-field where the world once hung in the balance, to follow in the path of some poet and learn for ourselves what it was that fed his genius, to explore the haunts of history, then, of course, nothing should stand in the way, and no poverty of home travel prevent the voyage; but if it is merely for the sake of excitement, to while away the time, to say one has been abroad, to see charming sights, then the desire is not so comprehensible. I have even heard other people declare that they would experience a sensation of shame to stand awe-struck underneath the dome of St. Paul's if they had never seen the white wonder of our own Capitol dome, or to be found admiring the bucketful of water tumbling over Lodore and have the curious stranger inquire concerning the Niagara which they had failed to see at home. The rest of the world, indeed, is beautiful, but those wiseacres who hold that the original Eden was in America are not so far out of truth's way as they might be; and for the rest, is it not written that "The eyes of the fool are in the ends of the earth?"

CHAPTER SEVENTEENTH.

Love of Others.

> In faith and hope the world will disagree,
> But all mankind's concern is charity.
> —*Pope.*

> His heart and hand both open and both free,
> For what he has he gives, what thinks he shows,
> Yet gives he not till judgment guides his bounty.
> —*Shakespeare.*

> Careless their merits or their faults to scan,
> Thus to relieve the wretched was his pride,
> And even his failings leaned to virtue's side.
> —*Goldsmith.*

> Alas for the rarity
> Of Christian charity
> Under the sun!
> —*Thomas Hood.*

> Blessed is he that considereth the poor.
> —*Psalms.*

> The destruction of the poor is their poverty.
> —*Proverbs.*

> He that hath pity upon the poor lendeth to the Lord.
> —*Proverbs.*

> Whene'er I take my walks abroad
> How many poor I see!
> What shall I render to my God
> For all His gifts to me?
> —*Dr. Watts.*

> I owe much; I have nothing; I give the rest to the poor.
> —*Rabelais.*

> I'm very lonely now, Mary,
> For the poor make no new friends;
> But oh they love the better still
> The few our Father sends!
> —*Lady Dufferin.*

There will be little happiness in our house after all, if it has been built and conducted only for ourselves, and if we have not comprehended that the rest of the world has a share in it, and have not given ourselves the happiness of giving—giving not indiscriminatingly but wisely and joyously. As the season approaches when want is most keenly felt by the poor, and begging children appear at every city alleyway and country door, we are tempted constantly to pay no heed to the rule we have been advised to form of giving no alms at the door, but of referring the applicant to the bureaus of associated charity, or to one society or another that stands ready to afford assistance where needed. But from this denial and cold reference the heart shrinks, whether or not reflection and reason show that in referring those asking help to these societies we in reality give them far more efficient help than it is possible for us to bestow ourselves. For certainly, in our large cities, charity has come under such a system, and philanthropy is so well organized as a business, with salaried agents, that it almost brings into being, as a counterpart, the profession of pauperism.

Associated Charities.

Let a person once prove himself in need and incapable of exertion, and bureaus with salaried officers make that person an object of solicitude; there are hospitals in which the destitute child can be born, asylums where it can be reared, schools where it can be educated, reformatories, if need be, where it can be trained, institutions from which later on it can be fed, and public fees at last with which it can be buried. In fact, being recognized and acknowledged as a pauper, it can be comfortably taken care of from the cradle to the grave.

It has, of course, been a question with many who desire the advancement of the human race as to how far such wide charities are calculated to advance it, and whether, indeed, they do not lower its average of usefulness, virtue, and intelligence. So long as the tender sympathy with suffering which exists in the heart of almost all who are themselves free from want and suffering will not allow the beholder to see this trouble without trying to alleviate it, the imprudent, the improvident, and the reckless will go on defiantly multiplying cares and wants, sure that they will be relieved in a community that can not be disgraced by the starvation of any of its members, and could not, from pure pity, suffer the thought of the starvation anyway, if brought to its notice, as such case would surely be. Yet the whole direction of this sort of thing, according to the opinion of the greater number of those who have made pauperism and charity a subject of scientific study, is to increase the proportion of paupers, and so to deteriorate the moral and mental condition, not only of scattered individuals, but of the race.

It is not to be doubted that all the modern ameliorations of life make life possible to those who in past generations would have died after a very short trial of existence. To-day these same examples live, but, for all that, they have not the strength to repel diseases that are, it may be said, the result of the intrinsic weakness of their own systems, and they transmit a vitiated organism to their descendants and again lower the average of health and vitality in the whole mass.

Transmission of Vitiated Organisms.

In spite of the terrible condition of the poor, this fact reaches over and touches them at many points. We can not, moreover, lower the average of health without making work more difficult to do, and livelihood the harder to obtain; and here we travel in a vicious circle, for the moment we encounter the inability to obtain a livelihood in poverty we encounter sickly conditions again, brains undeveloped, and bodies poorly nourished, in crowd and poisonous neighborhoods. It is known of every one who pays attention to the matter that extreme poverty is not favorable to the production of virtue; on the contrary that it is the hot-bed of vice, and cannot help being so. It is equally well known that there are instances of extreme wealth of the same nature, that there is more than one noble family in Europe, and wealthy family here, notorious for some one vicious trait, and that where the case is not so bad as this, in many instances the families die out and become extinct through too great indulgence in luxury. Yet for one such case among those in affluent circumstances there are countless ones to be found among the so-called pauper class. Be they rich or poor, the intemperate and the profligate, owing to their infringement of the laws of nature, will leave few of their race and name behind them; and those few are more likely than not to continue the sins and crimes of those who went before them, and so make sin hereditary. When the profligate rich continue to exist, it is because of an extraordinary original strength in the race, making a vitality hard to overcome; yet ordinarily they tend to extinction through other causes, as even in marrying they choose heiresses, the fact of whose wealth shows that they are the only daughters of their parents, and whose mothers perhaps were only daughters before them, if anything may be inferred from the accumulation of money in their single hands; and the pair start "housekeeping" with a hereditary tendency to keep their numbers small, while the tendencies of their manner of life are to disease and early death. Of course it will be claimed that they are those exceptions which prove the rule.

Extremes of Wealth and Poverty.

It would seem as if the two extremes either of great wealth or of extreme poverty are equally dangerous to the social structure and equally to be avoided. The one has no object in life but to dissipate time upon enjoyment, a new enjoyment being constantly to be invented to replace the enjoyment that palls. The other, also, has no object in life but enjoyment—enjoyment which in such instance can only be attained by wrong-doing of one kind or another. Honest poverty is quite another thing—poverty that works and that refuses alms, but meets on common ground with moderate wealth and comfort, each naturally supplying the wants of the other, each indispensable to the other, each holding up the pillars of the state, each liable to interchange conditions. It is not with that sort of wealth or poverty that the perplexed student of social science deals, and perhaps the time will come when it will enter upon the consideration of undue wealth as earnestly as upon that of undue poverty, and look about for methods that shall prevent the excess of either one or the other.

Giving at the Door.

It is a little hard on the good housewife that she can not hear the timid ring at her own gate, and see the wan, pinched face and shivering figure there, without finding herself launched on the great social problem of all ages. She will hardly be likely to adjust matters with any delicate balance between systems of philosophy or philanthropy; she will not pause to think whether she is fostering crime and increasing the wrong she wishes to cure. She sees, at any rate, that here is a child into whom a good meal will put needed life, and for whom a full basket will make joy, and she proceeds at once to incur the displeasure of all the scientific philanthropists by disobeying their advice and feeding the child. Perhaps afterward she takes notes of the case, and refers it to the especial society whose duty it is to look after it, and not feeling quite sure even then of aid and justice, takes it upon herself to see if that society has done its duty by personal inspection, altogether in ignorance that she is thus interfering with a satisfactory solution of the problem, and is destroying the efficacy of organized charity by interfering with the organization.

There is an old line familiar to most of us, "The poor ye have always with you," the force of which we seldom realize so much as in the bitter days when the sun runs low and his beams are so niggardly. But I think that most of us will leave the question of equivalents and ultimate perfection to the political economists and gradgrinds when a little shivering form stands in the porch some freezing day, with a blue and pinched face and trembling lips, and asks for a bit of bread, and we shall give her the bread whether we are at liberty or not! How else would we sit down to a sumptuous dinner after having refused a crust to the little wistful beggar? and do we not all feel that we would better be the victims of possible imposture than the instruments of certain cruelty?

Many of those who occupy our luxurious homes have but little conception of what poverty is. The French princess who, when she heard during a famine that the people had no bread, wondered if they could not eat cake, although really she simply meant oaten cake, is only an exaggerated representative of many of our women who have never entered the houses of the poor, and know nothing at all of the way the world treats them. If these ladies who have only "lived in the roses and lain in the lilies of life," whose hearts are full of kindness, yet who are ignorant of what real deprivation means, should leave their fortunate fastnesses and go down into the purlieus of poverty, penetrate reeking cellars, climb rickety stairs, see the parched fever patient burning out his delirium alone; see the consumptive on his straw, exposed to the draughts of leaky roof and broken window, without nourishment or dainty; see the hearty children hungry still on the daily division of a single loaf; see hopeless girls, wrapped in shawls and without fire, sewing for life, as if they saw the monsters that stalked behind them; see mothers aching for their children, and fathers empty-handed and cursing their fate; see all the horrid, piercing sights of want—of want whose neighbor on the one hand is death, and on the other is crime—then, we think, their hearts would be sore among their treasures unless they could do something to relieve a little share of the trouble with which every great city is catacombed. There are many of our wealthy women, let it be repeated, who, though they have heard of poverty, are so unacquainted with its actual resemblance as to be able to form no idea of the real state of things. But, on the other hand, there are just as many more who make it their business to be informed of all this dark and sad under-life, and who spend a good part of their days in giving and devising, and assuaging the pain there still must be in spite of them.

Lovely Examples.

Indeed, I know lovely ladies who, in simple garb, spend some, certain hours of every day, in alleviating all the suffering that they can reach, and who then, going home, put on their silken garments and tread their velvet floors, and give no intimation of the sights they have seen to sadden the guests, unless the assistance of those guests is needed.

To all other women of wealth, when in the arms of their own comforts they know how strongly fire and furs and hearty food are needed by themselves, let such examples be commended, not only since they will find their recompense in the act, but in remembrance of the assurance also that "Inasmuch as ye did it unto the least of these, ye did it unto Me!"

But for our part, those of us that are not wealthy, we cannot run the risk of letting even possible suffering and death load the winter with their dark weight without examining into the facts of the case, or else, provided the power to alleviate is ours, we shall feel that the blood of these sufferers is on our hands. There is always, we know, some one member of our family who is able to look into these matters; and once having the report, we are at ease; if the case of suffering is a forged one, our sympathies are relieved; if it is genuine, and if to lighten its load we are obliged to forego the new cloak, to delay the new silk, or abandon the opera tickets, we can be soothed by the consciousness that our heavenly robe will be all the brighter, and our souls will be all the more finely attuned by-and-by to the music of the stars singing together. Cold comfort, perhaps, but sure; for he that giveth to the poor lendeth to the Lord.

Still, it is usually possible to assuage the pain of poverty without depriving ourselves of enjoyment of real consequence, for the poor, it is said, are able to be happy on the superfluity of the rich, and the mistress of a single comfortable household has kept the wolf from the door of more than one penniless family during a whole winter.

It needs, perhaps, a little more oversight of store-room and cupboard than it is always agreeable to give, in order to make sure that this superfluity shall go in the right direction; a little more attention to the way of the cook with her friends who are not in such dire distress, thus to see for ourselves that the fragments of our feasts reach those in real need. Yet that is but a slight tax; and we shall be well rewarded in the rosy cheeks of the children who come daily with their baskets, when we reflect that but for our oversight, the cheeks would have been wan and pinched and blanched, even if their owners were not underground altogether.

A Degrading Course.

It may be that it would be more agreeable if we could sit down at our novel and our fancy-work, our little bit of piano practice or water-color, our entertainment of callers, our afternoon stroll, our evening gayety, enjoy life in sybaritic fashion, and know nothing of the presence of distress in the world. But if we reflected upon the results even to ourselves of such a course

STEPPING STONES TO HAPPINESS. 455

MORE AGREEABLE IF WE COULD SIT DOWN AT OUR FANCY WORK.

of life, we should see at once how injurious and degrading it would be; the flies, the butterflies live as valuable a one; the flowers that, at any rate, scatter their sweet perfume abroad, like the aroma of good deeds, and in so far add to the enjoyment and happiness, live, we might almost say, a better one. Never to have our sympathies called out, our active interest in the needs of others, our active assistance; never to be able to experience pity, that divine emotion which is but the pathetic side of love, which so enlarges and ennobles every soul that knows it; never to join in the sorrows of others—why, it is like living in a glare of everlasting sunshine, and never knowing the depth and glory of the darkness that sets the soul and the imagination free among the stars.

The Poor a Benison.

In fact for those of us who have a right to be classed on the other side, it is a good thing that there are the poor to be looked after; for the poor are, indeed, a benison bestowed upon us, though sometimes in disguise; and the community in which there are no poor is by no means one to be envied. "God's poor," an old writer has it; and to make them ours also is but another bond to the Divine love. That is necessarily but a selfish and one-sided life which has no outlet toward the majority of mankind, toward that dark and dreary lot which belongs to the larger number of our fellow-creatures; for great wealth is but a phenomenal thing, great comfort belongs to the very few, and though a modicum of comfort belongs to many, yet the by-places of the world are full of those who want and wait and weary in their suffering.

The brilliant flies, with wings of many colors, that we see disporting in the air are to be numbered, but the slugs and worms and blind beetles that live in the dark, and that we see in multitudes under any stone that is turned up in a pasture, are countless.

What the Poor Have Done.

But apart from the moral value of the poor to those in better circumstances, what in the world would be done without them? Who but the poor have built our railroads and tunneled our mountains and laid the piers of our bridges beneath the rivers? who but the poor have mined our coal, smelted our ores, sailed our ships, built our houses, tended our gardens, groomed our horses, made our garments? who but the poor have done our household work, and have, in fact, by their laborious existence made our easy and luxurious one possible? If we lived in the wilderness, and there were no poor about us, all the millions of Crœsus would not prevent the necessity of our laboring in order merely to keep the breath between our teeth; it is only by their neighborhood that we enjoy our ease where we are. In the city we scarcely appreciate this peculiar blessing of the poor, as the machinery of city life works in such wise that we hardly feel our wants before they are answered; but in the country what would become of us without a neighbor in less lucky circumstances than our own, who would run our errands, do our chores, lend a hand at the housework in time of need, wait on table at a pinch, take home

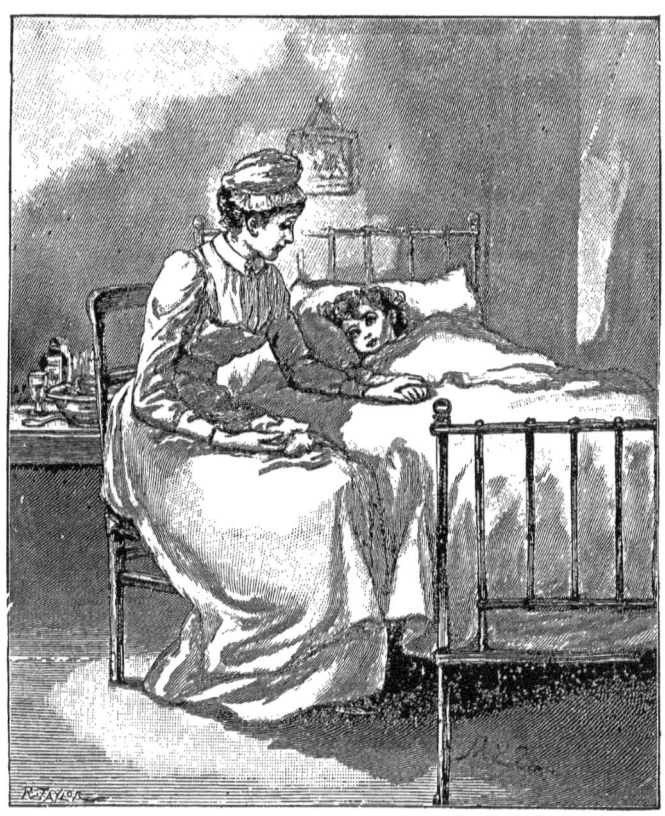

THE MOST WE CAN DO FOR THE POOR IS BUT A DEBT WE OWE.

the extra washing of a guest, dig the paths in winter, clear up the grounds in spring and fall, do all and every odd job, man and wife and child, at home and abroad? The money we pay that family is a pittance whose outgoing from time to time we do not feel, but whose incoming is to them a bounty and a theme for thanksgiving, while the service they do for us we can never quite appreciate till by some accident we are deprived of it. And since the poor are, as it would seem, of such value to us, would it not be a shame if the good done were all on one side, and were of no value to them? Indeed it may well be said—not only in view of the equities of the case through the bounty we have received from Heaven, but in view of the services the poor as a body render—that the most we can do for the poor is not a favor that we show them, but a debt we owe.

After all, where there is a will there is a way; and whether by associated or by personal endeavor, the poor are to be relieved, and relieved by us. We can not all do as Anstress Hermans did with her money, but we can all appreciate what she did and emulate her example, with large means if we have them, in lesser ways if those are all that are possible to us.

The Story of Anstress.

There had been large expectations in the city concerning the day when Anstress Hermans should come of age—expectations in which, it is not too much to say, almost every one within the circle of her radiation, so to speak, participated in a greater or less degree. Well-bred, well-educated, well-looking, of good disposition, the fact of her approaching majority caused the parents of eligible sons to count upon the advantages of her entrance into their respective families, caused the youths themselves—without, therefore, being coxcombs—to think of the possibility of grasping at once what few of them would ever grasp in all the course of their lives, and caused youths and maidens alike to rejoice in the prospect of the festivities with which, according to immemorial usage in such circumstances, the twenty-first birthday of the young heiress would most probably be celebrated.

Whether the festivities were to take place or not, the parents and the sons just mentioned might have spared themselves the trouble of hope or of conjecture; for the affections of Anstress had already been engaged by the son of her guardian, a companion of hers since childhood, and who if not, as yet, entirely arousing her deeper nature, had succeeded in making himself as altogether indispensable to her daily life as he found her to be to his, and the only reason why the engagement between them had not been announced was because Mr. Jeffreys, the father of the young gentleman, and the guardian of Anstress, had, in order, perhaps, to save appearances by-and-by, expressed a wish that nothing of the sort should be considered definite and irrevocable until after Anstress had become of age, in which case, of course, it was wisest that nothing at all should be said of it abroad—Mr. Jeffreys taking excellent care, in the mean time, to hedge her about in good measure from any too great intimacy with other suitors, and to have nearly all the small things which make the happiness of life reach her only through this son of his, the tall and quiet, grave John Jeffreys.

STEPPING STONES TO HAPPINESS.

Of course John could have nothing to do with bestowing upon her any of the material comforts which she enjoyed; those were the gift of her dead father, dead almost since her infancy; but it had been the policy of Mr. Jeffreys to afford those to her so stintingly, that when, through John's urgency, any greater largess and liberty were allowed to Anstress, it should seem like the gift of John himself. Of this, to be sure, John was totally unobservant and unaware, or it might have fared differently with Anstress, for the young student had some pride of character that would have proved a formidable obstacle to such course of treatment. But, as it was, Mr. Jeffreys could not think of letting Anstress undergo the expense of a coach and horses; but John represented her desire for an equipage so strongly, that, when it was at last allowed, it was quite as if John took her to drive with his own team, supposing that he had one; and when Mr. Jeffreys declared that his performance of his duty would be questionable if he suffered Anstress to purchase a set of sapphires on which her heart was fixed, it was John who had them sent to the house, and then displayed Anstress, decked in their sparkle, to his father, with such eloquence, that the guardian could not but relent, with much show of being overcome by the eloquence, but not at all by the sparkle, and it was quite as if John had given her the sapphires; and it was John who really took her to the theatre (this was before the day of chaperones), to the picture galleries, secured the best seat for her when any gay pageant was in procession, brought her the news, and rendered her all those pleasant unobtrusive flatteries which make a young girl think what a sweet thing life is. It was John, too, who gave Anstress something to busy herself about and to feel an occupying solicitude for. It was to make his pipe doubly pleasant to him that she spent months in embroidering a smoking-cap, with so much gold braid that it was top heavy; it was to prevent his taking cold that the silk dressing-gown was quilted in such stir and secrecy; it was for a pattern for John's satchel that she ransacked all the haberdasheries; it was to ornament his paper-cutter and book-marks that she learned to paint; it was with regard to his comfort or his welfare that she pursued almost every step of her quiet and guarded life—and very likely, in the first place and principally, because it was her nature to desire to be giving pleasure to somebody, and so far she had found nobody but John, and now it was a habit. She had lived in the same house with him as a child; after he went to the university, and while she attended to her studies with a governess, his casual return was something to look forward for, since it always was a holiday by Mr. Jeffreys' direction; the whole of his vacation was her vacation, too; and she was beaming and smiling with pride and enthusiasm, at last, on the day when he graduated with the highest honors, and every one admired and praised, and he brought it all to her. John was a sufficiently fine-looking and manly fellow, of a temperate disposition and habit of thought, and of quite the average power of mind, so that there would seem to be no reason for condemning Mr. Jeffreys' course in having arranged the matter as he had between his son and his ward, and which would most probably have arranged itself to the same end had he let it alone. Anstress was perfectly happy in the relation—John was the top and flower of chivalry to her appreciation; it was a great thing to be his handmaiden, to work his cravats and slippers, to learn his songs, to dance with him every other time at the parties that Mr. Jeffreys allowed her to attend on the promise of denying herself all the round-dances—a promise that he had no need to extort, since Anstress had a holy horror of round-dances, and, besides that, they made her dizzy. It was on driving home from one of these parties that Anstress, a happy little maiden, walled about by the security of wealth, and ignorant of any of the trouble in the world, was first awakened from her dream of youth, and into real life. Till that night suffering had never crossed her path, no one had demanded the exertion of her, and she had not troubled herself to think that every one in the world was not as comfortable and content as she was.

John had been away from town, and as he was to return in the midnight-train, she had left the little company—where, considering John's absence, she had been enjoying herself quite passably—something earlier than usual, and bade the coachman hurry home by the quickest route. The quickest route was by no means the pleasantest; indeed, it lay through the short-cut of a dozen squalid lanes, and Anstress, leaning back, with closed eyes, among her luxurious cushions, was startled by a yell and an oath, the shriek of a child, and then a loud tumult of cries. It was a drunken man, she afterward discovered, beating his child, and interfered with by the neighbors, till, in the general rough-and-tumble ensuing, the police brought peace about by carrying all the participants off to the station-house together. Anstress had made the coachman wait, in spite of his assurance that it was no place for the likes of her; her heart was beating with terror in one great pulse all over her; the vague things she had heard from Sunday to Sunday as to the presence of sin and horror in the world, without ever realizing them, became, all in a moment, living truths, and if suddenly a yawning chasm of the bottomless pit, across which flitted shapes of fire, had opened before her, she would have felt no otherwise than she felt that moment when these creatures rose and astonished her, by the glimmer of the street lights and the carriage-lamps—children that were incarnate disease, women that were only nightmares of women, men like wild beasts—all swarming to the scene of riot and around the white-faced lady in the coach.

"What does it mean?" asked Anstress, after the police has led away the originator of the disturbance.

"Mane?" cried the nearest woman. "That it's a free country where Pat O'Harrigan hasn't the right to bate his own b'y!"

"But he didn't know—he'd been drinking, they said"——

"Av coorse he had! And yese had been drinking yerself, an' the ould woman sint to the Island the same day, more betoken."

"To the Island?" asked Anstress, with a puzzled tone.

"Oh, yese a mighty foine lady," said the woman, turning off with a laugh. "But ye'll learn where the Island is sune enough, I'll warrant ye, if yese go round by day as naked as yese are by night!"

It is due to the coachman to say that at this point he had to conquer the inherited instincts of a long line of McMurphys in order to prevent himself from precipitating as fine a shindy as ever occurred out of Donnybrook Fair, but he struggled manfully, and like St. Anthony, overcame the temptation by fleeing away from it.

"What was that place where we stopped, James?—what street, I mean?" asked Anstress, when the coach drew up at Mr. Jeffreys' door, while she gathered closely now the cloak that had fallen from her forgetful shoulders when leaning from the carriage-window during the disturbance.

"'Dade, miss, and you mustn't be afther asking me," said James, "for 'twould be all my place is worth if the master found I been driving you acrost a bit uv the North End."

And not wanting to annoy him just then, Anstress went up the steps not very much enlightened after all. John had come, for there was his hat in the hall. She ran into the drawing-room, and, in passing, paused a moment before the long mirror, and with a glance the woman's last words came over her with redoubled force, and she looked at herself as she had never looked before—the white silk clinging to the form, with its atom of a waist, out of which the shoulders rose like those of a dryad from a flower, the gore and train drawing away the skirt from the shapely hip.

"Oh, I don't wonder the woman said so!" cried Anstress. "It is just like a piece of statuary! Why didn't somebody tell me? And all the others were the same."

And she darted away to her own room, with no thought of John or of anything else but sheltering darkness.

The next morning Anstress was down long before breakfast, clad in her simplest guise, and had summoned James, and bade him put one of the horses into the trap and drive to the place where he had taken her on the night before. James trembled for his situation, and assured her that indeed it wasn't safe; but as Mr. Jeffreys had not yet come down, the man had nothing to do but obey, which he did with better grace after Anstress had promised him perfect indemnity from Mr. Jeffreys' displeasure, no matter what happened; and driving to Messuage street, a little money easily melted the way before her, and Anstress had an initiation into a dark side of the world that her dreams had never visited. For when she entered a room in one of the houses of that dreadful district—a room several feet below the street, whose walls were stained with a perpetual ooze, under which the paper-hangings had rotted long ago, and the plaster had fallen in great patches; where, across the floor, the leakage of a water-pipe sent a perpetual gutter that gathered in a pool at the other end, above which a broken window was half blocked up with a heap of garbage; and in the damp and the dreary half-light a wizened-looking child of some dozen years was holding a gasping baby that had but a few moments to live—when Anstress, who knew nothing of poverty, who had hardly seen sickness, and never seen death, entered this cellar, it was only because she was determined not to do so that she did not faint away, for she grew sick and giddy at the sight and thought of it. The little girl seemed to be too absorbed or too unhappy to think the intrusion anything strange, for when Anstress, looking at the pinched and frosted face of the baby, asked hurriedly where the doctor was, the child sobbed out that her mother had gone for him, but he wouldn't come, or they'd have been here. Before she had finished speaking, Anstress was in the trap and away after the family physician of the Jeffreys; but when she triumphantly returned with him to the place, he was no longer needed—the baby had left it.

"I don't know what I wanted it to live for in such a place as this!" cried Anstress, never thinking of recoiling from the woman on whose shoulder her hand lay, and looking at the pitiful object in her arms with streaming eyes.

The woman turned away and held her dead baby in silence—she wanted at least the luxury of her grief alone. Anstress stayed a moment to try and soothe the little girl, who was crying wildly, and then laid the contents of her purse in her hands, and went out after the physician. As they closed the door of the cellar, the doctor began to reprove Anstress for being there.

"Do not talk to me," said she. "What have they been hiding such things from me for? Now that I am here, I am going to see all there is to see. I don't suppose they can be quite as bad off in the upper rooms. What is the place left in this fashion for—the pipes leaking, the drains open? The landlord ought to be whipped through the streets!" cried Anstress, in a passion. "Oh, to think of their living so, with puddles of water on the floor, and the children dying in convulsions!"

"It was no convulsions the child died of," said another woman, hurrying in and shoving by them in the narrow way. "'Twas starvation."

"Do you mean so?" cried Anstress, catching hold of her and letting go again.

"Indeed I do," replied the woman, hurrying on; "and 'tis no place for such as you, miss," she added, looking back, more kindly, "for the house is full of fever."

"I am not afraid of the fever," said Anstress. "And I am going upstairs. It can't be that I shall find death in every room." But afterward, Anstress said to herself that Death would have been a kinder visitant in those rooms than the squalor and the suffering, the sin and sorrow, that she found there. When she came out with the doctor into the free air again, the children on the sidewalk were saying that the little boy who was beaten last night had died this morning, and it seemed to her that the very sky had blackened since she went into that house.

When Anstress returned home, breakfast had been waiting nearly an hour; but that was of small consequence, for the reproofs her unexplained truancy received were only affectionate ones, since to-day was her birthday and the day of her majority. Anstress took all their congratulations very quietly, sitting by John's side, and silently revolving many things in her troubled mind.

"I am going to be told about my property to-day, am I not, John?" she asked, when they were alone.

"I suppose so," said John. "My father has been busy in the library with your papers," he said.

"Do you know how much it is, John?"

"Not exactly; but a large sum—seven figures, perhaps."

"What! millions?"

"I fancy so. Father said once that it was enough for the income alone to be a fortune."

"The income—that is, the interest? That is what other people pay for the use of it?"

"About that."

"Yes," said Anstress, reflectively; "I remember, in the arithmetic, the horrible things in percentage my governess used to drive me wild with. Six per cent.—and does one always receive six per cent. for everything?"

"Oh, no; sometimes less, sometimes more. Sometimes the money is not lying at idle interest as in loans, but is earning profits as in railroads and shipping. Savings-banks pay you a small per cent., because they are safe; buildings pay twice as much, on account of wear and tear."

"Why, I should think the interest paid to half the fortunes in the world would eat up all the other half some day!"

"So it would, according to figures. But, practically, there are found to be great offsets and drawbacks."

"Tell me about it, John. I ought to know—oughtn't I?"

"Certainly. But it is an intricate matter; you couldn't understand it, dear, all at once. I don't think I do myself. There is only one thing clear—that the rates of interest are exorbitant and that while philosophers quarrel as to what 'brought death into the world and all our woe,' it is certain that that, and nothing else, makes half the poverty and sin there is."

"There is something awful, then, in being very rich!" said Anstress, opening her eyes.

"Riches are certainly a great responsibility," answered John, gravely.

"Doesn't it make you afraid to marry me, John?"

"Few people," said John, laughing, "are afraid to marry an heiress. But your property is settled on yourself, and is to be always independent of all the husbands in creation."

"But you will have to take care of it for me, for you see I am completely ignorant, and don't know anything about any money except what I happen to have in my purse."

"Very well; and you will have to pay me a salary for doing so. I tell you beforehand, that my charges will be high."

Something made Anstress turn away quickly. Was it possible that John was mercenary?—that, after all, it was her money he meant to marry, or that salary belonging to the guardian of a fortune, rather than herself? Before the shadow had more than time to flit across her face, and bring with it and leave behind it a crowd of new thoughts, to add to all the others of the night and day, the bell rang, and a servant summoned her and John to Mr. Jeffreys, in the library.

"My dear Anstress," said Mr. Jeffreys, with great solemnity, when they were seated around the library-table, which was half covered with files of papers tied up and labeled, "to-day you become the unfettered mistress of one of the largest fortunes in the city. You have been an orphan for twenty years, and the property your father left you has been steadily increasing during that period. I think you will be satisfied with its management. Here are schedules of the items and receipts. I expect you to examine them all scrupulously, but at your leisure. You will see that the large amount withdrawn from mortgages, and invested in woolen manufactures, at the beginning of the war, has doubled and trebled itself, while the bonds, which were bought at forty cents on the dollar, have also as good as cleared themselves thrice over. With the other securities you will do as you please, but the bonds I shall still advise you to retain, in spite of any political clamor that may reach your ear, since, the coupons being negotiable, a million of the bonds may be shut up in one's safe, and so be practically exempt from all taxation, no one being the wiser, and they paying not a dollar's tax."

"But, Mr. Jeffreys"——began Anstress, and paused. Why did not John speak for her, she was asking herself. "I beg your pardon, sir, but—is that right? Of course, I don't know—but is it honest?"

Certainly Mr. Jeffreys had the right to be displeased, but instead of that, he laughed.

"Now, my dear Anstress," said he, "I must beg you, once and for all, to put away any quixotic notions you may entertain. Though, with your large fortune, you may deal heavy blows, yet, after all, you will find yourself fighting against a windmill, and get some backward buffet that will lay you flat. This is a matter of business. It is something very largely done"——

"But is it not against the law?"

"Why—strict construction—certainly"——

"And in accepting the protection and benefits of the law, we tacitly promise to obey it, do we not?'

"My child, nobody has time for such finely-drawn subtleties and Socratic questionings in a matter of business. I am very much afraid," said Mr. Jeffreys, with hesitation, "that you are not fit for the management of affairs of this magnitude."

"But I suppose, dear sir," said Anstress, gently, "that it will not ruin me, that it will do me no great harm if I pay the legal tax on my bonds?"

"No; but it will take the value of half a million out of your property, though—a good many thousands a year out of your income."

"Do you mean to say," cried Anstress, "that I have been cheating the Government out of—I beg your pardon, Mr. Jeffreys, of course you can't mean that—I am so stupid!"

Mr. Jeffreys wisely turned to something else, after having given John a searching look, for, to tell the truth, he was a little fearful that John was already as much of a doctrinaire as Anstress threatened to be.

"Here," said he, "is a statement of your lands and tenements"——

"What! do I own houses, too?" she exclaimed.

"Whole streets of them."

"Do I? Why, how rich I must be!"

"Yes, very rich, Anstress. And these are part of your most profitable possessions. Your father obtained mortgages of many of them, in payment of some outstanding bill, and so, one by one, a large part of the neighborhood falling into his hands, he purchased the rest, to have it all under his control."

"Ah, it must have been a poor neighborhood, then?"

"Quite poor—quite. Your father's grocery was about in its center when he begun"——

"My father's—I thought papa was a wholesale merchant."

"So he was, certainly, afterward. A wholesale grocer and liquor-dealer."

"Was he?"

"But wealth obliterates all distinctions, my child. To become enormously rich is a sort of death in the old Adam, and resurrection among the proud and long-descended families. And at the time of his death he was a banker, and running great lines of steamships and the whole of a Western railway."

"I don't know as I care about that," said Anstress. "It doesn't make any difference in our country, you know, whether you are grocers or idlers."

"Doesn't it?" said Mr. Jeffreys.

"But about the houses?" asked Anstress.

"The houses—yes. They are all of the poorer class, of course, but yielding better incomes than better buildings do?"

"Whereabouts are they?" asked Anstress, suddenly shivering a little, she knew not why.

"Conduit and Messuage streets, both sides; places you never saw, my dear.'

"Is it possible?" Anstress cried out. "Mine!—those dens!—oh, I felt what was coming! When I said the landlord deserved— Am I—is my father responsible for that fever, those white women, those deformed children? Do we make money out of their wretchedness? coin their groans"——

"Anstress, you surprise me," said Mr. Jeffreys.

"Oh, I had rather be one of them than stand in my place to-day! Why did you let me, sir—why did you let me—swelling my wealth with their rents, and that child starving! Oh, what did they make me rich for, and leave me such another inheritance? It poisons all the rest—it poisons life! Oh, John, what makes you silent? what shall I do?" And her voice broke down in a wild fit of weeping, that neither John nor Mr. Jeffreys could check, and she ran to her own room and locked herself in, and was seen no more by any one, until she sent for a servant, that day.

It was late in the evening when Anstress crept down-stairs again, and, finding no one in the drawing-room, went into the cozy little flower-room beyond, where she was pretty sure to find John reading among his brilliant pelargoniums and sweet geraniums. And there he was, not reading, but busy with pencils and sheets of cardboard.

"I hope you did not think me a wild barbarian this morning, John?" said Anstress, timidly. "I know Mr. Jeffreys did. But indeed I couldn't help it, and it was so sudden—and—oh, John! I was down in Messuage street, and saw a child just dead there not two hours before!"

"You were, my darling? You? Alone in that brutal region?"

"It has no business to be a brutal region. If anything had happened to me there, it would only have been a sort of poetical justice, a righteous retribution. But James was with me," said Anstress, as if it were necessary to believe his apprehensions concerning her danger. "I can't tell you the dreadful things I saw!" she added, with a sobbing breath. "I didn't know there were such things. There was a woman on the floor stupid with drink, there was—oh, John!—But there, I can't talk about it. I suppose Mr. Jeffreys is very angry with me?" she added, in a tone half question, half assertion, but one full of relief at having left her recent topic.

"No, not angry," said John. "Something puzzled—never having looked at it in your light. He and I have frequently talked about it—I urging something to be done, he not considering that he had any right, or that it was possible to improve the condition of such people."

"Have you, John?" A light swept over Anstress' cloudy face. "Oh, John," she said, "I am afraid I have been very ungrateful! But there is something I must tell you—something that I mean to do, at any rate; and you must let me know if you don't think it best." She paused a moment. She did not like to tell him that she was absolutely resolved to do it, let him think of it what he would, although, unconsciously, both to herself and to him, not measuring her words, she had said little less than that; and, whether or no, she could not tell him that she had made the light in which he might consider her new proposition a test of his affection, a touchstone of his honesty, an answer to the question that had harassed her and fevered her by fits and starts since yesterday—the question as to whether it were her fortune or herself that John desired to possess.

"I am listening, dear," said John, as she hesitated, giving her his chair, and half seating himself on a corner of the table before her. "What is it troubles your mind? Confession is good for it, as you have heard say."

"You know, John," she began a little doubtfully, "that if my father kept a corner grocery in the beginning and obtained possession of all these houses in Messuage and that other street by means of the bills that were run up there—you know what that means—people who own that sort of houses do not mortgage them for bread; I have asked James and Nora about the habits of such people in that relation, and they have told me a good deal—and it means that they drank, and grew thriftless, and the bill at the corner grocery discouraged them, and they drank more and it was 'chalked down' to them till the bill was swollen large enough to cover house and home, and heaven only knows what became of them then! And such bills as those were the foundation of all my fortune. I don't believe my father realized what he was doing—for every one says he was a good and just man—do you, John?"

"No, darling."

"Now of course I can never find those people—they are lost, they were lost long ago. But the people who live in Messuage and Conduit streets to-day are their representatives; and it is the duty of my father's heir to take care of them in different fashion from the way they are being cared for now. I don't want to be rash or quixotic, and after thinking about how I can relieve them almost all day the best way that has occurred to me is this: To buy land enough in the neighborhood on which to build nice tenement-houses, and let them have them for the same rent they pay now, or less; and then tear down these disgraceful sheds, out of which we shall first have moved the tenants into the new houses, and after that, build nice brick blocks in their place as fast as may be, with good water and drains and sleeping-rooms, and every facility for health and necessary comfort that rich people have and that in a city poor people ought to have just as much; and so go on until both sides of both these streets are clean and wholesome. What do you think, John?"

"You can never hope to have your money back, Anstress," said John looking at her steadily.

Anstress turned pale at the words. The money was nothing to her any more than if she had been a destitute girl without a cent for whom John would work and care and keep away the wolf. Was it after all the very worst that she had feared? Was she weighing John in the balance and finding him wanting? Was he going to endeavor to prevent this for the paltry sake of that money?

"If you carry out this plan, Anstress," said John, "and place the rents of the new buildings at as low a rate as the tenants now pay, or rather, I should say, at exactly what they now pay, deducting repairs, insurance and taxes, you will receive about one per cent., or one and a half on your investment, which would generally be considered madness in relation to any purpose, letting alone the disposal of perishable property. The erection of the buildings will, besides, absorb nearly the whole of your fortune. And I presume the scheme would be everywhere thought of the wildest and most wanton, and be frowned on by capitalists as threatening to produce trouble for other landlords, and there would be annoying paragraphs in the newspapers concerning the dissipation of a great fortune, and vexations without number."

"But we needn't care for any of that, need we, John?"

"Not in the least."

"And there is no law to hinder us?"

"Certainly not.'

"And then, what do you say to it, John?"

"Here is a plan for the buildings, that I have been drawing this afternoon"——

"What! Oh, John! have you really"—and Anstress fell upon his neck with tears and kisses. "How good you are!" she cried. "How wicked I am! I would rather have it than a thousand fortunes!"

"My love," said John, smoothing her tumbled hair, "could you think I would object to this plan? That, as a matter of personal pride I would not hail any such escape from the suspicion that must always fasten on a man in such circumstances, of having married a woman for her money? And that, on other grounds, I should not deem it the best and most desirable thing that you should use the means of relieving suffering which God has given you?"

"How good you are, John!" repeated Anstress. "Oh! I never knew how much I loved you! I don't deserve you!"

"Never mind, my darling; you deserve some one a great deal better. And now let us talk about the buildings, and understand exactly what we want."

"We want everything plain but good, John; the rooms, for instance, high enough to give good air to breathe, but not too high to keep warm in winter; and finished in hard wood, so as to avoid perpetual paint, but not in black-walnut or mahogany, or any foolishness."

"Very well. That is my plan, too. Built solidly, around a hollow square, with cellarage in which each family has a share that it is not possible for another family to interfere with; divided into tenements of varying size, but so arranged that there shall be a living-room, and a sleeping-room for every two persons, with water and gas and tubs set, and all such requisite conveniences; each floor having an entrance separate from the other floors, and an exterior elevator to lift provisions and coals, and take down garbage; and plenty of drying-room for the clothes of every family, on the piazza running round the backs of the building on the hollow square; and the hollow square itself to be common property for such of the tenants of the first floor as choose to sit there, or to raise a grapevine, or a row of sweet corn, or a bed of flowers. Here are rooms, too, for a janitor, who, in consideration of his rent, shall preserve order in the building, and collect the rents; and, for the rest, the act of obliging the tenants not to abuse the houses, but to keep them decently and decorously, will be as good a civilizer and reformer as you can desire; it will give the men that ambition and the women that pride which are found to be marvelous supports in well-doing, and by insisting upon it, your janitor will presently make a residence in these buildings a sure sign of respectability."

"And when a single person has a share of the world's goods so far exceeding most other people's shares, John, don't you think that one per cent. is enough to receive?"

"Yes, I do—in equity. But then I may not be a good judge, for I have some radical theories about the right of a single person to shut up the use and accumulation of money beyond his own power to enjoy; that is to say, if a person, with his family, can enjoy everything the world at present affords of reasonable luxury and comfort at ten thousand a year, I am not sure that he has a right to add another ten thousand a year to his idle hoard, instead of distributing it to those in need as it comes in."

"And one per cent. is the salary you would receive for taking care of my fortune for me, is it not?"

"I think you can take care of it yourself, with a little advice now and then. I shall practice my profession, my dear, and the salary I expect to have for my assistance is love and the sweet services of my wife." Anstress' blushes, as he spoke, were not those of maidenly modesty so much as of mortification to think she had so misjudged the best and noblest of lovers. But she conquered them by the aid of some shame-faced kisses and embraces, and after this skirmish with her color, returned valiantly to the business in hand.

"How much will one per cent. of the property be?" she asked.

"About thirty thousand."

"And that will certainly give us everything we can possibly want, and a great deal more for charity besides, won't it?"

"Everything."

"And are you quite sure, John, that you shall be satisfied with this arrangement?"

"Are you quite sure, Anstress, that you will be yourself? The owner of a large property must remember that he is not acting for himself only, but for those that come after him. And when his property comes to be divided among heirs, those heirs, brought up in the habit of having all that the whole income could yield, are suddenly reduced to very different circumstances, with a thousand wants created and fostered which now they are unable to gratify."

"People of great wealth, then, must live as if the division of their property had already been made, and they had but one share of it. But, whether they do or not, I don't think it is desirable for people to begin life any better off than you are now, John—do you? It crushes all aspiration and self-discipline and self-denial. Don't you think so, John?"

"It is very possible," said John, smiling at her rosy enthusiasm.

"I wonder what Mr. Jeffreys will say to all this," added Anstress, presently, and laughing in spite of herself while picturing her late guardian's horror at her intentions.

"He will be struck with consternation," said John, "and will think at first that we both ought to have strait-jackets instead of wedding-garments. But I think if you leave it to me, I can bring him round, and even make him think it was his own suggestion, and so secure his assistance and experience, things not to be laughed at. As for the rest of the world, no matter. Perhaps your action may teach them"——

"Our action, John!"

"Perhaps our action, dear, may teach them that all this wealth which they call theirs is really not theirs at all. But that the earth is the Lord's, and the fullness thereof; that they cannot take away this wealth with them when they go; that they are merely stewards of it for the time being, and must administer it to the Master's ends."

"John, dear, you ought to be a minister," said Anstress. "Do you really love me very much?"—the cheeks were like two carnations now. "For if you would like it—you won't think strange, my saying so? you asked me once, you know—the day the corner-stone of the first building is laid shall be our wedding-day." And that was the end of the expectations of the good outside people. and there is to-day nothing but an outcry over two such misers as John and Anstress Jeffreys.

CHAPTER EIGHTEENTH.

The Genial Temper.

> Oh blest with temper whose unclouded ray
> Can make to-morrow cheerful as to-day.
> —*Pope.*

Blessed is the healthy nature; it is the coherent, sweetly confidential, not incoherent, self-distracting, self-destructive one!—*Carlyle.*

Think not thy word, and thine alone, must be right.
—*Sophocles.*

Remember, when the judgment's weak the prejudice is strong.
—*Kane O'Hara.*

> To look up and not down,
> To look forward and not back,
> To look out and not in, and
> To lend a hand.
> —*Edward Everett Hale.*

> She was good as she was fair,
> None—none on earth above her!
> As pure in thought as angels are,
> To know her was to love her.
> —*Rogers.*

> No falsehood can endure
> Touch of celestial temper.
> —*Milton.*

> The world is good, and the people are good,
> And we're all good fellows together.
> —*John O'Keefe.*

> Ill habits gather by unseen degrees,
> As brooks make rivers, rivers run to seas.
> —*Dryden.*

> 'Tis well said again,
> And 'tis a kind of good deed to say well:
> And yet words are no deeds.
> —*Shakespeare.*

> Give unto me made lowly wise
> The spirit of self-sacrifice.
> —*Wordsworth.*

STEPPING STONES TO HAPPINESS.

> Manlike is it to fall into sin,
> Fiendlike is it to dwell therein,
> Christlike is it for sin to grieve,
> Godlike is it all sin to leave.
> —*Friedrich Von Logan.*

Before we reach our ideal shores of happiness we shall have learned to make sure of something besides the material advantages of life either for ourselves or others ; we shall have learned to make ourselves capable of receiving the ideal happiness, we shall have learned to cherish a sunny temper, and in doing that we shall also have learned to love humanity, and to put ourselves in relation to the claims of others, in some degree if not altogether out of sight. Many individuals possess what may be called an aptitude to suffer injury. They not only accept it at every turn and receive it at every pore, but actually seem to hunt it up and lie in wait for it. Nothing falls that does not hit them; nothing breaks that does not hurt them ; nothing happens anyway that they do not reap a golden harvest of wrong from it. These people are miserable, as a matter of course—that goes without saying; but they would be utterly and hopelessly miserable if they could not at any moment scrape the substance of an injury together to solace some heavy hour destitute of other excitement. If somebody has not backbitten them, somebody is just about to do so; if somebody has not cheated them, somebody would like to cheat them, and if the number of the ill-intentioned living is insufficient to feed the appetite for boasted suffering, there is always an ancestry—fortunate thing !—to fall back upon, whose wrong-doings have been innumerable, and the results of whose wrong-doings are incalculable.

Of course these injured beings never do anything to provoke injury. They never insinuate or whine; they never openly or underhandedly charge the innocent with outrage; they never weary the patient with complaining, or repay good intentions with unceasing reproach, or "nag" the worm till it turns; they never abuse anybody's friends; they never criticise anybody's person; they never make themselves so disagreeable that people avoid them and escape them in self-defense; and they are never by any means so insolent over imaginary injuries that it becomes impossible for those having any self-respect at all to explain the circumstances and do away with the error; they never in effect do anything but conduct themselves like suffering saints waiting for their translation.

Why, then, it may be asked, should anybody want to injure them ? But there is the mystery, the problem they are always trying to solve, and whose solution, though they reach it in twenty days, will never be other than to the satisfaction of their self-esteem; and they invariably fall back on a comforting belief that they receive the injury because of envy of their superior virtues, grace, beauties, or position.

An Unpleasant Idiosyncrasy.

These people, it may be seen, are possessed of a singular sort of folly, if it may be so mildly denominated, and it be not in reality an idiosyncrasy bordering on the nature of insanity. There is wisdom ordinarily in doing the utmost to have the world believe you to be well thought of, held in esteem, and treated with consideration. If people in general observe that you have the countenance of others, you are tolerably sure to stand well in their favor; but if others are found to regard you as worth nothing but injury, the natural inference may be that nothing but injury is what you deserve. It is only the beggars that exhibit their sores, and those that have any common sense with their vanity, and wish the world to hold whatever is said or thought of them of consequence, instead of parading the ill conceit that others have of them, will take every opportunity of making manifest precisely the contrary, and swelling their self-importance by the means of it. But no such idea enters the minds of these unfortunates; their vanity feeds on their martyrdom.

It is not always, either, that they are entirely satisfied with the ills they have; they would like to fancy themselves receiving some positive and tremendous wrong. If somebody would slap their faces they would have real exultation; if they could only be turned out of house and home, it would be triumph; if their wives would run away, if their husbands would try to take their lives, bliss—bliss, that is, of their melancholy kind—could hardly go farther with them.

Love of Injury.

In what the enjoyment of this sort of emotion consists it is not easy to say, nor even to imagine. If it were in the exhibition to spectators of the patience and meekness and fortitude with which the wrongs, real or fancied, are borne, one might comprehend something of it in view of the self-complacency gratified by such exhibition. But as the spectators see nothing of the sort, but, on the other hand, see every opposite method used—not fortitude, but whines, not meekness, but defiance, and no other patience than that simulated thing which is a mockery of those whom it accuses—it remains unexplained why there are people in the world who love to be injured, and who are happier the more injured they are—people who know that no one possesses such power of creating intense discomfort in the hearts and souls of those that mean to do right, such power to annoy, to humble, to worry, to sadden, to distress in every way, and who do not hesitate to exercise this power to its fullest extent, till one is ready to declare that there is no such instrument of torment in any home as one of these martyrs. For do what you will you can not avoid given the offense for which they lie in wait. They are always on the lookout for a slight; they scent it from afar as vultures scent their prey, and it is difficult to say when they are best pleased, whether in enjoying a sense of triumph when courted or flattered, or in nursing the sense of burning wrong when overlooked and forgotten. They imagine the slight, and believe in it, when it does not exist; and when it is really impossible to believe in it, content themselves by picturing what the case would be if it did exist, until the suitable emotions are kindled in their breast, and they have the dramatic species of pleasure nearly the same as if it had been founded on fact.

Perhaps it is their friend who has "slighted" them, omitted the personal mention of their name from some general invitation, forgotten in some pressure to send them cards at all, inadvertently turned the back upon them in the crowd, accidentally carried off a suitor, and accidentally swept them a triumphant glance; coolness, distrust, icy discomfort, stalk upon the scene, to be followed after a time by a sort of slurred-over forgiveness that circumstances, whether of affection or convenience, make necessary. But perhaps it is not their friend, but your friend, that has done this deed, and woe is you for the distress and annoyance that then become yours through the agency of the individual whom your friend has outraged, until fresh outrage wipes out the memory of the old one.

To be slighted—that gives one an opportunity for eloquence in stating the reasons why one should not have been slighted, or else for assumption of humility in stating the reasons why the slight was not undeserved. It gives one the opportunity, too, of feeding an old grudge with the indulgence of a righteous indignation called for by self-respect, of nourishing a hearty spite by the recital of any piquant scandal concerning the giver of the slight that otherwise it might not be permissible to recite, or else of a lofty show of magnanimity by merely hinting at the knowledge of such scandal, and without consenting to gratify the tantalized curiosity of the listener; and at all events it allows one to make an inventory of one's virtues, all by one's self, in wondering why an individual possessing such qualities should be made the victim of such wrong, and when the inventory is made, to feel doubly wronged, and to render uncomfortable every member of the household that does not entirely concur in the view taken of the slight.

Fancied Slights.

It is really both amusing and amazing to see how these fabulous injuries can be conjured up and made the most of with a morbid enjoyment, when every consideration of proper pride and self-respect ought to lead them to think it would be impossible for any one to dream of such a thing as slighting their claims to attention. Why should one slight them? Are they coarse, gross, vulgar, ill-bred, ill-mannered, ill-natured, so plain as to be disgusting, so simple as to be a bore, so spiteful as to be dangerous, so ignorant as to be a laughing-stock, so low-born and of so low associations as to be contaminating? And if for none of these, for what other reasons can they be slighted? From personal dislike? Yet why should one dislike them but for such or kindred qualities? From envy? One who supposes that hardly makes the listener a convert to belief in superior qualities calculated to excite envy; for one will not be envied unkindly, if rich, unless an unkind display of riches is flaunted in the face of those who have none; if well educated, unless contempt is shown for those less fortunate; if virtuous, unless the virtue is self-righteous; if beautiful, unless the beauty is spoiled by consciousness, flippancy, heartlessness, and the assumption of "top-lofty" airs. No, indeed; one would have an exceedingly erroneous opinion of the very nature of society if it were for a moment supposed that virtue, beauty, learning, good fortune, were not welcomed eagerly by it in the persons of the happy owners. There is not so much of any of these fine things abroad in the world that any can be dispensed with; they are the very elements of that charming society that feeds the wit and delights the eye, the forces that make it lovely and of good repute, and wherever they are seen they are gladly welcomed and made a part of it. Just as a hostess would hail with satisfaction the acquisition of a choice prima donna, with her singing, at her evening entertainment, so will society hail with satisfaction the advent of any who can add by one iota to its pleasure; and if one is not hailed, if one is slighted, it is fair to presume that one is destitute of the means of affording this pleasure.

Quid Pro Quo.

For if one receives pleasure from society one must in return render pleasure to society; and before complaining of slights it is no more than just to sit down and inquire what right one has to other treatment. Has one a home and the means of entertaining in it, and so of being a valuable factor in this society and returning something of all that is given? If not that, then has one such beauty as will be a perpetual feast at which the gazer asks no more? Or if not that, has one intellect to lead, to control, to illuminate society, to add to its gayety, to lend its instruction, to direct it toward noble pursuits; If one, in fact, has nothing at all to give, and only the power of holding up one's pitcher to receive, should one feel entitled to complain if the pitcher be not always full and runi. .ig over ? The inference is plain that one rather greedily holds too big a pitcher for one's share, and that less demand and less expectation would not find themselves slighted.

A jealous disposition and an inordinate vanity are the things at the root of the whole matter. The disposition that is not jealous is not perpetually hunting for hurts; takes life as it comes; aware of ill-will towards none, so suspicious of ill-will from none; if overlooked, seeing or supposing some perfectly good reason for it, desirous rather of the comfort of others than of the flattery of self; not too sensitive to wounds which are like the bruises of "dead men's pinches;" and always convinced of the truth of the old king's wisdom which declares, "Better is a handful with quietness than both hands full with travail and vexation of spirit." And the nature whose restless vanity is not always expecting and claiming will never smart for want of recognition of the claims, will scarcely dream of rights before the rights are acknowledged, can not live, indeed, in an atmosphere darkened by absurd conjecturings and imputings of evil intent. And to sum up the whole matter, one would suppose that the utter want of good taste in this complaint of fancied slights would repel the inordinate vanity as much as any other breach of the canons; and if one must needs fancy one's self slighted at every turn, one should go into training to get the better of the tendency, and should that be found impossible, at least have the sense to keep quiet about it, and not to vaunt one's shame. There is so much pain and trouble that is real in our few years of active life that it seems a sorry thing to add to it by all the weight of imagined trouble; and we should perhaps cease to care for such selfish tribulation if we once properly mused upon

"the little lives of men,
And how they mar this little by their feuds."

The Undisciplined Temper.

For living in the house with these and such as these is like being stung to death by flies. There is nothing calculated to work such havoc with nerves, for you are in the perpetual uncertainty and unrest of never knowing how the simplest action is going to be construed by one whose temper is undisciplined, or what may be the consequences; and you dance on this mental and moral tight-rope till every point is strained and sore, trembling now in momentary expectation of an outburst, springing up in relief that it did not come, bowing beneath it when it does; and if you do not at last find refuge in insanity, it is because you have already found it in indifference or dislike.

For the forms of this undisciplined temper are numberless as they are oppressive; they are not confined to that with the too quick sense of injury; there is the simply and nakedly tyrannical, which raises the lightest whim to visionary importance and overbears everything, feelings, scruples, beliefs, wishes, for its gratification. And the worst of this form is that when the gratification is assured a total change of sky takes place, the offender becomes altogether sunny, and insists upon it that there is no sweeter temper in existence than the one that was just bursting over your head, and proves it to the world by the circumstance that you who have just been outraged and trampled upon are not feeling so sweet and sunny yourself as might be. There is the sinister form of ill-temper, too, which works underground, flaring up at last like brushwood at the touch of a torch, that scorns to explain, broods over wrongs till wholly mad, whereupon it is clothed in a robe of fire, and its poor object is reduced to the condition of a slave. There, too, is the bitter one that lets the aqua-fortis bite deeper and deeper, and carries a raw spot that, singularly enough, causes you to feel as though some of the aqua-fortis had been thrown in your own face. There is the discontented one, that wearies heaven and earth with its whine. There is the severe one, with which the cutting tongue is a weapon that wounds and turns in the wound, sure always to condemn and never to condone. And there is the violent one, whose bolts fell you to the ground, and in dread of which you live as if you had a thunder-cloud in the house. And then there are all the infinity of the lesser varieties and combinations of these, with which, to quote an old saying, one lives "the life of a toad under a harrow."

The Sinners Themselves.

Often enough the unfortunate possessors of these tempers are as unhappy as the unfortunate victims, if not more so, for they live in a state of burning discomfort and suffering equal to that which they inflict, and it is all a thousand times aggravated by the real inner knowledge that they have nobody but themselves to blame for it. Every outbreak in which they indulge, and the habit of which has grown by indulgence uncontrollable at length, has to be followed by a corresponding fit of remorse, although, sooth to say, the remorse is quite as disagreeable and trying to the first victim as the offense before it was.

But these sinners are of a class that assuredly deserve their suffering, and they do not by any means deserve pity as they do who have to encounter the blow, are subject to the daily torture, and live and move and have their being with fluttering heart and bated breath; and if they do deserve it they do not have it. One thinks with far more interest than of this subject of his own despotism of the poor soul who is harrowed beyond bounds by the testy,

LOVE IS A POTENT SHIELD AGAINST MANY TROUBLES.

touchy mate to which it is chained, whether it be the husband or the wife of a house, the parent or child, sister or brother, mistress or maid—the soul originally inoffensive, glad and gladdening, that has been stirred to its depths by these cruel tempests, and made turbid with sense of injustice and resentment, till daily life is shipwrecked on desert islands, with gall and wormwood for all banqueting, with all sunshine darkened, all affection gone to the bottom, all sound impulses overwhelmed and turned to evil things, and with whom, under the daily and hourly wrongs, hatred has taken the place of everything but bald duty.

It is a perilous thing to belong, in another way, to such ill-doers as the owners of the tempers of which we speak, unless one is willing to receive a share of the condemnation; for those subject to them look with stern criticism upon one in such case, and grow to dislike not only the ill-doer, but those behind the ill-doer, who failed in early life to draw the fangs. For as hard a part of it as any is that it could in such measure have been prevented by proper effort in the beginning. It is something that comes home to mothers and nurses bitterly. For the child born with delicate and sensitive nerves could, with the watchful care it had a right to have, have been spared the irritation which increased the sensitiveness; and that child received the irritation and that child's victims bear their wrongs more largely than otherwise through the negligence and indulgence of guardians who gave to-day without thought and deprived to-morrow without reason, who found it easier to administer a slap than to make the exertion of hindering the necessity of the slap by observation, by warding off, by explanation, by caressing—for a caress, even when undeserved, has soothed many a sore spirit and led it to better resolves. Love is a potent shield against many troubles, and they who love their children better than they love themselves can go a great way in triumph in the effort even of overcoming nature. And certainly the distress occasioned by these undisciplined tempers in mature life is never lessened by the thought that it might all have been hindered, and homes that have been made deserts might have been Edens.

The Sulky Soul.

For, look you, you rise in the morning, the bird singing in your heart, sunshine all about you, with never an echo of discord in your thoughts, meaning kindly to all the world; you feel well and young and happy; you run lightly down the stairs; you open the door of the breakfast-room gayly—and as if a cloud fell on you, you are conscious, in a flash, of a different moral atmosphere,

IT IS NOT EASY TO THINK IT IS NOT AS FINE AS IT CAN BE. (481)

one of blackness and gloom and bitterness, let the sun sparkle on glass and silver and china never so brightly. What is the matter? No one knows. One solitary individual of the family has retreated into a shell—not that, indeed, for if it were merely a retreat into a shell it could be endured; but it would seem nearer the truth to say that that individual's soul has left its body, and h is been replaced for the time being by a sour and evil spirit. At any rate, all this blackness and bitterness is infused into the bright and happy, atmosphere of the house, till it is as dark as doom, from that solitary individual. What occasioned it? Again, nobody knows. It is, perhaps, a case of what children used to call "getting up wrong end first." Some inexplicable offense has been taken; some unremembered contradiction has rasped the sensitive nerves and been brooded over in the watches of the night till it has seemed to be the throwing down of a gage; some careless remark has been misinterpreted and kept rankling; some real injury has been unforgiven, unforgotten, and swollen into quintuple proportions; or else some too rich morsel has produced a heavy indigestion, and *hinc illæ lachrymæ*.

We are not quite sure that a mind at rest with itself, conscious of no blame in the matter, can have—if it is able to overlook the annoyance of a disturbed equilibrium of the household—much more amusement afforded it than is afforded by the conduct of such a person. The affected haughtiness of composure, the cutting silence, except for now and then more cutting speech, which is frequently so double-bladed as to cut the cutter, and the dignity magnificent as Malvolio's, are all frequently as good as a play to the "looker-on in Venice." For the person who is in the sulks unavoidably betrays all the workings of the mind so plainly that they are as quickly and thoroughly read as one moving about in a lighted room is visible to the watcher in the dark outside; and if surprise at the pettiness gives pain, entertainment at the pettishness quite counteracts it, provided one does not become so provoked at the silly childishness as to lose temper one's self. In fact, in a large house full of people, when amusement begins to flag, a bad fit of the sulks does not come in at all amiss, and it would lend quite an agreeable variety in the way of fun if it were not that one is apt to feel as the ancients used to do concerning one "possessed," that the person is sacred in its possession either by angelic or demoniac power.

If this were the end of it, a fit of the sulks would not, perhaps, be so bad as it is painted; for one could bear having silence brought about where there used to be pleasant converse, could bear the impending sneer, the descending fleer, for a day or so, although that day or so is then like something blotted out of the year by an ink spot; but the sulking disposition is also the suspicious one; and one is conscious, whenever it has a kindred soul to answer it among the other inhabitants, of living in the midst of conspiracy, so that one fears to grow like one's surroundings, and presently suspects hidden meanings in innocent words, evil in the handling of a chair, poison in a cup.

Yet when we have made the best of it, a person with this sulking liability is a very uncomfortable companion, in no way to be relied on for comfort or enjoyment, since so likely to fail you at a pinch. And it seems to us that when the fit comes on, if the person has not discretion enough to withdraw voluntarily, a request should be made in the name of the household for that individual's retirement to the secrecy of a private room till the inner weather has cleared; for no one has a right, through any reason under heaven, to poison the peace of those who have not offended in order to retaliate upon the one who does offend, even if the offense is real; and when the offense is imaginary, the sulking party is no better than the insane, and can not complain of such mild restraint. Of course it goes without saying that when the poor soul descends at last with a smile, no notice should be taken of the past.

Nevertheless, every wrong brings its own right, and the sulker is punished in the sulks themselves, since the gloom and bitterness must be all but unbearable to the person who suffers them inwardly, and finds all the world as black as if followed up by a cuttle-fish. And the punishment is the more felt because, owing to the very law of compensations, the one most subject to the sulks is often sparkling, vivacious, and pleasure-loving enough, when not jostled out of bias, to make light hours and gladness chase each other about the house.

A Remedy.

But if our lot is inextricably mingled with that of these owners of vicious tempers we have two things to do—one to help them to overcome the demon that possesses them, and the other to walk in the paths of right ourselves, considering these among the trials that are to work for our blessing if we treat their temptation with the strength that overcomes. For no man lives to himself alone. The world is such a vast affair with its mighty physical agencies and its interwoven co-relations of vitality, that the most of us would shrink back awed at the idea that we had anything to do with the task of helping it on its ascent to perfection. All the more as our first thought about it is that it is already perfection. But we ourselves are in reality a part of this beautiful world, not parasites on it; and as we do not yet claim perfection for ourselves, why should we claim it for others, or for the less noble and more material objects of nature?

In truth, there are few things in the world completely perfect, although everything may be on the road to be so. The wild flower it is possible to take and train to fuller development, the wild fruit may be grafted, the jewel may be set free and faceted and polished, the savage may be cultivated, and the earth, we know, is to be reduced and the wilderness made to blossom like a rose. All that is comparatively simple work, though; it is material, and to be done by material means energized by the spiritual determination, will, pluck, endeavor.

The Perfection of the World.

It is not easy to look up at the infinite hue of the sky flooded with sunshine, and think it is not as fine as it ever can be; to look up through the deep vaults of night and measure off heaven after heaven with the near and distant stars, and fancy improvement possible; to see in what the landscape from the mountainside, with its sea of hills, its long levels, and its melting colors, can be made more glorious. Yet if it is not possible to our eyes, more perfect eyes may see the need, more perfect powers be shaping the means. For why else was the huge gaseousness of the sun compressed and its planets sent rolling off, to what else are we to suppose the earth goes forward on her way in space, to what other end than ultimate perfection can the whole solar system be moving up with all its stellar mates to its central point, and the great pendulum of the starry motions be swinging backward and forward with boundless ages for one motion, but that at each long swing the whole shall be finer than it was before, that the little earth itself become the fitter for the throne it bears in the thousand years of peace?

And if this is so, can we suppose that there is one particle of matter or of spirit that has not its portion of the work to do, is not directed upon that work, whether consciously or not, and is obedient to the great purpose only just so far as it obeys this direction?

If we find it impossible to imagine what part can be given us, with our infinitesimally small powers, in the perfection of the universe or the refining of the planet—for we know, of course, it does not mean we are merely to keep our flower beds bright and make two blades of grass grow where one grew before —perhaps we may find it worth while to consider whether it does not mean that by truth, patience, unselfishness, through countless generations, we are to transmute the very dust of the earth into the dust of heroes, martyrs and saints. If the earth is to be reduced, are we not a part of the earth? and is there to be no reducing in our own system as well as in the solar system?

Protoplasm and Dust.

For the religionist and the scientist have but one story to tell when it is sifted down to its last statement, and the protoplasm of one can claim to be nothing more than the dust of the earth of the other. Being made of the dust of the earth, with all her strange currents kneaded through us, her magnetic, her electric, her finer and her grosser ones, and with her impetus upon us, when we return that dust to her shall it have gained nothing for our possession of it, shall the grosser have endured no refinement, the finer not have become finer still, until in its own vast period all the substance of the great globe itself shall be the better and richer for the life our souls have lived in it?

Whatever be the especial part of the work assigned to humanity, we know that some work it is, since it is contrary to the economy of nature, manifested everywhere else, that we should be here for any idle purpose; and all we have to do is to follow the open passage and perform the work we find at hand, feeling very sure that if we are doing wrong in nothing else, we are doing right in this, and not only reducing the earth and our portion of it, but, it may be, sending out some of the vital energy of our well-doing to regions beyond—who shall say?

Let what will be false and fanciful, this must be true—that he who does persistent wrong, he who is treacherous, mean, cowardly, cruel, animal, and base, is rebellious to the directing power, is betraying his trust, can not be helping forward the great ends which tend only to light and goodness. While just as true is it that he who is pure and noble, self-forgetting and faithful, gentle and sympathetic, scorning falsehood, disdaining sensualism, can not but live in obedience to that directing power, can not but so have put himself into communication with all the channels of goodness that virtue runs like the blood in his veins, and, little as it may be, he lends his share of strength to the work of lifting the universe toward its perfect consummation, although it be as insensibly as any single ray of light helps in bringing about the dawn.

Right and Light.

For if we had no other instruction we should know by instinct and observation that the ways of right were the ways toward light, and those of wrong toward darkness. We know how smooth truth makes the way for our feet, and how entangling falsehood is; we know whether curse or blessing follows theft; we know what pleasure we receive in giving pleasure, what absence of pleasure, to say the least, and sometimes what suffering of remorse, in refusing it; we know how cruelty can recoil upon ourselves in pain, and what bodily evil and degradation sensuality drags after it, and if there were no other monitor to tell us of the heavenly sweetness and light, observation of these facts alone might do it. It is easy, then, for us to see that in doing right every individual is helping to work out the Divine purpose; and we find a fresh dignity belonging to the humblest soul on earth when we think of the share it bears in the work— the beggar who is too proud to steal and too ill to work sending out some virtue to wide nature, and the little child that resists the temptation of the sweetmeat jar is lending his mite in the resistance to this upward flight of the stars, as relatively as the saint and martyr who lays down his life for his faith. It gives us all a proud sense of value ; but it gives us at the same moment one of humility, as we remember that loathsome beggar and little child can bear the burden as well as we, and that our most earnest endeavor at great crises being to us exactly what their earnest endeavor in small crises is to them, they are transmuting common clay into heroic dust with the same vigor, and are lending their energy to the energy of the stars. For circumstances may make crises small or great, but we can only fill them with the measure of our nature and will, and their mite may help forward as much as our largess, if it is not, indeed, their largess and our mite.

> "O power to do ! O baffled will !
> O prayer and action ! Ye are one.
> Who may not strive may yet fulfill
> The harder task of standing still,
> And good but wished with God is done."

Transmuting Clay.

We shall do little then in our effort at transmuting clay to more angelic material till we have attained at least something like self-forgetfulness. "There is no cross," says Fénélon, "when there is no self to suffer under it." Those of us who are in the sad habit of complaining of this world as a dreary abode, a dark pilgrimage, a place of graves, a mere halt between ante-natal gloom and the gloom of the tomb, would find it a very difficult thing if for any portion of the time while we are in it we could but forget ourselves.

Self - Forgetfulness.

Forget ourselves ? That is, to remember other people till their trials, if they do not crowd out our personal trials, occupy equal place with them, till their identity looms up and corresponds with our own ; or simply, and in better words, to love our neighbors as ourselves. Without doubt we are privileged to take our choices of the neighbor, the point being only to make sure of the neighbor at all odds—the neighbor whose benevolent conducting power leads away from us all that surplus introspection and brooding, all that energy for sympathy, which, directed only upon our own affairs, work havoc there.

It is not to be supposed that in a phase of existence where good is still to be wrought out of evil on its upward way, and where so many various elements are still clashing, that any individual condition can be perfectly and permanently happy. The little child, surrounded by love, without a care, the young person just pausing on the threshold of maturity, to whom the future is wrapped in a golden haze of hope and expectation, are the only ones to whom life seems bright and faultless; are the only ones who, if you asked them, would be positively and absolutely sure that life was something to be thankful for; the only ones filled with satisfaction through the " mere joy of living."

The Child's Troubles.

But to some even of these young beings the little cloud upon the horizon overshadows that heaven of theirs: the apparition of the multiplication table rises and shakes its horrid hair, in its train a long procession of evils—the fearful ten to be carried, the awful mystery of the possessive case, the necessity of learning how to spell *phthisic*, and eventually *metempsychosis*, the deprivation of dainties with which elder people provoke younger palates, the obligation to work when sunshine invites to play, to go to bed just as the lamps are lighted and everything is bright as fairyland down stairs, the subjection of the will to another's in all respects and at all times, the reaching forward to that haven of rest, the condition of the "grown up:" too soon do these troubles, and such as these, adulterate the happiness with which the child opens its innocent eyes upon life, and too soon do corresponding troubles beset the youth or maiden who has found, so far, Pippa's satisfaction with life, but to whom, as the years fly by, come disappointments in love, in hopes, comes blasting of ideas and aims, comes the sense that it needs, indeed, another world to complete this.

Another World to Complete This.

And so it happens that there are few, if any, human beings among us who are completely and rapturously happy for any length of time. Lovers in each other's arms, benefactors relieving suffering, mothers clasping their babies, actor and poet under the fresh laurels of triumph—all these know surely what the ecstasy of bliss is. But the child leaves the mother's arms, the benefactors receive ingratitude, the lovers weary or deceive or die, the actor or the artist finds that one warm heart had been better than the hollow ring of all

TO GO TO BED JUST AS THE LAMPS ARE LIGHTED.

those plaudits; and the ecstasy with all has been brief. And that is what the moan is about—that it can not last to all time, as if in a world that "spins forever down the ringing grooves of change," every moment, with its invisible forces, must not pull the present combination apart to effect a new one, and as if it were anything but childish kicking against a wall to remonstrate or complain of the inevitable; for by submitting and trying to make the best of it, something, at any rate, is to be gained.

It being conceded, then, that every lot in life has its bitterness, while "laughter shall be mingled with sorrow, and mourning take hold of the end of joy," that corroding cares beset the possession of our best earthly treasures, it becomes a self-evident truth that the chief relief from that lot is to cease to consider it. "As a moth doeth by a garment, and a worm by the wood, so the sadness of a man consumeth the heart," says the old Latin Vulgate; and we can forget our own sadness best by grieving over the sadness of another, by rejoicing over another's joy.

Changing Our Condition for Another's.

In the one case we shall find that ours is not an isolated instance, but that each soul bends beneath the weight of its own especial cross, and that light as such cross seems to us in comparison with our own, yet if we took the temperament and situation of its bearer with it, we should find it just as grievous. We see some woman of genius, at whose voice, with whose beauty, beneath whose power, every night a multitude thrills; we contemplate her brilliant destiny; we envy her while we admire her; we wonder at partial fate, and laugh at the idea that this fortunate creature has any cross at all to bear: we do not know that she has given her heart and her happiness into the keeping of an unworthy man, so neglectful and so base that her honors, her genius, her beauty, are mere dross to her, and that whenever she lies down to sleep she would be grateful if she were never to wake up. We see a man before whom senates tremble, who moves a nation so that as his heart beats, the hearts of all its people beat, whose name resounds to the farthest parts of the earth. We ask could he have more?

But we do not know how he suffers under the wide slanders that falsely persecute him, and while they seem to us mere gnat stings, eat up his happiness like a canker. Or we see another, on whom fortune waits, who handles states like pawns, who is the personification of power, whose station would be to us as impossible as Alnaschar's dream. We do not know the secret shame for some ill deed that follows him like a Nemesis; of the future moment of horror that darkens all the splendid moments now, when at his death, if not before, the bubble of his fair fame shall be pricked; or else of the hidden trouble in his home that makes all success mean failure; or yet of the unwhispered disease that gnaws, vulture-like, at his vitals, and for which we can have no pity nor sympathy, since it is death to a politician's hopes to be known to suffer from disease at all. We see a lovely woman rolling by in her luxurious coach: her velvets, her jewels, her flowers, her hosts of friends, her devoted

ROLLING BY IN HER LUXURIOUS COACH.

husband, her life at home like a chapter in the beatitudes, all move us to imagine what ill thing shall befall her, and so make matters even. We do not know that an ill thing has already befallen her; that her way has lain over graves, that her heart aches and longs for the children that are denied her, and that without them all the rest is naught. This—the knowledge of all this—is, perhaps, but bitter consolation for one's own grief.

Rejoicing in Another's Joy.

Yet, nevertheless, it hinders one from supposing any particular malevolence on the part of the powers of the universe directed at one's self, and affords one, as we have said, the opportunity—in bringing amusement to these others, relief, oblivion for the moment—of forgetting one's self and one's own burden. And in the other case—that of rejoicing in the joy of the fortunate possessor of that blessing—the very exertion of casting aside envy, of refusing to listen to the evil suggestion concerning injustice, brings back a shadow of that joy on us; a ray of happy satisfaction, it may be also, with our own virtue, which is cheering, and gives us certainly pleasant and heart-warming sensations that we should not otherwise have known.

For whether we are glad on our own account or on another's, gladness is gladness, and it raises the barometer of the soul to the mark of fair weather there; while so long as we have felt that throb of sympathy, have identified ourselves with that other joyous soul, so long, at any rate, we have known self-forgetfulness and have mastered happiness. There is one light of the stars and another of the moon, but it is all light, whether it be direct or reflected.

The Golden Time for Love.

It is Margaret Sangster's sweet spirit that sees in all times the time to forget ourselves and love our neighbor, saying:

"When is the golden time you ask—
  The golden time for love;
The time when earth is green beneath
  And skies are blue above;
The time for sturdy health and strength,
  The time for happy play,
When is the golden hour? you ask;
  I answer you, 'To-day.'

To-day, that from the Maker's hand
  Ships on the great world sea
As stanch as ever ship that launched
  To sail eternally;
To-day, that wafts to you and me
  A breath of Eden's prime,
That greets us, glad and large and free—
  It is our golden prime.

For Yesterday hath veiled her face,
  And gone as far away
As sands that swept the pyramids
  In Egypt's ancient day.
No man shall look on Yesterday,
  Or tryst with her again;
Forever gone her toils, her prayers,
  Her conflicts, and her pains.

* * * * * * * *

You ask me for the golden time—
  I bid you seize the hour,
And fill it full of earnest work,
  While yet you have the power.
To-day the golden time for joy
  Beneath the household eaves;
To-day the royal time for work,
  For bringing in the sheaves.

> To-day the golden time for peace,
>   For righting older feuds;
> For sending forth from every heart
>   Whatever sin intrudes
> To-day the time to consecrate
>   Your life to God above;
> To-day the time to banish hate,
>   The golden time for love."

Even if we desire the boon of self-forgetfulness for no special grief or outrage, for no worse trouble than a well-grown disgust of ourselves, a sense of fatigue with our own personality, there is no other way to get it than to go into the personality of others. The anchorite has practiced this truth in desert caves, ceasing the remembrance of his unworthiness in the contemplation of beings and states beyond this mortal sphere; the dweller in cities seeks the crowd to lose himself there. That is a very vain and very shallow nature which is so satisfied with itself as to need no change of view; for so imperfect are we yet that the only permanent happiness to be acquired, the only tranquillity of soul, must come through this thorny path of self-forgetfulness.

On Tranquil Heights.

Only when we have reached, if not the very consummation of self-abnegation and forgetfulness, yet at any rate such a height that we can see the way clear that leads to the heights beyond, will our eyes be opened, and will we see the work about us as it is, and see our fellow-wayfarers as they are, knowing, then, that full often and all unaware, we go hand in hand with angels.

Hand in Hand with Angels.

> Hand in hand with angels,
>   Through the world we go;
> Brighter eyes are on us
>   Than we blind ones know;
> Tenderer voices cheer us
>   Than we deaf will own;
> Never, walking heavenward,
>   Can we walk alone.
>
> Hand in hand with angels,
>   In the busy street,
> By the winter hearth-fires—
>   Everywhere—we meet,

STEPPING STONES TO HAPPINESS.

Though unfledged and songless,
  Birds of Paradise;
Heaven looks at us daily
  Out of human eyes.

Hand in hand with angels,
  Oft in menial guise;
By the same straight pathway
  Prince and beggar rise.
If we drop the fingers
  Toil-imbrowned and worn,
Then one link with heaven
  From our life is torn.

Hand in hand with angels:
  Some are fallen—alas!
Soiled wings trail pollution
  Over all they pass.
Lift them into sunshine!
  Bid them seek the sky
Weaker is your soaring
  When they cease to fly.

Hand in hand with angels;
  Some are out of sight,
Leading us, unknowing,
  Into paths of light.
Some dear hands are loosened
  From our earthly clasp,
Soul in soul to hold us
  With a firmer grasp.

Hand in hand with angels—
  'Tis a twisted chain
Winding heavenward, earthward,
  Linking joy and pain.
There's a mournful jarring,
  There's a clank of doubt,
If a heart grows heavy,
  Or a hand's left out.

Hand in hand with angels
  Walking every day;—
How the chain may lengthen
  None of us can say;
But we know it reaches
  From earth's lowliest one
To the shining seraph
  Throned beyond the sun.

> Hand in hand with angels!
>   Blessed so to be!
> Helpéd are the helpers;
>   Giving light, they see.
> He Who aids another
>   Strengthens more than one;
> Sinking earth he grapples
>   To the Great White Throne.

Earth indeed sinks from us when we have gone so high. We wonder at the trifles we have pursued, and at the false relations these trifles have held for us—the honors, the achievements, the riches.

The Riches of Angels.

"What," asks Lucy Larcom, "what can an angel regard as riches? Certainly nothing that is appreciable by our mortal senses—not such things as we see with covetous eyes, and touch with miserly hands, and lock away from thieves in tomb-like coffers. Milton has drawn for us a fancy sketch of one such sordid angel, among the rebellious host:

> 'Mammon, the least erected spirit that fell
> From heaven, for even in heaven his looks and thoughts
> Were always downward bent, admiring more
> The riches of heaven's pavement, trodden gold,
> Than aught divine or holy else enjoyed
> In vision beatific.'

"But the messengers of God, who fly abroad on His errands through the universe, cannot travel with their winged thoughts weighted by any material burden. An angel's riches are the messages he bears—messages of love and truth from the heart of God to His creatures. The messenger knows that he is the bearer of inestimable wealth, but he has no desire regarding it except that it may reach its destination, and bless the souls for whom it was intended. If any selfish hoarding of truth and love were possible, the truth would turn to falsehood, and love to hate—and heaven would be hell. The heavenly riches must be given away, freely as the air we breathe, or it is no longer heavenly. Again the plural gives the pronoun its value. 'All things are *yours*.' We are not the real possessors of things earthly or heavenly, while we persist in saying, 'They are mine;' the only permanent claim we have upon them is that they are *ours*. God never gives us anything for our individual self alone. The divineness of His gifts is proved by our desire to share them with others. It is only perishable objects that we can hold selfishly, and in so holding them, they and we perish together."

True Happiness at Last.

It is only the soul that has reached these tranquil levels where self has been over-lived, and the love of man and the love of God has filled it with serenity, that can know true happiness, that has ceased from concern, that can live unashamed before its own scrutiny and assoiled before the heavenly gaze; and so having lived, so can die—die as sweetly and as calmly as in Matthew Arnold's beautiful poem, "A Wish," it is desired to die, passing from one life to another, and from one mansion of the Father's house to the next.

Matthew Arnold's Wish.

"I ask not that my bed of death
    From bands of greedy heirs be free ;
For these besiege the latest breath
    Of fortune's favored sons, not me.

I ask not each kind soul to keep
    Tearless, when of my death he hears ;
Let those who will, if any, weep !
    There are worse plagues on earth than tears.

I ask but that my death may find
    The freedom to my life denied ;
Ask but the folly of mankind,
    Then, then at last, to quit my side.

Spare me the whispering, crowded room,
    The friends who come, and gape, and go
The ceremonious air of gloom—
    All that makes death a hideous show !

Nor bring, to see me cease to live,
    Some doctor full of phrase and fame,
To shake his sapient head and give
    The ill he cannot cure a name.

Nor fetch, to take the accustomed toll
    Of the poor sinner bound for death,
His brother doctor of the soul,
    To canvass, with official breath,

The future and its viewless things—
    That undiscovered mystery
Which one who feels death's winnowing wings
    Must needs read clearer, sure, than he!

Bring none of these! but let me be,
  While all around in silence lies,
Moved to the window near, and see
  Once more before my dying eyes,

Bathed in the sacred dews of morn
  The wide aerial landscape spread—
The world which was ere I was born,
  The world which lasts when I am dead;

Which never was the friend of *one*,
  Nor promised love it could not give,
But lit for all its generous sun,
  And lived itself, and made us live.

There let me gaze, till I become
  In soul with what I gaze on wed!
To feel the universe my home;
  To have before my mind—instead

Of the sick room, the mortal strife,
  The turmoil for a little breath—
The pure eternal course of life,
  Not human combatings with death.

Thus feeling, gazing, let me grow
  Composed, refreshed, ennobled, clear;
Then willing let my spirit go
  To work or wait elsewhere or here!"

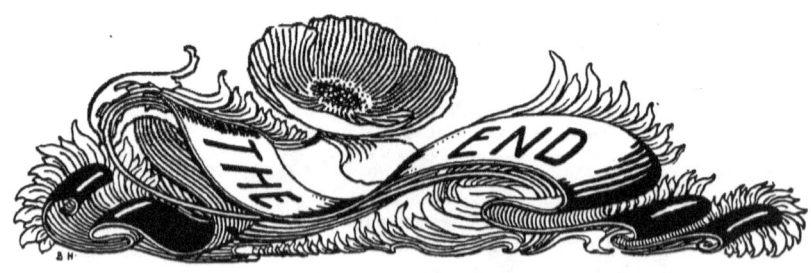

www.ingramcontent.com/pod-product-compliance
Lightning Source LLC
Chambersburg PA
CBHW031322230426
43670CB00006B/212